THE PATH TO ENLIGHTENED INVESTOR STEWARDSHIP

The Path to Enlightened Investor Stewardship begins from a transformative premise: that institutional investors, as custodians of capital, bear enduring responsibilities not only to their proximate clients and beneficiaries but also to end-investors and to the financial, social, and ecological systems in which they operate. Yet stewardship remains a contested and fragmented field of norms, practices, and expectations. Focusing on the UK as a paradigmatic site, this book traces the historical, conceptual, and regulatory evolution of stewardship from its shareholder-centric roots to an expansive, system-aware model. Drawing on original analysis of stewardship disclosures and activist interventions, and informed by interdisciplinary insights, it develops a typology of investor stewardship – multi-level, multi-actor, multi-asset, multi-means, and multi-aim. At its heart is the model of enlightened investor stewardship: a relational and purposive framework that charts a path from fragmented duties to coherent accountability, and from procedural compliance to transformative responsibility.

DIONYSIA KATELOUZOU is Reader in Law at King's College London, a Research Associate at the Centre of Business Research at the University of Cambridge and a Research Member of The European Corporate Governance Institute (ECGI). She specialises in comparative and transnational corporate law, corporate governance, and financial regulation. Internationally recognised for her interdisciplinary research and policy engagement, she leads the Global Investor Stewardship project and has secured major research grants.

'A brilliant reimagining of institutional investor power for our systemic age. Essential reading on how stewardship can balance private returns with public purpose.'

Marco Becht, Goldschmidt Chair Professor, Solvay Brussels School; Executive Director, European Corporate Governance Institute (ECGI)

'Stewardship has over the past 15 years become a key buzzword in corporate governance and investment circles. Dionysia Katelouzou's book is now the definitive work on point and is essential reading for anyone interested in how companies are run and in how investment intermediaries address their myriad responsibilities.'

Brian R. Cheffins, S.J. Berwin Professor of Corporate Law, Faculty of Law, University of Cambridge

'Like many fashionable notions, "stewardship" is a term which can mean different things to different people. And regulators, who rush to take the concept up, rarely tarry to define it. This book undertakes the task of saving stewardship from the charge of vacuity. It is difficult to think of anyone better than Professor Katelouzou to undertake this task. She has worldwide knowledge of the instantiation of stewardship, has developed an analytical apparatus which is second to none, and applies with vigour to this most tricky of problems.'

Paul Davies, Senior Research Fellow, Harris Manchester College, University of Oxford

'Institutional investors controlling trillions face pressure to address climate change, inequality, and systemic risks beyond short-term returns. This groundbreaking book develops "enlightened stewardship", redefining investor responsibility across time, stakeholders, and systems. Drawing on extensive UK data, it proposes transforming stewardship from a compliance exercise into a credible mechanism of investor accountability.'

Luca Enriques, Professor of Business Law, Bocconi University

'A perfect work by the world's most influential scholar Dionysia Katelouzou on investor stewardship. With insightful observation and analysis of all issues and proposed solutions, this is a great book suitable for anyone and countries that are serious in pursuing better corporate governance regime.'

Andrew Jen-Guang Lin, Professor, National Taiwan University

'Dionysia Katelouzou has long been a leading voice in the area of investor stewardship. In this book, *The Path to Enlightened Investor Stewardship*, she breaks new ground in seeking to address key challenges of the age. The book examines the past, present, and, most importantly, the future of what

Dr Katelouzou terms "enlightened stewardship". It will be of interest to the legal and business communities, as well as policymakers in the United Kingdom and internationally.'

Jennifer Hill, Professor, Bob Baxt AO Chair in Corporate and Commercial Law, Faculty of Law, Monash University

'A must-read book on stewardship by Prof. Dionysia Katelouzou that brings the much-needed conceptual clarity about stewardship and reimagines it beyond shareholder centric model. She proposes a fundamental rethinking of the normative and institutional architecture of stewardship along with the model of enlightened investor stewardship.'

Dr. Harpreet Kaur, Professor, Vice-Chancellor, National Law University, Jodhpur, India

'In a time in which governments around the world turn a blind eye to reality, the future welfare and well-being of billions depend on a rather small number of institutional investors. Professor Dionysia Katelouzou advances a novel analytical framework of *enlightened stewardship* for their roles and responsibilities. The legal and policy analyses in her account are bold and ambitious yet uniquely lucid, sober, and well-grounded, which together yield an important contribution.'

Amir N. Licht, Professor, Harry Radzyner Law School, Reichman University

'Dionysia Katelouzou is the world's leading authority on investor stewardship, and this book is her magnum opus. With analytical precision and regulatory insight, she redefines stewardship as a vital public function – grounded in law, informed by data, and responsive to systemic risk. This is essential reading for anyone serious about corporate governance in the 21st century.'

Dan Puchniak, Yong Pung How Chair Professor of Law; Director, Centre for Commercial Law in Asia, Singapore Management University

'*The Path to Enlightened Investor Stewardship* is a landmark contribution to the field of corporate governance and shareholder engagement. With conceptual depth, empirical rigour, and normative clarity, Dionysia Katelouzou reframes investor stewardship as a public responsibility fit for the 21st century. This is not merely a book about shareholder rights – it is a compelling call to rethink the institutional role of capital in shaping resilient, accountable, and inclusive markets. An essential read for scholars, policymakers, and practitioners navigating the complex intersection of law, finance, and sustainability.'

Georg Ringe, Professor, Director of the Institute of Law & Economics, University of Hamburg

INTERNATIONAL CORPORATE LAW AND FINANCIAL MARKET REGULATION

Corporate law and financial market regulation have major implications for how the modern economy is organized and regulated and for how risk is managed and distributed – domestically, regionally and internationally. This Series seeks to inform and lead the vibrant scholarly and policy debate in this highly dynamic area by publishing cutting-edge, timely and critical examinations of the most pressing and important questions in the field.

THE PATH TO ENLIGHTENED INVESTOR STEWARDSHIP

DIONYSIA KATELOUZOU
The Dickson Poon School of Law, King's College London

CAMBRIDGE
UNIVERSITY PRESS

CAMBRIDGE
UNIVERSITY PRESS

Shaftesbury Road, Cambridge CB2 8EA, United Kingdom

One Liberty Plaza, 20th Floor, New York, NY 10006, USA

477 Williamstown Road, Port Melbourne, VIC 3207, Australia

314–321, 3rd Floor, Plot 3, Splendor Forum, Jasola District Centre, New Delhi – 110025, India

Cambridge University Press is part of Cambridge University Press & Assessment, a department of the University of Cambridge.

We share the University's mission to contribute to society through the pursuit of education, learning and research at the highest international levels of excellence.

www.cambridge.org
Information on this title: www.cambridge.org/9781009279468

DOI: 10.1017/9781009279499

When citing this work, please include a reference to the DOI 10.1017/9781009279499

First published 2026

Cover image: Andriy Onufriyenko / Moment via Getty Images.

A catalogue record for this publication is available from the British Library

Library of Congress Cataloging-in-Publication Data
Names: Katelouzou, Dionysia author
Title: The path to enlightened investor stewardship / Dionysia Katelouzou, The Dickson Poon School of Law, King's College London.
Description: Cambridge, United Kingdom ; New York, NY : Cambridge University Press, 2026. | Series: ICFM international corporate law and financial market regulation | Includes index.
Identifiers: LCCN 2025045192 | ISBN 9781009279468 hardback | ISBN 9781009279444 paperback | ISBN 9781009279499 ebook
Subjects: LCSH: Capital investments – Law and legislation – Great Britain | Capitalists and financiers – Legal status, laws, etc. – Great Britain | Stockholders – Legal status, laws, etc. – Great Britain | Corporate governance – Law and legislation – Great Britain | Corporation law – Great Britain | Financial institutions – Law and legislation – Great Britain
Classification: LCC KD1774 .K38 2026
LC record available at https://lccn.loc.gov/2025045192

ISBN 978-1-009-27946-8 Hardback

To Karolos and my mum

CONTENTS

FIGURES

TABLES

ACKNOWLEDGEMENTS

This book has been a long journey – intellectually, personally, and reflectively. Its origins lie in the first Global Shareholder Stewardship Conference, held at The Dickson Poon School of Law, King's College London in 2019. That gathering – bringing together scholars, regulators, institutional investors, and civil society voices from around the world – crystallised many of the questions that continue to animate this book. What began as a focused inquiry into shareholder stewardship evolved into a broader reflection on how institutional investors shape, and are shaped by, wider governance systems. Since then, the Global Investor Stewardship project has hosted numerous events, each generating valuable conversations that indirectly informed this work. I am grateful to all who contributed to the intellectual and institutional environment in which this book took shape.

I am especially indebted to colleagues, students, and non-academic interlocutors who engaged with my work at various stages – formally and informally. Their questions, critiques, and provocations sharpened the arguments and broadened the horizons of what stewardship can and should mean. Particular thanks go to those directly involved in the Global Investor Stewardship project, whose insights created a vibrant interdisciplinary context – even if necessarily at some remove from the solitary process of writing.

Over the years, I have benefitted from presenting parts of this research at conferences, workshops, and seminars hosted by academic and policy institutions across the UK, the US, Europe, Asia and beyond. The feedback received in those settings – from engaged audiences of scholars, practitioners, policymakers, and students – helped test, challenge, and deepen many of the book's core claims.

I am also grateful to the institutional investors, regulators, policymakers, proxy advisors, and civil society organisations who generously shared their time, disclosures, and reflections. Their engagement provided not only rich empirical material but also practical perspectives that grounded the research in real-world complexities and tensions.

This research was supported by several institutions whose backing I gratefully acknowledge: the British Academy Mid-Career Fellowship Award (2022), the British Academy 2020 Special Research Awards: Covid-19 Scheme, the British Academy/Leverhulme Small Research Grant (2019), the Economic and Social Research Council (ESRC) Social Impact Fund, and The Dickson Poon School of Law at King's College London. I am also thankful for the King's Undergraduate Research Fellowship (KURF) Scheme, which enabled the contributions of exceptional student research assistants. The European Corporate Governance Institute (ECGI) provided a vital platform for exchange and visibility, hosting events that showcased various strands of this project. My sincere thanks go to the editorial and production teams at Cambridge University Press for their thoughtful guidance and care in bringing this manuscript to life.

Finally – and most importantly – my deepest thanks go to my family, for your patience, joy, and unwavering love. This book was written amid sleepless nights, noisy days, and the quiet hope that ideas still matter.

Dionysia Katelouzou, London, May 2025

ABBREVIATIONS

1G UK Code	First-Generation UK Stewardship Code
2G UK Code	Second-Generation UK Stewardship Code
3G UK Code	Third-Generation UK Stewardship Code
ARGA	Audit, Reporting, and Governance Authority
ASCOR	Assessing Sovereign Climate-Related Opportunities and Risks
AUM	Assets under Management
CEO	Chief Executive Officer
CFO	Chief Financial Officer
COP	Conference of the Parties
CSR	Corporate Social Responsibility
DB	Defined Benefit
DC	Defined Contribution
EFAMA	European Fund and Asset Management Association
ESG	Environmental, Social, and Governance
ETF	Exchange-Traded Fund
EU	European Union
FCA	Financial Conduct Authority
FRC	Financial Reporting Council
FTSE	Financial Times Stock Exchange
G20	Group of Twenty
GFC	Global Financial Crisis
GRESB	Global Real Estate Sustainability Benchmark
ICCR	Interfaith Center on Corporate Responsibility
ICGN	International Corporate Governance Network
IIGCC	Institutional Investors Group on Climate Change
ISC	Institutional Shareholders' Committee
ISS	Investment Strategy Statement
LAPFF	Local Authority Pension Fund Forum
LDA	Latent Dirichlet Allocation
LGPS	Local Government Pension Scheme
LSE	London Stock Exchange
M&A	Mergers and Acquisitions
NLP	Natural Language Processing

NZAOA	Net-Zero Asset Owner Alliance
NZAM	Net-Zero Asset Managers Initiative
OECD	Organisation for Economic Co-operation and Development
ONS	Office for National Statistics
PRI	Principles for Responsible Investment
SDGs	Sustainable Development Goals
SFDR	Sustainable Finance Disclosure Regulation
SIP	Statement of Investment Principles
SRD II	Shareholder Rights Directive II
STM	Structural Topic Modelling
TCFD	Taskforce on Climate-Related Financial Disclosures
TCI	The Children Investment Fund
TNFD	Taskforce on Nature-Related Financial Disclosures
TPI	Transition Pathway Initiative
UK	United Kingdom
UN	United Nations
UNEP	United Nations Environment Programme
US	United States
USD	United States Dollar

1

Why Stewardship, Why Now? The Stakes, the Puzzle, and the Path Forward

1.1 The Stakes: Reframing the Stewardship Debate

What happens when those entrusted with guarding the world's capital fail – not only in delivering financial value but also in grappling with the broader responsibilities their power now entails? The global financial system stands at a crossroads – not only because of deepening systemic risks but also because the dominant model of 'shareholder capitalism', which prioritises shareholder value as the overriding purpose of the firm, has faltered.[1] Once justified by promises of efficient capital allocation and widespread wealth creation, it now faces mounting criticism for delivering short-term financial gains at the expense of long-term resilience, social cohesion, and planetary boundaries.

At the heart of this system is the rise of institutional investors – a defining feature of financialisation.[2] Pension funds, sovereign wealth funds, insurance companies, and the asset managers who act on their behalf now control vast pools of capital.[3] They invest across asset classes and geographies, shaping corporate behaviour across both public and

[1] See e.g. Gerald F Davis, *Managed By the Markets: How Finance Re-Shaped America* (Oxford University Press 2009), 64 (identifying 'a large gap between the theory of shareholder capitalism as an arm's-length meritocracy . . . and how the system operates in practice'). For an attempt to reimagine capitalism as a system which is in harmony with environmental realities, social justice and equality, and democratic institutions, see Rebecca Henderson, *Reimagining Capitalism in a World of Fire* (Penguin 2020).

[2] For accounts of financialisation and its implications for corporate governance and capital markets, see Gerald A. Epstein *Financialization and the World Economy* (Edward Elgar Publishing, (2005); Ronald Dore, 'Financialization of the Global Economy' (2008) 17 *Industrial and Corporate Change* 1097; Paddy Ireland, 'The Financialization of Corporate Governance' (2009) 60 *Northern Ireland Legal Quarterly* 1.

[3] For example, the UK asset management industry oversees approximately £11 trillion in assets – including shares, bonds, and alternative investments – making it the second largest globally after the US. See Financial Conduct Authority, *Updating and Improving the UK Regime for Asset Management* (DP23/2, February 2023) at [2.2]. For global figures, see

private markets. Despite the diversity of their mandates and time horizons, they share a common trait: they manage 'other people's money'.[4] Yet they do so within a fragmented governance architecture that often obscures accountability and purpose.

Traditionally, institutional investor influence has been most visible through equity holdings in listed companies – what this book terms *shareholder governance* – exercised through proxy voting, shareholder resolutions, board engagement, and behind-the-scenes dialogue.[5] These tools have positioned institutional investors as central actors in corporate governance, particularly in jurisdictions such as the UK and the US, where dispersed ownership structures prevail and shareholder oversight functions as a key mechanism of accountability.[6] Yet the stakes of shareholder governance are not merely financial. They are institutional and societal, as the capacity to hold corporate power to account increasingly depends on how institutional investors engage with the companies in which they hold shares.[7]

The legitimacy and limits of shareholder governance have long been contested. At its core lies a fundamental tension: should shareholders be regarded as ultimate owners endowed with governance rights, or as financial stakeholders whose interests are mediated through boards and managerial discretion? This debate, famously articulated in Berle and Means' foundational account of the separation of ownership and control, was later formalised by Fama and Jensen's agency theory, which positioned shareholders as residual claimants and market-disciplined monitors.[8] Within this framework, corporate governance became

Adriana De La Cruz, Alejandra Medina, and Yun Tang, *Owners of the World's Listed Companies* (OECD Capital Market Series 2019).

4 John Kay, *Other People's Money: Masters of the Universe or Servants of the People?* (Profile Books 2015).

5 Generally on the role of institutional shareholders in corporate governance, see Geof P. Stapledon, *Institutional Shareholders and Corporate Governance* (Clarendon Press 1998).

6 See e.g. L. C. B. Gower, 'Some Contrasts between British and American Corporation Law' (1956) 69 *Harvard Law Review* 1369, 1373 (noting that '[t]he subjecting of corporate management to some sort of control by the stockholders' has been conceived as one of the main problems that both the UK and the US faced during the twentieth century).

7 For a taxonomy of ownership engagement by institutional investors, see S. Çelik and Mats Isaksson, 'Institutional Investors as Owners: Who Are They and What Do They Do?' OECD Corporate Governance Working Papers 21–34 <https://doi.org/10.1787/5k3v1dvmfk42-en>

8 Adolf A. Berle and Gardiner C. Means, *The Modern Corporation & Private Property* (2009 ed., Transaction Publishers 1932); Eugene F. Fama and Michael C. Jensen, 'Separation of Ownership and Control' (1983b) 26 *Journal of Law and Economics* 301.

a matter of aligning managerial action with shareholder interests, primarily through mechanisms of exit, voice, and incentive alignment.[9]

Within this paradigm, *shareholder activism* emerged as a more assertive expression of shareholder governance. Activist investors – including hedge funds, institutional shareholders, and coalitions focused on environmental, social, and governance (ESG) issues – began to intervene directly in corporate governance, strategy, and capital allocation. While some forms of activism promoted accountability and long-term value, others drew criticism for reinforcing short-termism and privileging narrow financial interests over broader stakeholder concerns.[10] As activist tactics proliferated, so too did questions about the legitimacy, consistent and long-term value of investor influence.

Even early corporate theorists approached shareholder control with caution.[11] More recent scholarship has deepened this scepticism, pointing to power asymmetries, accountability gaps, and the normative narrowness of corporate governance models that elevate shareholder oversight above all else.[12] Some critics argue that amplifying shareholder voice – especially through intermediated institutional investors – may displace, rather than remedy, corporate accountability failures.[13] Recurrent crises – from corporate scandals and financial collapses to

[9] Frank H. Easterbrook and Daniel R. Fischel, *The Economic Structure of Corporate Law*, (1996 ed., Harvard University Press 1991).

[10] See e.g. Iman Anabtawi, 'Some Skepticism about Increasing Shareholder Power' (2006) 53 *UCLA Law Review* 561.

[11] For an early critique, see Richard Eells, *The Government of Corporations* (The Free Press 1962), at 69 and 253 (describing shareholder control as 'probably the foundation stone of the most widely held dogmas about corporate governance', but acknowledging that 'corporate governors . . . try to "balance the interests" of the competing groups, and in doing so they engage in a complicated system of bargaining'.)

[12] Margaret M. Blair and Lynn A. Stout, 'A Team Production Theory of Corporate Law' (1999) 85 *Virginia Law Review* 247; Martin Gelter, 'The Dark Side of Shareholder Influence: Managerial Autonomy and Stakeholder Orientation in Comparative Corporate Governance' (2019) 50 *Harvard International Law Journal* 129; Ruth V. Aguilera, Cynthia Williams, John M. Conley, and Deborah E. Rupp, 'Corporate Governance and Social Responsibility: A comparative analysis of the UK and the US' (2006) 14 *Corporate Governance: An International Review* 147; Dionysia Katelouzou and Peer Zumbansen, 'The Transnationalization of Corporate Governance: Law, Institutional Arrangements, & Corporate Power' (2021) 38 *Arizona Journal of International and Comparative Law* 1.

[13] As Roe argued, shifting power 'upstairs' from corporate managers to institutions risks replicating managerial problems at a higher level, since 'a partial shift to empowered but usually noninterventionist institutions . . . would merely mean that the problems would shift only partly'. See Mark J. Roe, *Strong Managers Weak Owners: The Political Roots of American Corporate Finance* (Princeton University Press 1994), 236.

climate breakdown, rising inequality, and geopolitical destabilisation – have exposed the limits of firm-level oversight and short-term value maximisation in addressing systemic fragilities.[14] These failures make clear that institutional investor power is no longer merely a technical matter of governance; it is a public concern.[15]

Beneath these critiques lies a deeper structural insight: the architecture of contemporary capital markets renders traditional dyadic agency models inadequate. In corporate governance discourse, institutional investors have long been positioned as principals, holding corporate managers to account. Yet they are also agents, bound by fiduciary, contractual, and regulatory duties to their proximate clients and beneficiaries. This dual characterisation, foundational to the idea of 'agency capitalism', captures an important tension but ultimately oversimplifies the role of institutional investors.[16]

The reality is more complex. In what has been termed 'fiduciary capitalism',[17] and more recently 'asset manager capitalism',[18] a small number of institutional investors – especially large asset managers – exercise growing influence over corporate governance and market outcomes, despite their delegated and intermediated position in the investment chain. Operating as custodians of other people's money, they are embedded in complex and opaque systems of delegation, often with little transparency or public oversight.[19]

[14] See e.g. Alan Dignam, 'The Future of Shareholder Democracy in the Shadow of the Financial Crisis' (2013) 36 *Seattle University Law Review* 639; Beate Sjafjell 'Achieving Corporate Sustainability: What Is the Role of the Shareholder?' in Hanne Birkmose (ed.), *Shareholder's Duties* (Kluwer Law International 2017), 377–404; Curtis J. Milhaupt, 'Corporate governance in an era of geoeconomics' (2025) 52 *Journal of Corporate Law Studies* 281.

[15] Dionysia Katelouzou, 'Shareholder Stewardship: A Case for (Re)Embedding the Institutional Investors and the Corporation?' in Beate Sjåfjell and Christopher M. Bruner (eds.), *The Cambridge Handbook of Corporate Law, Corporate Governance and Sustainability* (Cambridge University Press 2019), 581–595.

[16] Ronald J. Gilson and Jeffrey N. Gordon, 'The Agency Costs of Agency Capitalism: Activist Investors and the Reevaluation of Governance Rights' (2013) 113 *Columbia Law Review* 863.

[17] James Hawley and Andrew Williams, 'The Emergence of Fiduciary Capitalism' (1997) 5 *Corporate Governance: An International Review* 206.

[18] Benjamin Braun, 'Asset Manager Capitalism as a Corporate Governance Regime' in Alexander Hertel-Fernandez and others (eds.), *The American Political Economy: Politics, Markets, and Power* (Cambridge University Press 2021).

[19] Generally on the embeddedness of corporate socially responsibility and corporate governance, see Luc Fransen, 'The Embeddedness of Responsible Business Practice: Exploring the Interaction Between National-Institutional Environments and Corporate Social Responsibility' (2013) 115 *Journal of Business Ethics* 213; Dionysia Katelouzou and

In the UK, institutional investors have become central to the state's broader economic agenda, with policymakers increasingly viewing investor engagement as a lever for responsible governance, capital attraction, and market competitiveness.[20] Simultaneously, investors are being called upon to mitigate systemic risks – from climate change and biodiversity loss to inequality and public health.[21] The stakes of failing to move beyond narrow conceptions of oversight have never been higher.

Ideas of 'shareholder democracy' have added a layer of normative aspiration to the institutional investors' role in corporate governance.[22] In the UK, it took political form in the 1980s through the project of a 'share-owning democracy' – an effort to democratise capital by expanding retail participation in equity markets. Prime Minister Margaret Thatcher famously declared her ambition to build a society 'where owning shares is as common as having a car'.[23] While the rhetoric resonated across the political spectrum,[24] the structural realities of financial intermediation soon displaced this vision. The expansion of institutional ownership, fragmented accountability, and short-term investment strategies all revealed the limits of shareholder governance and activism as tools for meaningful oversight.

It is against this backdrop that *shareholder stewardship* emerged – not merely as an extension of shareholder rights but also as a more expansive vision of investor responsibility.[25] As institutions supplanted individuals

Peer Zumbansen, 'The New Geographies of Corporate Governance' (2020) 42 *University of Pennsylvania Journal of International Law* 1, respectively.

20 See HM Treasury, *Edinburgh Reforms* (2022); House of Commons Treasury Committee, *FCA and PRA Secondary Competitiveness and Growth Objective* (2024); UK Finance, *Plan for Growth* (March 2025).

21 World Bank Group, *World Development Report: Finance for an Equitable Recovery* (2022); World Economic Forum, *Global Risks Report 2024* (2024).

22 Dalia Tsuk Mitchell, 'Shareholders as Proxies: The Contours of Shareholder Democracy Symposium: Understanding Corporate Law through History' (2006) 63 *Washington and Lee Law Review* 1503.

23 Margaret Thatcher, Speech to Conservative Party Conference, 11 October 1985, available at www.margaretthatcher.org/document/106145. For a discussion of shareholder democracy as a political project during the Thatcher era, see Colin Crouch, *Post-Democracy* (Polity Press 2004), especially ch. 3.

24 See 'Brown speech: 'Politics as a moral duty' *Financial Times* (26 September 2005).

25 On shareholder stewardship and engagement, see generally contributions to Dionysia Katelouzou and Dan W. Puchniak (eds.), *Global Shareholder Stewardship* (Cambridge University Press 2022) and Harpreet Kaur, Chao Xi, Christoph Van der Elst, and Anne Lafarre (eds.), *The Cambridge Handbook of Shareholder Engagement and Voting* (Cambridge University Press 2022).

as dominant market actors, stewardship was proposed as a normative response to short-termism and the inadequacies of traditional governance.[26] The first-generation UK Stewardship Code (1G UK Code), introduced by the Financial Reporting Council (FRC) in 2010 and revised in 2012, sought to institutionalise this vision by promoting more effective engagement by institutional investors in the wake of the global financial crisis of 2007–09. As a soft-law instrument grounded in disclosure, the Code framed stewardship primarily in terms of firm-specific oversight, encouraging signatories to explain how they exercised their responsibilities as shareholders.[27]

While the UK Stewardship Code has often been described as a global 'gold standard', its real-world impact remains contested.[28] In the years that followed, rising demands for 'stakeholder capitalism', climate action, and sustainable finance began to redefine the expectations placed on institutional investors, situating them within a broader debate over corporate purpose and the responsibilities of capital.[29] Responding to

[26] See e.g. Stephen M. Davis, Jon Lukomnik, and David Pitt-Watson, 'Active Shareowner Stewardship: A New Paradigm for Capitalism' (2009) 2 *Rotman International Journal of Pension Management* 10; John Kay, *The Kay Review of UK Equity Markets and Long-Term Decision Making* (July 2012).

[27] Financial Reporting Council, *The UK Stewardship Code 2012* (2012).

[28] Financial Reporting Council, *The Influence of the UK Stewardship Code 2020 on Practice and Reporting* (July 2022), 9.

[29] See e.g. The World after Covid-19 – By Invitation: Mark Carney on How the Economy Must Yield to Human Values, *Economist* (18 April 2020); Barbara Nock, A Fundamental Reshaping of Finance (16 January 2020) Harvard Law School Forum on Corporate Governance, https://corpgov.law.harvard.edu/2020/01/16/a-fundamental-reshaping-of-finance/. The debate over the corporate has intensified since 2019 on both sides of the Atlantic with proposals from the Business Roundtable, the US association of corporate chief executive officers, and the British Academy. See *Statement on the Purpose of a Corporation*, Business Roundtable (19 August 2019), https://opportunity.businessroundtable.org/wp-content/uploads/2019/12/BRT-Statement-on-the-Purpose-of-a-Corporation-with-Signatures.pdf, and *Principles for Purposeful Business: How to Deliver the Framework for the Future of the Corporation*, British Academy (November 2019), www.thebritishacademy.ac.uk/documents/224/future-of-the-corporation-principles-purposeful-business.pdf. The academic debate over the corporate purpose has been also intensified. See e.g. Lucian A. Bebchuk and Roberto Tallarita, 'The Illusory Promise of Stakeholder Governance' (2020) 106 *Cornell Law Review* 91; Colin Mayer, 'Shareholderism versus Stakeholderism – A Misconceived Contradiction: A Comment on "The Illusory Promise of Stakeholder Governance", by Lucian Bebchuk and Roberto Tallarita Essay' (2020) 106 *Cornell Law Review* 1859; Alex Edmans, *Grow the Pie: How Great Companies Deliver Both Purpose and Profit* (Cambridge University Press 2020); Brian R. Cheffins, 'The Past, Present and Future of Corporate Purpose' (2025) 48 *Delaware Journal of Corporate Law* 387; Klaus J. Hopt, 'Corporate Purpose and Stakeholder Value: Historical, Economic, and Comparative Law Remarks on the Current Debate, Legislative Options, and Enforcement Problems' in Jens-

this evolving context – and to critiques of the 1G UK Code's narrow scope, procedural emphasis, and lack of enforcement – the second-generation UK Stewardship Code (2G UK Code), effective from 2020, significantly expanded the normative framing of stewardship.[30] It shifted the focus beyond shareholder oversight towards long-term value creation, ESG integration, and accountability for the financial and societal systems in which investors are embedded.[31]

Yet the promise of shareholder stewardship remains unevenly realised. Despite its expanded ambitions, stewardship continues to operate within fragmented institutional structures, constrained legal mandates, and inconsistent investor practices. In many cases, it has failed to generate meaningful shifts in accountability or long-term value orientation.[32] These limitations point to a deeper challenge: stewardship, in its current form, lacks the normative clarity, conceptual coherence, and institutional grounding needed to guide consistent and credible practice across the investment landscape.

Today, many institutional investors are universal owners, with globally diversified portfolios that expose them to both firm-level risks and broader systemic externalities and interdependent shocks.[33] In this context, a growing constellation of systemic risks – ranging from climate breakdown, biodiversity loss, and geopolitical instability to social inequality, digital vulnerability, public health crises, and political polarisation – shapes the very conditions under which long-term value can be generated and preserved.[34]

Hinrich Binder (ed.) *Corporate Purpose, CSR, and ESG* (Oxford University Press 2024), 17–54 and the contributions to: Elizabeth Pollman and Robert B. Thompson (eds.), *Research Handbook on Corporate Purpose and Personhood* (Edward Elgar Publishing 2021). See also Dorothy S. Lund, 'Toward a Dynamic View of Corporate Purpose' (2025) 109 *Minnesota Law Review* 2089 (arguing for a context-sensitive and evolving understanding of purpose that reflects changing stakeholder and market conditions).

30 Financial Reporting Council, *The UK Stewardship Code 2020* (2019).

31 On the contested meaning and evolution of ESG, see Ann Lipton, 'ESG Investing, or, if You Can't Beat 'em, join 'em' in Pollman and Thompson (eds.), Research Handbook on Corporate Purpose and Personhood; Elizabeth Pollman, 'The Making and Meaning of ESG' U of Penn, Inst for Law & Econ Research Paper No 22-23, European Corporate Governance Institute – Law Working Paper No 659/2022 <https://ssrn.com/abstract=4219857>.

32 See e.g. John Kingman, *Independent Review of the Financial Reporting Council* (December 2018).

33 James Hawley and Andrew Williams, 'Universal Owners: Challenges and Opportunities' (2007) 15 *Corporate Governance: An International Review* 415.

34 See e.g. Financial Stability Board, *Holistic Review of the March Market Turmoil* (2020); International Sustainability Standards Board, *IFRS S1 and S2 Standards* (2023); OECD

It is in response to these challenges that this book proposes a new conceptual model: *enlightened shareholder* – and more broadly, *investor* – *stewardship*. The model calls on institutional investors to move beyond narrow monitoring of corporate performance and to act as custodians of capital – with enduring responsibilities not only to their proximate clients and beneficiaries (those to whom duties are directly owed) but also to end-investors and to the financial, social, and ecological systems in which their decisions are embedded.[35]

This concept underpins the book's broader argument: that for institutional investors to fulfil their expansive, other-regarding responsibilities with credibility and effectiveness, a fundamental recalibration is needed – one that retains the discipline of fiduciary accountability while recognising the systemic, multi-relational nature of investor power. Enlightened investor stewardship does not abandon the historical foundations of shareholder governance or the legal realism of fiduciary, contractual, and regulatory duties. Instead, it recasts them in light of today's interdependent risks, fragmented accountabilities, and the interests of 'unseen others' indirectly affected across the investment chain and beyond.

At its core, this model of stewardship is about rebuilding *trust* – not only between shareholders and corporate managers but also across the entire investment system: among asset managers, asset owners, and the beneficiaries they serve.[36] It recognises that institutional investors differ in mandate, capacity, and strategy, yet insists that all stewardship be grounded in a framework of other-regarding responsibility – a normative orientation that takes seriously the broader impacts of capital allocation.

Enlightened investor stewardship conceives of stewardship as a multi-level practice, encompassing micro-level corporate oversight, portfolio-level allocation and monitoring, engagement with system-wide risks, and contributions to macro-level societal resilience. It calls for a mode of investor responsibility that is not only financially sound but also systemically informed, socially attuned, and publicly credible. It does not require all investors to act as activists or assume quasi-regulatory

(2023), *Long-Term Investment and the Role of Institutional Investors*; World Economic Forum, *Global Risks Report* (2024).

35 On the concept of custodianship as a model of institutional investor behaviour, see Andrew Johnston, Rachelle Belinga, and Blache Segrestin, 'Governing Institutional Investor Engagement: From Activism to Stewardship to Custodianship?' (2022) 22 *Journal of Corporate Law Studies* 45.

36 On the role of trust in the financial markets, see generally Colin Mayer, *Firm Commitment: Why the Corporation Is Failing Us and How to Restore Trust in It* (Oxford University Press 2013).

functions. But it does demand that they consider the wider implications of their decisions – without abandoning their core duties as fiduciaries and stewards of capital.

This responsibility has never been more urgent.[37] As expectations of stewardship expand, so too must the conceptual clarity, institutional support, and regulatory coherence needed to make it meaningful – not only to protect long-term value but also to sustain the conditions for inclusive and sustainable growth. Yet what meaningful stewardship requires – how it should be defined, institutionalised, and regulated – remains deeply contested. It is to that puzzle – and to the purpose of this book – that we now turn.

1.2 Framing the Puzzle: Power, Purpose, and Ambiguity

Investor stewardship, in its earliest form as shareholder stewardship, gained traction in the aftermath of the global financial crisis of 2007–09 – not merely as a technical enhancement of engagement practices but also as a response to growing concerns over investor accountability and long-term value protection. Its most influential articulation came in the 1G UK Code, which sought to improve investor–company engagement following the market failures of that period. Rooted in the work of the Institutional Shareholders' Committee (ISC), the 1G UK Code emphasised transparency in voting and firm-specific oversight but ultimately reinforced a shareholder-centric conception of stewardship – one focused on firm-level governance, with limited attention to broader structural or systemic dynamics.[38]

The 2G UK Code marked a significant conceptual shift – from shareholder stewardship to a broader model of investor stewardship. It widened the normative framing of stewardship beyond shareholder oversight to other asset classes and strategies to encompass long-term value creation, ESG integration, and systemic risk oversight. Under this expanded view, institutional investors were no longer cast solely as

[37] See e.g. *Edelman Trust Barometer 2025: Global Report* (Edelman, January 2025), which finds that business is now viewed as both the most competent and the most ethical institution and is increasingly expected to lead on societal challenges such as climate change, inequality, and misinformation. These rising expectations, this book argues, also extend to institutional investors.

[38] Dionysia Katelouzou, 'Something Old, Something New: Cultivating Institutional Investor Engagement through Shareholder Stewardship' in Luca Enriques and Giovanni Strampelli (eds.), *Board-Shareholder Dialogue: Policy Debate, Legal Constraints and Best Practices* (Oxford University Press 2024), 185, 198–201.

monitors of corporate behaviour, but as stewards of the broader systems in which investment is embedded.

Yet this evolution has introduced new conceptual and operational tensions. The current stewardship landscape is defined by a central paradox. Institutional investors are increasingly expected to address far-reaching challenges – climate breakdown, biodiversity loss, social inequality, and market fragility – yet the tools and governance frameworks available to support this expanded mandate have not kept pace. Inherited assumptions of shareholder primacy, the dominance of large asset managers, narrow constructions of materiality, and a tradition of regulatory deference continue to constrain the scope and credibility of current stewardship practices.[39]

While the pluralisation of stewardship across asset classes, strategies, and jurisdictions has fostered innovation, it has also exposed a central disjuncture: stewardship's expanding normative and operational ambitions have outpaced the legal, regulatory, and conceptual scaffolding on which they rest. What began as a modest tool for improving shareholder engagement now risks becoming conceptually overloaded and operationally incoherent.

This widening gap between aspiration and implementation gives rise to the central puzzle that animates this book: 'How can investor stewardship regimes credibly support long-term, other-regarding responsibilities in an institutional landscape marked by tensions between private governance and public consequence, fragmented regulation, and a reliance on soft-law disclosure – often in the absence of normative clarity or enforceable standards?'

Answering this question demands more than incremental reform. It requires a fundamental rethinking of the normative and institutional architecture of investor stewardship – first conceived in shareholder-centric terms, but now stretched across a more complex and contested terrain of responsibilities, actors, and risks.

As this book's historical, conceptual, and empirical analysis will show, stewardship has evolved from a narrow tool of corporate oversight into a wide-ranging – yet at times amorphous – set of expectations encompassing governance, sustainability, and systemic resilience.[40] But this

39 See e.g. Anna Tilba and Arad Reisberg, 'Fiduciary Duty under the Microscope: Stewardship and the Spectrum of Pension Fund Engagement' (2019) 82 *The Modern Law Review* 456.

40 Generally on the relationship between sustainability and corporate governance, see Andrew Johnston, 'Integrating sustainability into corporate governance' in

evolution has not been matched by regulatory coherence or conceptual clarity. Frequently invoked as a symbol of investor responsibility, investor stewardship remains under-defined, raising urgent questions about its legitimacy, effectiveness, and future direction.[41]

This conceptual looseness is reflected in the wide variation in how stewardship is defined and practised. Across policy, industry, and academic discourse, terms such as stewardship, engagement, and active ownership are often used interchangeably – typically to denote firm-level monitoring and dialogue.[42] For some, stewardship is reduced to a set of practices or tools, including ESG integration; for others, it signals a broader fiduciary ethos – a philosophy of accountability across time and stakeholders.[43] Among institutional investors, interpretations vary widely: some adopt a narrow, governance-focused lens, while others embrace a more expansive, sustainability-oriented approach.[44] For beneficiaries, workers, and the wider public, stewardship often appears as a vague promise – laden with normative appeal but lacking institutional clarity or enforceable commitments.[45]

Absent firmer conceptual foundations, investor stewardship risks becoming both protean in meaning and performative in application – frequently invoked, inconsistently applied, and ultimately ineffective in guiding investor conduct.[46]

Christopher M. Bruner and Marc T. Moore (eds.), *A Research Agenda for Corporate Law* (Edward Elgar 2023), 57–82.

41 On the broader disparity between the rhetoric of corporate responsibility and the practical mechanisms for accountability, see Colin Mayer, *Prosperity: Better Business Makes the Greater Good* (Oxford University Press 2018).

42 See e.g. Directive (EU) 2017/828 of the European Parliament and of the Council of 17 May 2017 amending Directive 2007/36/EC as regards the encouragement of long-term shareholder engagement, OJ L 132, 20.5.2017, Article 3g (referring to 'engagement'); Principles for Responsible Investment, *Stewardship*, https://public.unpri.org/investment-tools/stewardship (equating stewardship with 'active ownership').

43 See e.g. The Law Commission, *Fiduciary Duties of Investment Intermediaries* (Law Com No 350, 2014), xiv.

44 Dionysia Katelouzou, 'The Rhetoric of Activist Shareholder Stewards' (2021) 18 *New York University Journal of Law & Business* 665.

45 Cameron Gilchrist, Lucy Hayes, Cherryl Ng, Patrick Sholl, and Jackie Sprang, *Matter of fact-sheets: Improving consumer comprehension of financial sustainability disclosures* (Financial Conduct Authority, Occational Paper 62, October 2022), 5, 29.

46 Recent AGM seasons have further highlighted this performativity, revealing a persistent disconnect between formal mechanisms of engagement and genuine accountability. See e.g. ECGI, *'Shareholder Meetings: A Necessary Change of Tone'*, ECGI Blog (2024) www.ecgi.global/publications/blog/shareholder-meetings-a-necessary-change-of-tone (highlighting the growing call to recalibrate the tone and practice of shareholder meetings – from scripted exchanges to spaces for deliberative, constructive, and forward-

This book intervenes by confronting three foundational questions:

- What is the normative purpose of investor stewardship? Is it a mechanism for enhancing shareholder oversight, managing ESG risks, fostering sustainable capital markets, or all of these? And when these aims come into tension, how should they be balanced and prioritised?
- Who are the appropriate actors and intended beneficiaries of investor stewardship? While fiduciary and contractual frameworks emphasise duties to proximate clients and beneficiaries, investor decisions often affect a wider network of 'unseen others' – including investee companies, workers, communities, ecosystems, and future generations. How should these broader responsibilities be conceptualised, justified, and institutionalised?
- Can soft-law frameworks such as stewardship codes meaningfully support this expanded vision of investor responsibility? What do evolving disclosure practices under the first- and second-generation UK Stewardship Codes reveal about the possibilities – and limits – of stewardship reporting as a regulatory tool?

To answer these questions, the book develops a recalibrated model of *enlightened investor stewardship* – one that retains fiduciary and contractual realism but reframes them in light of intergenerational equity, systemic risk, and public legitimacy. While acknowledging diversity in investor type and strategy, it argues that all stewardship practices must be grounded in a shared normative and regulatory infrastructure.

Investor stewardship, in this view, is not a singular or uniform activity. It unfolds across four levels: micro (firm-specific oversight), portfolio (capital allocation and design), system (market-wide risks and norms), and macro (engagement with policy and institutional frameworks beyond the market). It is carried out by a heterogeneous ecosystem – asset owners, asset managers, proxy advisors, data providers, and others – whose varied roles shape the content, credibility, and accountability of stewardship. Practices range from compliance-driven monitoring to system-aware, values-driven engagement, reflecting differences in ambition, capacity, and responsibility. These complexities demand a stewardship model that is attuned to both the diversity of investor strategies and the systemic conditions that shape long-term outcomes.

looking dialogue). On the role of AGMs, see generally Anne Lafarre, *The AGM in Europe: Theory and Practice of Shareholder Behaviour* (Emerald Insight 2017).

Addressing this terrain requires a broader conceptual shift. Originally developed to curb short-termism in public equity markets, *shareholder stewardship* must now transition into *investor stewardship* – a broader, more inclusive model capable of addressing diverse asset classes, stewardship strategies, and systemic risks. This book adopts *enlightened shareholder stewardship* as a starting point – recognising the historical and legal roots of shareholder influence but insisting that the concept must evolve. Enlightenment here signals not a moral aspiration, but an institutional awareness – an orientation that integrates investor duties with attention to long-term value, systemic resilience, and public trust.

This shift is already underway. In 2023, one major UK public pension fund recalibrated its climate strategy – not by divesting from high-emitting companies, but by intensifying engagement on credible transition plans and long-term adaptation.[47] Another opted for divestment, citing systemic risk and public legitimacy.[48] A global asset manager voted against hundreds of firms failing short on climate and governance, linking these actions to both fiduciary duty and systemic sustainability.[49] While their approaches differ, these examples reflect a common recognition: that institutional investors – particularly public pension funds and large asset managers – are beginning to act not only as monitors of corporate behaviour but also as stewards of the broader systems affected by capital allocation.[50]

This emerging pattern reflects the essence of enlightened investor stewardship. It does not require all investors to become activists or planetary and societal guardians, nor to take on quasi-regulatory roles.[51] But it does require them to recognise the systemic dimensions of investment, respond to other-regarding impacts, and act with

47 Brunel Pension Partnership, *Climate Change Policy 2023–2030*.

48 Chris Flood, 'Nest Dumps ExxonMobil over Climate Change Risks' *Financial Times* (20 December 2021).

49 Thomas Cox, 'LGIM Votes against 32 Firms in "Say on Climate" proposals' *Environmental Finance* (25 April 2023).

50 See e.g. European Corporate Governance Institute (ECGI), 'This AGM Season, It's Time for Asset Owners to Step Up', ECGI Blog (2024) www.ecgi.global/publications/blog/this-agm-season-its-time-for-asset-owners-to-step-up (asserting that asset owners must not remain passive observers but instead assert leadership, setting expectations and aligning stewardship with long-term public value).

51 But see Paul Davies, 'The UK Stewardship Code 2010–2020: From Saving the Company to Saving the Planet?' in Dionysia Katelouzou and Dan W. Puchniak (eds.), *Global Shareholder Stewardship* (Cambridge University Press 2022), 44–66.

integrity, transparency, and accountability – without abandoning core regulatory and legal commitments.

Supporting this evolution requires more than incremental reform. A third-generation UK Stewardship Code (3G UK Code) is needed – not simply as an update, but as a principled and pragmatic response to stewardship's expanding remit. Properly designed, such a Code can serve as both a normative anchor and an institutional scaffold. But to do so, it must move beyond aspirational language, offering differentiated expectations, robust interpretive guidance, and credible mechanisms for learning, challenge, and accountability.

This book charts that path. Grounded in the UK context but globally relevant, it weaves historical analysis, conceptual development, empirical evidence, and regulatory critique into a coherent framework. It makes the case for transforming investor stewardship from aspirational rhetoric into a credible institution – capable of governing capital responsibly in an era of interdependence, uncertainty, and systemic risk.

1.3 Stewardship Reimagined: Normative, Empirical, and Regulatory Contributions

This book introduces a reimagining of investor stewardship – conceptually, empirically, and regulatorily – as part of a broader argument for redefining how institutional investor responsibility is understood and enacted. Rather than treating stewardship as a narrow mechanism of shareholder engagement or compliance-driven oversight, the book develops a multidimensional account that reflects the systemic, relational, and normative pressures reshaping capital markets today. Drawing on conceptual analysis, empirical data, and regulatory critique, it sets out how stewardship must be reconceived – and institutionalised – in a world of financial, ecological, and social interdependence.

Conceptually, the book advances a foundational rethinking of investor stewardship that moves beyond its shareholder-centric origins. While it begins with the institutional and historical development of shareholder governance – augmented by new empirical insights into evolving forms of shareholder activism in the UK – this is not to reinforce a narrow paradigm, but to illuminate how the nature, scope, and significance of institutional investor power have transformed over time.

At the core of this reconceptualisation lies a tripartite understanding of investor stewardship as a form of *power*: exercised by institutional investors, *on behalf of others* (their proximate clients and beneficiaries), and *for the benefit of others* who are often 'unseen' – a term used to capture the diffuse and indirect constituencies affected by investment decisions – including end-investors, investee assets, and the broader social, environmental, economic systems shaped by capital allocation.[52] This perspective casts investor stewardship not merely as a delegated responsibility grounded in legal, fiduciary, and contractual relationships but also as a public function shaped by the systemic consequences of investment decisions.[53]

Building on this, the book develops a four-part relational model that maps investor accountability across four overlapping domains: proximate clients/beneficiaries (*client stewardship*), end-investors across layers of intermediation and over time (*end-investor stewardship*), investee assets (*asset stewardship*), and the wider financial, environmental, and social systems in which investment is embedded (*sustainability stewardship*). These domains are neither static nor discrete; they are continually shaped by legal mandates, institutional design, and shifting expectations around risk, return, and responsibility. Their interaction – frequently marked by friction, asymmetry, and entanglement – calls for a more expansive understanding of fiduciary, contractual, and public duty: one capable of mediating tensions between short-term financial performance and long-term resilience, between private value and public values.

This relational lens is operationalised through a typology of investor stewardship that captures its *multi-level*, *multi-actor*, *multi-asset*, *multi-means*, and *multi-aim* character. Stewardship today unfolds across four interrelated levels: micro-level oversight of firms and other assets, portfolio-level capital allocation and design, system-level engagement with market-wide norms and systemic risks, and macro-level interaction with policy and insitutional frameworks. It is carried out by a diverse field of actors – including asset owners, asset managers, and proxy advisors – spanning both direct and delegated investment structures. It spans a wide array of asset classes, from public equities to private markets, sovereign debt, and infrastructure, each with distinct governance logics and accountability norms.

The means of investor stewardship range from downstream tools – such as engagement, voting, and escalation – to upstream mechanisms embedded in mandates, benchmark selection, and fee structures.

52 On the concept of the 'unseen', see Dionysia Katelouzou, 'The Unseen "Others": A Framework for Investor Stewardship' (2024) 77 *Current Legal Problems* 295.

53 On the broader tension and blurring lines between 'private power' and 'public authority', see A. Claire Cutler, *Private Power and Global Authority: Transnational Merchant Law in the Global Political Economy* (Cambridge University Press 2003).

These upstream levers are especially important for aligning incentives and embedding coherent stewardship practices across the various functions and decision points within an institutional investor. The aims of investor stewardship range from value-oriented goals focused on financial performance to ESG-integrated approaches, and more expansive system-aware aims that address market resilience, environmental sustainability, and broader societal well-being.

What emerges is a pluralistic and evolving field of practice, shaped not only by legal duties and market incentives but also by institutional interpretation, strategic framing, and normative aspiration. By weaving together the tripartite and relational models with the typological framework, the book offers a reconceptualisation of investor stewardship that is both theoretically grounded and responsive to contemporary realities. This is where the concept of enlightened investor stewardship – and, within the realm of public equities, enlightened shareholder stewardship – takes shape.

What distinguishes the enlightened investor steward is not a departure from fiduciary, contractual, or regulatory mandates, nor a displacement of financial performance metrics, but a principled engagement with these obligations in light of broader and longer-term considerations. Enlightened investor stewardship does not require systemic or intergenerational concerns to override core duties; rather, it involves a reasoned deliberation of competing interests and temporal claims. This role entails navigating persistent tensions between legal duty and public value, short-term metrics and long-term system resilience, and private mandates and systemic impact. It is an inherently pluralistic model: some stewards may foreground sustainability or systemic risk, while others may frame their expanded responsibilities through fiduciary, governance, or market-based logics. What unites them is a shared orientation towards embedding broader accountability within the institutional architecture of investment – pushing the boundaries of legally defined mandates without discarding them.

This conceptual architecture underpins the book's empirical and regulatory proposals and its core claim: that investor stewardship must be reimagined not only in scope and ambition but also in the very terms by which it is defined, institutionalised, and held to account.

Empirically, the book begins by analysing how institutional investor power is exercised in practice, with a focus on the evolving forms of shareholder activism in the UK. Drawing on a curated dataset of publicly reported activist interventions between 2010 and 2020, it shows how traditional governance concerns – such as board composition and executive pay – are increasingly entangled with environmental, social, and systemic issues. While hedge funds and activist boutiques often dominate public narratives, the findings highlight the growing involvement of mainstream institutional investors – especially large asset managers and pension funds – in both collaborative and confrontational forms of shareholder engagement. This analysis offers a textured account of how shareholder stewardship is operationalised 'on the ground', revealing a continuum of influence from value-oriented to values-driven strategies.

Building on this foundation, the book then turns to how investor stewardship is disclosed and institutionalised through the UK Stewardship Code. It presents a mixed-methods analysis of public disclosures under the 2012 and 2020 iterations of the Code, combining qualitative coding, textual metrics, and structural topic modelling. This is the most systematic empirical account to date of the UK regime's implementation. The findings reveal both innovation and inertia. While some institutional investors articulate forward-looking, system-aware approaches aligned with long-term sustainability goals, others fall back on generic, backward-looking narratives that prioritise procedural over substantive engagement.

This variation is not merely a matter of institutional capacity or reporting style. It exposes deeper structural and normative tensions about what investor stewardship entails, whom it serves, and how it should be evaluated. As the analysis shows, without clearer purpose, interpretive alignment, and institutional enforcement, the reliance on stewardship reporting as a regulatory tool risks reinforcing opacity rather than promoting transparency. The pluralism captured in the book's typology of the varieties of investor stewardship thus becomes a double-edged sword: a space for institutional innovation but also a site of conceptual drift and regulatory fragmentation.

Regulatorily, the book responds to these tensions by advancing a reform agenda for a 3G UK Code. It diagnoses key shortcomings of the current regime – notably definitional ambiguity, narrative overload, and uneven implementation – that constrain the 2020 Code's ability to fulfil its ambition. In response, the book articulates a model of *enlightened investor stewardship* that remains faithful to legal, fiduciary, and contractual realism, while expanding its interpretive horizon to include the 'unseen others': from end-investors to investee assets and the broader systems – economic, environmental, and social upon which sustainable value depends.

Stewardship codes, in this light, should be reimagined not simply as disclosure tools or voluntary standards, but as *norm entrepreneurs*: regulatory instruments that articulate, align, and institutionalise evolving societal expectations about the role of capital in the economy. Positioned at the intersection of law, market practice, and public policy, a 3G UK Code can serve as both a normative anchor and a scaffolding for credible practice. To fulfil this role, it must offer a clearer definitional foundation, differentiated expectations across investor types and asset classes, and mechanisms for learning, challenge, and accountability – thereby enabling stewardship to function not as a performative label, but as a meaningful public responsibility.

This contribution engages and advances multiple scholarly and policy literatures. It speaks to corporate governance by rethinking shareholder power and board accountability; to fiduciary law's evolving understanding of investor obligations; to sustainable finance's efforts to integrate ESG and system-level risk; and to regulatory theory's analysis of soft-law, principles-based regulation, and the expressive function of legal norms. It also contributes to empirical legal studies through a methodologically rich account of stewardship disclosures; to institutional theory and the political economy of corporate governance by tracing how investor norms evolve under conditions of pressure and uncertainty; and to transnational legal and regulatory governance by analysing how domestic stewardship regimes shape – and are shaped by – global norms and practices.

By weaving these strands together, the book offers not merely a synthesis but also a conceptual reframing. It develops a new lens for governing capital in the public interest – one that does not sidestep the constraints of legal obligation, but reinterprets them through a more systemic, relational, and pluralistic account of institutional responsibility.

In short, *The Path to Enlightened Investor Stewardship* makes the case for a reimagined stewardship regime – one that is intellectually rigorous, empirically grounded, and institutionally credible. It begins with the legacy of shareholder stewardship, but rethinks its scope, purpose, and application in light of the evolving responsibilities that institutional investors now face – not only to their proximate clients and beneficiaries but also to end-investors, investee companies, broader stakeholders, and the systems within which markets operate. While retaining the legal, fiduciary, and contractual duties that underpin their legitimacy, this reframing opens the door to a more expansive and accountable vision of stewardship. This, in turn, sets the stage for enlightened investor stewardship: the conceptual model developed and advanced throughout the book.

1.4 Mapping the Book: From Shareholder Governance to Enlightened Stewardship

This book unfolds in three interconnected parts, tracing the evolution of shareholder – and more broadly, investor – stewardship from its intellectual foundations to its regulatory manifestations and empirical realities, culminating in a reform agenda grounded in the model of enlightened investor stewardship. It moves from conceptual genealogy to practical diagnosis to normative reconstruction.

Chapters 2 and 3 lay the historical and intellectual groundwork of shareholder governance as the precursor to contemporary shareholder – and, more broadly, investor – stewardship. Chapter 2 revisits the classical debates surrounding the separation of ownership and control, the rise of the managerial firm, and the shifting status of the shareholder – from entrepreneurial owner to passive risk-bearer to empowered institutional investor. It traces the evolution of shareholder governance across economic, legal, and political paradigms, clarifying foundational tensions between shareholder control and managerial discretion, efficiency and legitimacy, and private interest and public responsibility.

Chapter 3 extends this foundation by examining the rise of institutional investors and the transformation of shareholder activism. Drawing on empirical data from UK activist campaigns, it explores how once-passive actors have become key participants in corporate governance – deploying voice across firm-level, portfolio-level, and system-level strategies. In doing so, the chapter marks the pivot point in the book from traditional shareholder governance towards the broader responsibilities associated with investor stewardship.

Chapters 4 and 5 turn to the anatomy and regulation of investor stewardship. Chapter 4 develops a conceptual framework grounded in a tripartite model: institutional investors exercise power *on behalf of others* (their proximate clients and beneficiaries) and *for others* (the broader stakeholders and systems affected by their decisions). It introduces four interconnected stewardship relationships: *client stewardship*, which centres on aligning stewardship activities with the contractual and fiduciary duties owed to proximate clients and beneficiaries; *end-investor stewardship*, which recognises obligations to the ultimate savers and beneficiaries; *asset stewardship*, which focuses on the responsible oversight of investee companies and other assets; and *sustainability stewardship*, which extends responsibility to ecosystems, systemic risks, and future generations.

Throughout the book, references to 'clients and beneficiaries' reflect the language of stewardship codes and disclosures. Analytically, however, client stewardship concerns contractual and legal obligations to proximate clients or beneficiaries, depending on institutional form, while end-investor stewardship captures responsibility to ultimate beneficiaries. Together, these overlapping and sometimes conflicting responsibilities illustrate how institutional investors must navigate multiple accountabilities, shifting norms, and growing expectations within and beyond the investment chain.

Chapter 5 turns to the UK Stewardship Code as both a national experiment in soft-law governance and a global reference point in the transnational diffusion of stewardship norms. It traces the Code's evolution from its origins in investor-led best-practice statements, through the 1G UK Code (2010/2012) to the 2G UK Code (2020). The chapter analyses how this trajectory reflects a progressive broadening of regulatory ambition: from micro-level shareholder engagement to portfolio- and system-level stewardship; from a narrow focus on listed equities to all asset classes; and from monitoring corporate governance to shaping market-wide norms and public outcomes. At the same time, it interrogates the persistent limitations of soft law and the tensions between normative ambition and non-binding, disclosure-based enforcement. It shows how the Code's effectiveness ultimately hinges not on legal compulsion, but on reputational incentives, institutional uptake, and interpretive coherence across a heterogeneous investment landscape.

Chapters 6–8 shift from conceptual and regulatory foundations to empirical insight and reform. Chapter 6 presents a systematic textual and computational analysis of stewardship disclosures submitted under the 2012 and 2020 iterations of the UK Stewardship Code. Employing a multi-method Natural Language Processing (NLP) framework – including lexical analysis, similarity scoring, Structural Topic Modelling (STM), and regression analysis – it traces the evolution from the relatively uniform, compliance-driven narratives of the 1G UK Code to the more varied and rhetorically ambitious disclosures of the 2G regime. STM reveals a rhetorical shift towards *other-regarding stewardship* among large, UK-based, and experienced signatories, but also highlights fragmentation, vagueness, and raises concerns about *stewardship washing*.

Chapter 7 synthesises these patterns – enriched by a qualitative analysis of the 2020 stewardship disclosures – into a typology of the varieties of investor stewardship, arguing for a plural, differentiated understanding of stewardship in practice. It distinguishes between levels of intervention (micro, portfolio, system, and macro), types of actors (direct and indirect stewards), asset classes (listed equity, fixed income, real assets, and private markets), motivations (value, ESG/risk, and systemic), and operational mechanisms from upstream capital allocation to downstream engagement and escalation.

Chapter 8 advances a forward-looking reform agenda. It calls for a 3G UK Code, grounded in the model of *enlightened investor stewardship*. This model recognises the legal and fiduciary constraints institutional investors face but insists on their responsibility to address systemic risks and long-term societal outcomes. Stewardship codes, the chapter argues, should serve as *normative entrepreneurs* – enabling institutional coordination, guiding accountability, and expanding the boundaries of legitimate investor conduct. Drawing on lessons from the 2G UK Code and Section 172 of the Companies Act 2006, it proposes a redefinition of stewardship, improved reporting standards, and a differentiated, capacity-sensitive regulatory approach. While grounded in the UK context, the argument gestures towards a global shift: from investor stewardship as a procedural disclosure exercise to stewardship as a credible expression of investor responsibility for the public interest.

This intervention comes at a critical juncture. Across markets, institutional investors are being asked to shoulder new responsibilities for climate resilience, human rights, and inclusive growth, amid mounting scepticism over the legitimacy of financial governance. The UK's 2024 consultation on the Stewardship Code underscores this urgency.[54] As the gap between aspiration and implementation widens, so too does the need for a principled and practicable stewardship regime.

This book responds to that moment. It is written for scholars, policy-makers, and practitioners committed to understanding – and shaping – the evolving role of institutional investors in an age of systemic risk, interdependence, and public accountability. It provides a conceptual, empirical, and regulatory foundation for reimagining investor stewardship not as a narrow tool of compliance, but as a dynamic institution of governance.

The Path to Enlightened Investor Stewardship does not claim to offer a single blueprint. Rather, it sets out a framework for reform that is legally grounded, operationally viable, and normatively ambitious. It recognises that law alone cannot deliver legitimacy, nor can stewardship codes by themselves transform investor behaviour. But it insists that how we

[54] Financial Reporting Council, *UK Stewardship Code Consultation* (November 2024).

define, institutionalise, and enact investor stewardship matters – and that doing so with greater coherence, ambition, and integrity is both necessary and possible.

Without clearer normative anchoring, investor stewardship risks becoming a rhetorical exercise – rich in ambition but shallow in implementation. Is stewardship, to borrow Shakespeare's phrase, 'a tale . . . full of sound and fury, signifying nothing'?[55] Perhaps – but only if we allow it to remain conceptually vague and operationally weak.

This book argues otherwise.

[55] William Shakespeare, *Macbeth* act 5, sc 5.

2

Ownership, Control, and Shareholder Governance

Theoretical Roots and Institutional Shifts

2.1 Introduction

Shareholders have long held a prominent place in corporate governance literature.[1] However, the concept of *shareholder governance* – referring to the overall system of rules, processes, and practices that govern the relationship between shareholders and company 'management'[2] – has not featured prominently in the evolving trajectory of company law, which has oscillated between public regulatory frameworks and private contractual models.[3]

This chapter explores how theoretical perspectives from neighbouring fields such as economics, finance, and management have shaped understandings of shareholder governance over the past two centuries, with significant influence on legal scholarship. Spanning more than 200 years of intellectual history, it begins by retracing the historical role of shareholders in corporate governance, dating back to the eighteenth century when the roles of owners-entrepreneurs and risk bearers were closely

[1] A Google Scholar search for the term 'shareholder(s)' in article titles returned approximately 23,300 results as of 13 May 2025, indicating the term's widespread academic usage.

[2] Managers or management are used broadly to include both senior officers and board directors who carry out company business and make decisions on behalf of the company. For a similar broad definition, see Adolf A. Berle and Gardiner C. Means, *The Modern Corporation & Private Property* (2009 ed., Transaction Publishers 1932), 196 (defining 'management' as 'that body of men who, in law, have formally assumed the duties of exercising domination over the corporate business and assets. It thus derives its position from a legal title of some sort. Universally, under the American system of law, managers consist of a board of directors and the senior officers of the corporation').

[3] See e.g. Victor Brudney, 'Corporate Governance, Agency Costs, and the Rhetoric of Contract' (1985) 85 *Columbia Law Review* 1403, 1409 (arguing that the effect of the privatisation of company law was to disconnect shareholders from ownership and 'dependence upon state authority for their power'). For a recent account of the 'legal pluralist' configuration of company law and corporate governance, see Dionysia Katelouzou and Peer Zumbansen, 'The New Geographies of Corporate Governance' (2020) 42 *University of Pennsylvania Journal of International Law* 14.

intertwined. This overlap blurred the boundaries between ownership and property on the one hand, and control and power on the other.[4] That entanglement began to unravel in the early twentieth century, as the now-famous separation of ownership and control came into sharper focus.

While shareholder governance remained relatively subdued in the UK during the mid twentieth century, the rise of the market for corporate control from the late 1950s onwards marked the resurgence of shareholders as key actors in corporate governance. This period witnessed a shift from a traditional focus on ownership rights to an emphasis on market efficiency as the foundation of shareholder governance. Contractarian (economic) theories of the firm reinforced the shareholders' right to exit, portraying them as 'principals' to managerial 'agents' and recasting them as residual claimants or risk bearers – without necessarily endorsing active *shareholder engagement*. At this stage, shareholder involvement was largely reactive and transactional. The idea of shareholder engagement – understood as the active participation of shareholders in dialogue with company management to express opinions, concerns, and expectations – was not yet a central feature of governance practice.

The decline of hostile takeovers in the 1990s called into question the efficiency of passive shareholder ownership. At the same time, the ascent of institutional shareholders revitalised shareholder governance, making it a central feature of today's corporate governance landscape.

In concluding this journey through the theoretical and historical foundations of shareholder governance, this chapter re-evaluates how the evolving relationship between ownership and control continues to shape – and at times constrain – the role of shareholders. While the dispersion of share ownership challenged traditional conceptions of power, economic theories helped rescue shareholder governance by redefining it in terms of efficiency and contract, yet they also contributed to the marginalisation of participatory shareholder control. The rise of institutional investors has added a further layer of complexity: shareholder control – particularly the transient or 'migrant' influence of large asset managers – has become even more elusive.

[4] In addition to ownership/property and power/control, a third aspect of the corporate governance relationship between managers and shareholders relates to 'entitlement', that is, 'what shareholders are legally entitled to expect' from a company and its management. This aspect, which remains at the periphery of this chapter, has attracted scholarly attention and continues to provoke debate and controversy. For an account of shareholder entitlements under UK law, see Sarah Worthington, 'Shares and Shareholders: Property, Power and Entitlement' (2001) 22 *Company Lawyer* 258.

2.2 The Historical Foundations of Shareholder Governance

2.2.1 From Entrepreneurs to Risk Bearers: Shareholders in the Eighteenth and Nineteenth Centuries

Historically, before the prominence of the company form in Britain, what is now referred to as the shareholder (or stockholder in American terms) was often entwined with the 'entrepreneur'. Adding to the complexity, the 'entrepreneur' was sometimes termed an 'undertaker' or an 'adventurer' in early eighteenth-century English economic literature.[5] During this period, the 'joint stock company'[6] form was limited to large enterprises operating in the public interest under state-granted privileges. Entrepreneurs were identified with the 'proprietor' or 'owner' of shares, while smaller businesses operated as common law partnerships or sole proprietorships, with sole owners or partners serving as both entrepreneurs and managers.[7]

It was only in the late eighteenth and early nineteenth centuries that the three distinct roles of 'proprietor' (or 'capitalist'), 'entrepreneur', and 'manager' began to be delineated. Entrepreneurs started investing in other enterprises, becoming 'sleeping partners' or 'co-partners' who provided capital without managing.[8] The Companies Act 1844 and subsequent reforms accelerated the adoption of the company form, covering larger, previously unincorporated operations and smaller companies.[9] This

5 Bert F. Hoselitz, 'The Early History of Entrepreneurial Theory' in Joseph J. Spengler and William R. Allen (eds.), *Essays in Economic Thought: Aristotle to Marshall* (Rand McNally 1960), 240–3 (elaborating the English concepts designating entrepreneurial activity in the seventeenth and early eighteenth centuries).

6 For the distinction between the joint stock company as an *economic* form and the incorporated company as a *legal* form, see Paddy Ireland, 'The Rise of the Limited Liability Company' (1984) 12 *International Journal of Sociology of Law* 239.

7 Adam Smith, *An Inquiry into the Nature and Causes of the Wealth of Nations* (1776), 740 (preserving the quasi-public joint-stock company form – in which the management by 'a court of directors' is insufficiently controlled by 'a general court of proprietors' – for large companies operating in specific sectors).

8 See Brian R. Cheffins, *Corporate Ownership and Control: British Business Transformed* (Oxford University Press 2008), 156, 164 (elaborating that in most of the eighteenth century entrepreneurs or 'industrialists' remained sceptical or even belligerent to outside investment and tracing the key transition to the divorce of ownership and control in Britain to 'the 1845/46 railway mania').

9 See, among others, Ron Harris, 'The Private Origins of the Private Company: Britain 1862–1907' (2013) 33 *Oxford Journal of Legal Studies* 339, 342–50 (tracing the history of companies in Britain from the few and large joint-stock companies of the seventeenth and early eighteenth centuries to the more and smaller private companies); R. A. Bryer, 'The Mercantile Laws Commission of 1854 and the Political Economy of Limited Liability'

transition eroded the traditional understanding of entrepreneurs as both capital owners and managers.

English economic literature was slow to adapt, often equating entrepreneurs with 'capitalists', who provided and accumulated capital. This view contrasted with Cantillon's perspective of the 'risk-bearer' entrepreneur or Say's 'mediator in production'.[10] English classical economists, from Smith to Marshall, expected entrepreneurs to provide capital. The function of capital provision, fulfilled by 'owners', 'quasi-partners', or 'proprietors',[11] was not seen as distinct from that of business leaders or managers in joint stock companies.[12] However, by the late nineteenth and early twentieth centuries, it became clear that those making pivotal decisions often contributed little or no capital. This shift redefined *shareholders* as *risk bearers.*[13] As Marshall noted, '[t]he shareholders bear the risks, but delegate nearly the whole of their functions, as owners of the business, to the directors and other employees'.[14]

This shift in the conceptualisation of shareholders, transitioning from proprietors to risk bearers, carried significant legal implications. Until the mid nineteenth century, the joint stock company, resembling 'extended partnerships', was closely identified with its members (shareholders).[15] Incorporation did not, at that time, entail a 'complete separation' between companies and their members; instead, the

(1997) 50 *The Economic History Review* 37, 55 (attributing the rise of listed companies and the 'socialization' of capital to the introduction of limited liability in 1855).

10 Hoselitz, 'The Early History of Entrepreneurial Theory', 234–57 (tracing the history of the entrepreneurial theory in English and French economic literature from the beginning of the seventeenth century).

11 Ross Grantham, 'The Doctrinal Basis of the Rights of Company Shareholders' (1998) 57 *Cambridge Law Journal* 554, 557–9 (for a succinct elaboration of the proprietarian view of the shareholder over the nineteenth century).

12 Philip L. Williams, *The Emergence of the Theory of the Firm: From Adam Smith to Alfred Marshall* (The Macmillan Press Ltd. 1978), 12–14 (explaining that English economists of that period had no concept of the 'entrepreneurial function'). See also Fritz Redlich, 'The Business Leader in Theory and Reality' (1949) 8 *The American Journal of Economics and Sociology* 223, 234 (elaborating that it was in the second half of the nineteenth century that the manager was theoretically discovered as distinct from the entrepreneur).

13 P. Sargant Florence, *The Logic of British and American Industry: A Realistic Analysis of Economic Structure and Government* (Routledge & Kegan Paul Ltd 1953), 299–300 (attributing the detachment of the concept of the entrepreneur as a profit-maker from the capital provider to post-Keynesian writings).

14 Alfred Marshall, *Industry and Trade: A Study of Industrial Technique and Business Organization; and of their Influences on the Condition of Various Classes and Nations* (MacMillan 1919) 311.

15 Paddy Ireland, Ian Grigg-Spall, and Dave Kelly, 'The Conceptual Foundations of Modern Company Law' (1987) 14 *Journal of Law and Society* 149, 158.

incorporated company was understood as a collective of shareholders merged into a single legally distinct body.[16] Although shareholders had become 'co-partners' with limited active involvement in management, their shares, following partnership principles, were still regarded in law as equitable (direct proprietary) interests in the company's assets, rather than distinct property.[17]

However, with the rapid increase in joint stock companies, the diffusion of share ownership among individual investors (now known as 'retail' investors), and the growing tradability of shares in the mid nineteenth century, shares transformed into a form of 'fictitious capital', representing a claim to profit independent of the company and its tangible assets.[18] This transformation of shareholders from entrepreneurs and co-partners to risk bearers and owners of intangible share capital laid the foundation for modern doctrines of separate legal personality and limited liability.[19] By the early twentieth century, the separation between shareholders – the owners of capital – and the 'company', whether 'public' or 'private',[20] had become well-established both *economically* and *legally*. Consequently, the conception of shareholders as *risk bearers*, divorced from the control of the company, gained significant traction.

[16] Ibid., 150–1 (highlighting the different wordings of the 1856 and 1862 Companies Acts, which marked the depersonalisation of the incorporated company and rejecting the conventional view that 'complete separation is a function of the legal act of incorporation'). See also Paddy Ireland, 'Company Law and the Myth of Shareholder Ownership' (1999) 62 *Modern Law Review* 32, 39.

[17] For a comprehensive analysis of the transformation of the share in the eighteenth and nineteenth centuries, see Paddy Ireland, 'Capitalism without the Capitalist: The Joint Stock Company Share and the Emergence of the Modern Doctrine of Separate Corporate Personality' (1996) 17 *Journal of Legal History* 41, 50 (noting that 'the view of shares as equitable interests in the company property and of shareholders as equitable co-owners of it persisted well into the nineteenth century').

[18] Ireland *et al.*, 'The Conceptual Foundations of Modern Company Law', 159. The seminal case here is *Bligh v Brent* (1837) 2 *Y & C Ex* 268, 295 (holding that 'the individual members of a corporation are quite as distinct from the metaphysical body called the corporation') and 297 (concluding that the shares are 'personal property').

[19] Walter Horriwtz, 'Historical Development of Company Law' (1946) 62 *Law Quarterly Review* 375 (reviewing the history of the development of limited liability between the 1850s and 1940s). For a similar development in the US and the development of the 'entity theory', see Morton J. Horwitz, 'Santa Clara Revisited: The Development of Corporate Theory' (1986) 88 *West Virginia Law Review* 173.

[20] The seminal *Salomon v Salomon & Co Ltd* [1897] AC 22 was critical in the 'triumph of the company legal form' among smaller business organisations. See Ireland, 'The Rise of the Limited Liability Company', 251–5.

2.2.2 *The Separation of Ownership and Control: Berle and Means Revisited*

The separation of ownership and control, or 'the managerial function'[21] in Weberian terms, has characterised large public companies in 'Anglo-American'[22] corporate governance systems for most of the twentieth century and remains prevalent today. Berle and Means' book *The Modern Corporation & Private Property* is widely recognised for elucidating this phenomenon, and a public company without a controlling shareholder is often referred to as a 'Berle-Means corporation'.[23]

Notwithstanding the enduring legacy of *The Modern Corporation & Private Property*, the idea consolidated by Berle and Means had circulated within academic, practitioner, and policymaking circles for years prior.[24] For instance, in 1904, Thorstein Veblen noted that 'the management is separated from the ownership of the property, more and more widely as the scope of finance widens . . . [and] this alienation of control on the parts of the owners may be, by so much, irrevocable'.[25] In the 1920s, Veblen revisited the theme of the 'absentee ownership', noting that 'the effectual control and management of any corporate business has passed into the hands of a relatively smaller minority of the ultimate owners'.[26] Frank Knight, writing

[21] Max Weber, *Theory of Social and Economic Organization* (trans. A. M. Henderson and Talcott Parsons, Free Press 1947), 248–9 (elaborating the practical implications of 'the separation of managerial functions from appropriated ownership' for the interests the firm pursues).

[22] While there are significant differences between the US and UK 'outsider' corporate governance systems, scholars most often lump these together in comparative analysis to distinguish them from the insider systems of Continental Europe and Japan. On this distinction, see e.g. Colin Mayer, 'Financial Systems and Corporate Governance: A Review of the International Evidence' (1998) 154 *Journal of Institutional and Theoretical Economics (JITE) / Zeitschrift für die gesamte Staatswissenschaft* 144.

[23] Brian R. Cheffins, 'The Rise and Fall (?) of the Berle-Means Corporation' (2018) 42 *Seattle University Law Review* 445, 445–6.

[24] Berle and Means themselves specifically referred to Rathenau's 1918 book *Von Kommenden Dingen* (*In Days to Come* transl.) and quoted 'No one is a permanent owner. The composition of the thousand-fold complex which functions as lord of the undertaking is in a state of flux. . . . This condition of things signifies that ownership has been depersonalised'. See Berle and Means, *The Modern Corporation & Private Property*, 309.

[25] Thorstein B. Veblen, *Theory of Business Enterprise* (Charles Scribner 1904), 157, 175–6.

[26] Thorstein Veblen, *Absentee Ownership and Business Enterprise in Recent Times: The Case of America* (George Allen & Unwin, Ltd. 1924), 292, 331–2. For an account of Berle and Means' *Modern Corporation* in light of Veblen's work of evolutionary institutional economics, see Charles R. T. O'Kelley, 'Berle and Veblen: An Intellectual Connection Berle II' (2010) 34 *Seattle University Law Review* 1317.

in 1921, emphasised 'the combination of diffused ownership with concentrated control' as a hallmark of the modern corporation.[27] British economists, from John Atkinson Hobson in the late 1890s to Dennis Holmes Robertson and John Maynard Keynes in the 1920s, also described the widening of share ownership and diminishing power of shareholders in large corporations before the publication of *The Modern Corporation & Private Property*.[28]

Despite these earlier discussions, Berle and Means' book remains the most famous, authoritative, and cited work on the topic, likely due to its detailed empirical data on the dispersion of stock ownership in America's largest corporations in 1929. This evidence substantiated their claim of a separation of ownership from the control in the 'modern', 'quasi-public' corporation.[29]

The chronology of the separation of ownership and control has been extensively debated on both sides of the Atlantic.[30] In Britain, the extent of this separation during the period *The Modern Corporation & Private Property* was written has been contentious. Business historian Leslie Hannah saw Britain as having 'persistent wide shareholding' early in the 1900s,[31] while Cheffins acknowledged dispersed ownership in UK railways and banks by World War I, but challenged the extent of this separation in

[27] Frank H. Knight, *Risk, Uncertainty and Profit* (Houghton Mifflin Company 1921), 291. But for Knight, what he terms as the separation between 'risk' and control is only an 'illusory' one ('arising from the failure to recognize the fundamental fact that in organized activity the crucial decision is the selection of men to make decisions . . . the control of enterprise falls into the hands of the owner (or owners) of a part of the productive service used in the enterprise'). See ibid., 293–9. For an analysis of Knight's theory of the entrepreneur and its links with Berle and Means' thesis, see Charles R. T. O'Kelley, 'Berle and the Entrepreneur' (2009) 33 *Seattle University Law Review* 1141.

[28] John Atkinson Hobson, *The Evolution of Modern Capitalism: A Study of Machine Production* (Walter Scott Ltd 1895); Dennis Holmes Robertson, *The Control of Industry* (1943 ed., Nisbet. 1923), 65; John Maynard Keynes, *The End of Laissez-Faire* (The Hogarth Press 1926), 42–3.

[29] Berle and Means, *The Modern Corporation & Private Property*, 5 (defining the quasi-public corporation as 'a corporation in which a large measure of separation of ownership and control has taken place through the multiplication of owners') and 47–65, 84–111 (providing statistics on ownership dispersion). Another explanation for its legacy is that the book was directly cited by agency theorists as discussed in Section 2.4.2.

[30] For the US, see Maurice Zeitlin, 'Corporate Ownership and Control: The Large Corporation and the Capitalist Class' (1974) 79 *American Journal of Sociology* 1073 (for a review of discrepant empirical findings supporting that the separation of ownership and control is a 'pseudofact'); Cheffins, The Rise and Fall (?) of the Berle-Means Corporation, 448–54.

[31] Leslie Hannah, 'The "Divorce" of Ownership from Control from 1900 Onwards: Re-calibrating Imagined Global Trends' (2007) 49 *Business History* 404.

industrial companies before 1914.[32] This aligns with the 'conventional' view among business historians that the US, rather than the UK, led the 'separation of ownership from management', attributed by Chandler to Britain's persistent 'family capitalism'.[33]

Despite differing opinions on the extent of blockholding in early twentieth-century UK industrial companies, the separation of 'ownership' – today clearly understood as mere property interests in shares[34] – from 'control' gradually became the norm in larger UK companies post World War II. Parkinson's study of major UK publicly quoted companies in the early 1940s and Florence's data on 'very large' industrial and commercial companies for the years 1936 and 1951 show a clear trend towards this separation, although large UK companies were less dispersed than their US counterparts.[35] By the mid twentieth century, UK shareholders had transformed from proprietary entrepreneurs to risk bearers and from 'owners' with 'rights and privileges' to 'beneficial owners' with expectations for dividends and limited voting rights.[36]

[32] Cheffins, *Corporate Ownership and Control*, 225–51.

[33] Alfred D. Chandler, *Scale and Scope: The Dynamics of Industrial Capitalism* (Harvard University Press 1990), 286 ('Throughout the late nineteenth century British entrepreneurs continued to view their businesses in personal rather than organizational terms, as family estates to be nurtured and passed on to heirs') and 335 ('The development of British organizational capabilities was held back not only by less vigorous competition between firms but also by the desires of the founders and their families to retain control').

[34] But the nature of shares and shareholding is not easily defined. For the conceptual difficulties of defining shares as a legal matter, see Robert R. Pennington, 'Can Shares in Companies Be Defined?' (1989) 10 *Company Lawyer* 140, 144 (concluding that shares can be at best defined as 'a species of intangible movable property which comprise a collection of rights and obligations relating to an interest in a company of an economic and proprietary character, but not constituting a debt'). See also Ireland, 'Company Law and the Myth of Shareholder Ownership', 44–7 (concluding that the share is 'a particular and distinctive form of money capital; property in the form of a claim on the company's profits').

[35] Hargreaves Parkinson, *Ownership of Industry* (Eure & Spottiswoode 1951), 58 (reporting '[a]n aggregate of £347 millions (nominal) of industrial capital is shared among £1,113,000 holdings (in round figures)'); P. Sargant Florence, *Ownership, Control and Success of Large Companies* (Sweet & Maxwell Limited 1961), 186, 188–9. See also Cheffins, *Corporate Ownership and Control*, 303–6 (acknowledging that despite the limitations with Florence's research, the pattern of the steady decline of family ownership in British companies is verified by other empirical studies).

[36] Berle and Means, *The Modern Corporation & Private Property*, xxxi. Several other scholars confirmed that blockholders had become the exception to the rule in publicly traded UK companies by the 1970s. For a snapshot of the empirical studies on the ownership patterns of British companies between 1920 and mid-2000, see Cheffins, *Corporate Ownership and Control*, 11–17.

To fully grasp the impact of the shareholder's evolving status on shareholder governance, it is essential to contextualise this shift within broader inquiries into the 'nature' of the modern corporation and the challenges posed by the influence of large publicly quoted companies and their managers. The following two sections explore shareholder governance in the UK against the backdrop of two foundational theories on business structure and behaviour: managerialism and the 'nexus of contracts' theory.

2.3 The Rise of Managerialism and Shareholder Passivity

2.3.1 Shareholders in the Managerial Company

The separation of ownership (that of risk-taking shareholders) and control had significant ramifications in the field of 'managerialism', a body of theory premised on 'management control', and had spawned a wide range of hypotheses about business structure and behaviour among both conservative and Marxist scholars.[37] Extensive literature has explored the chronology of the managerial company, the explanations of its rise and the potential consequences for how managers–controllers might regard their objectives and responsibilities.[38] However, the implications that managerialism had on the understanding of the corporate governance role of shareholders during the mid twentieth century, when managerialism was predominant, are less discussed. This is the focal point of the current analysis.

[37] The literature on 'managerialism' is vast. Some of the seminal contributions include Robin Marris, *The Economic Theory of 'Managerial' Capitalism* (MacMillan 1964); John K Galbraith, *The New Industrial State* (New American Library 1968); Alfred D. Chandler, *The Visible Hand: The Managerial Revolution in American Business* (Harvard University Press 1977); and more recently Brian R. Cheffins, *The Public Company Transformed* (Oxford University Press 2019). For an account of major managerial thinkers, see John Child, *The Business Enterprise in Modern Industrial Society* (Collier-Macmillan Canada Ltd 1969), 38–44; Edward S. Herman, *Corporate Control, Corporate Power: A Twentieth-Century Fund Study* (Cambridge University Press 1981), 9–14 and Theo Nichols, *Ownership, Control and Ideology* (George Allen and Unwin Ltd 1969), 21–30. For an account of Marxist writing on the subject of the separation of ownership and control, see Michel De Vroey, 'The Separation of Ownership and Control in Large Corporations' (1975) 7 *Review of Radical Political Economics* 1.

[38] See e.g. Cheffins, 'The Rise and Fall (?) of the Berle-Means Corporation', 454–72 (summarising the reasons behind the rise of the Berle-Means corporation); Herman, *Corporate Control, Corporate Power: A Twentieth Century Fund Study*, 242–301 (stressing a number of themes on the control and power of large corporations and arguing that despite the corporate responsibility debate the impact of managerialism has been the creation of 'a larger, more bureaucratic and rational profit-seeking entity').

Descriptively, Berle and Means provided empirical, albeit not unequivocal, evidence that share ownership had been separated from control in large American corporations. In Britain, this separation occurred a few decades later.[39] Normatively, the centralisation of control to managers and the transformation of shareholders into risk bearers and beneficial owners significantly changed corporate behaviour as the interests of owners and managers diverged.[40] This led Berle and Means to two conclusions: firstly, that directors and managers have only 'powers in trust' which are 'at all times exercisable only for the rateable benefit of all the shareholders'.[41] Secondly, because the nineteenth-century logic of private property cannot apply to the ownership of shares, the shareholders – as owners of only 'passive property' – 'have surrendered the right that the corporation should be operated in their sole interest' so that '[t]he modern corporation' can 'serve not alone the owners or the control but all society'.[42] While these two conclusions appear to hold incompatible implications – especially in light of today's regenerated corporate purpose debate – any normative contradictions should be understood by referring to the context in which *The Modern Corporation & Private Property* was written and Berle's scholarly thinking between the 1920s and the 1960s.[43]

It is misleading to associate *The Modern Corporation & Private Property* with modern shareholder primacy.[44] For Berle, the scattered shareholders

[39] See Section 2.2.2.

[40] Berle and Means, *The Modern Corporation & Private Property*, 7.

[41] Ibid., 220.

[42] Ibid., 312.

[43] See e.g. William W. Bratton and Michael L. Wachter, 'Shareholder Primacy's Corporatist Origins: Adolf Berle and the Modern Corporation' (2008) 34 *Journal of Corporation Law* 99, 118–22 (illustrating that while Book II of *The Modern Corporation & Private Property* reflects the shareholder primacy mode of the earlier work of Berle's *Powers in Trust*, the final chapter of Book IV offers a 'new concept of the corporation' which overlaps the 'New Individualism' speech that Berle wrote for FDR and turns the trust model to its head, concluding that the corporation should serve societal goals); John W. Cioffi, 'Fiduciaries, Federalization, and Finance Capitalism: Berle's Ambiguous Legacy and the Collapse of Countervailing Power Berle II: The Second Annual Symposium of the Adolf A. Berle Jr. Center on Corporations, Law & Society' (2010) 34 *Seattle University Law Review* 1081 (examining some ambiguities and tensions within Berle's thinking before and during the New Deal era). See also William W. Bratton, 'The Modern Corporation and Private Property Revisited: Gardiner Means and the Administered Price' (2018) 42 *Seattle University Law Review* 591, 598–608 (explaining these contradictions by references to Means' contribution to *The Modern Corporation & Private Property*).

[44] Fenner Jr. Stewart, 'Berle's Conception of Shareholder Primacy: A Forgotten Perspective for Reconsideration during the Rise of Finance Berle II: The Second Annual Symposium of the Adolf A. Berle, Jr. Center on Corporations, Law & Society' (2010) 34 *Seattle University Law Review* 1457.

who lost control to managers were the American working and middle classes.[45] Berle's championing of managerial accountability to the shareholder group is, therefore, best viewed as a tool to democratise control of managerial power and can be associated with what he later termed 'Collectivism' or 'People's Capitalism'.[46] Notably, for Berle and Means in 1932, the alternative of managers serving the interests of society at large was only a much-hoped-for possibility rather than an actual feature of the managerial capitalism of the time.[47] In subsequent writings, Berle further advanced his analysis of the 'quasi–public corporation' as a 'conscience-carrier of twentieth-century American society',[48] an idea that aligns with his view of the corporation as a 'public' rather than 'private' institution and its managers as 'civil servants'.[49]

A clear answer to the accountability problem raised by the increasing power of those who direct and control large companies cannot be found in *The Modern Corporation & Private Property*. However, the key takeaway from this book is not so much in the separation of ownership and control itself – which had been remarked upon much earlier[50] and consolidated much later[51] – but rather the extent to which this separation gave rise to a new type of *internal* relationship between management and shareholders. In Berle and Means' eyes, the separation of ownership and control and the

45 Ibid., 1465.

46 Adolf A. Berle, *Power without Property: A New Development in American Political Economy* (Harcourt, Brace & World Inc. 1959), 19. For a review of post-war sociologists adopting a similar view and praising managerialism as 'a harbinger of increased democracy', see Mark S. Mizruchi, 'Berle and Means Revisited: The Governance and Power of Large U.S. Corporations' (2004) 33 *Theory and Society* 579, 582–4.

47 Berle and Means, *The Modern Corporation & Private Property*, 312.

48 Adolf A. Berle Jr, *The 20th Century Capitalist Revolution* (Harcourt, Brace 1954), 182.

49 Adolf A. Jr. Berle, 'Constitutional Limitations on Corporate Activity – Protection of Personal Rights from Invasion through Economic Power' (1951) 100 *University of Pennsylvania Law Review* 933, 953. For an analysis of the 'new (public) concept of the corporation' as this was advanced by Berle, see Olivier Weinstein, 'Ownership and the Business Firm: Implications for Corporate Governance and Social Responsibility' (2012) 2 *Accounting Economics, and the Law* 1, 10–14.

50 See Section 2.2.2. See also Smith, *An Inquiry into the Nature and Causes of the Wealth of Nations*, 740–41 (noting the separation between the 'court of directors' and the 'court of proprietors': 'The trade of a joint stock company is always managed by a court of directors. This court, indeed, is frequently subject, in many respects, to the control of a general court of proprietors. But the greater part of those proprietors seldom pretend to understand anything of the business of the company, and when the spirit of faction happens not to prevail among them, give themselves no trouble about it, but receive contentedly such half-yearly or yearly dividend as the directors think proper to make them').

51 See Cheffins, 'The Rise and Fall (?) of the Berle-Means Corporation', 451.

growing power and size of the largest corporations shifted the focus on the balance of power *within* the corporation between managers and dispersed shareholders. Hence the key question: what was the role of shareholders in the managerial company?

A key feature of the managerial or Berle-Means corporation is its status as an *autonomous* entity: shareholders cannot be considered akin to the nineteenth-century proprietors of the company; they own shares which they can sell, but they do not own the assets of the company. As Berle and Means put it, the 'atom of ownership' was split 'into its component parts, control and beneficial ownership'.[52] This split found legal expression, as noted above, in the principles of separate legal personality ('entity shielding') and limited liability ('owner shielding'), together labelled as 'asset partitioning'.[53] Shareholders 'lock-in' their capital and 'yield control' over the business operations to a board of directors that was – and still is, to a much lesser degree – controlled by managers.[54] This so-called governance separation[55] of the roles of contributing capital and operating the business – stemming in part from the limited-liability protection shareholders enjoyed and the transferability of their shares on the stock market – played a key role in the transfer of power and control from shareholders to management, pejoratively called 'the new princes' by Berle and Means.[56] The weakening of shareholder control together with an almost exclusive reliance on internal capital markets were among the factors that facilitated the centralisation of power in the hands of non-propertied, full-time, experienced, and salaried management in US large companies. This shift has been praised by

[52] Berle and Means, *The Modern Corporation & Private Property*, 8.

[53] Henry Hansmann and Reinier Kraakman, 'The Essential Role of Organizational Law' (2000) 110 *Yale Law Journal* 387.

[54] For the significant and almost independent powers of 'full-time salaried executives' in US businesses for most of the twentieth century, see the seminal Chandler, *The Visible Hand*, 415–18, 450–4, 482–3. For an earlier account of the 'shirtsleeve' directors in the US, see William O. Douglas, 'Directors Who Do Not Direct' (1933) 47 *Harvard Law Review* 1305. On the rise of independent directors in the US, see Jeffrey N. Gordon, 'The Rise of Independent Directors in the United States, 1950–2005: Of Shareholder Value and Stock Market Prices' (2006) 59 *Stanford Law Review* 1465. In Britain, the monitoring board model was 'imported' from the US with the Cadbury Report in 1992, but the series of reforms focusing on the composition and the role of board of directors, including the emphasis on independent, non-executive directors, that followed made the UK the leading 'exporter' of best corporate governance norms and practices. See Brian R. Cheffins, 'The Rise of Corporate Governance in the UK: When and Why' (2015) 68 *Current Legal Problems* 387.

[55] Margaret M. Blair, 'Locking in Capital: What Corporate Law Achieved for Business Organizers in the Nineteenth Century' (2003) 51 *UCLA Law Review* 387, 393.

[56] Berle and Means, *The Modern Corporation & Private Property*, 116.

Alfred Chandler as the 'visible hand' which replaced Adam Smith's 'invisible hand' of the market and contributed to the rise and success of companies with centralised, hierarchical management.[57]

Over the same period in Britain, the separation of ownership and control may not have been as extensive as in the US, but shareholder assiduity over corporate affairs started to fade away. Sealy suggests that as long as the liability remained unlimited, shareholders took a much greater supervisory interest in their investments, but he notes that in the first years after the introduction of limited liability in 1855, 'shareholders continued to take their role seriously'.[58] Even though scholars disagree on the extent of meaningful shareholder engagement in large companies,[59] shareholder supervision of management has steadily declined as shareholder ownership widened. Legally, this weakening of shareholder control was reflected in, and reinforced by, the departure from the nineteenth-century view that a majority of the shareholders at the general meeting was the company, leading to a decline in their right to intervene in the day-to-day management.[60]

Berle and Means were not concerned with day-to-day supervision of management but with the ability of shareholders to 'control' management by electing the board directors.[61] Fragmented ownership negatively impacted shareholders' abilities and incentives to exercise their legal rights, including voting. Ownership dispersion turned shareholders into passive risk bearers who often opt for liquidity and diversification.

The *passive shareholder*'s position in the managerial company cannot be fully understood without referencing the two variants of managerialism, termed by Nichols as 'sectional' and 'non-sectional' managerialism.[62] Sectional managerialists, such as Robert Aaron Gordon, argue that without shareholder control, management pursues its self-interest, driven by financial and non financial incentives.[63] Burnham, known as 'the popularizer of managerialism', asserted that '[o]wnership means control; if

[57] Chandler, *The Visible Hand*, 1.

[58] Len Sealy, 'Perception and Policy in Company Law Reform' in David Feldman and Frank Miesel (eds.), *Corporate and Commercial Law: Modern Developments* (Lloyds 1996), 25.

[59] Ireland, 'Company Law and the Myth of Shareholder Ownership', 42 (stressing that 'the great majority of joint stock company shareholders had never in any meaningful sense acted like participating industrial capitalists *inside* the association') (emphasis in the original).

[60] *Automatic Self-Cleansing Filter Syndicate Co. Ltd v. Cuninghame* [1906] 2 Ch. 34.

[61] For a detailed analysis of the notion of control, see Section 2.6.2.

[62] Nichols, *Ownership, Control and Ideology*, 53–5.

[63] Robert Aaron Gordon, *Business Leadership in the Large Corporation* (The Brookings Institution 1945), 327–8.

there is no control, then there is no ownership'.[64] He identified 'control' with 'managers' and viewed shareholders as 'passive' recipients of dividends with 'subordinate' ownership rights.[65] Burnham and other sectional managerialists believed that the managerial 'ruling class' would inevitably exercise power in their self-interest.[66] In the 1960s, sectional managerialists like Marris and Williamson drew on Nobel Laureate Herbert Simon's 'bounded rationality' to view management as 'satisficing' rather than profit-maximising – that is, managers seek a 'good enough' level of profits rather than shareholder utility maximisation.[67]

On the other hand, non-sectional managerialists, like Berle, consider managers as 'trustees' on behalf of the public.[68] In Britain, Crossland and Child shared Berle's view, contending that the transfer of power to socially motivated managers can serve social goals.[69] In the US, Drucker saw the divorce of ownership and control as not only 'natural' but also 'in the social interest'.[70] Economists like Kaysen, who spoke of a 'soulful corporation', also fall into this group.[71]

The ubiquity of non-sectional managerial assumptions is evident in the prevailing 'social responsibility' sentiment of the mid twentieth century and the triviality of the 'shareholder democracy' movement during the same period. However, there is little evidence that managers in the mid twentieth century governed their firms for the benefit of society or cared less about

[64] James Burnham, *The Managerial Revolution* (3rd ed., Putnam 1944), 87–88.

[65] Ibid., 81 and 89.

[66] For a critical analysis of Burnham's influential *The Managerial Revolution*, see Nichols, *Ownership, Control and Ideology*, 31–39.

[67] Marris, *The Economic Theory of 'Managerial' Capitalism*, 107–8 and 266–88 (developing a satisficing theory for managerial behaviour); Oliver E. Williamson, *The Economics of Discretionary Behavior: Managerial Objectives in a Theory of the Firm* (1974 ed., Kershaw 1964), 38–60 (developing what he calls 'managerial discretion models of the business firm' which are based on the assumption that management have the discretion to extend the company's preference function to involve 'staff' expenses and personal 'emoluments', and thereby seek 'discretionary profit' rather than profit per se).

[68] Berle, *Power without Property*, 19 (contending the American economic system as one of 'People's Capitalism').

[69] Antony Crossland, *The Future of Socialism* (2006 ed., Constable 1956), 16–21; John Child, *British Management Thought: A Critical Analysis* (George Allen and Unwin Ltd 1969), 219–220.

[70] Peter F. Drucker, *The New Society: The Anatomy of Industrial Order* (1993 ed., Transaction Publisher 1950), 35 (arguing that the separation of ownership from control 'expresses clearly the idea that the enterprise cannot and must not be operated in the interest of any one group; stockholders, workers or consumers, but in the interest of society, that is, as we shall see, in the interest of economic performance').

[71] Carl Kaysen, 'The Social Significance of the Modern Corporation' (1957) 47 *The American Economic Review* 311, 314.

maximising profits.[72] Nichols' study of directors and senior managers in a northern English city does not support non-sectional managerialism.[73] Even during the peak of social responsibility in the 1960s and 1970s, British managers believed that 'the profit making process is itself a beneficent one'.[74]

Managerialism, as Nichols puts it, 'has a Berlian tradition and a Burnhamian one'.[75] Despite their disagreements on management objectives and policies and the degree to which managers serve shareholder interests, both sectional and non-sectional managerialists held common assumptions about management/shareholder relations. Both saw the firm as a hierarchical 'structure' dominated by management due to its organisational expertise. Both conceded that managers, relying on internal capital markets, had fewer reasons to maximise shareholder profits. And both viewed shareholders as passive risk-bearers. Whether because managers tend to 'satisfice' within the concept of bounded rationality or because they serve as 'statemen' considering a wide range of resources, both sectional and non-sectional managerialists were sceptical of companies maximising shareholder profits and questioned the direct role of shareholders in corporate affairs.

2.3.2 *Dissenting Voices: Shareholders as 'Demos'*

What the analysis has revealed so far is that between Berle and Means' 1932 book, which highlighted the separation of ownership and control as a central issue in company law, and the rise of the law-and-economics work of the 1970s, which marked the decline of managerialism that shaped the legal-academic field during the 1950s and 1960s, shareholders had little influence in corporate governance. During this era, often referred to as 'heroic' managerialism, only a few lonely voices defended shareholder

[72] Child, *The Business Enterprise in Modern Industrial Society*, 57. For a similar argument in the US, see Harwell Wells, 'Corporation Law Is Dead: Heroic Managerialism, Legal Change, and the Puzzle of Corporation Law at the Height of the American Century' (2012) 15 *University of Pennsylvania Journal of Business Law* 305, 330 (calling the optimistic, non-sectional version of managerialism as 'heroic').

[73] Nichols, *Ownership, Control and Ideology*, 225 (concluding that the managerial 'conceptions of social responsibility did not necessitate the introduction of policies at odds with those general objectives of growth and profitability which is to be expected that most companies will set themselves').

[74] Ibid., 229.

[75] Ibid., 55.

control amidst widespread optimism about management and hostility towards shareholder governance.[76]

Dissenting commentators, viewing shareholders as the Greek 'demos' (the common people), employed terms like 'corporate democracy' and 'shareholder democracy' to draw analogies between corporate and political spheres.[77] The analogy was inspired by the fragmentation of share ownership among individual shareholders. According to Cheffins, individuals owned over 80 per cent of the securities traded on the London Stock Exchange by the early 1930s, and by 1949, the number of people owning shares in UK public companies was approximately 1.25 million, almost double the number at the beginning of the twentieth century.[78] Contemporaries dubbed this shift the 'democratization' of share ownership, though it was mainly the wealthy and upper-middle class who invested in shares at that time.[79]

The political implications of the terms 'shareholder democracy' or 'property-owning democracy' are clear. In an era when large companies were transforming into 'social institutions'[80] and rivals to the state, the

[76] Wells, 'Corporation Law Is Dead: Heroic Managerialism, Legal Change, and the Puzzle of Corporation Law at the Height of the American Century', 339–44 (analysing how the dominant managerialist assumptions during this period fended off the shareholder democracy movement).

[77] For a contemporary analysis of the terms 'shareholder democracy' and 'corporate democracy' and their inaccurate political connotations, see Ray Garrett, 'Attitudes on Corporate Democracy – A Critical Analysis' (1956) 51 *Northwestern University Law Review* 310, 310–12. For more recent critiques, see Usha Rodrigues, 'The Seductive Comparison of Shareholder and Civic Democracy' (2006) 63 *Washington and Lee Law Review* 1389 and Ann K. Buchholtz and Jill A. Brown, 'Shareholder Democracy as a Misbegotten Metaphor' in Maria Goranova and Lori Verstegen Ryan (eds.), *Shareholder Empowerment: A New Era in Corporate Governance* (Palgrave Macmillan 2015), 81–102.

[78] For detailed statistical data on the share ownership of individuals between 1880 and 1939, see Cheffins, *Corporate Ownership and Control*, 191, 267, 269.

[79] Leslie Hannah, *The Rise of the Corporate Economy* (Methuen 1976), 64 (noting that 'what happened over the period since 1911 was not that a significantly larger proportion of families had become large shareholders, but rather that the minority of wealthy families no longer held their wealth in single companies in which they were also directors, choosing instead to spread their wealth over a wider range of assets'. Similarly, Cheffins, *Corporate Ownership and Control*, 269 (elaborating that it was mainly due to the upper middle that share ownership was more widely distributed up until the 1950s). But see Janette Rutterford, David R. Green, Josephine Maltby, and Alastair Owens, 'Who Comprised the Nation of Shareholders? Gender and Investment in Great Britain, c. 1870–1935' (2011) 64 *The Economic History Review* 157, 181 (providing evidence of the growing number of individual investors, including women).

[80] Berle and Means, *The Modern Corporation & Private Property*, 3 (opening Chapter I as follows: 'The corporation has, in fact, become both a method of property tenure and a means of organizing economic life. Grown to tremendous proportions, there may be said to have evolved a "corporate system" – as there was once a feudal system – which has

analogy to democratic governance mechanisms of the state was significant. What is paradoxical about this rhetoric is that shareholder democracy parallels were mostly used by shareholders' advocates, particularly in the US, to support greater shareholder governance rather than promoting the interests of society at large in a Berlian, pro-sectional managerialist sense.[81]

In the US, shareholder democracy gained traction among scholars through Emerson and Latcham's homonymous book.[82] Writing in the 1950s, Emerson and Latcham defended shareholder proposals by proxy and supported shareholder suffrage during a period when the influence of managerialism was at its height. Defining shareholder democracy in broad terms as 'the restoration of some measure of control to the stockholder-owners', they made a vigorous thesis for greater shareholder participation in management.[83] During the same period, others defined shareholder democracy in more moderate terms as 'the shareholder's right to speak, congregate, communicate with other shareholders, and to know what is going on'.[84] Even though shareholder democrats were careful not to frame their calls for greater direct shareholder participation in corporate affairs as a direct polemic against managerialism and the dominant view of the large company as a social institution,[85] this movement faced significant resistance.

Shareholder democracy was often dismissed as 'a slightly old-fashioned ring'[86] and a 'misconceived',[87] 'unreal'[88] effort, due to the observed passivity

attracted to itself a combination of attributes and powers, and has attained a degree of prominence entitling it to be dealt with as a major social institution'). See also Gerald F. Davis, 'The Twilight of the Berle and Means Corporation' (2011) 34 *Seattle University Law Review* 1121, 1122–6 (on how managerialists and sociologists understood the large corporation as a 'social institution' in the mid-twentieth century).

81 Berle and Means, *The Modern Corporation & Private Property*, 312.

82 Frank D. Emerson and Franklin C. Latcham, *Shareholder Democracy: A Broader Outlook for Corporations* (The Press of Western Reserve University 1954).

83 Ibid., 8.

84 A. Joseph. Livingston, *The American Stockholder* (J.B. Lippincott Company 1958), 76.

85 See e.g. Emerson and Latcham, *Shareholder Democracy: A Broader Outlook for Corporations*, 150 (defending shareholder voting by proxy as a means for 'affording a broader social outlook in solving corporate issues').

86 L. C. B. Gower, 'Shareholder Democracy: A Broader Outlook for Corporations' (1955) 68 *Harvard Law Review* 922, 927 (reviewing Frank D. Emerson and Franklin C. Latcham's homonym book).

87 Abram Chayes, 'The Modern Corporation and the Rule of Law' in Edward S. Mason (ed.), *The Corporation in Modern Society* (Harvard University Press 1959), 40 (arguing that shareholder democracy is 'misconceived because the shareholders are not the governed of the corporation whose consent must be sought').

88 Eugene V. Rostow, 'To Whom and for What Ends Is Corporate Management Responsible?' in Edward S. Mason (ed.), *The Corporation in Modern Society* (Harvard University Press 1959), 53–4 (arguing that in what he calls the 'endocratic' corporation – where because of

of shareholders, including many women.[89] Even apologists of shareholders, such as Livingston, recognised that '[s]tockholders, for the most part, are doctors, lawyers, executives, schoolteachers first, and stockholders second. They are investors, who, for the most part, do not wish to be bothered – except by dividends'.[90] Stronger critiques blamed shareholder democracy from diverting legal scholarship 'away from the developments actually taking place'.[91] Others more emphatically dismissed the idea that the key to ensuring managerial responsibility lay in shareholder voting. Berle, for example, believed that dispersed share-ownership reduced the shareholder vote to a 'ceremonial status' and questioned in his 1959 book, *Power Without Property*, its effectiveness in choosing managers or locating power.[92] Others, like Drucker and Manning, even suggested eliminating shareholder voting rights in large publicly held companies.[93]

Despite this resistance, shareholder democrats drew inspiration from the activities of the 'corporate gadflies' or 'militant shareholders' of the 1940s and 1950s in the US, including the Gilbert brothers, Wilma Soss, Father David Bayne, and a handful of other social issues activists. These early shareholder activists legitimised and used shareholder resolutions with the aim of promoting 'a more democratic society'.[94] Among them Lewis D. Gilbert 'has earned the title of America's No. 1 Militant Shareholder'.[95] In his words, 'stockholder action at annual meetings'

the widely diffused ownership management controls the corporate elections – shareholder democracy is 'not addressed to prevailing reality').

89 On how the dominant shareholder-passivity thesis relied on gender stereotypes, see Sarah C. Haan, 'Corporate Governance and the Feminization of Capital' (2022) 74 *Stanford Law Review* 515.

90 Livingston, *The American Stockholder*, 38.

91 J. A. C. Hetherington, 'Fact and Legal Theory: Shareholders, Managers, and Corporate Social Responsibility' (1968) 21 *Stanford Law Review* 248, 274.

92 Berle, *Power without Property*, 63 and 107.

93 Drucker, 'The New Society: The Anatomy of Industrial Order', 341; Bayless Manning, 'Review of Livingston, the American Stockholder' (1958) 67 *Yale Law Journal* 1477, 1490 (advocating for a shareholder position 'quite similar to that of a voting trust certificate-holder with all economic rights in the deposited stock but no power to elect or replace the trustees by vote'). See also Bayless Manning, 'Corporate Power and Individual Freedom: Some General Analysis and Particular Reservations' (1960) 55 *Northwestern University Law Review* 38, 42 (dismissing shareholder democracy as an 'involuted-Marx-upside-down-argument').

94 Richard Marens, 'Inventing Corporate Governance: The Mid-Century Emergence of Shareholder Activism' (2002) 8 *Journal of Business & Management* 365, 373 (tracing the ancestries of modern shareholder activism to these early 'gadflies').

95 Livingston, *The American Stockholder*, 81.

plays 'a very important role in developing a real people's capitalism'.[96] The activities and language used by the corporate gadflies are symptomatic of the shareholder democracy movement or 'corporate democracy' in the words of Lewis D. Gilbert.[97] The real effect of the activities of corporate gadflies may be debatable,[98] but certainly they facilitated shareholder networking and paved the way for social activists in the 1960s and 1970s – a period which in the US has been labelled as the 'age of corporate responsibility'.[99]

In Britain, however, shareholder militancy of the kind developed in the US in the mid twentieth century was limited. Attendance at shareholder meetings was relatively high (even though lower than in previous decades), but compared to their American counterparts, shareholders in Britain remain largely passive, especially in relation to corporate governance issues.[100] In 1951, Hargreaves Parkinson wrote that whereas in theory shareholders are perceived, consciously or unconsciously, as a '*demos* or electorate', in practice

> [o]nly a handful of shareholders attend annual meetings, or appoint voting delegates, and their function is mainly to be a rubber stamp for the decisions of the Directors. It must be admitted that, in the ordinary way, the stockholder is *not* an interested party, in the sense of one who takes an intelligent, even if discontinuous, interest in the company's affairs. As a rule, he neither understands them nor makes any attempt to understand them. ... Today there is only one bond of union between shareholders – a common desire to obtain as high dividend as possible. (emphasis in the original)[101]

96 Lewis D. Gilbert, 'An Independent Shareholder Appraisal' (1956) 34 *University of Detroit Law Journal* 558, 573. For the battle of corporate gadflies against the restrictions SEC placed on the shareholder proposal rule 14A-8 in the 1950s, see David C. Bayne, 'Around and beyond the SEC–The Disenfranchised Stockholder' (1950) 26 *Indiana Law Journal* 207; Lewis D. Gilbert, 'The Proxy Proposal Rule of the Securities and Exchange Commission' (1955) 33 *University of Detroit Law Journal* 191.

97 Livingston, *The American Stockholder*, 68 (attributing the term 'corporate democracy to Lewis D. Gilbert and Robert H. O'Brien, a member of the SEC').

98 Contrast Livingston, *The American Stockholder*, 72 (claiming that the 'vocalism and histrionics' of militant shareholders 'have transformed annual meetings from routine nobody-shows affairs to town meetings') and 99 (concluding that 'Gilbert has had a modest effect on the affairs of corporations' and his 'power is not commensurate with his energy, because he is trying to lead an army that prefers dividends and quite to contumely in defense of rights they do not care about') with Marens, Inventing Corporate Governance: The Mid-Century Emergence of Shareholder Activism, 384–5 (highlighting the various achievements of these early activists).

99 Herman, *Corporate Control, Corporate Power: A Twentieth Century Fund Study*, 251.

100 Janette Rutterford, 'The Shareholder Voice: British and American Accents, 1890–1965' (2012) 13 *Enterprise & Society* 120, 130–1, 140–3.

101 Parkinson, *Ownership of Industry*, 99–100.

The passivity of British shareholders has been attributed to the stronger legal position they enjoy,[102] the lack of cooperative engagement,[103] and the absence of corporate gadflies who were eager to use shareholder meetings to air their views. Julian Hodge, a Welsh accountant who intervened in companies facing a takeover bid with the aim to obtain a higher price from the bidder, seems to be the only exception to the rule of shareholder passivity and has been heralded as 'a solitary figure on the British battle-ground for corporate democracy'.[104]

Contributing to, and possibly symptomatic of, shareholder passivity in Britain – lamented as 'Capitalism's Trojan Horse'[105] – was the fact that the debate over the role of shareholders in corporate governance remained peripheral as the issue of industrial democracy took precedence in the 1970s.[106] During this period, efforts were directed at increasing the power and participation of employees rather than shareholders to address issues related to unaccountable management and underperformance.[107] In sharp contrast to the US debate, the significance of the fragmentation of share ownership and the rise of the 'small investor' were not seen as reasons to grant more participatory powers to shareholders. Instead, the separation of ownership and control was analysed in the context of the successive nationalisations of 'the ownership of the means of production' that took place in post-World War II Britain.[108] Parkinson attributed below-market-value nationalisations to 'shareholder inertia' and called on the 'million-and-a-quarter' individual shareholders to mobilise against their shift in status, from 'the owner of risk capital' to 'a rentier' through nationalisations.[109]

Some scholars even proposed extreme measures, suggesting the creation of an organisational structure that resolves shareholder–management

[102] Rutterford, 'The Shareholder Voice: British and American Accents, 1890–1965', 122. On shareholder rights in the UK, see generally David Kershaw, *Company Law in Context* (2nd ed., Oxford University Press 2012) Chapters 6 and 8; Paul L. Davies and Sarah Worthington, *Gower: Principles of Modern Company Law* (11th ed., Sweet & Maxwell 2022), Chapter 15.

[103] Tom Hadden, *Company Law and Capitalism* (2nd ed., Weidenfeld and Nicolson 1972), 329.

[104] Alex Rubner, *The Ensnared Shareholder* (Penguin Books Ltd. 1965), 139, 152.

[105] Candidus in Investors' Chronicle, 19 November 1955, cited in Crossland, *The Future of Socialism*, 304.

[106] Hadden, *Company Law and Capitalism*, 439; Cheffins, The Rise of Corporate Governance, 399–404.

[107] Alan Bullock, *Report of the Committee of Inquiry on Industrial Democracy* (1977) Cmnd. 6706.

[108] Parkinson, *Ownership of Industry*, 1.

[109] Ibid., 101–4.

relationship challenges by '*totally abolishing the shareholders*' (emphasis added).[110] This view, along with the dominance of Keynesian economics in British politics after World War II and the focus on industrial democracy rather than shareholder democracy, explains why journalists, politicians, and academics in mid-century Britain generally saw shareholders as having no priority over other stakeholders and dismissed the idea of shareholder democracy as a 'Good Thing'.[111]

2.4 The Contractarian Turn in Corporate Governance

2.4.1 Market Revival and the Shareholder's Right to Exit

About fifty years after Berle and Means predicted that the separation of ownership and control would lead to shareholder losses,[112] a different perspective emerged at a Hoover Institution conference in Palo Alto. It was argued that 'the separation of ownership and control no longer presented a problem, if indeed it ever had'.[113] This shift was heavily influenced by the rise of law-and-economics in the 1970s, which profoundly impacted this conclusion.[114]

The 'nexus of contracts' or contractarian theory of the firm represents a groundbreaking attack on managerialism. While acknowledging the diffusion of share ownership, contractarians diverge significantly from the managerial perspective by rejecting the hierarchical and non-market characteristics of the managerial company. They also distance themselves from the social and public nature attributed to large public corporations by non-sectional managerialists. For contractarian theorists, there are no hierarchies, and management is constrained by market forces. The company is seen as an apolitical, economic, and private institution dedicated to advancing shareholder interests.

110 L. C. B. Gower, 'Some Contrasts between British and American Corporation Law' (1956) 69 *Harvard Law Review* 1369, 1374.

111 See e.g. Gower, 'Shareholder Democracy', 927 (highlighting that 'he is not sure that their [Emerson's and Latcham's] idea of shareholder democracy is a Good Thing or that the proxy rules seek to accomplish it'). See also Hadden, *Company Law and Capitalism*, 84–6 (writing in the early 1970s that the most significant limitations on managerial powers are organised labour and involvement of government rather than the shareholders).

112 Berle and Means, *The Modern Corporation & Private Property*, 293 and 312.

113 Bratton, 'Modern Corporation and Private Property Revisited', 595.

114 James J. Park, 'From Managers to Markets: Valuation and Shareholder Wealth Maximization' (2021) 47 *Journal of Corporation Law* 435 (critically analysing the 'conventional' explanations for the replacement of managerialism with the shareholder wealth principle).

Before delving into the implications of the contractarian theory for shareholder governance, it is essential to place Henry Manne's work from the 1950s and 1960s (long before the contractarian theory of the firm gained prominence) in the broader context of the 'reprivatisation of the public company'[115] that unfolded in the 1970s and dominated legal literature in the early 1980s.

In the 1950s, Manne expressed concern about the dominance of non-sectional, Berlian managerialism, asserting that a corporation's 'conscience', when not guided by the market or the courts, was 'a problematic safeguard at best'.[116] In 1961, he introduced the agency-theory vocabulary aimed at aligning conflicting interests, a framework that would shape scholarship in the post-1970s era.[117] Manne dismissed Berle and Means' contention that management could secure financing internally by reinvesting business earnings, thus freeing itself from market constraints.[118] He challenged their assumptions regarding private property and profit distribution,[119] arguing that a shareholder, as 'owner', had 'the right to delegate its control . . . within a private property, free contract system'.[120] Manne concluded that the separation of ownership and control posed 'no substantial danger to the shareholders of large corporations', which were 'basically and primarily' profit-maximising entities.[121]

However, Manne's belief that companies aimed to maximise shareholder profits did not support contemporary claims to restore 'control' to shareholders. For Manne, making management more responsive to shareholders did not require active shareholder participation in corporate management. In his assessment of shareholder democracy, Manne concluded that 'neither

[115] See also Paddy Ireland, 'Defending the Rentier: Corporate Theory and the Reprivatisation of the Public Company' in John Parkinson, Andrew Gamble and Gavin Kelly (eds.), *The Political Economy of the Company* (Hart 2000), 141, 152.

[116] Henry Manne, 'Book Review of Richard Eells, Corporation Giving in a Free Society' (1956) 24 *University of Chicago Law Review* 194, 197.

[117] Henry Manne, 'Current Views on the Modern Corporation' (1961) 38 *University of Detroit Law Journal* 559, 562 ('There is a sort of running conflict of interests between the shareholders and management with the managers generally receiving more for their services than traditional theory about "hiring" these employees would indicate that they should').

[118] Henry Manne, 'The "Higher Criticism" of the Modern Corporation' (1962) 62 *Columbia Law Review* 399, 400. For empirical evidence refuting Berle and Means's thesis in the late 1950s, see John Lichtner, 'The Financing of Corporations' in Edward S. Mason (ed.), *The Corporation in Modern Society* (Harvard University Press 1959).

[119] Manne, 'Current Views on the Modern Corporation', 561–2.

[120] Manne, 'The "Higher Criticism"', 407.

[121] Ibid., 402.

the advocates nor the critics of corporate democracy have fully comprehended the interplay of share voting and share transferability'.[122] Instead, he highlighted the economic aspects of voting and the disciplinary role of proxy fights, later revisited in his seminal work on the 'market for corporate control'.[123] Therefore, Manne dismissed claims for participatory shareholder democracy and legitimised the *sale of shares* as a 'proper' shareholder action if dissatisfied with management.[124] This position contradicted both advocates and opponents of direct shareholder democracy.

In his subsequent work, Manne outlined an economic theory for large public companies, arguing that the primary role of shareholders was 'to put out money at risk for use by entrepreneurs and managers'.[125] He believed management selection was the 'function of the entrepreneur, and not of the capitalist investors'.[126] Manne viewed management's responsiveness to shareholder interests not as a result of direct shareholder participation but as a function of optimal capital allocation and the market for corporate control.

Manne asserted that the market for corporate control is premised on 'a high positive correlation between corporate managerial efficiency and the market price of shares'.[127] Poor management would lower a company's share price relative to its industry or the market, facilitating a takeover.[128] In an active market for corporate control, shareholders could 'trade in a company's stock in order constantly to correct the share price', conditioning managers to align with shareholder interests.[129] Economist Robin Marris developed a similar 'theory of take-over'.[130] The common thread between the Manne and Marris hypotheses was that a shareholder could

[122] Ibid., 410–13.

[123] Ibid., 410–13. The seminal work is Henry Manne, 'Mergers and the Market for Corporate Control' (1965) 73 *Journal of Political Economy* 110.

[124] Of course, Manne recognises that the larger the shareholder the greater impact of a stock sale on the market price. See Henry Manne, 'Review of J A Livingston, the American Stockholder' (1958) 5 *Saint Louis University Law Journal* 309, 312.

[125] Henry G. Manne, 'Our Two Corporation Systems: Law and Economics' (1967) 53 *Virginia Law Review* 259, 273.

[126] Ibid., 261.

[127] Manne, 'Market for Corporate Control', 112. But whether the share price accurately reflects managerial performance is an empirical question. See e.g. Michael C. Jensen and Kevin J. Murphy, 'Performance Pay and Top-Management Incentives' (1990) 98 *Journal of Political Economy* 225 (finding only weak statistical links between CEO pay and shareholder returns).

[128] Manne identifies three basic techniques for taking over control of companies: proxy fights, direct purchases of shares, and mergers. See ibid., 114–19.

[129] Manne, 'Our Two Corporation Systems', 266 and 274.

[130] Marris, *The Economic Theory of 'Managerial' Capitalism*, 29–40.

exercise 'control' merely by selling its share – or by exercising what Hirschman would later famously refer to as the 'exit option'.[131]

In summary, Manne's early work legitimised shareholder governance, including the right to exit, not by viewing shareholders as 'owners' but in terms of *market efficiency*. This shift from controlling managers and passive owners to markets as the primary driver of corporate governance arrangements laid the foundation of the 'nexus of contracts' or contractarian theory of the firm. This paradigm has dominated for the past four decades and continues to shape shareholder governance today.

2.4.2 Contractarian Theory and the Recasting of Shareholder Governance

The nexus of contracts theory, also known as the contractarian or 'new economic' theory of the firm, conceptualises the company (or firm)[132] as a 'nexus' of contracts, with profound implications for corporate law, economics, and management. It particularly informs our understanding of corporate governance, stakeholder relationships, and the role of contracts in shaping organisational behaviour. While the implications for shareholder roles in corporate governance may seem ambiguous, a deeper exploration is warranted.

The nexus of contract theory comprises two variants, as outlined by Bratton: the neoclassical and the institutional.[133] The neoclassical, or 'strong', variant applies neoclassical microeconomics to depict the firm as a 'nexus' of explicit and implicit 'contracts'[134] among individual factors of production.[135]

[131] Albert O. Hirschman, *Exit, Voice and Loyalty: Responses to Decline in Firms, Organizations and States* (Harvard University Press 1970), 4.

[132] In this chapter the terms 'firm' and 'company' or 'corporation' are used interchangeably. But see Charles R. T. O'Kelley, 'Coase, Knight, and the Nexus-of-Contracts Theory of the Firm: A Reflection on Reification, Reality, and the Corporation as Entrepreneur Surrogate' (2012) 35 *Seattle University Law Review* 1247 (explaining the differences in the use of these two terms).

[133] William W. Bratton, 'The New Economic Theory of the Firm: Critical Perspectives from History' (1989) 41 *Stanford Law Review* 1471, 1477–82.

[134] The terms 'contract' and 'contractual' are not used by economists according to their legal meaning. For the different notions of contract employed by lawyers and economists, see William W. Bratton, 'The "Nexus of Contracts" Corporation: A Critical Appraisal' (1989) 74 *Cornell Law Review* 407, 446–51.

[135] Armen A. Alchian and Harold Demsetz, 'Production, Information Costs, and Economic Organization' (1972) 62 *American Economic Review* 777, 778, 794–5; Michael C. Jensen and William H. Meckling, 'Theory of the Firm: Managerial Behavior, Agency Costs and Ownership Structure' (1976) *Journal of Financial Economics* 305, 310–11. See also

In this view, the firm operates as a 'highly specialised surrogate market' for exchanging inputs and outputs, with no inherent distinction between 'insiders', such as shareholders, managers, and employees, and 'outsiders', such as suppliers, or customers.[136] Management is seen as one of many production factors rather than holding a unique strategic position.[137]

Conversely, the institutional, or 'weak', variant shares the neoclassical view of the firm as a contractual entity but emphasises Coasean 'transaction-cost economizing', distinguishing between internal and external relations.[138] Here, the 'entrepreneur',[139] being *inside* the firm, has authority over resources, while factors of production, including investors, are *outside* the firm and transact through price mechanisms.[140] Scholars like Williamson draw from interdisciplinary work – including Chandler, Hayek and Arrow, and Simon – to depict the company as a means of reducing transaction costs, grounded in managerial discretion in a market characterised by 'bounded rationality' and 'opportunism'.[141] Institutionalists legitimise the hierarchical, authoritarian view of the managerial corporation as a 'governance structure' with authority that is meaningfully distinct from market contracting.[142]

Eugene F. Fama and Michael C. Jensen, 'Separation of Ownership and Control' (1983) 26 *Journal of Law & Economics* 301, 302.

136 Jensen and Meckling, 'Theory of the Firm: Managerial Behavior, Agency Costs and Ownership Structure', 311. See, however, Edward B. Rock and Michael L. Wachter, 'Islands of Conscious Power: Law, Norms, and the Self-Governing Corporation' (2001) 149 *University of Pennsylvania Law Review* 1619, 1628–9 (characterising this 'emptiness' of the firm as the main weakness of the nexus of contracts theory).

137 Alchian and Demsetz, 'Production, Information Costs, and Economic Organization', 777 (viewing the hierarchical, managerial model of the firm as a mere 'delusion'). See also Eugege F. Fama, 'Agency Problems and the Theory of the Firm' (1980) 88 *Journal of Political Economy* 288, 290 (describing management as 'a type of labor but with a special role – coordinating the activities of inputs and carrying out the contracts agreed among inputs').

138 Ronald H. Coase, 'The Nature of the Firm' (1937) 4 *Economica* 386, 390–5 (explaining 'firms' and 'markets' as alternative forms of 'organization', with the 'costs of organising' (transaction costs) determining the choice between the two methods of allocating resources). For a forceful critique of the conflation of the firm and the market by contractarian theorists, see Geoffrey M. Hodgson, 'The Legal Nature of the Firm and the Myth of the Firm-Market Hybrid' (2002) 9 *International Journal of the Economics of Business* 37.

139 Coase, 'The Nature of the Firm', 388 and 392. See also Ronald H. Coase, 'The Nature of the Firm: Meaning Lectures' (1988) 4 *Journal of Law, Economics & Organization* 19, 31.

140 O'Kelley, 'Coase, Knight, and the Nexus-of-Contracts Theory of the Firm', 1257–8.

141 Oliver E. Williamson, 'The Modern Corporation: Origins, Evolution, Attributes' (1981) 19 *Journal of Economic Literature* 1537–45.

142 Ibid., 1539. For a comprehensive analysis of the differences between the Coasean firm and the nexus-of-contracts version, see O'Kelley, 'Coase, Knight, and the Nexus-of-Contracts Theory of the Firm', 1259–64. See also Stewart J Schwab, 'Coase's Twin Towers: The Relation between the Nature of the Firm and the Problem of Social Cost'

Despite their differences, both variants share fundamental concepts from the law and economics of contracts, prioritise market primacy, and view the firm as a private, cost-reducing device.[143] They concur on the firm's role in maximising profits for shareholders, albeit with different rationales: in the neoclassical variant, shareholders claim profits based on residual rights, while in the institutional variant, the asset-specific nature of shareholders' investment justifies their entitlement to profits.[144] Both regard the board of directors as a monitoring governance structure responsible for safeguarding shareholder interests.[145] Given these similarities, both variants are sufficiently similar for analysing the role of shareholders in corporate governance.[146]

However, understanding the implications of contractarianism for shareholder governance requires considering agency theory. Rooted in neoclassical economic assumptions, agency theory extensively addresses the challenge of managerial 'negligence and profusion'[147] arising from widely dispersed ownership. It provides an economic framework for analysing management–shareholder relationships, recognising that managers as agents to shareholder *principals* have incentives to 'shirk' responsibilities and prioritise self-interests over shareholders' interests.[148] Agency theorists emphasise market-induced monitoring devices, both external and internal, such as the stock market, the market for corporate control, the managerial labour market, the board of directors, and executive compensation packages, albeit with less focus on shareholder governance as an internal monitoring device.[149]

From the agency theory perspective, shareholders are one of the many parties entering into contracts within the firm's nexus, sharing contractual space with other corporate constituencies such as managers,

18 *The Journal of Corporation Law*, 359, 365–7 (elaborating that contractarian theorists have criticised the Coasean firm).

143 Bratton, 'The 'Nexus of Contracts' Corporation', 421–2, 439–42; Bratton, 'Theory of the Firm', 1481–2.

144 For the differences between the two contractarian variants in this regard, see Lynne L. Dallas, 'Two Models of Corporate Governance: Beyond Berle and Means' (1989) 22 *University of Michigan Journal of Law Reform* 19, 48–63.

145 Ibid., 70.

146 See also Ireland, 'Defending the Rentier', 142.

147 Smith, *An Inquiry into the Nature and Causes of the Wealth of Nations*, 741.

148 Jensen and Meckling, 'Theory of the Firm: Managerial Behavior, Agency Costs and Ownership Structure', 308.

149 Fama, 'Agency Problems', 293–305; Fama and Jensen, 'Separation of Ownership and Control', 311–314 and 322–323.

directors, employees, customers, creditors, and suppliers. Fama states that while shareholders contribute equity capital, ownership of capital does not equate to ownership of the firm, making the notion of the corporation being *owned* by shareholders or anyone else becomes 'irrelevant'.[150] This challenges Berle's notion of 'passive' ownership and the managerial literature stemming from it.[151]

Despite the downgraded standing of shareholders within the contractarian firm, they retain significance in the neoclassical model as residual claimants or residual risk bearers to the firm's income stream. Alchian and Demsetz state: '[t]he specialist who receives the residual rewards will be the monitor of the members of the team'.[152] In their model, the manager-monitor self-disciplines due to their stake in the firm and role as a residual claimant.[153] Jensen and Meckling also assign monitoring responsibilities to residual claimants, but in their model, the manager-monitor owns 100 per cent of the residual claims.[154] This recalls the nineteenth-century entrepreneur-owner-manager concept.[155] However, neither model applies directly to large companies with diffused ownership and non-propertied managers.[156]

Fama, and later Fama and Jensen, addressed this gap by extending the agency framework to corporations where ownership (capital) is separate from control. In their framework, shareholders assume the role of 'residual claimants' or 'residual risk bearers', bearing the 'residual risk' as 'the difference between stochastic inflows of resources and promised payments to agents'.[157] Shareholders, with rights to the firm's residual earnings ('what is left over'), have an inherent incentive to maximise firm performance and mitigate management shirking.[158] Fama and Jensen also distinguished between 'decision management', involving the 'initiation' and 'implementation' of decisions, and 'decision control', encompassing

150 Fama, 'Agency Problems', 290.

151 See Section 2.3.1.

152 Alchian and Demsetz, 'Production, Information Costs, and Economic Organization', 782.

153 Ibid., 785.

154 Jensen and Meckling, 'Theory of the Firm: Managerial Behavior, Agency Costs and Ownership Structure', 312.

155 See Section 2.2.1.

156 Jensen and Meckling, 'Theory of the Firm: Managerial Behavior, Agency Costs and Ownership Structure', 356 (acknowledging this limitation) and Alchian and Demsetz, 'Production, Information Costs, and Economic Organization', 794 (calling the 'central agent' in the team production 'the firm's owner and the employer').

157 Fama and Jensen, 'Separation of Ownership and Control', 302–303; Fama, 'Agency Problems', 291–292.

158 Fama and Jensen, 'Separation of Ownership and Control', 303.

the 'ratification' and 'monitoring' of decisions. They emphasised that in addressing agency issues within large companies, these three functions – decision management, decision control, and residual risk bearing – should not be consolidated within the same agent(s).[159] This separation of roles helps ensures checks and balances, reducing conflicts of interest.

The question then arises as to who controls management when ownership is dispersed. Agency theorists, drawing on modern portfolio theory, argue that shareholders, as risk bearers, tend to diversify rather than closely monitor individual firms.[160] Dispersed shareholders indirectly monitor by selling their shares on the capital market, leading to declines in stock prices.[161] Similar to Manne's approach, where management discipline relies on the market for corporate control, agency theorists assert that the separation of ownership and control is efficient due to the disciplinary forces of various markets, including capital, product, management, and labour.[162] Thus, although shareholders are dispersed and unlikely to engage in direct oversight, contractarian theory holds that they exert discipline indirectly through market mechanisms – primarily by trading their shares, which influences stock prices and, in turn, managerial behaviour.

Corporate law underwent a significant shift in the 1980s, heavily influenced by contractarian assumptions. Scholars speak of a 'revolution'[163] in corporate law during this period, with nearly every aspect, including

159 Ibid., 303–4 and 307.

160 Fama, 'Agency Problems', 295 (highlighting that '[w]hen management and risk bearing are viewed as naturally separate factors of production, looking at the market for risk bearing from the viewpoint of portfolio theory tells us that risk bearers are likely to spread their wealth across many firms and so not be interested in directly controlling the management of any individual firm').

161 Alchian and Demsetz, 'Production, Information Costs, and Economic Organization', 788 (noting that '[r]ather than try to control the decisions of the management … unrestricted salability provides a more acceptable escape to each stockholder from continued policies with which he disagrees'); Fama, 'Agency Problems', 292 (stressing that 'although an individual security holder may not have a strong interest in directly overseeing the management of a particular form, he has a strong interest in the existence of a capital market which efficiently prices the firm's securities. The signals provided by an efficient capital market about the values of a firm's securities are likely to be importance for the managerial labor market's revaluations of the firm's management').

162 Note, however, that agency theorists emphasise different markets as external monitoring devices. See e.g. Fama, 'Agency Problems', 294–5 (setting Manne's market for corporate control aside as a 'last resort' and emphasising instead the discipling role of the managerial labour markets).

163 Roberta Romano, 'After the Revolution in Corporate Law' (2005) 55 *Journal of Legal Education* 342. See also Bratton, 'The 'Nexus of Contracts' Corporation', 409 (highlighting that the impact of the nexus of contracts theory is such that the theory has been accorded 'the weight of scientific truth').

fiduciary duties, takeovers, and minority shareholder protection, redefined through a contractarian and market perspective.[164] Easterbrook and Fischel's 1991 book, *The Economic Structure of Corporate Law*,[165] is credited with establishing modern finance and economics as 'the conventional analytical approach to corporate law'.[166] Integrating contract law and agency theory, it presents a contractarian view of corporate law.[167] In the UK, Cheffins's work further synthesised contractarian ideas, applying efficiency arguments to analyse company workings.[168] Since then, a vast, economically oriented corporate law literature has emerged, premised on the idea that agency costs are the central problem that corporate law needs to address.[169] Easterbrook and Fischel's economic analysis of shareholder voting is particularly significant for our purposes, forming the basis of renewed economic interest in earlier calls for increased shareholder participation in corporate governance.

[164] See e.g. Ralph K. Jr. Winter, 'State Law, Shareholder Protection, and the Theory of the Corporation' (1977) 6 *Journal of Legal Studies* 251 (providing an economic analysis of the production of state corporate law and dismissing proposals to increase shareholder power via federal regulation); Frank H. Easterbrook and Daniel R. Fischel, 'The Proper Role of a Target's Management in Responding to a Tender Offer' (1981) 94 *Harvard Law Review* 1161 (integrating the agency theory into Manne's 1965 seminal work on the market for corporate control to advocate managerial passivity and a reform of fiduciary standards in the event of hostile takeovers); Jonathan R. Macey, 'Fiduciary Duties as Residual Claims: Obligations to Non-shareholder Constituencies from a Theory of the Firm Perspective' (1999) 84 *Cornell Law Review* 1266 (providing a contractarian account of fiduciary duties).

[165] Frank H Easterbrook and Daniel R Fischel, *The Economic Structure of Corporate Law*, (1996 ed., Harvard University Press 1991).

[166] Romano, 'After the Revolution in Corporate Law', 351. See also Ian Ayres, 'Making a Difference: The Contractual Contributions of Easterbrook and Fischel' (1992) 59 *University of Chicago Law Review* 1391, 1392 (praising in his review the book as 'the best book ever written about corporate law').

[167] The authors had already contributed to this perspective through published articles in the 1980s. See e.g. Frank H. Fischel Easterbrook, and R. Daniel, 'Corporate Control Transactions' (1981) 91 *Yale Law Journal* 698; Frank H. Easterbrook and Daniel R. Fischel, 'Mandatory Disclosure and the Protection of Investors' (1984) 70 *Virginia Law Review* 669; Frank H. Fischel Easterbrook, and Daniel R. Fischel, 'The Corporate Contract' (1989) 89 *Columbia Law Review* 1416.

[168] Brian R. Cheffins, *Company Law: Theory, Structure and Operation* (Oxford University Press 1997). For an economic account of the history of English company law, see Michael J. Whincop, *An Economic and Jurisprudential Genealogy of Corporate Law* (Ashgate 2001).

[169] A highly influential book – now in its third edition – which applies the agency theory understanding of corporate law in a comparative context is Renier Kraakman, John Armour, Paul Davies, *et al.*, *The Anatomy of Corporate Law* (3rd ed., Oxford University Press 2017).

2.4.3 Shareholder Voting and the Economic Foundations of Shareholder Governance

At the core of the contractarian perspective lies the assertion that shareholder voting is not inherent or political, but fundamentally contractual – a tool justified by shareholders' role as residual risk bearers.[170] From this view, shareholder governance, expressed primarily through voting, is warranted because shareholders bear the firm's residual risk and thus have the strongest incentive to monitor management. Voting, Easterbrook and Fischel argue, 'exists in corporations because someone must have the residual power to act (or delegate) when contracts are not complete'.[171] Shareholders, as residual claimants to the firm's income, are therefore considered the best-positioned actors to exercise that residual authority.[172]

When voting is legally mandated, as in cases of fundamental changes such as mergers, contractarian scholars see it as a high-stakes monitoring device.[173] Voting in such cases helps to fill the inevitable gaps in incomplete contracts. However, where shareholder voting mechanisms are mandated by law – as with shareholder proposals under US federal regulation or the right to remove directors under UK law – Easterbrook and Fischel argue that these mechanisms displace voluntary arrangements and impose costs that likely exceed their benefits.[174] Given that shareholders in dispersed ownership structures are typically risk-averse and diversified, they are unlikely to engage in costly monitoring and more likely to adopt a passive stance.[175]

This expectation of minimal shareholder engagement is often explained through the free-rider and collective action problems. Individual shareholders bear the costs of becoming informed and voting but capture only a small fraction of the resulting benefit, which accrues to all shareholders.[176] As a result, it is rational for shareholders to remain passive – benefitting

170 Easterbrook and Fischel, *The Economic Structure of Corporate Law*, 66 (asserting that '[t]he right to vote is the right to make all decisions not otherwise provided by contract – whether the contract is express or supplied by legal rule').
171 Ibid., 67.
172 Ibid., 68.
173 Ibid., 79–80.
174 Frank H. Easterbrook and Daniel R. Fischel, 'Voting in Corporate Law' (1983) 26 *Journal of Law & Economics* 395, 423.
175 Daniel R. Fischel, 'Corporate Governance Movement' (1982) 35 *Vanderbilt Law Review* 1259, 1276.
176 Oliver Hart, 'Corporate Governance: Some Theory and Implications' (1995) 105 *Economic Journal* 678, 681.

from others' efforts without contributing themselves.[177] Rather than voice concerns through participation, dissatisfied shareholders typically choose the more efficient response: exit, by selling their shares. According to Fischel, failing to recognise these structural incentives is the '[t]he fundamental error of the proponents of shareholder democracy'.[178]

Consistent with the neoliberal assumption that markets allocate resources more efficiently than organisations, contractarian theorists see limited value in shareholder governance where ownership is widely dispersed.[179] This perspective resonates with earlier managerial theories of passive shareholders.[180] Yet contractarians concede that shareholder voting, while irrelevant to most day-to-day decisions, can serve a functional role in extreme situations. They justify legal rules mandating shareholder approval for fundamental changes as efficient 'gap-filling' mechanisms in the 'corporate contract'.[181]

The idea of voting as a narrowly functional, last-resort mechanism may not satisfy advocates of greater shareholder participation. But the 1970s marked a turning point. During this period, agency theory recast management as the agent of shareholders – a conceptual shift that had lasting consequences. First, portraying managers as agents overstated shareholders' control over corporate decision-making and legitimised the rhetoric of shareholder value maximisation – a view most famously championed by Milton Friedman.[182] While 'agency' was originally used in a non-legal economic sense, its adoption into legal scholarship imbued it with 'a life of its own'.[183] Second, the notion that agency costs represented a drag on

177 For an extended analysis of the collective action problem of diversified shareholders, see Edward B. Rock, 'The Logic and (Uncertain) Significance of Institutional Shareholder Activism' (1991) 79 *Georgetown Law Journal* 445, 453–63.

178 Fischel, 'Corporate Governance Movement', 1276.

179 See e.g. Michael C. Jensen, 'The Modern Industrial Revolution, Exit, and the Failure of Internal Control Systems' (1993) 48 *The Journal of Finance* 831 (advocating the ineffectiveness of internal control mechanisms).

180 See Section 2.3.1.

181 Easterbrook and Fischel, 'Voting in Corporate Law', 402, 415–17. In English company law, see Cheffins, *Company Law: Theory, Structure and Operation*, 238 (arguing that 'shareholder voting is by and large a sensible system').

182 Milton Friedman, 'A Friedman Doctrine – The Social Responsibility of Business Is to Increase its Profits' *The New York Times* (13 September 1970) SM 17.

183 David Millon, 'Radical Shareholder Primacy' (2013) 10 *University of St Thomas Law Journal* 1013, 1032 (terming the introduction of the agency idea to the corporate law scholarship 'radical shareholder primacy').

shareholder value led to renewed emphasis on shareholder voting as a mechanism for monitoring managerial discretion.[184]

Still, the effectiveness of shareholder voting remained contested. Collective action problems, rational apathy, and shareholder passivity persisted. Moreover, the broader question of whether shareholders alone should exercise ultimate control – especially at the expense of other stakeholders – remained unresolved.[185] What is clear, however, is that the reconceptualisation of voting as part of shareholders' residual risk-bearing role, and the framing of management as their agent, transformed the view of shareholders from passive owners to active governance participants.[186]

By the early 1980s, the previously dominant scepticism towards shareholder governance in legal scholarship had begun to recede.[187] The shareholder value ideology gained traction, supported by the contractarian depiction of shareholders as residual claimants and principals. Despite criticism,[188] the assumptions of agency theory maintained influence due to their heuristic clarity. The nexus-of-contracts theory reinforced this shift, legitimising the separation of ownership and control, while refuting older, ownership-based views of shareholder governance. By emphasising the relationship between risk-bearing and governance rights, the principal-agent model placed shareholders firmly at the centre of corporate oversight.

[184] Easterbrook and Fischel, *The Economic Structure of Corporate Law*, 79–80.

[185] For a critical view see e.g. Lynn A. Stout, *The Shareholder Value Myth: How Putting Shareholders First Harms Investors, Corporations and the Public* (Berrett-Koehler Publishers 2012).

[186] See also Harwell Wells, 'A Long View of Shareholder Power: From the Antebellum Corporation to the Twenty-First Century' (2015) 67 *Florida Law Review* 1033, 1087–8.

[187] For a remnant of this scholarship in the late 1970s see J. A. C. Hetherington, 'When the Sleeper Wakes: Reflections on Corporate Governance and Shareholder Rights' (1979) 8 *Hofstra Law Review* 183, 190–221, 254 (arguing that calls for shareholder democracy do not serve the interests of shareholders but 'those who speak for investors without their consent', including 'academicians', 'public interest reformers', and the Securities Exchange Commission).

[188] See e.g. Daniel J. H. Greenwood, 'Fictional Shareholders: For Whom are Corporate Managers Trustees, Revisited' (1995) 69 *Southern California Law Review* 1021 (for a critique of the agency metaphor based on the argument that shareholders are fictional); Simon Deakin and Giles Slinger, 'Hostile Takeovers, Corporate Law, and the Theory of the Firm', *Journal of Law and Society* 24 (1997), 124–51, 129 (challenging the view that shareholders bear the residual risk on the basis of evolutionary theories of the firm); Simon Deakin, 'The Corporation as Commons: Rethinking Property Rights, Governance and Sustainability in the Business Enterprise' (2011) *Queen's Law Journal* 339; David Ciepley, 'The Anglo-American Misconception of Stockholders as 'Owners' and 'Members': Its Origins and Consequences' (2020) 16 *Journal of Institutional Economics* 623.

Yet positioning shareholders as residual claimants and principals did not necessarily lead to greater engagement by shareholders. By the early 1980s, even proponents of shareholder democracy acknowledged its practical limits. One advocate conceded in 1983 that 'shareholder participation ordinarily is not capable of decisive influence in determining corporate affairs' and that 'participation through the voting process is of dubious cost and effectiveness'.[189]

This scepticism was soon overshadowed by developments in the 1980s – known as the 'Deal Decade' – which saw a wave of hostile takeovers on both sides of the Atlantic.[190] These takeovers appeared to provide an effective substitute for shareholder governance by disciplining managers through the threat of being replaced.[191] If share price was assumed to reflect performance, then underperforming management teams became targets for acquisition. The market for corporate control thus offered a 'constant and unrelenting' form of accountability, in contrast to the sporadic and uncertain nature of shareholder voting or proxy battles.[192]

In this context, shareholder passivity was not seen as problematic. The effectiveness of the takeover threat depended, however, on legal rules preventing directors from unilaterally adopting defensive measures.[193] In the UK, unlike in the US, directors were restricted from using post-bid defences

[189] Donald E. Schwartz, 'Shareholder Democracy: A Reality or Chimera?' (1983) 25 *California Management Review* 53, 60, 62, 65. See also Brudney, 'Corporate Governance, Agency Costs, and the Rhetoric of Contract', 1428–1430 (writing in the US context that 'there are severe limitations on the power of dispersed stockholders to "control" or "ratify" decisions initiated by management').

[190] Margaret M. Blair, *The Deal Decade: What Takeovers and Leveraged Buyouts Mean for Corporate Governance* (Brookings Institution Press 1993). On the rise of hostile takeovers, see Michael C. Jensen, 'Takeovers: Folklore and Science' (1984) November-December *Harvard Business Review* 109 (for the US) and Cheffins, *Corporate Ownership and Control*, 360–70 (for the UK).

[191] The literature is voluminous. See e.g. Easterbrook and Fischel, *The Economic Structure of Corporate Law*, 171–3; Michael C. Jensen, 'Takeovers: Their Causes and Consequences' (1988) 2 *The Journal of Economic Perspectives* 21, 28–9; Michael C. Jensen, 'The Takeover Controversy: Analysis and Evidence' (1986) 4 *Midland Corporate Finance Journal* 1; John C. Coffee, 'Shareholders versus Managers: The Strain in the Corporate Web' (1986) 85 *Michigan Law Review* 1, 55 (attributing the 'deconglomeration' movement that took place in the US in the 1980s to the takeover threat). *Cf.* Mike Burkart, 'Economics of Takeover Regulation' LSE Financial Markets Group Discussion Paper No 256, 12–4 (reviewing the relevant empirical literature and suggesting that the evidence is still inconclusive to resolve the debate over the likely efficiency effects of the takeover threat).

[192] Coffee, 'Shareholders versus Managers', 63.

[193] See the seminal work of Easterbrook and Fischel, 'The Proper Role of a Target's Management in Responding to a Tender Offer', 1164 (arguing that 'legal rules allowing

without prior shareholder approval, increasing their accountability and reinforcing the takeover mechanism as the primary disciplinary force.[194]

But this model began to falter in the 1990s.[195] The decline of hostile takeovers exposed the fragility of relying solely on market forces to align shareholder and managerial interests. The assumption that markets alone could substitute for shareholder engagement came under increasing strain. As the next section will explore, this coincided with a significant transformation in the ownership landscape: the rise of institutional investors as dominant shareholders.

2.5 The Rise of Institutional Investors: The UK Shareholder Landscape from the 1970s Onwards

2.5.1 The Reversal Begins: Early Trends in Institutional Ownership

Berle and Means predicted in 1932 that ownership dispersion and the separation of ownership and control would increase over time.[196] However, this prediction did not fully materialise. In 1959, Harbrecht, examining the growing influence of pension funds in the US, identified a 'new tendency' towards a 'convergence of control' in the hands of institutional investors.[197] This trend was driven by the shift of equity ownership from individuals to institutional investors and the collective power wielded by institutional investors due to the concentration of their holdings.[198] Berle himself noted a similar counter-trend towards the concentration of control within institutional investors, particularly pension funds and mutual funds.[199]

the target's management to engage in defensive tactics in response to a tender offer decrease shareholders' welfare').

194 For a comprehensive account of the differences in the regulation of defensive tactics across the Atlantic, see John Armour and David A. Skeel Jr., 'Who Writes the Rules for Hostile Takeovers and Why – The Peculiar Divergence of U.S. and U.K. Takeover Regulation' (2007) 95 *Georgetown Law Journal* 1727.

195 Michael C. Jensen, 'The Eclipse of the Public Corporation', (1989) 5 *Harvard Business Review*, 61–75.

196 Berle and Means, *The Modern Corporation & Private Property*, 47 (predicting that dispersion in ownership '[h]as already proceeded far, it is rapidly increasing, and appears to be an inevitable development').

197 Paul P. Harbrecht S. J., *Pension Funds and Economic Power* (Twentieth Century Fund Inc. 1959), 33.

198 Ibid., 23–4, 32 and 34.

199 Berle, *Power without Property*, 41–54.

A comparable but more significant reduction in individual ownership was observed in Britain during the same period. Before World War II, individual investors predominantly held UK public equity. Business historians have highlighted that institutional investors were not heavily involved in equity investments during this time.[200] In 1951, a study of the ownership structure of thirty 'representative' companies listed on the London Stock Exchange concluded that ownership was characterised by 'fragmentation' and was regarded as an 'ineradicable' trend.[201] However, this conclusion was soon proven wrong. Between the 1950s and the 1970s, individual investors began selling company securities, which were subsequently acquired by institutional investors.[202] Evidence provided by the London Stock Exchange to the Wilson Committee in 1977, which reviewed the operations of UK financial institutions, indicated that '. . . for over twenty years . . . [t]he main change in the supply of savings has therefore been the increasingly dominant role of independent savings institutions and the reduction of the direct market participation by individual investors'.[203]

Individual investors collectively retained the majority of shares in British companies until the mid 1960s (Figure 2.1). In 1957, one estimate indicated that individual investors owned approximately 65.8 per cent of UK-quoted ordinary shares,[204] and by 1963, they were reported by the Office for National Statistics (ONS) to own 54 per cent of UK-quoted shares (Figure 2.1). However, by 1970, individuals had ceded the majority of shares to institutional investors and, by 1975, their collective share had decreased to 37.5 per cent of all quoted (ordinary) shares of UK

200 Nigel Morecroft and Craig Turnbull, 'Institutional Equity Investing in Britain from 1900 to 2000' (2019) 26 *Financial History Review* 1, 8, 13 (reporting that equity allocations by British insurance companies increased from 3 per cent in 1913 to 10 per cent in 1937 and 23 per cent in 1965). A similar trend is discernible in relation to pension funds which redirected their investment strategies from fixed-interest securities to equities following the success of the Imperial Tobacco pension funds and his manager George Ross Goobey. See Leslie Hannah, *Inventing Retirement: The Development of Occupational Pensions in Britain* (Cambridge University Press 1986), 73–5.

201 Parkinson, *Ownership of Industry*, 100.

202 S. J. Prais, *The Evolution of Giant Firms in Britain* (2nd ed., Cambridge University Press 1976), 115–16 and 120; Cheffins, *Corporate Ownership and Control*, 343–4.

203 Wilson Committee, *Committee to Review the Functioning of Financial Institutions: Evidence on the Financing of Industry and Trade (Volume 3)* (1978), 208–9.

204 John Moyle, *The Pattern of Ordinary Share Ownership 1957–1970* (Cambridge University Press 1971), 18.

Figure 2.1 Percentage of shares of UK and US public companies owned by individual and institutional investors, 1953–1970.

Sources: Compiled using data from Moyle (1971) and the Office for National Statistics for the UK and O'Sullivan (2000) for the US.

Note: The data for the 1950s was calculated based on the years 1957 for the UK and 1955 for the US. The data for the 1960s was calculated based on the years 1963 and 1965 for the UK and the US, respectively.

companies. During this same period, individual shareholders in the US also saw a decline in majority shareholding (Figure 2.1).[205]

As individual investors reduced their direct investments in shares, institutional share ownership was significantly increasing on both sides of the Atlantic. This was due to the growth in the funds available to institutional investors and an increase in the percentage of their assets invested in public equity.[206] In the UK, the proportion of public equity held by institutional investors, including insurance companies, pension funds, unit trusts, and other 'financial institutions', approximately doubled over two decades

205 See, further, Mary A. O'Sullivan, *Contests for Corporate Control: Corporate Governance and Economic Performance in the United States and Germany* (Oxford University Press 2000), 155–6.

206 For the UK see Prais, *The Evolution of Giant Firms in Britain*, 114–20 (reporting an increase in the total holdings of financial institutions from £12,900 million in 1938 to £43,310 million in 1972, and an increase in the percentage invested in public equity from 33 per cent in 1957 to 57 per cent in 1972). For the US, see Melvin A. Eisenberg, *The Structure of the Corporation: A Legal Analysis* (Beard Books 1976), 53.

(between the mid 1950s and mid 1970s).[207] In the US, the share ownership held by institutional investors rose from 9.2 per cent in 1955 to 14 per cent in 1965, and further increased to 36.7 per cent in 1975 (Figure 2.1).

The growth in the equity holdings of institutional investors was believed to significantly impact the separation of ownership and control. As early as 1928, John Maynard Keynes, the then chairman of the National Mutual Life Assurance Society, expressed concern about the 'complete impotence' of fragmented individual shareholders and advocated for collaborative action among institutional investors.[208] In 1959, Berle referred to institutional investors as 'centres of powers'. While acknowledging their underutilised voting power, he optimistically predicted that '[t]omorrow these centres will be able, without having to ask assistance from individual stockholders, to deliver a controlling vote at will'.[209]

The optimism about the monitoring role of institutional shareholders was echoed in popular writings. Business editor Livingston, in his 1958 book, concluded:

> Most shareholders – most of the nearly nine million – are like spectators at a ball game. They can boo the umpires; boo the players; or applaud. But they do not have much effect on the play. The institutional investors do. They can influence the rules of the game; the comportment of the players. But they can do it by silence; by being simple investors, first, last and always. They have to have a sense of trusteeship. . . . They are permanent shareholders: as permanents as the corporations they invest in. . . . When policies are right, the institutional function is to keep them right; when policies are wrong, to make them right – in the institution's and the general stockholder's interest. That is a moral obligation institutions shoulder when they become investment trustees.[210]

Livingston recognised that institutional shareholders did not function as Gilbert-like militant shareholders, but he had faith in their monitoring capacities, exercised through both voice and exit.[211] Similarly, corporate

[207] For details on the categories of holders and owners, see Moyle, *The Pattern of Ordinary Share Ownership 1957–1970*, 31–3.

[208] John Maynard Keynes, Principles of Investment Policy, (address to) National Mutual Life Assurance Society, London, 25 January 1928, cited in Rubner, *The Ensnared Shareholder*, 150–1. For the impact of Keynes' ideas in life insurers' allocations on equity in the mid-twentieth century, see Morecroft and Turnbull, Institutional Equity Investing in Britain from 1900 to 2000, 4–8.

[209] Berle, *Power without Property*, 53.

[210] Livingston, *The American Stockholder*, 247–8.

[211] Ibid., 156–7 and 162–3.

law scholar Melvin Eisenberg, in a 1976 book, expressed hopes that institutional investors could create a 'countervailing force to management'.[212]

However, these hopes were not realised until several decades later. For the most of the mid twentieth century, institutional shareholders remained largely passive, or, in Berle's words, 'passive-receptive'.[213] When dissatisfied with management, they often chose to sell their shares.[214] A 1965 study of the UK 'ensnared shareholder' painted a gloomy picture of institutional investors as 'passive investors' who rather than fighting in public, they often sell their investments at a loss to avoid public spectacle.[215]

Several critical factors contributed to this passivity. First, individual investors owned a majority of shares in public companies until 1970 (Figure 2.1). The widespread diffusion of ownership among individual investors, often referred to as 'property-owning democracy'[216] or 'People's Capitalism',[217] left little room for institutional investors' mobilisation. Despite gaining prominence in UK publicly quoted companies quicker than in the US,[218] individual investors remained a significant source of corporate equity until the last decades of the twentieth century.

Second, the increase in shares owned by institutional investors did not result in sizable blocks of shares in a few companies capable of shifting control from management to institutional shareholders. Despite early optimism about the 'convergence of control' into institutions' hands, data confirmed that institutional shareholders did not amass significant stakes (over 5 per cent or more) in publicly traded companies.[219]

Third, there was no collaborative action among minority institutional shareholders during this period that could have significantly reduced the

212 Eisenberg, *The Structure of the Corporation: A Legal Analysis*, 61–2.
213 Berle, *Power without Property*, 74.
214 Ibid., 55. See also Peter F. Drucker, *The Unseen Revolution: How Pension Fund Socialism Came to America* (Heinemann 1976), 82–3 (arguing that 'the pension funds are not "owners", they are investors. They do not want "control"; indeed, they are disqualified from exercising it. The pension funds are "trustees". It is their job to invest the beneficiaries' money in the most profitable investment. They have no business trying to "manage". If they do not like a company or its management, their duty is to sell the stock').
215 Rubner, *The Ensnared Shareholder*, 151.
216 Crossland, *The Future of Socialism*, 306.
217 Berle, *Power without Property*, 19.
218 O'Sullivan, *Contests for Corporate Control: Corporate Governance and Economic Performance in the United States and Germany*, 156 (reporting that between 1945 and 1980, individual investors dominated the registry of US public-traded companies, only for their stake to decrease to 48.6 per cent by 1985).
219 Cheffins, *The Public Company Transformed*, 121.

separation of ownership and control.[220] The absence of collective action and a formal organisational framework until the mid 1970s contributed to this reticence.[221] However, this institutional reticence, sometimes described as 'the British anomaly',[222] did not persist for long.

2.5.2 *The Dominance of Institutional Investors in UK Public Equity*

The transformation of the ownership structure of UK publicly listed companies over the last seven decades is remarkable. As shown in Table 2.1, between 1957 and 1981, individual share ownership halved, and by 2008 it reached a record low of 10.2 per cent. By the end of 2020, individuals owned only 12 per cent of UK-listed equity either directly or through nominee accounts.[223] In contrast, indirect investment and the institutionalisation of UK public equity increased significantly. British institutional investors – insurance companies, pension funds, investment and unit trusts, and other non-financial institutions – saw their investments in listed equity rise from 20 per cent in 1957 to 47.3 per cent in 1981, peaking at 60.6 per cent in 1992.

Pension funds, in particular, grew their holdings from 4.4 per cent in 1957 to a record high of 32.4 per cent in 1992, driven by a broader shift towards equities, known as the 'cult of equity'.[224] However, in the following decade, pension funds halved their holdings of UK-listed equities, a trend that continues today due to portfolio 'de-risking', changes in the treatment of dividends and actuarial valuations, and international diversification.[225] By the end of 2020, domestic pension

220 Ibid., 121–2.

221 See Rubner, *The Ensnared Shareholder*, 153 (describing the failed attempts to establish investors' associations between the 1930s and 1950s).

222 Ibid., 152.

223 It is concerning that over half of these shares (50.6 per cent) are held through multiple-ownership pooled nominee accounts. See Office for National Statistics, *Ownership of UK-Quoted Shares: 2020* (2022). On the implications of intermediation, and for the differences between direct and indirect individual holdings in terms of shareholder interest and engagement, see Department for Business Innovation & Skills, *Exploring the Intermediated Shareholding Model* (2016), 27–85.

224 Yally Avrahampour, 'Cult of Equity: Actuaries and the Transformation of Pension Fund Investing, 1948–1960' (2015) 89 *Business History Review* 281.

225 Ibid., 303; Cheffins, *Corporate Ownership and Control*, 388–390. For data on UK defined benefit pension funds' asset allocation, see Pension Protection Fund, *The Purple Book 2020: DB pensions universe risk profile* (2020), 5, 36 (reporting a decrease in the proportion of schemes' assets invested in equities from 61.1 per cent in 2006 to 20.4 per cent in 2020, from which 13.3 per cent are UK-listed. Meanwhile, the schemes' assets invested in bonds rose from 28.3 per cent in 2006 to 69.2 per cent in 2020).

funds held only 1.8 per cent of the UK-listed market, the lowest on record. Similarly, British insurance companies' equity holdings peaked in the mid 1970s,[226] and plateaued around 20 per cent until the early 2000s, after which they declined due to market and legal factors, reaching a record low of 2.5 per cent by the end of 2020 (Table 2.1).[227]

Unit trusts (open-end funds) and investment trusts (closed-end funds) are significant players in the institutional market. While investment trust allocation towards equities has remained low,[228] British unit trusts reached a record high of 9.6 per cent in 2018, making them the third-largest beneficial owner.[229] This rise is attributed to effective marketing, the introduction of open investment companies (OEICs), and the growth in the size of the mutual fund industry over the past two decades.[230] However, by the end of 2020, unit trusts' share in the UK-listed market fell to 7.4 per cent, making them the fourth-largest beneficial owner, following other financial institutions such as index funds, exchange-traded funds, hedge funds, socially responsible funds, and ethical funds. These other financial institutions, which held a relatively small percentage of UK-listed equity in the 1990s, saw a sharp increase in the 2000s, reaching 12.3 per cent in 2010, and recovered to 12.8 per cent by the end of 2020, the highest on record.

Overall, the trends for investment in UK-listed companies by domestic institutional investors are largely negative. On average, domestic institutional investors now own almost the same percentage of UK public equity

[226] Morecroft and Turnbull, 'Institutional Equity Investing in Britain from 1900 to 2000', 8–11 (linking this shift to the actuarial community).

[227] Cheffins, *Corporate Ownership and Control*, 387–8 (attributing the net selling of equity by insurers in the 2000s to changes in accounting practices and market regulation favouring a higher degree of certainty with liabilities).

[228] But see Janette Rutterford and Leslie Hannah, 'The Rise of Institutional Investors' in David Chambers and Elroy Dimson (eds.), *Financial Market History: Reflections on the Past for Investors Today* (CFA Institute Research Foundation 2016), 248 (elaborating that up until the 1960s investment trusts dominated unit trusts by asset size).

[229] Since 2012, OEICs have been included within the unit trust category. It is also worth noting that the ONS beneficial ownership data in Table 1 do not reflect updated allocations of beneficial ownership within pooled nominee accounts between 1998 and 2008, likely underestimating the share of holdings attributable to unit trusts during that period. See, further, Office for National Statistics (2022), 2.

[230] A. Joseph Warburton, 'Competition in Financial Services: Evidence from British Mutual Funds' (2012) 9 *J Empirical Legal Stud* 827, 830–40 (providing data on the increase of the British mutual fund industry, a degree of which is attributed to the permission of OEICs in 1997). On differences between unit trusts and OEICs, see A. Joseph Warburton, 'Should Mutual Funds Be Corporations? A Legal & Econometric Analysis' (2007) 33 *Journal of Corporation Law* 745. For a similar growth in the mutual fund industry in the US, see Rutterford and Hannah, 'The Rise of Institutional Investors', 248.

Table 2.1 *Percentage of total market value of UK-quoted shares by beneficial owner, 1957–2020*

Category of Beneficial Owner	1957	1963	1975	1981	1992	2001	2008	2010	2012	2018	2020
Insurance companies	8.8	10	15.9	20.5	19.5	20	13.4	8.8	6.2	3.9	2.5
Pension funds	3.4	6.4	16.8	26.7	32.4	16.1	12.8	5.6	4.7	2.2	1.8
Rest of the world	4.4	7	5.6	3.6	13.1	35.7	41.5	43.1	53.3	55.7	56.3
Banks	0.9	1.3	0.7	0.3	0.5	1.3	3.5	2.5	1.9	2.1	3.1
Other financial institutions	2.5	11.3	10.5	6.8	0.4	7.2	10	12.3	6.6	8.2	12.8
Public sector	3.9	1.5	3.6	3	1.8	–	1.1	3	2.5	0.9	0.7
Unit trusts	0.5	1.3	4.1	3.6	6.2	1.3	1.8	8.8	9.5	9.4	7.4
Investment trusts	5.2	–	–	–	2.1	1.6	1.9	2.1	1.7	1.3	1
Charities	1.9	2.1	2.3	2.2	1.8	1	0.8	0.9	0.6	0.9	0.9
Private non-financial companies	2.7	5.1	3	5.1	1.8	1	3	2.2	2.3	2.1	1.4
Individuals	65.8	54	37.5	28.2	20.4	14.8	10.2	10.6	10.6	13.3	12

Sources: Compiled using data from Moyle (1971) and Office for National Statistics.

Notes:

Note 1: Other financial institutions include investment trusts for 1975 and 1981.

Note 2: Public sector comprises local government, central government, and public corporations.

Note 3: Components may not sum to the total due to rounding.

as they did sixty years ago, and less than half the percentage they held in the 1990s.[231] The most significant decline is observed in the equity ownership by domestic pension funds and insurance companies, which both appear to have been reducing their holdings of UK-listed equity, contributing to the 'capital leakage' faced by UK-listed companies.[232] However, this does not mean that the institutionalisation of UK-listed equity is on the decline.

As shown in Table 2.1, the most substantial increase in beneficial ownership has been in the category of 'Rest of the world', which surged from 4.4 per cent in 1957 to 35.7 per cent in 2001, reaching 55.7 per cent in 2018. At the end of 2020, overseas investors owned a record high of 56.3 per cent of UK-quoted shares, totalling £1.22 trillion in market value.[233] Of these overseas investors, 46 per cent were based in North America in 2020 (down from 51.3 per cent in 2018). By type of beneficial owner, 56.3 per cent of the North American shareholdings are in the hands of unit trusts, followed by 24.3 per cent held by other financial institutions and 15 per cent by pension funds.[234] Overall, North American institutional investors drive the institutionalisation of UK-listed equity, comprising as high as 96.7 per cent of all North American beneficial owners at the end of 2020.[235] More than 70 per cent of these non-UK beneficial owners are institutional investors.[236]

Data from the OECD confirms that institutional investors dominate UK-listed equity, holding 62 per cent of the market capitalisation in the UK as of the end of 2020, slightly less than the 68 per cent they owned in the US, and significantly higher than the 37 per cent average in Europe.[237] Taking into account some of the free float held by institutional investors, their holdings are estimated to be as high as 70 per cent.[238] While the OECD data attribute slightly higher ownership to domestic institutional investors compared to

[231] According to the data provided in Table 2.1 domestic institutional investors together owned 20.4 per cent and 25.5 per cent in 1957 and 2018, respectively.

[232] ONDRA, *Britain plc in liquidation* (October 2023) <www.ondra.com/assets/pdfs/Britainplc_131023.pdf> (estimating that the liquidation of pension and insurance equity holdings resulted in the loss of £200 billion from UK-listed equity).

[233] For detailed data, see www.ons.gov.uk/releases/ownershipofukquotedshares2020.

[234] Office for National Statistics (2022).

[235] Own calculations based on ONS data. See ibid., Figure 9 and Table 3.

[236] Office for National Statistics, *Ownership of UK quoted shares: 2018* (2020).

[237] OECD, *The Future of Corporate Governance in Capital Markets Following the COVID-19 Crisis* (2021); Figure 2.32.

[238] Ibid. See also Adriana De La Cruz, Alejandra Medina, and Yun Tang, *Owners of the World's Listed Companies* (OECD Capital Market Series 2019), Figure 10.

the ONS data,[239] they both confirm that the current domestic investors holdings in the UK are much lower in the 1990s, with foreign investors dominating UK-listed equity.[240]

US institutional investors, particularly US mutual funds, are the largest foreign investors in UK public equity. According to Orient Capital data from 2021, US mutual funds owned £1 in every £6 of UK shares, up from just £1 in £9 in 2013, making them the largest shareholders in UK publicly listed companies. This share is twice as large as individual shareholders, who owned £1 in every £12, and even greater than UK unit trusts, which owned £1 in every £7 as of 2021.[241]

Neither the fact that institutional investors hold the majority of UK-listed shares nor that the institutionalisation of equity is driven by foreign (mainly US) investors are new developments. What is new is that a relatively small group of institutional investors can today collectively exercise significant voting control. Figure 2.2 illustrates the average combined holdings of the largest three, ten, and twenty institutional investors in UK- and US-listed companies. Notably, the average combined holdings of the top three largest institutional investors are high in both countries, standing at 23 per cent in the UK and 24 per cent in the US. Additionally, the largest twenty institutional investors, on average, own 42 per cent and 49 per cent in UK and US companies, respectively.

A corollary trend in ownership structures with significant implications for shareholder governance is the relatively high degree of ownership concentration observed at the company level in both the UK and the US.[242] Figure 2.3 illustrates that the three largest owners hold over 30 per cent in 56.7 per cent of UK companies and between 10 per cent and 29 per cent in 41.9 per cent of the listed companies. This ownership concentration pattern in UK companies exceeds that in US companies, where investors hold over 30 per cent in 42 per cent of listed companies.[243] When this trend towards more concentrated ownership

[239] Domestic institutional investors hold 25.5 per cent (as of 2018) and 30 per cent (as of 2020) according to the ONS and OECD data, respectively.

[240] According to OECD data, 73 per cent of foreign investors in the UK are institutional investors. De La Cruz, *Owners of the World's Listed Companies*, 12.

[241] Orient Capital, *Foreign Investors Take an Increased Stake in UK plc* (2021).

[242] For a critical view on the implications of this trend, see John C. Coates, *The Problem of Twelve: When a Few Financial Institutions Control Everything* (Columbia Global Reports 2023).

[243] It is noteworthy, however, that the UK concentration pattern is much lower than the global ownership distribution. Globally, the three largest shareholders own above 30 per cent in 71 per cent of the listed companies. See OECD 2021, Figure 2.33.

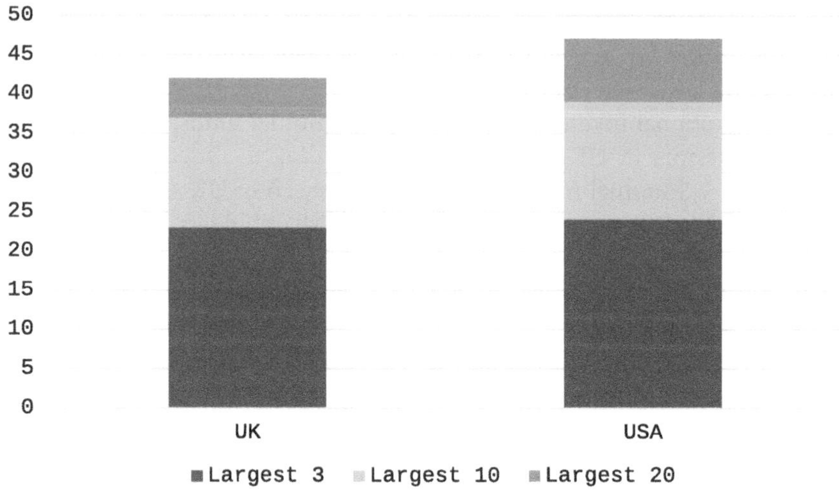

Figure 2.2 Largest institutional investors' holdings (%) at the company level. Source: OECD 2021.

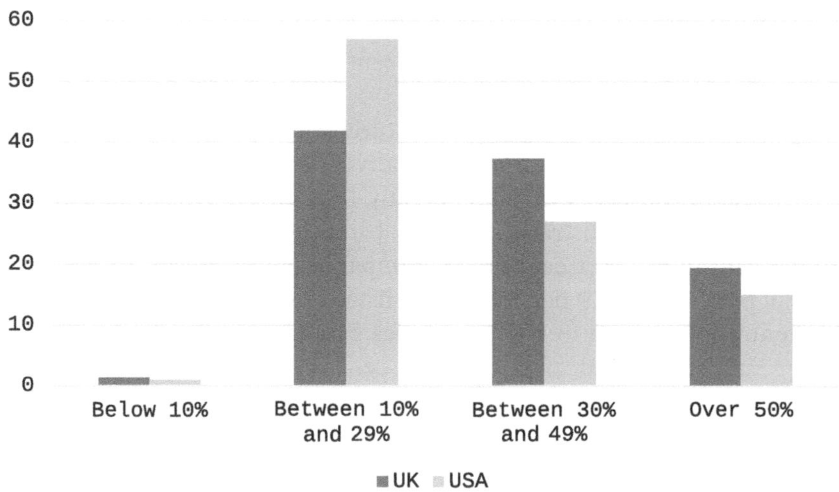

Figure 2.3 Average ownership share of the three largest owners, as of end 2020. Source: OECD 2021.

structures is combined with the overall institutionalisation of UK public equity and the fact that institutional investors collectively hold substantial ownership stakes at the company level, it becomes clear that an institutional nucleus of ownership is emerging. While such ownership concentration in the hands of institutional investors is not the global norm,[244] it underscores that the long-held perception of widely dispersed ownership in UK companies is no longer tenable.

Whether institutional investors are inclined to engage with companies and exercise meaningful stewardship is a question addressed in later chapters. For now, three key reflections emerge from the ownership data outlined in this section. First, there is a clear and accelerating trend towards the institutionalisation of UK-listed equity ownership, driven largely by foreign – particularly US-based – institutional investors. This development forms part of a broader global shift towards institutional dominance in capital markets.[245] Second, institutional investors not only hold a dominant share of UK public equity but also, taken together, possess the aggregate voting power to influence – or potentially control – the majority of UK-listed firms. Third, while direct individual ownership of UK equities remains low, many individuals participate in the market indirectly through intermediated structures such as pension schemes, investment trusts, and unit trusts. These layers of intermediation obscure the identity of ultimate beneficiaries and raise fundamental questions about the transmission of shareholder rights and the potential for effective engagement.

Taken together, these developments carry significant implications for the structure and legitimacy of shareholder activism – a subject taken up in Chapter 3. Before turning to that discussion, however, it is necessary to revisit the conceptual foundations of ownership and control in corporate governance.

2.6 Rethinking Shareholder Governance: Power, Ownership, and Control

Having contextualised the role of shareholders in corporate governance amid conflicting ideologies, evolving theories, shifting market conditions, and changing ownership patterns, the next step is to delve deeper into the nuanced notions of 'ownership' and 'control'. This exploration is crucial for understanding the evolving nature of shareholder governance,

244 Ibid., Figure 2.34 (providing data that in jurisdictions outside the UK and the US the largest twenty institutional investors do not surpass 25 per cent).

245 According to recent data by the OECD, institutional investors are the dominant category of investors holding at least 43 per cent or USD44 trillion of the global market capitalisation. Ibid. Figure 2.31.

particularly in light of recent trends towards the institutionalisation of UK-listed equity.

2.6.1 Rethinking Ownership: How Economic Theories Reframed Shareholder Governance

'Ownership' is undeniably 'one of the characteristic institutions of human society'.[246] While ownership of physical assets – such as land, buildings, or personal possessions – is typically clear-cut and legally well-defined, the concept of ownership in relation to companies is far more complex. In corporate contexts, 'ownership' is frequently treated as synonymous with the holding of shares, yet this equation masks important ambiguities and competing definitions.

In discussions of the separation of ownership and control, the terms 'ownership' and 'property' are often used interchangeably. Berle and Means, in their seminal 1932 analysis, questioned whether the traditional logic of property still applied to shareholders who had surrendered control of their wealth. This surrender of control, they argued, might fundamentally alter the nature of ownership.[247] Berle later revisited these themes in his 1959 book *Power Without Property*, where he contended that the rise of dispersed beneficial ownership had eroded the classical conception of ownership as inherently tied to control. The resulting disjunction between formal ownership and actual control, he suggested, calls for a fundamental rethinking of both legal and normative assumptions underpinning corporate governance.[248]

From a legal perspective, 'property' and 'ownership' are not synonymous. 'Property' refers both to the 'objects' of ownership and to the 'rights exercised' over them, while 'ownership' pertains specifically to the latter.[249] In his celebrated 1961 essay, Honoré identified eleven key attributes of ownership pertaining to an asset or 'thing', including the right to possess, use, manage, and benefit from an asset.[250] Importantly, Honoré's concept

[246] See the seminal work of Antony M. Honoré, 'Ownership' in Antony Gordon Guest (ed.), *Oxford Essays in Jurisprudence: A Collaborative Work* (Oxford University Press 1961), 107.

[247] Berle and Means, *The Modern Corporation & Private Property*, 297.

[248] Berle, *Power without Property*, 53–4.

[249] A. Irving Hallowell, 'The Nature and Function of Property as a Social Institution' (1942) 1 *Journal of Legal & Political Sociology* 115, 119, 120 (analysing the 'triadic' relation of property as a 'social institution' which involves 'rights, duties, powers, privileges, forbearances, etc., of certain kinds').

[250] Honoré, 113.

of 'full' ownership is not absolute; it encompasses a 'bundle of rights' that may be fragmented and constrained by legal or institutional limitations.[251]

When applied to the corporation, this typology reveals that a firm cannot be owned in the same way as a tangible asset. Shareholders, even as holders of shares, resemble claimants rather than full owners.[252] Their rights – limited in scope and contingent on legal, contractual, and institutional structures – fall short of the comprehensive control implied by classical notions of ownership.[253]

However, Honoré's definition of ownership differs significantly from that of economists like Alchian, who focus on the probability that a person's decision about resource use will dominate others.[254] This economic perspective tends to emphasise 'possession' rather than genuine property rights.[255] In contrast, Honoré's account positions property rights as just one component of a broader 'bundle of rights' that collectively constitute ownership in law.[256]

Economists' accounts of shareholder ownership align more closely with the structure of large, widely dispersed companies, contrasting with the full ownership model seen in small, concentratedly owned companies of the nineteenth and early twentieth centuries.[257] The contractarian theory of the firm has reinforced his perspective arguing that shareholders' status as *residual claimants* justifies, from an efficiency perspective, their rights of (indirect) control over the company and its assets, even though the firm itself cannot be owned.[258]

251 Ibid., 113 and 134.

252 John Kay and Aubrey Silberston, 'Corporate Governance' (1995) 153 *National Institute Economic Review* 84, 87–8; Virgile Chassagnon and Xavier Hollandts, 'Who Are the Owners of the Firm: Shareholders, Employees or No One?' (2014) 10 *Journal of Institutional Economics* 47, 54–5. See also Richard Eells, *The Government of Corporations* (The Free Press 1962) 260–1 (describing shareholder as 'a claim holder, with legal rights to some of the fruits of the enterprise when, as, and if the directors agree that the tree is ripe of shaking').

253 For instance, shareholders' entitlement to the income of their shares (dividends) is subject to the decision of the board of directors. See, further, Chassagnon and Hollandts, 'Who Are the Owners of the Firm: Shareholders, Employees or No One?' 55 (discussing the limitations on other ownership incidents related to shares).

254 Armen A. Alchian, 'Some Implications of Recognition of Property Right Transactions Costs' in Karl Brunner (ed.), *Economics and Social Institutions: Insights from the Conferences in Analysis and Ideology* (Martinus Nijhoff Publishing 1979), 237.

255 Geoffrey M. Hodgson, 'Editorial Introduction to "Ownership" by A. M. Honoré (1961)' (2013) 9 *Journal of Institutional Economics* 223.

256 Ibid., 224.

257 See Section 2.2.1 and Ireland, 'Company Law and the Myth of Shareholder Ownership', 52.

258 Section 2.4.2.

Another development in economic theory is the shift from viewing firms solely as nexuses of contracts to seeing them as combinations of contracts and assets, often described as 'a nexus of contracts about assets'.[259] Grossman and Hart, key figures in this shift, define ownership as the 'purchase' of the 'residual rights of control', meaning the rights not explicitly allocated to others by contract.[260] In the 'property rights approach' or 'property rights theory' of the firm, the 'owner' of an asset holds 'residual control rights', granting them decision-making authority over all potential uses of the asset, except where constrained by prior contractual obligations, established custom, or legal obligations.[261]

This 'residuary essence of property rights' aligns with Honoré's eleventh incident of ownership, referred to as the 'incident of residuarity'.[262] Thus, property rights theorists and lawyers share a similar understanding of ownership.[263] However, the property rights account of ownership differs significantly from contractarian theories that equate ownership with residual income.[264] Residual control rights are crucial when contracts are incomplete, but they differ from the right to residual returns. In widely held companies, shareholders typically do not exercise residual control rights; instead they delegate 'authority' to a board of directors and managers,[265] which weakens the explanatory power of property rights theory in such contexts. At the same time, as Armour and Whincop highlight, there is also 'joint sharing' of residual

259 John Armour and Michael J. Whincop, 'The Proprietary Foundations of Corporate Law' (2007) 27 *Oxford Journal of Legal Studies* 429, 431.

260 Sanford J. Grossman and Oliver D. Hart, 'The Costs and Benefits of Ownership: A Theory of Vertical and Lateral Integration' (1986) 94 *Journal of Political Economy* 691, 692. See also the seminal work of Oliver Hart and John Moore, 'Property Rights and the Nature of the Firm' (1990) 98 *Journal of Political Economy* 1119.

261 Oliver Hart, *Firms, Contracts and Financial Structure* (Clarendon Press 1995), 29–30. On the differences between the property rights theory and the other economic theories of the firm, including the agency theory and the transaction cost approach of Coase and Williamson, see Oliver Hart, 'An Economist's Perspective on the Theory of the Firm' (1989) 89 *Columbia Law Review* 1757, 1765–71.

262 Armour and Whincop, 'The Proprietary Foundations of Corporate Law', 437–8.

263 Ibid., 438.

264 Hart, *Firms, Contracts, and Financial Structure*, 63–6. See also Raghuram G. Rajan and Luigi Zingales, 'Power in a Theory of the Firm' (1998) 113 *Quarterly Journal of Economics* 387, 388, 390, 422 (highlighting access, defined as 'the ability to use, or work with, a critical resource', as 'an alternative way of conferring power', and favouring 'third-party ownership').

265 Hart, *Firms, Contracts, and Financial Structure*, 61–3.

aspects of ownership among shareholders that are not delegated to managers.[266] The recent re-concentration of ownership in institutional investors' hands expands institutional shareholders' entitlements to decision-making.

What, then, are the implications of property rights theory for shareholder governance? When considering a proprietary understanding of the firm and company law, the implications extend beyond the firm's boundaries, especially regarding third-party claims.[267] However, internally, like agency theory, property rights theory posits that allocating control rights among firm's participants mitigates agency costs.[268]

The argument extends further: several economic theories of the firm – including the nexus of contracts, transaction cost economics, agency theory, and property rights theory – appear to converge in their conceptualisation of shareholder governance.[269] Despite differing premises, these approaches consistently position shareholders' residual right to remove directors as a critical mechanism for mitigating managerial agency costs and aligning managerial interests with those of shareholders. In this sense, economic theory has played a pivotal role in reasserting shareholder governance against the dominance of managerialism – whether by emphasising shareholders' entitlement to residual income (as in contractarian theory) or by affirming their residual control rights (as in property rights theory). With this analytical foundation in place, the discussion now turns to the more nuanced and contested concept of shareholder 'control'.

2.6.2 The Elusive Nature of Shareholder 'Control': Power and Institutional Influence

When examining shareholder governance, complexities surrounding control and power quickly arise. *What* exactly constitutes control over a company, *who* and *why* should possess it, and *how* it is acquired and

266 Armour and Whincop, 'The Proprietary Foundations of Corporate Law', 438–41 (analysing of the entitlement-sharing arrangements in a typical public company).

267 For an excellent analysis of the distinction between 'contracts about assets' and 'the partition of property rights to assets', see ibid., 431 and the earlier work of Hansmann and Kraakman, 'The Essential Role of Organizational Law'.

268 Armour and Whincop, 'The Proprietary Foundations of Corporate Law', 439.

269 For a more general 'convergence' argument between the economic theories, see Hart, 'An Economist's Perspective on the Theory of the Firm', 1774.

maintained are all challenging questions, particularly as control, closely tied to power, remains an elusive concept in the social sciences.[270] Coase famously described firms as 'islands of conscious power' within the vast ocean of market transactions.[271] Within the firm, power and control predominantly evolve through the continuous interplay between shareholders and management. Among corporate stakeholders, shareholders occupy a distinct position in the ongoing debate of 'who controls the company', shaped by regulatory, socio-historical, and scholarly forces.[272]

Initially, shareholder control was equated with entrepreneurial control, reliant on nearly total or majority ownership. When a single shareholder or group holds the majority of voting power, ownership and control are often treated as interchangeable.[273] However, as dispersed ownership became more prevalent, control could no longer be simplistically equated with voting power. The threshold for minority (voting) control depends on the dispersion of remaining shares, with some scholars suggesting that an ownership stake as low as 5 per cent, or even less, can exert significant influence.[274]

Yet, as Margaret Blair argues, asserting shareholder control on the basis of ownership claims is a 'semantic trap'.[275] Economic theories of the firm

[270] On how political scientists consider the concept of power within a firm, see generally Peter A. Gourevitch and Peter Shinn, *Political Power and Corporate Control: The New Global Politics of Corporate Governance* (Princeton University Press 2005); John W. Cioffi, *Public Law and Private Power: Corporate Governance Reform in the Age of Finance Capitalism* (Cornell University Press 2010).

[271] Ronald H. Coase, 'The Nature of the Firm' (1937) 4 *Economica* 386, 388.

[272] On how both the natural entity theory and the aggregate theory supported a shareholder-centred view of corporate governance, see David Millon, 'Theories of the Corporation' (1990) *Duke Law Journal* 201. A prominent example of the influence of shareholder-centred legal scholarship is Henry Hansmann and Reinier Kraakman, 'The End of History for Corporate Law' (2001) 89 *Georgetown Law Journal* 439 (contending that corporate law has undergone convergence, moving towards a shareholder-oriented model of corporate governance). For a critical view, see Lilian Moncrief, 'A Different Kind of "End of History" for Corporate Law' in Emilios Christodoulidis, Ruth Dukes and Marco Goldoni (eds.), *Research Handbook on Critical Legal Theory* (Edward Elgar 2019).

[273] See e.g. Knight, *Risk, Uncertainty and Profit*, 332 and 294–298 (contending that the 'separation between control and uncertainty-bearing' is illusory).

[274] John Scott, *Corporate Business and Capitalist Classes* (Oxford University Press 1997) 43.

[275] Margaret M. Blair, *Wealth Creation and Wealth Sharing: A Colloquium on Corporate Governance and Investments in Human Capital* (The Brookings Institution 1996), 6. For a significant challenge to the casual use of the term 'owners' to describe the status of shareholders, particularly considering the firm-specific investments made by employees, see also Margaret M. Blair, *Ownership and Control: Rethinking Corporate Governance for the Twenty-First Century* (The Brookings Institution 1995); 'Firm-Specific Human

have played a crucial role in legitimising minority shareholder control – or more accurately, minority shareholder power – by framing shareholders as 'control claimants', even as management largely remained immune to shareholder influence throughout the twentieth century.[276] Shareholders' residual rights over control and profit appropriation do not automatically translate into the routine exercise of those rights.[277] In reality, shareholders generally refrained from actively exercising their governance rights, making their ownership – in the economic rather than strict legal sense – 'passive' and 'nominal' rather than 'active' and 'effective'.[278]

Furthermore, the question of *who* wields control over a company may oversimplify decision-making.[279] American economist Herman, in his book *Corporate Control, Corporate Power* introduces a crucial distinction between mechanism(s) of control (*how* control is maintained) and locus of control (*who* wields it).[280] He further differentiates 'literal control' – the direct power to make company decisions – from 'the power to constrain', which limits certain decision choices.[281] In widely held companies, shareholders often possess only the latter, while management retains literal control. However, even this ability to constrain decisions represents a form of partial control.[282] Herman also distinguishes between 'active' and 'latent' power, where institutional investors with sizeable stakes hold 'latent' but significant influence, primarily through board selection and trading decisions.[283] In contrast, widely dispersed shareholders wield negligible 'latent' power,

Capital and Theories of the Firm' in Margaret M. Blair and Mark J. Roe (eds.), *Employees and Corporate Governance* (Brookings Institution Press 1999), 58.

276 See Section 2.4.2. In the US, Bainbridge's director primacy theory presents an alternative to positive and normative accounts of shareholder control. See, generally, Stephen Bainbridge, *The New Corporate Governance in Theory and Practice* (Oxford University Press 2008).

277 Despite the limited participation of minority shareholders, including institutional shareholders, in exerting control until quite recently, most economists have advocated for the allocation of control rights to shareholders, even when they may not be able to effectively exercise these rights. See e.g. Henry Hansmann, *The Ownership of Enterprise* (Harvard University Press 1996), 11–12.

278 See Berle and Means, *The Modern Corporation & Private Property*, 304 and Scott, *Corporate Business and Capitalist Classes*, 37, respectively.

279 Nichols, *Ownership, Control and Ideology*, 147.

280 Herman, *Corporate Control, Corporate Power: A Twentieth Century Fund Study*, 24.

281 Ibid., 17–20.

282 Ibid., 19–20.

283 Ibid., 21 and 25–6. Notably later literature continued to put weight on these two shareholder rights. See e.g. Julian Velasco, 'The Fundamental Rights of the Shareholder' (2006) 40 *UC Davis Law Review* 407, 409 (viewing the right to elect directors and the right to sell shares as 'the fundamental rights of the shareholder').

making their role as 'constraints' largely ineffective.[284] In large companies, the overall dynamic can be described as one of 'shared power', where '[t]hose possessing latent power share it with those who have active power, which is exercisable within limits, under constraints, and on a contingent basis'.[285]

The rise of institutional investors – first pension funds, later large asset managers – has added further complexity to the evolving dynamics of corporate ownership and control. As early as the 1950s, Berle identified pension trustees, mutual fund managers, and insurance company executives as emerging 'nuclei of power', foreshadowing the growing influence of financial intermediaries.[286] In the US, scholars raised concerns about a 'migration of power' away from original shareholders – the beneficiaries – and into the hands of pension trustees.[287] Father Harbrecht described this shift as the 'paraproprietal society', in which 'power' over property was transferred, even as legal ownership remained unchanged.[288]

In the UK, similar concerns were voiced. The Cohen Committee in 1945 warned that individual investors risked becoming increasingly disengaged from their investments, particularly when investing through collective vehicles such as unit trusts.[289] Yet these concerns were initially tempered by the fact that pension fund trustees rarely exercised their power actively.[290] For much of the twentieth century, institutional investors remained largely passive, particularly in firms with widely dispersed ownership. Scholars have offered various explanations for this passivity, including weak incentives, diversification strategies, conflicts of interest, engagement costs, and persistent free-rider and collective action problems.[291]

Another crucial feature of institutional ownership is its delegated structure: institutional investors act on behalf of others. In the case of pension funds, the beneficiaries are typically workers and retirees who contribute

284 Herman, *Corporate Control, Corporate Power: A Twentieth Century Fund Study*, 23.

285 This can still be of concern to management, however, because of the workings of the market for corporate control. Ibid., 23.

286 Berle, *Power without Property*, 53.

287 Eells, *The Government of Corporations*, 262–3.

288 Harbrecht S. J., *Pension Funds and Economic Power*, 285–7.

289 *Report of the Committee on Company Law Amendment (Cohen Report)* (1945), para 124.

290 Eells, *The Government of Corporations*, 44.

291 On the factors behind shareholder passivity, see e.g. Fischel, 'Corporate Governance Movement', 1277; Bernard S. Black, 'Shareholder Passivity Re-examined' (1990) 89 *Michigan Law Review* 520; John C. Jr. Coffee, 'Liquidity versus Control: The Institutional Investor as Corporate Monitor' (1991) 91 *Columbia Law Review* 1277; Roberta Romano, 'Public Pension Fund Activism in Corporate Governance Reconsidered' (1993) 93 *Columbia Law Review* 795.

to, and depend on, these schemes.[292] This model of mediated ownership, combined with post-war welfare state ideology, gave rise to the notion that employees were gradually becoming indirect owners of corporate capital. In 1976, Peter Drucker famously described this development as an 'unseen revolution', claiming that the 'employees of America' were becoming 'the true owners of the means of production' through their pension funds.[293] In the UK, Sir Harold Wilson, the then Chairman of the Committee to Review the Functioning of Financial Institutions, argued that pension fund investment in corporate equities represented not only an 'extension of nationalisation' but also the potential foundation for a broader 'transformation of society'.[294] In 1980, Minns summarised this idea, noting that the revolutionary nature of pension funds lay in their origins: employee contributions, scale, and growth positioned them as a unique vehicle of ownership, distinct from other financial institutions.[295]

Yet this so-called revolution had significant limitations. In a 1976 study of the hundred largest UK manufacturing companies, Prais observed that, despite the increasing concentration of ownership through financial intermediaries, institutional investors largely treated their holdings as tradable assets rather than as stakes demanding active oversight or managerial involvement.[296] While some argued that institutions engaged more than commonly assumed – albeit discreetly – their interventions rarely translated into visible governance changes.[297]

Even where formal shareholder rights were exercised, the ultimate beneficiaries remained at the distant end of an extended investment chain, far removed from meaningful control. Whether the institutionalisation of UK-listed equity has in fact led to stronger shareholder governance – either formal or informal – remains contested. Historically and today, concerns persist that the re-concentration of ownership has not bridged the long-standing separation between ownership and control. Instead, the ascent of institutional investors has, in many respects, pushed the 'true owners' – clients, beneficiaries, and ultimately end-investors – further removed from the levers of corporate influence. Recent efforts to reframe institutional

[292] Regarding how this element of acting on behalf of others has later influenced the development of the investor stewardship movement, see Section 4.3.2.

[293] Drucker, *The Unseen Revolution: How Pension Fund Socialism Came to America*, 2.

[294] Richard Minns, *Pension Funds and British Capitalism: The Ownership and Control of Shareholdings* (Heinemann 1980), 8–9.

[295] Ibid., 11.

[296] Prais, *The Evolution of Giant Firms in Britain*, 113–4.

[297] Child, *The Business Enterprise in Modern Industrial Society*, 46.

investment as a source of democratic empowerment – for example, through public pension funds and union-affiliated investors in the US – have sought to revive this promise. But even this more activist vision of the 'working-class shareholder' faces significant institutional and structural barriers.[298]

2.7 Conclusion: From Control to Influence – The Evolving Logic of Shareholder Governance

This chapter has traced the theoretical and historical trajectory of shareholder governance, from its origins in concentrated entrepreneurial control to the challenges posed by dispersed ownership and the rise of managerialism. Economic theories, particularly contractarian and agency perspectives, helped re-legitimise shareholder governance by recasting shareholders as residual claimants and control claimants. Yet, these same frameworks also contributed to the marginalisation of participatory shareholder control, as institutional ownership structures deepened and shareholder influence became increasingly abstracted through layers of intermediation.

The ascent of institutional investors – initially pension funds and now large asset managers – has reshaped the contours of corporate power, introducing new dynamics of latent influence and passive control. Despite their growing presence in UK public equity, institutional shareholders remained largely disengaged for much of the twentieth century, constrained by structural, economic, and ideological factors. The promise of a pension-led revolution in corporate ownership ultimately gave way to a more market-oriented form of financial intermediation, leaving beneficiaries further removed from decision-making and control.

Today, concentrated shareholder power in the hands of institutional investors remains more relevant than ever. Unlike mid twentieth-century pension trustees, today's key players include a small number of large asset managers – such as BlackRock, State Street, and Legal & General – alongside major asset owners and activist investors. These actors resemble what Berle once described as 'naked power vehicles', wielding significant influence over investable assets.[299] Yet this power is *migrant*: shaped by market fluctuations, exercised selectively, and often without direct accountability. Meanwhile, the ultimate beneficiaries of these investments – end-investors – have become increasingly *distant owners*, structurally and

298 David Webber, *The Rise of the Working-Class Shareholder* (Harvard University Press 2018).

299 Adolf A. Berle, *Economic Power and the Free Society: A Preliminary Discussion of the Corporation* (The Fund for the Republic 1957), 13.

informationally disconnected from the corporate decisions made on their behalf.[300]

As a result, institutional investors now occupy an ambiguous position in the governance ecosystem: powerful yet remote, influential yet selectively engaged. This ambiguity has shifted the discourse from questions of ownership and control towards questions of legitimacy, responsibility, and strategic intervention. As the boundaries of shareholder power blur, a new paradigm has begun to emerge – one focused not merely on legal rights or economic entitlements, but on *how* shareholders, particularly institutional ones, intervene in corporate affairs.

The next chapter explores this shift in detail by examining the rise of institutional shareholder activism. It unpacks how activism has evolved from firm-level interventions to broader systemic engagements, and how new actors, strategies, and motivations are redefining the practice of shareholder governance in the twenty-first century.

300 Michel De Vroey, 'The Owners' Interventions in Decision-Making in Large Corporations: A New Approach' (1975) 6 *European Economic Review* 1, 6 (theorising about the different degrees of ownership and control in the 1970s and characterising the end-investors as 'distant owners').

3

Institutional Shareholder Activism

Evolving Actors, Strategies, and Influence

3.1 Introduction

Shareholder activism has moved from the margins of corporate governance to its mainstream. Once dismissed as the province of dissident shareholders and corporate raiders, activism is now central to how shareholder governance is understood and practised – particularly in markets with high institutional ownership.[1] While early critiques focused on 'functionless shareholders' and 'absentee owners',[2] today's landscape is defined by a growing array of activist interventions, spanning firms, industries, and entire financial systems.

This chapter examines the institutionalisation and diversification of shareholder activism, tracing its transformation from a firm-specific response to managerial underperformance into a multi-level and multi-actor governance practice. It explores how hedge funds pioneered offensive, targeted campaigns at the firm level, while institutional investors – including index funds, common owners, and pension funds – have increasingly embraced broader forms of portfolio-level, industry-wide, and symbolic activism. These developments reflect a strategic recalibration of shareholder engagement, shaped by shifts in market structure, corporate governance norms, and risk management priorities.

As the boundaries of activism expand, so too does its economic rationale. What began as a narrow cost–benefit exercise has matured into a more complex logic that accounts for systemic risk, reputational capital, and the interplay between financial and sustainability goals. This chapter draws on new empirical data from the UK to explore the actors,

[1] For empirical evidence on institutional ownership, see Adriana De La Cruz, Alejandra Medina, and Yun Tang, *Owners of the World's Listed Companies* (OECD Capital Market Series 2019).

[2] Thorstein Veblen, *Absentee Ownership and Business Enterprise in Recent Times: The Case of America* (George Allen & Unwin, Ltd. 1924). See also Section 2.2.

objectives, strategies, ownership patterns, and outcomes that define contemporary institutional shareholder activism. It also situates these developments within broader policy debates, including the competing imaginaries of the institutional investor – as 'Engaged Shareholder', 'Transient Shareholder', or the emerging figure of the 'Steward', whose legitimacy rests on long-term accountability and systemic responsibility.

By unpacking the modalities, motivations, and institutional logics of shareholder activism, this chapter provides a framework for understanding activism not simply as a tool of shareholder governance, but as an evolving institutional practice with strategic, regulatory, and normative implications.

3.2 Setting the Stage: The Expanding Scope and Economic Logic of Shareholder Activism

3.2.1 *From Exit to Voice: The Foundations of Shareholder Activism*

At the core of shareholder governance lies Albert O. Hirschman's organisational theory of *voice*, *exit*, and *loyalty*, which introduced a nuanced relationship between the options of voice (shareholder engagement) and exit (divestment).[3] Hirshman defined voice as any effort to *change* a firm's practices, policies, or outputs,[4] describing it as a 'residual of exit' – a mechanism used when selling shares is not a viable option.[5] However, he also suggested that voice can serve as a substitute for exit.[6] According to Hirschman, while the availability of exit can strengthen voice by providing leverage, an overly accessible exit option may discourage shareholder engagement by making voice less necessary or impactful.[7]

For much of the twentieth century, these propositions held true. The liquidity-driven environment of the Deal Decade favoured exit over voice, with limited exceptions, such as politically motivated shareholder activism in the 1960s and 1970s, where disinvestment remained a peripheral tactic.[8] However, as explained in Chapter 2, market structural changes – particularly

[3] Albert O. Hirschman, *Exit, Voice and Loyalty: Responses to Decline in Firms, Organizations and States* (Harvard University Press 1970), 83.
[4] Ibid., 30.
[5] Ibid., 33.
[6] Ibid., 77–8 and 82–3.
[7] Ibid., 83.
[8] For the evolution of public interest proxy resolutions in the US, see David Vogel, 'Trends in Shareholder Activism: 1970–1982' (1983) 25 *California Management Review* 68.

the decline of takeovers and the rise of institutional investor ownership – heightened the importance of the voice mechanism.[9] Institutional shareholders began adopting more systematic forms of shareholder governance, collectively referred to as *shareholder activism*, which has since become central to corporate governance, particularly in publicly listed companies.

Shareholder activism broadly refers to deliberate shareholder actions aimed at influencing corporate policies, management, corporate governance, or environmental and social issues.[10] It is characterised by two key features. First, it requires equity ownership, distinguishing it from bondholder activism, where influence is exercised through debt holdings.[11] Second, it involves active engagement, setting it apart from looser forms of shareholder monitoring that may not necessarily include direct intervention to address managerial shortcomings.[12]

Initial scholarship, building on Hirschman's framework, framed exit and voice as a trade-off, favouring exit as the primary means of shareholder influence.[13] More recently, it has been recognised that the threat, either actual or implied, of exit can often reinforce voice.[14] This has led some management scholars to distinguish between 'voice activists' and 'exit activists'.[15] However, the latter term can be misleading, as exit is typically a last resort rather than a core activist strategy. What

9 Sections 2.4.3 and 2.5.

10 Stuart L. Gillan and Laura T. Starks, 'A Survey of Shareholder Activism: Motivation and Empirical Evidence' (1998) *Contemporary Finance Digest* 10; Maria Goranova and Lori Verstegen Ryan, 'Shareholder Activism: A Multidisciplinary Review' (2014) 40 *Journal of Management* 1230; Kevin Chuah, Mark R. DesJardine, Maria Goranova, and Witold J. Henisz, 'Shareholder Activism Research: A System-Level View' (2024) 18 *Academy of Management Annals* 82.

11 Michelle M. Harner, 'The Corporate Governance and Public Policy Implications of Activist Distressed Debt Investing' (2008) 77 *Fordham Law Review* 703. For an account of bondholder apathy, see Jonathan Brogaard and Yesha Yadav, 'The Broken Bond Market' Vanderbilt Law Research Paper No 21–43 <https://ssrn.com/abstract=3941941>, 47–51.

12 Edward B. Rock, 'The Logic and (Uncertain) Significance of Institutional Shareholder Activism' (1991) 79 *Georgetown Law Journal* 445, 453 (distinguishing 'discipline' from the more common term 'monitoring' which, according to Rock, may not necessarily involve 'doing something' to address poor management).

13 John C. Jr. Coffee, 'Liquidity versus Control: The Institutional Investor as Corporate Monitor' (1991) 91 *Columbia Law Review* 1277, 1289; Edward S. Herman, *Corporate Control, Corporate Power: A Twentieth-Century Fund Study* (Cambridge University Press 1981), 153.

14 Anat R. Admati and Paul Pfleiderer, 'The "Wall Street Walk" and Shareholder Activism: Exit as a Form of Voice' (2009) 22 *The Review of Financial Studies* 2645.

15 Janet H. Marler and Christophe Faugère, 'Shareholder Activism and Middle Management Equity Incentives' (2010) 18 *Corporate Governance: An International Review* 313, 314.

fundamentally distinguishes activists from other shareholders is their reliance on voice, rather than exit, to exert pressure on management.[16]

Early academic discussions on shareholder activism centred on the monitoring role of large shareholders and other market participants, such as corporate raiders and merger arbitrageurs, identifying key factors influencing activist interventions.[17] However, as institutional ownership expanded and market-based disciplinary mechanisms weakened, the role of shareholder voice became increasingly critical as a check on management.[18] Since the mid 1980s, it has been *minority* institutional investors – rather than large shareholders or corporate raiders – who have driven this transformation, embracing voice over exit as their primary governance tool.[19] This shift has reshaped corporate governance dynamics, but the extent to which institutional investors engage in shareholder activism ultimately depends on their cost–benefit considerations.

[16] Recent literature examines how the interplay of voice and exit as alternative governance mechanisms affects strategic communication in activism, highlighting that the decision not to exit, rather than the exit or its threat, enhances the activist's credibility. See Doron Levit, 'Soft Shareholder Activism' (2018) 32 *The Review of Financial Studies* 2775, 2780.

[17] Anat R. Admati, Paul Pfleiderer, and Josef Zechner, 'Large Shareholder Activism, Risk Sharing, and Financial Market Equilibrium' (1994) 102 *Journal of Political Economy* 1097; Patrick Bolton and Ernst-Ludwig Von Thadden, 'Blocks, Liquidity, and Corporate Control' (1998) 53 *The Journal of Finance* 1; Charles Kahn and Andrew Winton, 'Ownership Structure, Speculation, and Shareholder Intervention' (1998) 53 *The Journal of Finance* 99; Ernst Maug, 'Large Shareholders as Monitors: Is There a Trade-Off between Liquidity and Control?' (1998) 53 *The Journal of Finance* 65.

[18] Bernard S. Black, 'Agents Watching Agents: The Promise of Institutional Investor Voice' (1992) 39 *UCLA Law Review* 811; John Pound, 'The Rise of the Political Model of Corporate Governance and Corporate Control' (1993) 68 *New York University Law Review* 1003; Bernard S. Black and John C. Coffee, 'Hail Britannia? Institutional Investor Regulation under Limited Regulation' (1994) 92 *Michigan Law Review* 1997. For a review of early empirical evidence on the effectiveness of institutional shareholder monitoring, see Stuart L. Gillan and Laura T. Starks, 'Corporate Governance, Corporate Ownership, and the Role of Institutional Investors: A Global Perspective' (2003) 13 *Journal of Applied Finance* 4.

[19] Amil Dasgupta, Vyacheslav Fos, and Zacharias Sautner, 'Institutional Investors and Corporate Governance' (2021) 12 *Foundations and Trends in Finance* 276. For a bibliometric review of shareholder activism literature between 1983 and 2022, see Dionysia Katelouzou, Yanqiu Ren, and Marti Sagarra, 'A Bibliometric Analysis of Four Decades of Shareholder Activism Research' (2025) 33 *Corporate Governance: An International Review*, 946, 960, 967, 972 (confirming that most of the shareholder activism literature focuses on activism initiated by institutional investors).

3.2.2 Firm-Level Shareholder Activism: From Cost–Benefit Constraints to Hedge-Fund-Style Influence

Shareholder activism is fundamentally a cost–benefit undertaking, where the activist's anticipated gains must outweigh the expected costs of the campaign. Traditionally assessed at the firm level, early literature suggested that when an activist's ownership stake is relatively small, the potential financial gains may not justify the associated costs.[20] In more formal terms, firm-specific shareholder activism is considered a rational strategy only when the activist's expected profits (P_{f_i}) from engaging with a target company exceed the expected costs of the campaign (C_f):

$$P_{f_i} > C_{f_i}. \tag{3.1}$$

Since an activist's ability to capture value is directly linked to their ownership stake, this condition can be rewritten as:

$$a_{f_i} \Delta V_{f_i} > C_{f_i}, \tag{3.2}$$

where a_f represents the activist's ownership stake in company i and ΔV_{f_i} represents the expected increase in the firm's value resulting from the activist's campaign.

For decades, the cost–benefit analysis of shareholder activism has suggested that for most institutional investors the expected profits from firm-specific activism did not justify the associated costs.[21] This assumption fuelled what became known as the 'passivity story' – the notion that most institutional investors lacked sufficient incentives to engage actively with their investee companies and, even when they did, had little impact

[20] See e.g. Kahn and Winton, 'Ownership Structure, Speculation, and Shareholder Intervention', 109–10. But see Thomas H. Noe, 'Investor Activism and Financial Market Structure' (2002) 15 *The Review of Financial Studies* 289, 305, 310 (refuting a monotonic relationship between the probability of activism and the size of shareholding).

[21] For the various costs of shareholder activism, see Dionysia Katelouzou, 'Worldwide Hedge Fund Activism: Dimensions and Legal Determinants' (2015) 17 *University of Pennsylvania Business Law Review* 798, 797–802, 852 (elaborating that the costs of firm-specific shareholder activism include entry costs (that is, search costs associated with identifying the potential candidate target company), financing and transaction costs involved in acquiring an ownership stake, and the costs of actually executing an activist campaign (disciplining costs). See also Nickolay Gantchev, 'The Costs of Shareholder Activism: Evidence from a Sequential Decision Model' (2013) 107 *Journal of Financial Economics* 610, 611 and 624 (providing evidence that the proxy context had the highest cost equal to $5.94 million for the average campaign in a hand-collected sample of hedge fund activism in the US between 2000 and 2007).

on corporate governance and firm performance.[22] Activist hedge funds were the key exception. Their structural advantages – such as capital lock-up periods, performance-based compensation, and financial engineering capabilities – provided strong incentives for firm-level activism.[23] Empirical evidence suggests that hedge fund activism can generate significant short- and medium-term value for target firms, with some indications of positive real effects.[24]

As hedge fund activism gained momentum in the 2000s, institutional investors also began adopting more active engagement strategies, leading to the emergence of distinct forms of shareholder activism. A common classification distinguishes between 'defensive' and 'offensive' shareholder

[22] Bernard S. Black, 'Shareholder Passivity Re-examined' (1990) 89 *Michigan Law Review* 520524. For the US, see e.g. Bernard S. Black, 'Shareholder Activism and Corporate Governance in the United States' in Peter Newman (ed.), *The New Palgrave Dictionary of Economics and the Law*, vol 3 (Palgrave Macmillan 1998) (finding little evidence that institutional shareholder activism mattered); Stephen J. Choi and Jill E. Fisch, 'On beyond CalPERS: Survey Evidence on the Developing Role of Public Pension Funds in Corporate Governance Symposium' (2008) 61 *Vanderbilt Law Review* 315, 318 (concluding that 'their findings offer reasons to be skeptical of the so-called promise of institutional activism'). For the UK, see Brian R. Cheffins, *Corporate Ownership and Control: British Business Transformed*, (Oxford University Press 2008), 369 (illustrating the 'hands-off' approach of the UK institutional investors especially up to 1990).

[23] On short-selling by activists, the so-called negative activists, see Barbara A. Molk Bliss, Peter Partnoy, Frank, 'Negative Activism' (2019) 97 *Washington University Law Review* 1333; Peter Molk and Frank Partnoy, 'The Long-Term Effects of Short Selling and Negative Activism' (2022) 2022 *University of Illinois Law Review* 1.

[24] For literature reviews of the empirical literature in the US, see Alon Brav, Wei Jiang and Hyunseob Kim, 'Hedge Fund Activism: A Review' (2009) 4 *Foundations and Trends in Finance* 185; Alon Brav, Wei Jiang, and Hyunseob Kim, 'Recent Advances in Research on Hedge Fund Activism: Value Creation and Identification' (2015) 7 *Annual Review of Financial Economics* 579; John C. Jr. Coffee and Darius Palia, 'The Wolf at the Door: The Impact of Hedge Fund Activism on Corporate Governance' (2015) 41 *Journal of Corporation Law* 545, 551 (2016). For empirical evidence outside the US, see e.g. Marco Becht, Julian Franks, Jeremy Grant, and Hannes F. Wagner, 'Returns to Hedge Fund Activism: An International Study' (2017) 30 *The Review of Financial Studies* 2933. On the debate on the long-term effects of hedge fund activism, juxtapose Lucian A. Bebchuk, Alon Brav, and Wei Jiang, 'The Long-Term Effects of Hedge Funds Activism' (2015) 115 *Columbia Law Review* 1085 (finding improved operating performance of companies following activist interventions) with Martijn Cremers, Saura Masconale, and Simone M. Sepe, 'Activist Hedge Funds and the Corporation' (2016) 94 *Washington University Law Review* 261 (finding that hedge fund activism is associated with excessive risk-taking but has no significant impact on managerial accountability). On the real effects of hedge fund activism, see Alon Brav, Wei Jiang, and Rongchen Li, 'Governance by Persuasion: Hedge Fund Activism and the Market for Corporate Influence', *Oxford Research Encyclopedia of Economics and Finance* (2022).

activism.[25] Defensive activism occurs when an existing shareholder, dissatisfied with management, pushes for change. Offensive activism, by contrast, involves acquiring a stake – often only 1–3 per cent – with the specific intent of initiating firm-specific changes, not necessarily in an adversarial manner. Defensive activism is typically associated with mainstream institutional investors, such as pension funds and mutual funds, while activist hedge funds are commonly linked to offensive shareholder activism. The key distinction lies in the timing: defensive activists act ex post, responding to managerial underperformance, whereas offensive activists act ex ante, acquiring shares with a predetermined activist agenda.[26]

However, with the evolution of hedge fund activism, the line between offensive and defensive activists has blurred. Since the 2000s, the global expansion of US-spurred hedge fund activism and the rise of local activist investors have transformed activism into a mainstream investment strategy.[27] No longer confined to activist hedge funds, traditional institutional investors have adopted similar tactics. A 2017 JP Morgan report noted that shareholder activism 'is no longer the preserve of aggressive hedge funds but is now a tactic used by a host of traditional institutional shareholders'.[28]

With hedge fund activism gaining traction among investors with diverse investment styles and approaches, the rigid distinction between defensive and offensive activists has become less relevant. While some activist hedge funds continue to engage exclusively in the purely offensive activism described by earlier literature – launching campaigns without prior stakes – others may already hold small shareholdings before initiating activism. Moreover, the label offensive activism, with its confrontational connotation, does not fully capture the approach of many activists, especially those outside the US, who often engage more

[25] Brian R. Cheffins and John Armour, 'The Past, Present and Future of Shareholder Activism by Hedge Funds' (2011) 37 *Journal of Corporation Law* 51, 56–7.

[26] Marcel Kahan and Edward B. Rock, 'Hedge Funds in Corporate Governance and Corporate Control' (2007) 155 *University of Pennsylvania Law Review* 1021, 1069.

[27] See e.g. Ruth V. Aguilera, Ryan Federo, and Yuliva Ponomareva, 'Gone Global: The International Diffusion of Hedge Fund Activism' in Douglas Cumming, Sofia Johan, and Geoffrey Wood (eds.), *The Oxford Handbook of Hedge Funds* (Oxford Academic, Oxford University Press 2021) and data in Section 3.3.1.

[28] Ben Martin, 'Activism "Is no Longer the Preserve of Big Hedge Funds"' Daily Telegraph (13 July 2017) 8. See also Lazard's Shareholder Advisory Group, *Review of Shareholder Activism* (2018) 6 (reporting that a record forty 'first timers' launched activist campaigns in 2018).

discreetly and collaboratively with target companies. As activism adapts to different market contexts and regulatory environments, the term *hedge-fund-style activism* better reflects the broader uptake of hedge fund tactics by a wider range of institutional investors.[29] This broader adoption has also contributed to a shift beyond firm-level activism, as institutional investors – particularly those with diversified portfolios – recognise the need to shape governance and market dynamics across their entire portfolio.

3.2.3 Beyond the Firm: The Rise of Portfolio-Level and Systemic Activism

For much of the twentieth and early twenty-first centuries, shareholder activism primarily centred on firm-level interventions, where investors sought to influence governance, management, and financial performance within individual companies based on a cost–benefit analysis. However, this firm-specific approach often failed to align with a diversified investment strategy and presented challenges to the business models of intermediary institutional investors, including active funds, index funds, and pension funds, as the financial gains from firm-specific activism are largely tied to an investor's ownership stake in a single company.[30]

By the early 1990s, scholars began to explore shareholder activism beyond the firm level, arguing that while diversified institutional investors had limited incentives to improve firm-specific governance and performance, they could still play a role in shaping the broader 'corporate governance system' by influencing market-wide standards and practices.[31] Nearly a decade later, in a review article, Ryan and Schneider expanded the definition of shareholder activism, describing

[29] For a broad definition of the term activist hedge funds, see Dionysia Katelouzou, 'Myths and Realities of Hedge Fund Activism: Some Empirical Evidence' (2013) 7 *Virginia Law & Business Review* 459, 468–73.

[30] See e.g. Roger M. Baker and Iris H-Y Chiu, *Corporate Governance and Investment Management: The Promises and Limitations of the New Financial Economy* (Edward Elgar 2017), especially Chapters 4 and 5 (discussing the limitations of firm-specific engagement for diversified institutional investors); Assaf Hamdani and Sharon Hannes, 'The Future of Shareholder Activism' (2019) 99 *Boston University Law Review* 971, 977–83 (highlighting the structural disincentives for institutional investors to engage in costly activism when holding widely diversified portfolios).

[31] Ronald J. Gilson and Reinier Kraakman, 'Reinventing the Outside Director: An Agenda for Institutional Investors' (1991) 43 *Stanford Law Review* 863, 866; John E. Parkinson, *Corporate Power and Responsibility: Issues in the Theory of Company Law* (Oxford University Press 1995), 174.

it as 'the use of power by an investor to either influence the processes or outcomes of a given firm or to *invoke large-scale change* in process or outcomes *across multiple firms* through the symbolic targeting of one or more firms' (emphasis added).[32]

This concept of *symbolic activism* refers to interventions where an activist's primary objective is not necessarily to enact direct change within the targeted firm but to send a broader signal to the market. By selecting a high-profile company, activists can pressure firms across an industry – or even the entire market – to adopt certain governance or sustainability practices.[33]

By contrast, *industry-wide activism* involves engagement with multiple firms in the same sector, often driven by institutional investors who hold stakes across competing firms. This form of activism is particularly prevalent in sectors with high horizontal shareholding – such as airlines, banking, and pharmaceuticals – where common owners seek to influence firms collectively rather than through firm-specific interventions.[34] Unlike symbolic activism, which relies on reputational pressure and signalling, industry-wide activism leverages direct engagement, voting strategies, and collaborative investor efforts to drive systemic change.

At an even broader scale, *portfolio-level activism* – also known as *beta activism*[35] or *systematic risk activism*[36] – extends beyond specific industries

[32] Lori Verstegen Ryan and Marguerite Schneider, 'The Antecedents of Institutional Investor Activism' (2002) 27 *Academy of Management Review* 554, 555.

[33] For instance, in 2018, activist hedge fund JANA Partners and the California State Teachers' Retirement System (CalSTRS) jointly sent a public letter to Apple Inc. to address concerns about children's overuse of technology. See Robert G. Eccles, 'Why an Activist Hedge Fund Cares Whether Apple's Devices Are Bad for Kids' *Harvard Business Review* (16 January 2018). Another notable example of symbolic activism is the shareholder resolution filed by the UK's largest charity fund manager CCLA Investment Management, in collaboration with US-based investor Trillium Asset Management, Dutch pension manager PGGM and green bank Triodos, demanding that Nike provide an independent report on its methods for identifying and addressing human rights abuses in its supply chains. See Kristen McGachey, 'CCLA, Trillium Rally Nike Shareholders for Showdown over Workers' Rights' *Financial News* (15 August 2024).

[34] See e.g. Einer Elhauge, 'Horizontal Shareholding Essay' (2015) 129 *Harvard Law Review* 1267.

[35] Jon Lukomnik and James P. Hawley, *Moving Beyond Modern Portfolio Theory: Investing That Matters* (Routledge 2021), 41, 97–110; Frederick H. Alexander, 'The Benefit Stance: Responsible Ownership in the Twenty-First Century' (2020) 36 *Oxford Review of Economic Policy* 341.

[36] John C. Jr. Coffee, 'The Coming Shift in Shareholder Activism: From "Firm-specific" to "Systematic Risk" Proxy Campaigns (and How to Enable Them)' (2021) 16 *Brooklyn Journal of Corporate, Financial & Commercial Law* 45.

to address systemic risks that affect the entire market, such as climate change, biodiversity loss, or social inequality. Large institutional investors may engage in portfolio activism to mitigate risks that affect the overall financial system and long-term portfolio performance.[37] Unlike firm-specific activism, which seeks to improve governance or performance at individual companies, portfolio activists focus on driving structural policy changes, regulatory reforms, and stewardship initiatives that shape corporate behaviour on a market-wide scale.

The financial rationale for portfolio-level activism can be understood through an aggregate cost–benefit analysis across an investor's entire holdings. The expected profits of portfolio-level, beta-focused activism (P_p) can be expressed as the sum of the expected firm-specific (adjusted-risk) returns across the investor's portfolio:

$$P_p = \sum_{i=1}^{n} P_{f_i}, \tag{3.3}$$

where P_{f_i} represents the expected profit from activism at firm *i*.

Given that P_{f_i} are contingent on the activist's ownership stake, each P_{f_i} is a function of the activist's shareholding in that firm (Equation 3.2). Substituting this relationship into Equation (3.3), the expected profits of portfolio-level activism can be expressed as:

$$P_p = \sum_{i=1}^{n} (a_{f_i} \Delta V_{C_i}), \tag{3.4}$$

where a_{f_i} represents the activist's ownership stake in firm i and ΔV_{C_i} represents the change in firm value due to engagement.

For example, consider a portfolio consisting of Companies A, B, C, and D. If Company A sacrifices £200 in profit to reduce pollution following a portfolio-level activist's campaign, this results in a £100 increase for each of the other three companies, resulting in a net market-wide benefit of £100.[38] A beta-focused activist with an evenly allocated portfolio (i.e., 25 per cent invested in each company) would bear 25 per cent of Company A's £200 loss (£50) while benefitting from 25 per cent of each £100 gain in Companies B, C, and D (a total of £75). This results in a net profit of £25. Meanwhile,

[37] However, on the limitations of portfolio-level activism, see Roberto Tallarita, 'The Limits of Portfolio Primacy' (2023) 76 *Vanderbilt Law Review* 511.

[38] This hypothetical is based on the assumption that firm-specific activism generates spillover effects on non-targeted firms within the activist's portfolio. See Wei Shi, Brian L. Connelly, Robert E. Hoskisson, and David J. Ketchen, Jr, 'Portfolio Spillover of Institutional Investor Activism: An Awareness–Motivation–Capability Perspective' (2020) 63 *Academy of Management Journal* 1865.

a shareholder with a concentrated portfolio in Company A would bear the full £200 loss. This example illustrates why systematic risk activists may still target individual companies (often a high profile one or those that contribute most to systematic risk), even if those companies' post-engagement value declines – so long as the expected financial return at the portfolio level is higher, on average, compared to similar portfolios.

Excluding large-scale activism driven by non-financial motives, portfolio-level shareholder activism is financially viable only if the expected portfolio-level profits (P_p) exceed the expected costs (C_p):

$$P_p > C_p. \tag{3.5}$$

This mirrors the cost–benefit logic of firm-specific activism, where interventions occur only when expected benefits exceed expected costs (Equation 3.1). However, for portfolio-level activism, the costs include both the intervention costs at the portfolio level and any firm-specific losses incurred as a consequence of activism.[39]

That said, firm-specific and portfolio-level activism are not mutually exclusive but often work in tandem. Portfolio-level activists frequently engage in firm-specific activism not solely to address individual corporate inefficiencies, but as a means of mitigating systemic ricks and enhancing long-term portfolio returns.[40] Accordingly, for portfolio-level activism to be financially justified, it must yield net portfolio-wide profits that are at least comparable to, and in relevant cases exceed, the net profits achievable through firm-specific activism addressing comparable risks.[41] This condition can be expressed as:

$$P_p - C_p > \sum_{i=1}^{n} (P_{f_i} - C_{f_i}), \tag{3.6}$$

which can be re-written as:

$$P_p > C_p + \sum_{i=1}^{n} (P_{f_i} - C_{f_i}). \tag{3.7}$$

If firm-specific activism yields higher net profits, portfolio-level activism may nevertheless be financially justified where it internalises negative externalities that firm-level interventions cannot address, reduces

39 See also Madison Condon, 'Externalities and the Common Owner' (2020) 95 *Washington Law Review* 164.

40 See e.g. Lukomnik and Hawley, *Moving Beyond Modern Portfolio Theory: Investing That Matters*, 41.

41 The assumption here is that a portfolio-level activist can pursue a firm-level activist campaign, but this is not always the case.

correlated risks across the portfolio, or generates indirect benefits, such as attracting capital to sustainability-focused investment products through branding or other strategic incentives.[42]

As shareholder activism continues to evolve, firm-specific and portfolio-level approaches are becoming increasingly interconnected. Targeted interventions at a single firm can create spillover effects, shaping corporate policies across an industry or even at a systemic level.[43] At the same time, the growing diversity of actors, shifting objectives, and more nuanced, multi-level engagement strategies are reshaping the activism landscape – a transformation explored in the next section.

3.3 Expanding the Playbook: Evolving Actors, Agendas, and Tactics

3.3.1 New Actors, New Influence: How Institutional Investors Shape Multi-level Activism

As shareholder activism expands beyond firm-specific interventions, institutional investors are playing an increasingly influential role in shaping industry-wide and portfolio-wide governance. While activist hedge funds have traditionally driven firm-level activism, institutional investors often display a form of 'rational reticence' – preferring to support activist campaigns led by others rather than spearhead them themselves.[44] Meanwhile, the rise of index funds and other large institutional investors has transformed the broader shareholder activism landscape, shifting the focus towards systemic issues and long-term value creation across entire portfolios.

[42] This is the case of Engine No.1's activist campaign in Exxon Mobil in which most of the profits did not come from the increase in the value of the share price of Exxon Mobil but from the huge marketing boost for Engine No.1's exchange-traded funds. See further Section 3.2.2.

[43] On portfolio spillover, see Shi *et al.*, Portfolio Spillover of Institutional Investor Activism: An Awareness–Motivation–Capability Perspective, 1865. On market spillover whereby firm-specific shareholder activism can affect the actions of competing firms in the same industry, see Hadiye Aslan and Praveen Kumar, 'The Product Market Effects of Hedge Fund Activism' (2016) 119 *Journal of Financial Economics* 226. More generally, on positive real externalities of hedge fund activism, see Nickolay Gantchev, Oleg Gredil, and Chotibhak Jotikasthira, 'Governance under the Gun: Spillover Effects of Hedge Fund Activism' (2019) 23 *Review of Finance* 1031.

[44] Ronald J. Gilson and Jeffrey N. Gordon, 'The Agency Costs of Agency Capitalism: Activist Investors and the Reevaluation of Governance Rights' (2013) 113 *Columbia Law Review* 863, 867, 895.

Unlike activist hedge funds, which can freely enter and exit positions, index funds are permanently tied to their holdings, making shareholder engagement their primary mechanism of influence. These funds, including exchange-traded funds (ETFs), track predefined financial indices, such as the FTSE 250 or the S&P 500, offering broad market exposure with relatively low fees. By 2021, US index funds' net assets reached $12.5 trillion, accounting for approximately 43 per cent of all long-term fund assets. In the UK, index-based investment strategies expanded from 22 per cent of total assets in 2011 to 32 per cent in 2021, reflecting the growing dominance of passive investing.

Because index funds prioritise a company's weighting within an index rather than its individual performance, their approach to corporate governance differs significantly from that of hedge funds and other active investors. Unlike hedge funds, which exert influence through both exit and voice, index funds cannot divest from underperforming companies and must instead rely entirely on engagement, proxy voting, and collaborative initiatives to shape corporate behaviour.[45]

However, critics argue that index funds and large asset managers – particularly the so-called 'Big Three' asset managers, BlackRock, Vanguard, and State Street Global Advisors – have weak incentives to exercise meaningful oversight due to agency costs and potential conflicts of interests.[46] Although their appetite for firm-specific activism tends to be modest, some scholars contend that index funds play a crucial role in portfolio-wide governance. Their substantial ownership stakes, long-term investment horizons, and competitive pressures – especially around fees and performance – motivate them to engage in ways that enhance overall portfolio value rather than targeting individual firms.[47] This broader focus, coupled with the rising demand from Millennial clients, has contributed to their growing involvement in ESG issues that extend beyond narrow shareholder interests.[48]

45 See e.g. Coffee, The Coming Shift in Shareholder Activism: From 'Firm-Specific' to 'Systematic Risk' Proxy Campaigns (and How to Enable Them), 50–1.

46 John D. Morley, 'Too Big to Be Activist' (2018) 92 *Southern California Law Review* 1407; Lucian Bebchuk and Scott Hirst, 'Index Funds and the Future of Corporate Governance: Theory, Evidence, and Policy' (2019) 119 *Columbia Law Review* 2029, 2050–75.

47 See e.g. Jill E. Fisch, Asaf Hamdani, and Steven Davidoff Solomon, 'The New Titans of Wall Street: A Theoretical Framework for Passive Investors' (2019) 168 *University of Pennsylvania Law Review* 17; Patrick Jahnke, 'Ownership Concentration and Institutional Investors' Governance through Voice and Exit' (2019) 21 *Business and Politics* 327.

48 Elroy Dimson, Oğuzhan Karakaş, and Xi Li, 'Active Ownership' (2015) 28 *The Review of Financial Studies* 3225; Michal Barzuza, Quinn Curtis, and David H. Webber, 'Shareholder Value(s): Index Fund ESG Activism and the New Millennial Corporate

Despite mixed empirical evidence on the effectiveness of index fund activism,[49] the growing dominance of index funds in capital markets has sparked regulatory debates. Some advocate for greater index fund activism to enhance corporate accountability, while others warn of the risks posed by concentrated voting power in the hands of a few dominant asset managers.[50]

Beyond the rise of index funds, the increasing concentration of institutional ownership has also fuelled industry-wide activism, particularly in sectors where major institutional shareholders hold stakes in multiple competing competitors, such as airlines, banking, pharmaceuticals, and technology.[51] The *common ownership theory* suggests that when institutional investors hold substantial stakes in competing firms, they may influence corporate strategies in ways that prioritise portfolio-wide returns rather than firm-specific performance.[52]

Regardless of ongoing debates about its economic implications and potential anticompetitive effects,[53] common ownership has significantly shaped corporate governance. Research indicates that institutional investors with stakes in multiple firms within an industry benefit from monitoring advantages, including better access to information and more

Governance' (2019) 93 *Southern California Law Review* 1243; Marco Becht, Julian R. Franks, Hideaki Miyajima, and Kazunori Suzuki, 'Does Paying Passive Managers to Engage Improve ESG Performance?' European Corporate Governance Institute – Finance Working Paper No 922/2023, HKU Jockey Club Enterprise Sustainability Global Research Institute – Archive <http://dx.doi.org/10.2139/ssrn.4506415>. However, for a critical view on the ESG investment stance of millennial, see Ken Costa, *The 100 Trillion Dollar Wealth Transfer: How the Handover from Boomers to Gen Z Will Revolutionize Capitalism* (Bloombury Continuum 2023).

49 Juxtapose e.g. Ian R. Appel, Todd A. Gormley, and Donald B. Kelm, 'Passive Investors, Not Passive Owners' (2016) 121 *Journal of Financial Economics* 111 with Davidson Heath, Daniele Macciocchi, Roni Michaely, and Matthew C. Ringgenberg, 'Do Index Funds Monitor?' (2021) 35 *The Review of Financial Studies* 91.

50 See e.g. Marcel Kahan and Edward B. Rock, 'Index Funds and Corporate Governance: Let Shareholders Be Shareholders' (2020) 100 *Boston University Law Review* 1771.

51 See Section 3.2.3.

52 For a critical analysis of what she describes as a 'controversial and broad-brush' theory, see Jennifer G. Hill, 'The Conundrum of Common Ownership' (2020) 53 *Vanderbilt Journal of Transnational Law* 881, 895.

53 There is an emerging yet still limited and inconclusive literature on the anti-competitive effects of common ownership. Juxtapose e.g. José Azar, Martin C Schmalz, and Isabel Tecu, 'Anticompetitive Effects of Common Ownership' (2018) 73 *The Journal of Finance* 1513 with Patrick Dennis, Kristopher Gerardi, and Carola Schenone, 'Common Ownership Does Not Have Anticompetitive Effects in the Airline Industry' (2022) 77 *The Journal of Finance* 2765.

coordinated voting patterns.[54] As institutional ownership continues to consolidate and expand, its influence on industry-wide governance is likely underestimated.[55] In Europe, research indicates that 67 per cent of all listed EU firms have common owners holding at least 5 per cent in each company with four major funds – BlackRock, Dimensional Fund, Norwegian Sovereign Fund, and Vanguard – holding significant stakes.[56]

Empirical research on mutual fund voting in US companies further highlights this trend, showing that funds within the same fund family rarely diverge in their voting decisions, with larger fund families having stronger incentives to vote actively, often applying tailored voting policies across all their holdings.[57] As a result, common owners are well-positioned to engage in industry-wide shareholder activism when facing industry-specific (idiosyncratic) risks that cannot be diversified or systematic risks that reduce risk-adjusted returns.[58]

While index funds and common owners play a dominant role in shaping corporate governance beyond the firm level, institutional shareholder activism remains far from monolithic. Even among institutional investors, significant variations exist in how activism is pursued, shaped by differences in investment structure, governance priorities, and engagement strategies. Activist pension funds, for example, adopt varied activist strategies depending on their investment approach.[59] Passively indexed pension funds often engage in portfolio-wide activism, using voting and engagement as levels to drive broad governance improvements. In contrast, actively managed pension funds are more likely to focus on individual companies, leveraging targeted engagement to bring about firm-level changes.

Similar distinctions emerge between internally managed funds and those delegating voting authority to external managers or proxy

54 Jun-Koo Kang, Juan Luo, and Hyun Seung Na, 'Are Institutional Investors with Multiple Blockholdings Effective Monitors?' (2018) 128 *Journal of Financial Economics* 576.

55 See e.g. Elhauge, 'Horizontal Shareholding Essay', 1277 (suggesting that 'there is good reason to think the phenomenon extends generally across many industries because institutional investors own 80% of all stock in S&P 500 corporations'). For Europe, see Nicoletta Rosati, 'Pietro Bomprezzi, Massimiliano Ferraresi, Annalisa Frigo, and Michela Nardo', *Common shareholding in Europe*, European Commission, Joint Research Centre (Publications Office 2020).

56 Rosati *et al.*, 'Common Shareholding in Europe', 5, 59.

57 Peter Iliev and Michelle Lowry, 'Are Mutual Funds Active Voters?' (2014) 28 *The Review of Financial Studies* 446, 455, 479.

58 Condon, 'Externalities and the Common Owner', 43–8 and 63–4.

59 Diane Del Guercio and Jennifer Hawkins, 'The Motivation and Impact of Pension Fund Activism' (1999) 52 *Journal of Financial Economics* 293.

advisors.[60] While some funds actively develop and execute their own governance policies, others rely on intermediaries, leading to differences in the consistency and intensity of engagement. These variations highlight the complexity of institutional shareholder activism, demonstrating that while large institutional investors and common owners wield significant influence, the strategies they adopt – and their overall effectiveness – vary widely across different fund types and investment models.

3.3.2 The Shifting Objectives of Shareholder Activism: From Financial Value to Sustainability Framing

The increasing diversity of shareholder activism – both in terms of levels and actors of engagement – is mirrored by significant variations in objectives and strategies. While the overarching goal, whether firm-specific or portfolio-wide, is ultimately the maximisation of fund value,[61] the means of achieving this objective have evolved. Institutional activist investors have long pursued a wide range of firm-specific objectives, including strategic realignment, financial restructuring, mergers and acquisitions, share buybacks, corporate governance reforms, and environmental and social initiatives.[62]

Early literature often framed value-oriented (financial) and social (non-financial) activism as distinct categories, emphasising a trade-off between financial returns and broader societal objectives.[63] However, the emergence of 'sustainability-oriented shareholder activism' reflects a growing blending of these objectives.[64] This evolving form of activism operates at both the

60 Ibid.

61 An exception, which does not concern us here, is the pursuit of social shareholder activism for not-for-profit, justice-derived motivations. On the competing for-profit and social justice logics of shareholder activism, see Leslie King and Elisabeth Gish, 'Marketizing Social Change: Social Shareholder Activism and Responsible Investing' (2015) 58 *Sociological Perspectives* 711.

62 Katelouzou, 'Myths and Realities of Hedge Fund Activism: Some Empirical Evidence', 484–8.

63 See e.g. Emma Sjöström, 'Shareholder Activism for Corporate Social Responsibility: What Do We Know?' (2008) 16 *Sustainable Development* 141; Huimin Chung and Till Talaulicar, 'Forms and Effects of Shareholder Activism' (2010) 18 *Corporate Governance: An International Review* 253.

64 Katelouzou *et al.*, 'A Bibliometric Analysis of Four Decades of Shareholder Activism Research', 947. For empirical literature on the effects of this activism, see Tamas Barko, Martijn Cremers, and Luc Renneboog, 'Shareholder Engagement on Environmental, Social, and Governance Performance' (2022) 180 *Journal of Business Ethics* 777; Andreas G. F. Hoepner, Ioannis Oikonomou, Zacharias Sautner, Laura T. Starks, and

firm and portfolio levels, targeting issues such as climate risk, social inequality, and economic resilience that increasingly bear on long-term financial performance.

Unlike the so-called ESG activism, which tends to focus on firm-level risks with clear financial implications, sustainability-oriented activism adopts a broader lens integrating financial and non-financial motivations to address both immediate (financial and non-financial) impacts and intergenerational effects.[65] A prominent strand within this trend is environmental and social (E&S) shareholder activism, which targets issues such as climate action, diversity, equity, and inclusion, and corporate social responsibility (CSR).[66]

While once led by specific investor groups, such as ESG funds,[67] E&S activism is increasingly gaining traction among a broader range of investors, including hedge-fund-style activists. For instance, The Children Investment Fund (TCI), once labelled a 'locust' for its aggressive 2005 campaign against Deutsche Boerse, has repositioned itself as a 'climate radical', now applying similarly assertive tactics to advocate for climate action.[68] Engine No. 1's high-profile activist campaign at ExxonMobil further illustrates that aggressive hedge fund activism and sustainability objectives are not necessarily at odds – particularly when framed as material financial concerns. Engine No. 1, a relatively small activist hedge fund, successfully secured three board seats at ExxonMobil, arguing that the company's lack of a credible climate strategy posed a financial risk to long-term shareholder value.[69] Unlike traditional ESG investors, Engine No. 1 framed its campaign on financial

Xiao Y. Zhou, 'ESG Shareholder Engagement and Downside Risk' (2023) 28 *Review of Finance* 483.

65 Katelouzou *et al.*, 'A Bibliometric Analysis of Four Decades of Shareholder Activism Research', 970.

66 E&S activism has a long history tracing back to the 1960s and early 1970s when non-profits and small, non-professional activists tried to push for social justice via shareholder resolutions. Today, however, the field of E&S shareholder activism has significantly grown and is dominated by sophisticated, for-profit investors. Sociologists refer to this transformation of social shareholder activism from a social movement to a profit-making industry as 'marketization'. See e.g. King and Gish, 'Marketizing Social Change: Social Shareholder Activism and Responsible Investing', 711, 713.

67 Marc Goergen, 'Governance Through Ownership and Sustainable Corporate Governance' in *Oxford Research Encyclopedia of Business and Management* (2022).

68 Edward Robinson, 'World's Most-Profitable Hedge Fund Is Now a Climate Radical' *Bloomberg News* (22 January 2022).

69 For a critical view of this campaign, see Bernard S. Sharfman, 'The Illusion of Success: A Critique of Engine No. 1's Proxy Fight at ExxonMobil' (2021) 12 *Harvard Business Law Review Online* 1.

performance, contending that Exxon's failure to transition towards cleaner energy threatened its competitiveness. A similar financial-risk framing was central to Bluebell Capital's 2021 campaign against Solvay, a Belgian chemicals company.[70] Bluebell accused Solvay of discharging toxic waste into the Mediterranean, arguing that the resulting legal liabilities and reputational damage posed significant financial risks.

The increasing reliance on financial-risk arguments in sustainability-oriented activism suggests that while hedge-fund-style activists have the expertise to conduct firm-level engagement, they tend to act only when environmental or social issues present direct financial implications – rather than out of an intrinsic commitment to sustainability goals.[71] At the same time, a deeper concern arises around what Christie terms *rational hypocrisy*: the tendency of large asset managers, particularly the Big Three, to publicly endorse ESG principles while overstating or selectively applying their commitments.[72] This performative engagement allows them to safeguard reputational capital without fundamentally altering their investment practices or challenging corporate behaviour that conflicts with long-term sustainability.

Recent political and regulatory resistance – particularly in the US – has further complicated the trajectory of sustainability-oriented activism.[73] Institutional investors appear increasingly cautious about supporting E&S-related shareholder proposals, particularly in industries facing economic or geopolitical uncertainty. Nonetheless, governance-focused activism – targeting board composition, executive compensation, and shareholder rights – remains a dominant force, reinforcing the view that governance serves as the foundation for broader corporate accountability.[74]

70 Peggy Hollinger, 'European Chemicals Group Solvay Declares Truce with Activist Bluebell' *Financial Times* (6 September 2022).

71 Sharon Hannes, Adi Libson, and Gideon Parchomovsky, 'The ESG Gap' (2023) 49 *Brigham Young University Law Review* 1137, 1168–73.

72 Anna Christie, 'The Agency Costs of Sustainable Capitalism' (2021) 55 *UC Davis Law Review* 875, 907–11.

73 See e.g. Patrick Temple-West and Attracta Mooney, 'Investors Pull Back Support for Green and Social Measures amid US Political Pressure' *Financial Times* (8 June 2023); Nives Dolsak and Aseem Prakash, 'The Rise and Fall of ESG' *Forbes* (23 April 2024); Tom C.W. Lin, 'The New Corporate Political Governance' (2024) 65 *Boston College Law Review* 834, 850–2; Leo E. Strine Jr, 'Ignorance Is Strength: Climate Change, Corporate Governance, Politics, and the English Language' (2025) 5 *Journal of Law and Political Economy* 170.

74 Recent activist campaigns directed at governance issues in the UK include the shareholder revolt over executive pay in The Restaurant Group (TRG), Astrazeneca and Centrica as well as shareholder concerns over the independence of a non-executive director in THG.

At the same time, a counter-movement has emerged in the form of 'anti-ESG activism'. This opposition is driven by investors who challenge sustainability-driven initiatives, arguing that they divert attention from financial performance and impose ideological or regulatory burdens on companies. Often framed as a defence of shareholder value, anti-ESG activists push for a return to a narrower focus on financial returns, frequently opposing corporate commitments to climate action, diversity, and other ESG-related policies.[75]

However, ESG considerations are not always rejected outright. Instead, specific sustainability commitments are often challenged when perceived as detrimental to profitability. This distinction is evident in Bluebell Capital Partners' campaigns against Danone in 2021 and BP in 2024.[76] In both instances, Bluebell challenged ESG initiatives it viewed as detrimental to financial performance, rather than opposing ESG principles entirely. This tension between ESG priorities and financial imperatives is further illustrated in BP's recent strategic shift. Under pressure from activist investors, including Elliott Management, BP announced plans to increase investments in oil and gas, responding to critiques that its earlier green transition may have been overly optimistic and potentially detrimental to shareholder value.[77]

Whether framed around sustainability, corporate governance, financial risk, or shareholder rights, activism is no longer a binary contest between financial and non-financial goals but rather a spectrum of strategies shaped by shifting market conditions and investor priorities. The next section examines how these evolving objectives are reshaping the strategies institutional investors deploy, ranging from engagement and voting to more assertive interventions.

See Oliver Barnes 'Waganama Owner Suffers Shareholder Revolt over Pay and Appointments' *Financial Times* 23 May 2023; Ian Johnston, 'AstraZeneca Shareholders Urged to Oppose Pay Plan for CEO Soriot' *Financial Times* 30 March 2024; Jillian Ambrose and Sarah Butler, 'British Gas Owner Suffers Shareholder Rebellion over CEO Pay Packet' *The Guardian* 8 May 2025; Laura Onita, 'UK Ecommerce Group THG Faces Shareholder Rebellion' *Financial Times* 10 June 2023, respectively.

75 Heidi Welsh, *Anti-ESG Proposals Surged in 2024 but Earned Less Support* (Harvard Law School Forum on Corporate Governance 2024) (reporting a surge in anti-ESG proposals during the 2024 proxy season in the US, though average shareholder report remained low at just 1.9 per cent).

76 Tom Wilson, 'BP Faces Activist Investor Pressure to Ditch Clean Energy Pledges' *Financial Times* (29 January 2024).

77 Malcolm Moore and Tom Wilson, 'BP Pivots Back to Oil and Gas after "Misplaced" Faith in Green Energy' *Financial Times* (26 February 2025).

3.3.3 *Activist Strategies: From Firm-Level Campaigns to Portfolio-Wide Influence*

To achieve their objectives, activist shareholders deploy a broad spectrum of strategies, ranging from targeted firm-level interventions to systemic, portfolio-wide influence. The intensity of these strategies varies, with some engagements focusing on direct confrontation with management, while others seeking gradual, industry-wide change through sustained engagement and voting practices.

At the firm level, activist investors rely on both *formal* shareholder rights mechanisms and *informal* engagement tactics to push for change.[78] Formal approaches include submitting shareholder proposals, exercising veto power over board initiatives, appointing or removing board directors, and initiating shareholder-driven litigation. Informal methods, by contrast, are often used to exert pressure before escalating to more aggressive tactics. These include vote-no campaigns to signal dissatisfaction with board nominees, withholding votes in director elections, engaging in public dialogue to shape investor sentiment, and participating in behind-the-scenes dialogue with company leadership or other investors. These strategies operate along a spectrum, ranging from softer, cooperative approaches to more confrontational tactics. While the use of formal and more confrontational strategies is

78 The literature on activist strategies is voluminous. See e.g. Willard T. Carleton, James N. Nelson, and Michael S. Weisbach, 'The Influence of Institutions on Corporate Governance through Private Negotiations: Evidence from TIAA-CREF' (1998) 53 *The Journal of Finance* 1335; Stuart L. Gillan and Laura T. Starks, 'Corporate Governance Proposals and Shareholder Activism: The Role of Institutional Investors' (2000) 57 *Journal of Financial Economics* 275; Jeanne M. Logsdon and Harry J. Van Buren, 'Beyond the Proxy Vote: Dialogues Between Shareholder Activists and Corporations' (2009) 87 *Journal of Business Ethics* 353; Yonca Ertimur, Fabrizio Ferri, and Stephen R. Stubben, 'Board of Directors' Responsiveness to Shareholders: Evidence from Shareholder Proposals' (2010) 16 *Journal of Corporate Finance* 53; Peter Cziraki, Luc Renneboog, and Peter G. Szilagyi, 'Shareholder Activism through Proxy Proposals: The European Perspective' (2010) 16 *European Financial Management* 738; Fabrizio Ferri, '"Low-Cost" Shareholder Activism: A Review of the Evidence' in Claire A. Hill and Brett H. McDonnell (eds.), *Research Handbook on the Economics of Corporate Law* (Edward Elgar Publishing 2013), 194–200; Joseph A. McCahery, Zacharias Sautner, and Laura T. Starks, 'Behind the Scenes: The Corporate Governance Preferences of Institutional Investors' (2016) 71 *The Journal of Finance* 2905; Tim Bowley, Jennifer G. Hill, and Steve Kourabas, 'Shareholder Engagement Inside and Outside the Shareholder Meeting' in Luca Enriques and Giovanni Strampelli (eds.) *Board-Shareholder Dialogue: Policy Debate: Legal Constraints and Best Practices* (Cambridge University Press 2024), 368–399.

more common in the US, activists in the UK and Europe generally regard them as a last resort.[79]

While firm-level activism focuses on company-specific interventions, portfolio-level activism seeks to drive broader change across multiple firms, particularly through engagement and voting strategies. Large institutional investors, especially index funds and asset managers, increasingly adopt portfolio-wide approaches to shape corporate practices on a systemic scale. A key example of this is thematic voting, where fund managers cast votes on resolutions across multiple portfolio companies to advance specific objectives. These objectives often include promoting board diversity, addressing climate change, or aligning with the United Nations Sustainable Development Goals.[80] Unlike firm-specific activism, which targets governance and strategic decisions within individual companies, portfolio-level activism aims to influence corporate behaviour at scale.

A critical enabler of both firm-specific and portfolio-level activism is coordinated activism, where investors collaborate – either formally or informally – to exert collective pressure.[81] Such coordination can occur within specific investor groups (*intra-group coordination*) or across different types of activist investors (*inter-group coordination*). A notable example of intra-group coordination at the firm level is *wolf-pack activism*, in which multiple hedge funds independently acquire minority stakes in a target company while subtly signalling their intentions to one another. By operating in parallel rather than through explicit agreements, these investors can exert significant pressure on management while avoiding regulatory disclosure requirements that could limit their influence.[82]

[79] Marco Becht, Julian Franks, Colin Mayer, and Stefano Rossi, 'Returns to Shareholder Activism: Evidence from a Clinical Study of the Hermes U.K. Focus Fund' (2008) 22 *The Review of Financial Studies* 3093.

[80] See e.g. Morningstar, *Proxy Voting: Managers Focus on Environmental and Social Themes* (2022).

[81] On informal 'cliques', see Alan D. Crane, Andrew Koch, and Sébastien Michenaud 'Institutional Investor Cliques and Governance' (2019) 133 *Journal of Financial Economics* 175.

[82] Anita Anand and Andrew Mihalik, 'Coordination and Monitoring in Changes of Control: The Controversial Role of Wolf Packs in Capital Markets Special Issue: Introduction to the Law and Markets: Regulating Controversial Exchange' (2016) 54 *Osgoode Hall Law Journal* 377; Yu Ting Forester Wong, 'Wolves at the Door: A Closer Look at Hedge Fund Activism' (2020) 66 *Management Science* 2347; Alon Brav, Amil Dasgupta, and Richmond Mathews, 'Wolf Pack Activism' (2022) 68 *Management Science* 5557.

Inter-group coordination tends to be more fluid and situational. Institutional investors often refrain from direct involvement in activist campaigns but may nonetheless provide crucial support. In some cases, hedge-fund-style activists work in tandem with mainstream institutional investors. Large asset managers – and passive funds in particular – typically do not initiate firm-specific activism, but their backing, especially through voting power, can be instrumental in determining the outcome of activist efforts.[83]

Scott's concept of a 'constellation' of shareholder power captures this loosely coordinated dynamic, highlighting the informal alliances between intermediary institutional investors and hedge-fund-style activists.[84] These relationships are reinforced by factors such as institutional investments in activist hedge funds and the circulation of corporate governance professionals among firms.[85]

Unlike the cohesive and coordinated nature of an activist wolf-pack, constellations of hedge-fund-style activists and institutional investors lack unity and have little potential for concerted action.[86] Their fundamentally different business models create competitive tensions, with each actor pursuing its own strategic priorities. As a result, intermediary

[83] This dynamic was notably evident in Engine No. 1's successful campaign against ExxonMobil. Despite being a relative small activist hedge fund, Engine No.1 leveraged the backing of major institutional investors – including BlackRock, Vanguard, and State Street – to secure board seats and advocate for a stronger climate strategy. See e.g. Was the Exxon Fight a Bellwether? (24 July 2021) Harvard Law School Forum on Corporate Governance, https://corpgov.law.harvard.edu/2021/07/24/was-the-exxon-fight-a-bellwether/.

[84] John Scott, *Corporate Business and Capitalist Classes* (Oxford University Press 1997) 48–9. See also Hamdani and Hannes, 'The Future of Shareholder Activism', 990–992 (providing a more nuanced account of the interactions between activist hedge funds and institutional investors).

[85] Edward Rock, 'Institutional Investors in Corporate Governance' in Jeffrey N. Gordon and Wolf-Georg Ringe (eds.), *The Oxford Handbook of Corporate Law and Governance* (Oxford Academic, Oxford University Press 2018), 363–386.

[86] Hand-collected data on public collective action underscores this trend: out of 6,221 activist campaigns, only 332 involved institutional investors publicly collaborating with hedge-fund-style activists. See Dionysia Katelouzou, 'Something Old, Something New: Cultivating Institutional Investor Engagement through Shareholder Stewardship' in Luca Enriques and Giovanni Strampelli (eds.), *Board-Shareholder Dialogue: Policy Debate, Legal Constraints and Best Practices* (Oxford University Press 2024), 197. But see Dan W. Puchniak and Umakanth Varottil, 'Climate-Related Shareholder Activism as Corporate Democracy: A Call to Reform "Acting in Concert" Rules' NUS Law Working Paper No 2023/023, European Corporate Governance Institute – Law Working Paper No 773/2024 <https://ssrn.com/abstract=4770897> (taking a more critical stance on acting in concert rules).

institutional investors are more likely to support hedge-fund-style activism when the activist's goal of firm value maximisation aligns with the institutional investor's broader objective of portfolio value maximisation.[87] This alignment is particularly likely when firm-specific activism produces 'governance externalities', encouraging other portfolio companies to adopt stronger governance practices to avoid becoming activist targets.[88] Recognising this, activist funds increasingly tailor their campaigns to appeal to passive investors, framing their proposals in terms of long-term financial and systemic risk mitigation rather than short-term gains.

The exercise of shareholder power by institutional investors is further reinforced through third-party coordination and collaborative investor networks. In the UK, the Investor Forum – comprising fifty-one institutional investors with £20 trillion in global assets under management – facilitates collaborative engagement on company-specific and thematic matters.[89] Globally, the 'Collaboration Platform' of the Principles for Responsible Investment (PRI) serves as a central hub for explicit investor coordination, particularly around portfolio-wide engagement and sustainability goals.[90]

Many of these collaborative initiatives, including Climate Action 100+, the PRI itself, and non-profits like ShareAction, promote joint action on systemic and industry-wide challenges such as climate risk, governance reform, and social responsibility.[91] These coalitions blend firm-level and portfolio-level activism: at the company level, tools such as shareholder resolutions, board nominations, letter-writing campaigns, and litigation are used; at the broader level, influence is exercised through coordinated voting, joint proposals, and public policy advocacy.

87 Luca Enriques and Alessandro Romano, 'Rewiring Corporate Law for an Interconnected World' (2022) 64 *Arizona Law Review* 51, 55 (arguing that intermediary institutional investors are 'portfolio value maximisers' rather than 'firm value maximisers').

88 Jeffrey N. Gordon, 'Systematic Stewardship' (2021) 47 *Journal of Corporation Law* 627, 638.

89 The Investor Forum Review 2024 (January 2025), https://www.investorforum.org.uk/wp-content/uploads/securepdfs/2025/01/Annual-Review-2024-FINAL.pdf

90 UNPRI, https://collaborate.unpri.org/. Jean-Pascal Gond and Valeria Piani, 'Enabling Institutional Investors' Collective Action: The Role of the Principles for Responsible Investment Initiative' (2013) 52 *Business & Society* 64. For empirical data, see Elroy Dimson, Oğuzhan Karakaş, and Xi Li, 'Coordinated Engagements' ECGI, Finance Working Paper No 721/2021 <https://ssrn.com/abstract=3209072> (analysing thirty-one PRI engagement projects between 2007 and 2015).

91 See e.g. Michael MacLeod and Jacob Park, 'Financial Activism and Global Climate Change: The Rise of Investor-Driven Governance Networks' (2011) 11 *Global Environmental Politics* 54.

Regardless of whether activism occurs at the firm level or the portfolio level, its overarching goal is typically to influence corporate behaviour rather than to acquire outright control. Even in board control-seat contests or takeover attempts, activists rarely seek full ownership. Instead, they aim to exert pressure and shape managerial decision-making.[92] As Cheffins and Armour describe, activists operate within the 'market for corporate influence', relying on persuasive rather than proprietary power.[93]

Firm-specific and portfolio-level activism should thus be viewed as points along a strategic spectrum rather than as entirely distinct categories. Activists frequently employ both approaches – for example, using a high-profile campaign to catalyse change not only within a targeted firm but also across the wider market. Recognising this strategic fluidity is essential to understanding how activist investors navigate the market for corporate influence, deploying both micro-level and macro-level strategies to achieve their objectives.

This broader understanding of activist strategies provides a useful lens for examining how public shareholder activism has evolved in the UK context.

3.4 Unveiling Trends: Institutional Shareholder Activism in the UK

3.4.1 Public Shareholder Activism in the UK: Growth and Key Players

Amid an evolving corporate governance landscape, firm-specific public shareholder activism (as opposed to private engagement) has emerged as a central and increasingly visible feature of the UK framework. Traditionally associated with private, behind-the-scenes shareholder engagement,[94] the UK market has witnessed a significant rise in public activist campaigns over the past twenty-five years. Early empirical research on hedge fund activism outside the US, focusing on the period between 2000 and 2010, captures this transformation. During that decade, UK companies were targeted in 128 activist campaigns, involving

[92] On firm-specific activism, see Katelouzou, 'Myths and Realities of Hedge Fund Activism: Some Empirical Evidence', 466, 484–5.

[93] Cheffins and Armour, 'The Past, Present and Future of Shareholder Activism by Hedge Funds', 55.

[94] Becht *et al.*, 'Returns to Shareholder Activism: Evidence from a Clinical Study of the Hermes U.K. Focus Fund', 3096.

274 distinct activist demands from 51 different activist hedge funds.[95] By comparison, Germany recorded thirty campaigns, while France and the Netherlands saw twenty-five and twenty campaigns, respectively.[96]

More recent data further reinforce the UK's prominence in European shareholder activism. Hand-collected data from Diligent Market Intelligence confirm that between 2013 and 2022, the UK saw 309 activist campaigns and 505 activist demands, accounting for 27.2 per cent and 29.18 per cent of all public activist demands and campaigns in Europe (Figure 3.1).[97] While the US remains the dominant market – recording 55.6 per cent of all activist demands in the same period – the UK continues to exhibit a high concentration of public activist demands relative to other European markets. Notable peaks occurred in 2019 (sixty-four demands) and 2021 (seventy-six demands), making up about 15 per cent of the total demands that year. This trend contrasts with the declining levels of public activist demands across the rest of

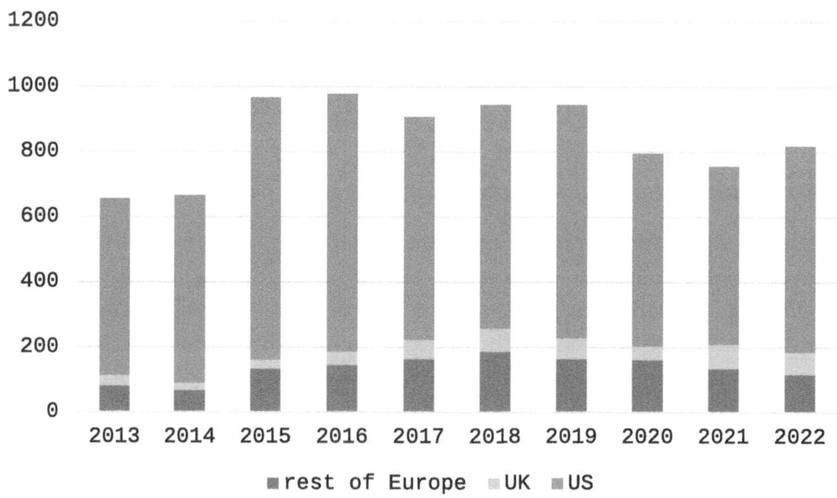

Figure 3.1 Public activist demands by region, 2013–2022.

[95] Dionysia Katelouzou, '*Hedge Fund Activism, Corporate Governance and Corporate Law: An Empirical Analysis across 25 Countries*' (PhD Thesis, University of Cambridge 2012), 93.

[96] Ibid., 94.

[97] The Diligent Market Intelligence (previously Insightia) is a subscription-based database, available here: www.insightia.com/

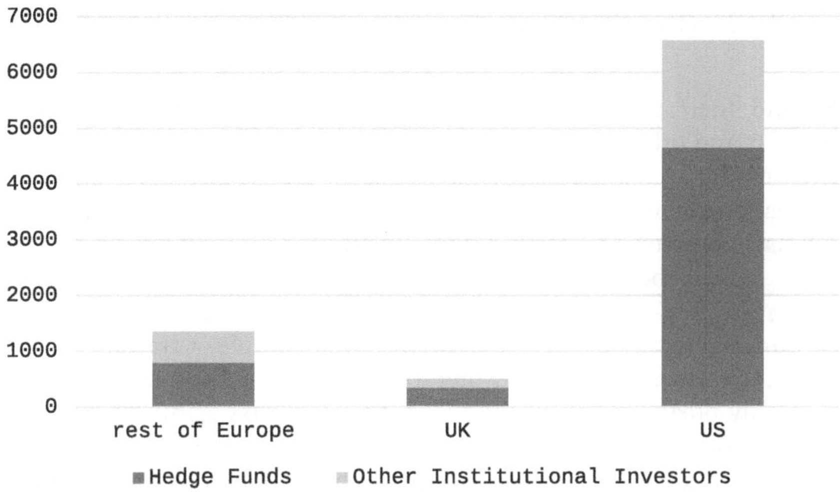

Figure 3.2 Public activist demands by investor type.

Europe, reinforcing the UK's position as a key hub for firm-specific shareholder activism.

A closer look at the key players driving this trend reveals the dominant role of hedge-fund-style activists. These investors account for the majority of institutional shareholder activism globally, accounting for 68.66 per cent of all cases (Figure 3.2). In the UK, their influence is even more pronounced, with hedge-fund-style activists initiating 346 demands – far surpassing the combined contributions of asset managers, private equity firms, venture capital funds, and pension funds – collectively referred to as 'other institutional investors' – which account for only 31.49 per cent.

UK companies have become prime targets for hedge-fund-style activists, with significant involvement from both US-based (42.77 per cent) and UK-based (35.26 per cent) insurgents. This dominance, particularly in comparison to the rest of Europe, may be attributed to several factors, including the highly institutionalised and dispersed ownership structure of UK public equity, the depth and liquidity of UK capital markets, and the strong shareholder rights embedded in UK company law.[98]

[98] On the legal determinants of hedge fund activism, see Katelouzou, 'Worldwide Hedge Fund Activism', 798.

3.4.2 Objectives, Strategies, and Success Rates of UK Activist Campaigns

Beyond their dominance in shareholder activism, hedge-fund-style activists and other institutional investors pursue a variety of objectives and employ distinct strategies. Table 3.1 (Panel A) provides a breakdown of the distinct objectives pursued by hedge-fund-style activists compared to other activist institutional investors.[99] Changes in personnel – both the removal and appointment of board members or key executives – emerge as the primary focus of shareholder activism accounting for 39.20 per cent of the total sample. Contrary to the prevailing assumption in US literature that hedge-fund-style activists primarily pursue personnel changes through proxy fights,[100] UK data suggests otherwise. Other institutional investors in the UK are more likely to seek such changes, with nearly half (49.69 per cent) of their demands targeting personnel shifts, compared to just over a third (34.39 per cent) for hedge funds.

Notably, activists in the UK overwhelmingly advocate for short–slate board representation rather than full board control, as shown in Panel C (Table 3.1).[101] Securing a board seat serves as a means to enhance board effectiveness and drive desired changes, such as improving operational performance, strengthening corporate governance, or advancing ESG initiatives.[102]

[99] Data for Table 3.1 are sourced from Diligent Market Intelligence and cover the period 2013–2022.

[100] April Klein and Emanuel Zur, 'Entrepreneurial Shareholder Activism: Hedge Funds and Other Private Investors' (2009) 64 *Journal of Finance* 187, 215 (studying activist hedge fund campaigns against US companies between 2003 and 2005 and finding that 40 per cent of the campaigns involve an actual (12 per cent) or threatened (28 per cent) proxy contest). Alon Brav, Wei Jiang, Frank Partnoy, and Randall Thomas, 'Hedge Fund Activism, Corporate Governance, and Firm Performance' (2008) 63 *The Journal of Finance* 1729, 1743 (analysing US data to 2006 and finding that activist hedge funds launched a proxy fight to gain board representation in 13.2 per cent of activist events). On the importance of proxy fights as a disciplinary mechanism, see generally Vyacheslav Fos, 'The Disciplinary Effects of Proxy Contests' (2017) 63 *Management Science* 655.

[101] See also Anna L. Christie, 'The New Hedge Fund Activism: Activist Directors and the Market for Corporate Quasi-Control' (2019) 19 *Journal of Corporate Law Studies* 1.

[102] See Gantchev, The Costs of Shareholder Activism: Evidence from a Sequential Decision Model, 610–31 and Katelouzou, 'Myths and Realities of Hedge Fund Activism: Some Empirical Evidence', 496 (both suggesting that board representation is a crucial step of an activist campaign, but not its ultimate objective).

Table 3.1 *Objectives and outcomes of institutional shareholder activism in the UK*

Panel A: Summary of Objectives								
Objectives	No. of Demands	% of Sample	Hedge Funds	Other Types of Investors	% Success	% Partial Success	% Failure	% Other Outcome
Appoint Personnel	109	21.58	75	34	64.22	3.67	20.18	11.93
Remove Personnel	89	17.62	44	45	42.70	5.62	34.83	16.85
Oppose M&A	84	16.63	55	29	55.95	1.19	32.14	10.71
Divestiture	51	10.10	45	6	31.37	9.80	37.25	21.57
Operational	42	8.32	29	13	30.95	11.90	38.10	19.05
Push For M&A	37	7.33	34	3	40.54		43.24	16.22
Governance	35	6.93	28	7	22.86	2.86	45.71	28.57
Return Cash to Shareholders	27	5.35	14	13	44.44	3.70	22.22	29.63
Remuneration	21	4.16	14	7	33.33		61.90	4.76
Capital Structure	6	1.19	6		83.33		16.67	
Environmental	4	0.79	2	2	50.00		50.00	

Table 3.1 *(cont.)*

Panel B: Success by Investor Type

Investor Type	No. of Demands	% of Sample	% Success	% Partial Success	% Failure	% Other Outcome
Hedge Fund	346	68.51	48.55	4.62	30.06	16.76
Others	159	31.49	40.88	3.77	40.88	14.47
Total	505		46.14	4.36	33.47	16.03

Panel C: Outcomes of Board-Control Seeking Activism

		Seats Gained								
Seats Proposed	No. Demands	0	1	2	3	4	5	6	Total Seats Gained	% of Full Success
1	57	10	47						47	82.46%
2	29	13	2	14					30	48.28%
3	6	1		1	4				14	66.67%
4	9	5		1		3			14	33.33%
5	1						1		5	100.00%
6	2	1						1	6	50.00%
7	1	1							0	0.00%

Beyond personnel changes, opposition to M&As is the second most prevalent activist demand. When combined with demands pushing for M&A activity – collectively referred to as 'corporate control activism'[103] – these account for 23.96 per cent of the total sample. Other common activist demands include divestitures and operational measures, such as asset sales, breakups, company divisions, and cost-cutting, which together constitute 18.42 per cent of the total sample. Hedge-fund-style activists play a dominant role in shaping the financial and strategic direction of target companies, initiating the vast majority of demands related to divestitures and operational changes (88.24 per cent and 69.05 per cent, respectively).[104]

In contrast, demands advocating for cash returns to shareholders, such as dividends and share repurchases, are less prominent in the UK.[105] Meanwhile, activism aimed at influencing corporate governance practices, such as increasing board independence and diversity and improving compensation structures, attracts substantial attention from both hedge-fund-style activists and other institutional investors.[106] Environmental demands, though present, have yet to take centre stage in the UK activist landscape, reflecting the diverse priorities of institutional shareholders.

Table 3.1 (Panel B), which reports success rates by investor type, reveals an impressive overall success rate of 50.5 per cent for activist demands, including both full and partial successes. Hedge-fund-style

[103] Katelouzou, 'Myths and Realities of Hedge Fund Activism: Some Empirical Evidence', 490. On M&A-related activism, see generally Royce D. Burnett, Li Xu, Marc Morris, and Ramon P. Rodriguez, 'Shareholder activism targets M&As' (2012) 23 *Journal of Corporate Accounting & Finance* 9; Robin Greenwood and Michael Schor, 'Investor activism and takeovers' (2009) 92 *Journal of Financial Economics* 362.

[104] Prior empirical literature substantiates the focus of activist hedge funds on what is referred to as 'corporate management activism'. See e.g. 'Katelouzou, Myths and Realities of Hedge Fund Activism: Some Empirical Evidence', 491–5; William W. Bratton, 'Hedge Funds and Governance Targets' (2007) 95 *Georgetown Law Journal* 1375; Brav *et al.*, 'Hedge Fund Activism, Corporate Governance, and Firm Performance', 1735–6.

[105] This contrasts e.g. with hedge fund activism in Japan which is often directed at the cash reserves of Japanese companies. According to hand-collected data, 15.72 per cent of the activist campaigns in Japan between 2000 and 2010 advocated for cash returns, as opposed to 8.76 per cent in the UK. Data with the author.

[106] On governance-related activism, see e.g. Yonca Ertimur, Fabrizio Ferri, and Volkan Muslu, 'Shareholder Activism and CEO Pay' (2011) 24 *The Review of Financial Studies* 535; Carol Marquardt and Christine Wiedman, 'Can Shareholder Activism Improve Gender Diversity on Corporate Boards?' (2016) 24 *Corporate Governance: An International Review* 443.

activists stand out as particularly effective, achieving a higher success rate (53.17 per cent) compared to other institutional investors (44.65 per cent). This confirms previous literature on the strategic acumen and assertiveness of hedge-fund-style activists in achieving their objectives.[107]

A deeper dive into the success rate of specific activist objectives reveals a dynamic and nuanced landscape. Demands for personnel appointments are particularly successful, with seventy recorded successes, significantly outperforming demands for removal (Table 3.1, Panel A). Activists opposing M&As achieve considerable success, while those advocating for M&As also see notable outcomes. Capital structure demands, though numerically limited, demonstrate a 100 per cent success or partial success rate. By contrast, demands for returning cash to shareholders yield mix results, with other outcomes, such as withdrawn demands or ongoing campaigns, accounting for 29.63 per cent. Divestiture-related demands show a balanced split between success and failure, while remuneration demands face the highest resistance, making them the least successful category. Governance-related activism produces varied outcomes, including successful interventions, unsuccessful attempts, and other results like negotiated settlements, reflecting the complexities of influencing corporate governance structures and policies. Environmental demands, though limited, are evenly divided between fully successful or unsuccessful outcomes, suggesting a growing but still uncertain influence on corporate environmental policies.

Given that demands for personnel appointment are the most prevalent, a closer examination of board-seat campaign outcomes in Table 3.1 (Panel C) provides valuable insights. Activists achieve the highest success rate when proposing a moderate number of board members, with a peak success rate of 82.46 per cent for campaigns seeking a single board seat. As the number of proposed seats increases, success rates fall sharply, dropping to 48.28 per cent for campaigns seeking two seats and to zero for those proposing seven. Notably, the total number of seats gained (116) exceeds the total number of demands (105), indicating that some campaigns resulted in multiple board appointments.

[107] For the US, see Brav *et al.*, 'Hedge Fund Activism, Corporate Governance, and Firm Performance', 1741–5. In the UK, hand-collected data confirm that almost 65 per cent of the activist hedge fund campaigns targeting UK companies between 2000 and 2010 have been partially or fully successful. Data on file with the author.

3.4.3 *Ownership Stakes, Investment Horizons, and Exit Patterns*

The effectiveness of shareholder activism is closely tied to the size of an activist's ownership stake, which reflects a fundamental cost–benefit trade-off.[108] Activists must balance the influence gained from a larger stake against the financial risks and reduced diversification that come with concentrated ownership. While seeking to influence corporate decision-making, they aim for change rather than outright control, typically remaining minority shareholders.[109] The analysis of activist ownership stakes in Table 3.2 (Panel A), which breaks down ownership thresholds by investor type, reinforces this. A significant proportion (47.24 per cent) of demands involve ownership stakes of less than 5 per cent, with activist hedge funds typically holding smaller stakes than other institutional investors. Specifically, 31.85 per cent of hedge fund demands are associated with ownership stakes below 3 per cent. In contrast, other institutional investors more frequently build larger stakes, exceeding 10 per cent or even 20 per cent.

The size of activist ownership is a key determinant of campaign success (Table 3.2, Panel B). Activists with ownership stakes between 5 per cent and 10 per cent achieve a notable success rate of 56.52 per cent, while those holding between 10 per cent and 20 per cent exhibit the highest success rate at 62.96 per cent. In contrast, campaigns led by activists with stakes below 5 per cent face higher failure rates, particularly within the 3 per cent and 5 per cent range. Interestingly, while success rates remain relatively high for activists holding more than 20 per cent (53.85 per cent), the significant failure rate (25.64 per cent) suggests that larger stakes do not necessarily guarantee higher success. For activists with holdings below 3 per cent, success and failure are almost evenly split. These findings indicate that while neither very small (<3 per cent) nor very large (>20 per cent) ownership stakes yield consistently high success rates, activists are most effective when holding between 5 per cent and 20 per cent.

Table 3.3 (Panel A), which reports campaigns by year of entry and exit, reveals a wide range of activist investment durations, spanning from as brief as a year to over a decade. Annual entry and exit events fluctuate, with 2018 seeing a surge in activist entries and 2021 marked by a high number of exits. As of July 2023, the end of the observation window, in

108 See Section 3.2.2.

109 Katelouzou, 'Myths and Realities of Hedge Fund Activism: Some Empirical Evidence', 490–1; Brav *et al.*, 'Governance by Persuasion: Hedge Fund Activism and the Market for Corporate Influence', 17.

Table 3.2 *Activist ownership*

Panel A: Activist Ownership by Investor					
Ownership	% of Sample	Hedge Fund		Other	
		No. of Demands	%	No. of Demands	%
<3%	26.76	43	31.85	14	17.95
3–5%	20.66	22	16.30	22	28.21
5.1–10%	21.60	37	27.41	9	11.54
>10%	12.68	12	8.89	15	19.23
>20%	18.31	21	15.56	18	23.08

Panel B: Activist Ownership and Success				
Ownership	% Success	% Partial Success	% Failure	% Other Outcome
<3%	45.61	3.51	47.37	3.51
3–5%	29.55	2.27	50.00	18.18
5.1–10%	56.52		21.74	21.74
>10%	62.96	7.41	18.52	11.11
>20%	53.85	2.56	25.64	17.95
Total	48.36	2.82	34.74	14.08

just over half of the cases (50.5 per cent), the activist is still invested in the target company, suggesting that many activists adopt a medium- to long-term perspective rather than exiting quickly after initiating change. Among these ongoing investments, nearly 60 per cent have lasted more than three years, challenging the perception that activist investors primarily adopt short-term strategies.

An analysis of 250 exit events (Table 3.3, Panel B) highlights key differences in the exit strategies of hedge-fund-style activists and other activist institutional investors, suggesting distinct approaches to value realisation. Hedge-fund-style activists primarily exit by selling shares in the open market or through acquisitions by listed companies, reflecting a liquidity-driven strategy similar to trends observed in US hedge-fund activism.[110] In contrast, other activist institutional investors exhibit a stronger preference for exits via transformative events, such as acquisitions, liquidations, or delistings. This distinction suggests that hedge-fund-style activists favour market transactions, while

[110] Brav *et al.*, 'Hedge Fund Activism, Corporate Governance, and Firm Performance', 1749.

Table 3.3 *Activist investment horizon*

Panel A: Entry and Exit Years

Entry Year	Exit Year 2013	2014	2015	2016	2017	2018	2019	2020	2021	2022	2023	Current	Total
1999									2				2
2003												1	1
2004							2						2
2005									1				1
2006				1		3						4	8
2008						3							3
2009	1	1		1	2							1	6
2010				2			1		1			4	8
2011		1	2			3	4					3	13
2012			5		1		1		3			2	12
2013	1	2		2	10	4	6	4	1	1		8	39
2014			4	1	2				7			15	29
2015			2	2	3	3	5	2	2	2		14	35
2016				3	3	5	2	2	1	9		31	56
2017					3	7	16		6			18	50
2018						2	7	7	14			41	71
2019							5	6	8			13	32
2020								1	8	5		28	42
2021									5	12		34	51
2022										1	5	38	44
Total	2	4	13	12	24	30	49	22	59	30	5	255	505

Table 3.3 (*cont.*)

Panel B: Breakdown of Exit			
	All Exit Events	Hedge Fund	Other
Purchased by listed company	15.25%	19.65%	5.66%
Company acquired/liquidated/entered administration/ delisted/merged/taken private	11.49%	8.38%	18.24%
Sold shares	13.66%	16.47%	7.55%
Purchased by private company	4.75%	4.62%	5.03%
Purchased by private equity Firm/another activist	4.36%	4.62%	3.77%
Still holding	50.50%	46.24%	59.75%

Panel C: Length of Holding Period (Days) for Completed Events			
Percentile	All Exit Events	Hedge Fund	Other
5%	90	119.1	72
25%	390.5	445.75	238
50%	923	892	1,093
75%	1,916.5	1,784	2,232
95%	3,795.25	3,225.15	5,366

Panel D: Length (Days) between Entry and Demand

Percentile	All Demands	Hedge Funds	Other
5%	0	0	0
25%	0	2	0
50%	129	143.5	70.5
75%	753.5	715.5	903.5
95%	2,777.8	2,359	2,893

Panel E: Length (Days) between Demand Outcome and Exit

Percentile	All Exit Events	Hedge Funds	Other	Successful	Unsuccessful
0.05	0	0	0	0	0
0.25	0	0	0	37.5	0
0.5	301	303	292.5	380.5	376
0.75	915	752	952.25	960	1,032
0.95	2,003.2	2,111.8	929	2,090.2	1,815.6

other institutional investors are more likely to leverage structural changes to realise value. Despite these differences, both groups exhibit a significant tendency to remain invested, with over 50 per cent still holding positions.

Among completed activist exits, Panel C of Table 3.3 shows that the mean (median) holding period from initial investment to exit is 1,496.65 (1,185) days, significantly exceeding the typical activist campaign duration observed in the US.[111] Hedge-fund-style activists generally have shorter median holding periods compared to other activist institutional investors (892 days versus 1,093 days). This disparity is even more pronounced at the 95th percentile, where hedge-fund-style activists exit after 3,225.15 days, whereas other institutional investors remain invested for up to 5,366 days. Interestingly, this pattern reverses at the lower percentiles (fifth and twenty-fifth), where hedge-fund-style activists exhibit longer holding periods than their institutional counterparts. This suggests that activist hedge funds may deploy varied engagement strategies depending on the firm or campaign objective – ranging from short-term interventions to prolonged involvement aimed at securing long-term value realisation.

The time between an activist's initial investment and the initiation of a demand confirms that distinguishing between offensive and defensive activism based solely on the presence or absence of an ex ante stake is no longer viable.[112] The average (median) duration for all events is 584.16 (129) days (Panel D, Table 3.3). Hedge-fund-style activists tend to hold shares longer before initiating a demand, with a median duration of 143.5 days but a longer average duration of 513.1 days. In contrast, other activist investors exhibit a shorter median duration (70.5 days) but a longer average duration (655.21 days), suggesting a greater degree of variation in their approach. These findings imply that while hedge-fund-style activists generally remain invested for a longer period before initiating activism, their holding periods are more skewed, with some exiting sooner than others.

Once activists achieve their objectives, their post-outcome holding periods provide further insights (Panel E, Table 3.3). The median post-outcome holding duration is 301 days, with hedge-fund-style activists exiting after 303 days on average, while other institutional investors exit

[111] Ibid.; Nicole M. Boyson and Robert M. Mooradian, 'Corporate Governance and Hedge Fund Activism' (2011) 14 *Review of Derivatives Research* 169, 177 (reporting an average of just over two years for aggressive forms of activism).

[112] See Section 3.2.2.

slightly sooner at 292.5 days. However, when considering average durations, hedge-fund-style activists tend to stay longer post-outcome (535.62 days) compared to other activist investors (472.59 days). These findings suggest that activists – regardless of type – typically maintain their investment for a significant period after achieving their objective, challenging the traditional narrative that they exit immediately after securing an outcome.[113]

Finally, successful activist demands are associated with longer post-demand holding periods than unsuccessful ones. The median (average) post-outcome duration for successful demands is 380.5 (596.39) days, compared to 376 (581.03) for unsuccessful demands. This suggests that activists who achieve their goals tend to stay involved with the company for longer periods, reinforcing their continued influence over corporate governance and performance.

3.5 Institutional Shareholder Governance in Policy Circles

Having examined empirical evidence on public firm-specific shareholder activism in the UK, it is now essential to shift focus to the broader policy discourse surrounding the corporate governance role of institutional investors. This discourse presents a diverse range of perspectives, shaping contrasting 'images' of institutional shareholders and their functions.[114] Understanding these perspectives is crucial for assessing how institutional investors are positioned within the UK governance ecosystem, the expectations placed upon them, and the evolving regulatory landscape that seeks to shape their role.

3.5.1 The Engaged Shareholder: Institutional Investors as Monitors and Governance Enforcers

One perspective presents an optimistic view, portraying institutional shareholders as 'virtuous' monitors – referred to as the 'Engaged

[113] See also Katelouzou, 'Myths and Realities of Hedge Fund Activism: Some Empirical Evidence', 478–83.

[114] Arguably, there is no single vision of shareholders that can be discerned in UK company law. On variations of shareholder images, see Jennifer Hill, 'Visions and Revisions of the Shareholder' (2000) 48 *The American Journal of Comparative Law* 39; Jennifer G. Hill, 'Images of the Shareholder – Shareholder Power and Shareholder Powerlessness' in Jennifer G. Hill and Thomas S. Randall (eds.), *Research Handbook on Shareholder Power* (Edward Elgar 2015), 53–73.

Shareholder'. This viewpoint is reflected in the strong participatory rights granted to shareholders under UK company law, grounded in the belief that shareholder empowerment helps mitigate challenges arising from the separation of ownership and control.[115] UK company law provides comparatively strong shareholder rights, including the ability to remove directors without cause and the authority to approve or veto key corporate decisions.[116] These rights are normatively framed as mechanisms to curb managerial discretion and enhance accountability – not only to shareholders but also to other stakeholders.[117] Consequently, while the Engaged Shareholder's primary role is to monitor companies and enhance shareholder value, it is also viewed as playing a broader role in promoting good corporate governance.

The origins of the Engaged Shareholder perspective can be traced to long-standing legal principles favouring shareholder rights and participation. However, it gained greater recognition in UK policy circles with the Cohen Committee's 1945 recommendations. The Committee advocated for stronger shareholder control in response to what it described as 'the illusory nature of the control theoretically exercised by shareholders over directors',[118] though it regarded direct intervention in individual companies as a last resort.[119]

It was not until the early 1990s – amid growing concerns over unaccountable management and corporate underperformance – that the Engaged Shareholder emerged as a prominent policy solution, shaping corporate governance reforms through both soft law (codes and guidelines) and hard law (legislative measures). The rise of institutional investors further reinforced this perspective, positioning them as key actors in enhancing corporate accountability and governance effectiveness.[120]

[115] See also Sections 2.4.2 and 2.4.3.

[116] Companies Act 2006, section 168. For other rights, see Companies Act 2006, sections 190–214, 226B, 239, 644, 693A, and 694. In addition, shareholders in the UK enjoy several procedural rights in relation to general meeting, including the right to initiate a meeting, to add an item on the agenda and the right to circulate a statement. See Companies Act 2006, sections 314–16 and 338.

[117] John Armour, 'Shareholder Rights' (2020) 36 *Oxford Review of Economic Policy* 314, 333–4 (considering the relationship between shareholders rights and social welfare more broadly).

[118] *Report of the Committee on Company Law Amendment (Cohen Report)* (1945), para 7(e).

[119] Ibid., para 124.

[120] Section 2.5.2.

However, the legitimacy of the Engaged Shareholder was not solely a product of shifting market dynamics – it was also anchored in distinct theoretical foundations. Agency theory played a crucial role in this process, asserting that institutional shareholder monitoring is an inherent aspect of risk-bearing – an extension of shareholders' status as residual claimants – and, in the absence of other market mechanisms, can help mitigate agency costs associated with widely held public companies.[121] Empirical studies grounded in principal-agent analysis further strengthened this view, presenting institutional shareholder activism as a potent, value-enhancing force in corporate governance.[122]

Beyond agency theory, the Engaged Shareholder perspective has been reinforced by the doctrine of shareholder value maximisation, which holds that a company's primary goal is to maximise shareholder wealth.[123] This principle aligns with the broader framework of shareholder primacy, which positions shareholders as the ultimate decision-makers in corporate governance.[124] As company law globally has increasingly converged around shareholder primacy,[125] the centrality of institutional investors in corporate governance is further solidified, reinforcing their role as active monitors of corporate performance.

While the doctrine of shareholder primacy has never fully dominated UK company law, the Engaged Shareholder perspective has significantly shaped the UK regulatory landscape, most notably through the Cadbury Report.[126] Developed in response to concerns over managerial accountability and corporate scandals, the report positioned shareholders – particularly

121 See Section 2.4.3. For a critical analysis, see Iris H-Y Chiu, 'The Meaning of Share Ownership and the Governance Role of Shareholder Activism in the United Kingdom' (2008) 8 *Richmond Journal of Global Law and Business* 117.

122 For a review of the empirical literature, see Matthew R. Denes, Jonathan M. Karpoff, and Victoria B. McWilliams, 'Thirty Years of Shareholder Activism: A Survey of Empirical Research' (2017) 44 *Journal of Corporate Finance* 405.

123 See e.g. William Lazonick and Mary O'Sullivan, 'Maximizing Shareholder Value: A New Ideology for Corporate Governance' (2000) 29 *Economy and Society* 13. For a recent critical approach, see Brian R. Cheffins, 'Stop Blaming Milton Friedman!' (2020) 98 *Washington University Law Review* 1607.

124 Jill E. Fisch, 'Measuring Efficiency in Corporate Law: The Role of Shareholder Primacy' (2005) 31 *Journal of Corporation Law* 637. See also Section 2.4.2.

125 Henry Hansmann and Reinier Kraakman, 'The End of History for Corporate Law' (2001) 89 *Georgetown Law Journal* 439.

126 The Committee on the Financial Aspects of Corporate Governance, *Report of the Committee on the Financial Aspects of Corporate Governance* (1992) (Cadbury Report hereinafter). For a critical examination of the use of codes in practice, see Donald Nordberg, *The Cadbury Code and Recurrent Crisis: A Model for Corporate Governance?* (Palgrave Macmillan 2020).

institutional investors – as key check on boards.[127] By emphasising shareholder accountability as the foundation of good corporate governance,[128] the Cadbury Report marked a shift from post-war managerial capitalism towards what has been coined as 'investor',[129] 'fiduciary',[130] or 'shareholder capitalism'.[131]

Recognising the substantial influence of institutional investors, the Cadbury Report emphasised their responsibility as 'owners' to actively hold boards accountable.[132] It called on them to adopt a proactive approach in corporate governance, which included maintaining regular dialogue with senior management, exercising voting rights judiciously, scrutinising board composition, and assessing corporate adherence to the report's voluntary recommendations.[133]

By embedding active ownership principles into the UK's corporate governance framework, the Cadbury Report institutionalised the Engaged Shareholder perspective. This trajectory was further reinforced by the Higgs-inspired revisions to the Combined Code in 2003, which strengthened investor influence by emphasising board independence and reinforcing directors' accountability to shareholders.[134] Subsequent revisions of the Combined Code – and later the UK Corporate Governance Code, particularly the 2010 revision – further advanced this framework by fostering a more relational form of accountability between boards and institutional shareholders.[135]

A key development was the formalisation of the 'comply-or-explain' mechanism, designed to position institutional investors as the primary

[127] See generally Laura F. Spira and Judy Slinn, *The Cadbury Committee: A History* (Oxford University Press 2013).

[128] Cadbury Report, para 6.1 (noting that '[t]he issue for corporate governance is how to strengthen the accountability of boards of directors to shareholders') and para 6.6.

[129] Michael Useem, *Investor Capitalism: How Money Managers Are Changing the Face of Corporate America* (BasicBooks 1996); Alfred F. Conrad, 'Beyond Managerialism: Investor Capitalism?' (1988) 22 *Journal of Law Reform* 117.

[130] James P. Hawley and Andrew T. Williams, *The Rise of Fiduciary Capitalism: How Institutional Investors Can Make Corporate America More Democratic* (University of Pennsylvania Press, Inc. 2000).

[131] Gerald F. Davis, *Managed by the Markets: How Finance Re-Shaped America* (Oxford University Press 2009).

[132] Cadbury Report, para 6.10.

[133] Cadbury Report, paras. 6.11, 6.15 and 6.16.

[134] Higgs, *Review of the Role and Effectiveness of Non-executive Directors* (2003).

[135] Nordberg, *The Cadbury Code and Recurrent Crisis: A Model for Corporate Governance?*, 12.

enforcers of corporate governance codes.[136] Under this approach, companies are invited or obliged to adhere to the Code's principles but are not bound to follow every provision. Instead, they may choose to deviate, provided they publicly explain their reasons for doing so. This framework assumes that engaged investors will scrutinise these explanations and hold companies accountable for any departures from governance best practices, reinforcing their role as active corporate monitors.[137] Throughout its various iterations, including the latest 2024 version, the UK Corporate Governance Code has consistently emphasised the relationship between boards and shareholders and encouraged institutional investors to engage constructively with boards of directors and leverage their shareholder influence to ensure companies uphold the Code's principles.[138]

Notably, the Engaged Shareholder perspective was not only embedded in soft law – primarily corporate governance reports and codes – but also reinforced through hard law reforms that strengthened the legal standing of shareholders.[139] Policymakers recognised that corporate governance frameworks alone would not suffice; legislative measures were necessary to provide shareholders with enforceable rights that incentivise active engagement.[140]

136 On the effectiveness of the comply-or-explain principle, see e.g. John Parkinson and Gavin Kelly, 'The Combined Code of Corporate Governance' (1999) 70 *Political Quarterly* 101; Sridhar Arcot, Valentina Bruno and Antoine Faure-Grimaud (2010) 'Corporate Governance in the UK: Is the Comply or Explain Approach Working?' 30 *International Review of Law & Economics* 193 (empirically examining the compliance levels to the UK Combined Code of Corporate Governance and finding that while most companies comply with the code, those that do not comply only provide poor explanations); Virginia Harper Ho, '"Comply or Explain" and the Future of Nonfinancial Reporting' (2017) 21 *Lewis & Clark Law Review* 317 (arguing that incorporating a comply-or-explain approach is more effective than voluntary ESG reporting in the US).

137 On the comply-or-explain model as a form of 'market-controlled' regulation, see David Kershaw, 'Corporate Law and Self-Regulation' LSE Legal Studies Working Paper No 5/2015 <https://ssrn.com/abstract=2574201>. For a critical view of the role of institutional investors in evaluating companies' compliance with the code, see Marc T. Moore, '"Whispering Sweet Nothings": The Limitations of Informal Conformance in UK Corporate Governance' (2009) 9 *Journal of Corporate Law Studies* 95.

138 UK Corporate Governance Code 2024, at 4 and Principle D.

139 Dionysia Katelouzou, 'Reflections on the Nature of the Public Corporation in an Era of Shareholder Activism and Stewardship' in Barnali Choudhury and Martin Petrin (eds.), *Understanding the Company: Corporate Governance and Theory* (Cambridge University Press 2017), 135–7.

140 However, despite several legislative measures aimed at strengthening shareholders' status within the corporation, the level of 'formal' shareholder protection worldwide did not change dramatically in the years following the financial crisis. For relevant

The rationale behind these legislative changes was that effective shareholder activism – and shareholder governance more broadly – depends on robust legal rights and a regulatory framework that incentivises active engagement.[141] One of the most notable hard law reforms was the introduction of shareholder approval mechanisms for executive remuneration policies, commonly referred to as 'say-on-pay'. This measure, which can take the form of binding or non-binding votes, was designed to curb excessive executive pay and enhance corporate accountability. By giving shareholders a direct voice in remuneration decisions, say-on-pay reinforced the expectation that institutional investors would act as responsible monitors, aligning executive compensation with long-term corporate performance.

The UK was a pioneer in adopting say-on-pay,[142] setting a precedent that later influenced its global diffusion, including its incorporation in the revised Shareholder Rights Directive.[143] This reform has fuelled increased shareholder activism on executive pay both domestically and internationally.[144] Beyond say-on-pay, further regulatory initiatives sought to lower barriers to shareholder engagement and collaboration, reinforcing shareholder governance and facilitating more active investor participation in corporate decision-making. Key measures included the introduction of electronic proxy voting, which streamlined voting processes and improved transparency, and the clarification of acting-in-concert rules, which provided institutional

statistics, see Dionysia Katelouzou and Mathias Siems, 'Disappearing Paradigms in Shareholder Protection: Leximetric Evidence for 30 Countries, 1990–2013' (2015) 15 *Journal of Corporate Law Studies* 127.

141 Katelouzou, 'Worldwide Hedge Fund Activism', 818.

142 Companies Act 2006, sections 226B, 226C, 439, and 439A.

143 Directive (EU) 2017/828 of the European Parliament and of the Council of 17 May 2017 amending Directive 2007/36/EC as regards the encouragement of long-term shareholder engagement [2017] OJ L132/1 (SRD II), Arts. 9a and 9b. For a comparative study encompassing eight jurisdictions, see Randall S. Thomas and Christoph Van der Elst, 'Say on Pay around the World' (2014) 92 *Washington University Law Review* 653. A shorter overview for eleven European countries can be found in Roberto Barontini, Stefano Bozzi, Guido Ferrarini and Maria Christina Ungureanu, 'Directors' Remuneration before and after the Crisis: Measuring the Impact of Reforms in Europe' in Massimo Belcredi and Guido Ferrarini (eds.), *Boards and Shareholders in European Listed Companies* (Cambridge University Press 2013), 251, tbl.1.

144 See e.g. Konstantinos Stathopoulos and Georgios Voulgaris, 'The Importance of Shareholder Activism: The Case of Say-on-Pay' (2016) 24 *Corporate Governance: An International Review* 359 (for the UK) and Randall S. Thomas, Alan R. Palmiter, and James F. Cotter, 'Dodd-Frank's Say on Pay: Will It Lead to a Greater Role for Shareholders in Corporate Governance Symposium: Financial Regulatory Reform in the Wake of the Dodd-Frank Act' (2011) 97 *Cornell Law Review* 1213 (for the US).

investors with greater confidence to coordinate on governance issues without triggering unintended regulatory consequences.[145]

Notwithstanding the substantial influence of the Engaged Shareholder perspective on UK corporate governance, questions remain about its long-term effectiveness in addressing corporate governance challenges. While shareholder empowerment has strengthened board accountability and facilitated more active institutional oversight, concerns persist regarding the extent to which institutional investors fulfil this role. The next section examines the competing perspectives that have emerged in response to perceived shortcomings of the Engaged Shareholder model, shedding light on the shifting expectations surrounding institutional investor governance.

3.5.2 The Transient Shareholder and Regulatory Adaptation

The optimistic portrayal of institutional shareholder governance embedded in the Engaged Shareholder perspective faced significant challenges following the global financial crisis of 2007–09. Mainstream institutional investors, including pension funds, were criticised as 'sleeping giants' for their failure to curb excessive corporate risk-taking.[146] The Walker Review, which examined corporate governance failures in financial institutions, highlighted that major investors had been largely ineffective in restraining excessive risk-taking of banks before the crisis, pointing to a failure of engagement at critical moments.[147] This critique reinforced broader concerns that institutional investors had, at times, prioritised short-term financial performance over long-term governance oversight, raising questions about their effectiveness as corporate monitors.

At the same time, the increasing prominence of hedge-fund-style activists sparked debate over their influence on corporate strategy and management. While these activists have been credited with improving efficiency, unlocking shareholder value, and addressing entrenched managerial underperformance, their interventions have also raised concerns about short-term financial pressures. Critics argue that hedge-fund-style activism, in some cases, prioritises immediate financial gains over

[145] See SRD II, Art. 3c and Takeover Panel, Practice Statement No. 26 (9 September 2009), respectively.

[146] Sharon Hannes, 'Brave New World: A Proposal for Institutional Investors' (2015) 16 *Theoretical Inquiries in Law* 245, 248.

[147] David Walker, *A Review of Corporate Governance in UK Banks and Other Financial Industry Entities: Final Recommendations* (2009), 70.

sustainable long-term value creation, potentially leading to corporate decision-making that emphasises short-term stock performance.[148] This debate became particularly relevant in discussions on whether public companies were becoming increasingly vulnerable to activist pressures driven by near-term returns.

As concerns over both institutional investor passivity and shareholder-driven short-termism gained traction, a counter-narrative emerged, portraying institutional shareholders as the 'Transient Shareholder' – investors with a short-term, fleeting approach to share ownership.[149] To counteract short-termism, some policymakers advocated for differentiated voting rights, such as loyalty shares, which grant additional voting power to long-term shareholders as an incentive to retain their investments.[150] While several European countries adopted loyalty shares,[151] the UK historically adhered to the 'one share, one vote' principle, in part due to resistance from institutional investors.[152]

Nevertheless, these concerns were increasingly reflected in subsequent regulatory shifts in the UK listing rules. Rather than introducing loyalty shares, the UK opted for dual-class share structures, designed to shield

[148] Alan Dignam, 'The Future of Shareholder Democracy in the Shadow of the Financial Crisis' (2013) 36 *Seattle University Law Review* 639; Leo E. Strine Jr., 'Can We Do Better by Ordinary Investors; A Pragmatic Reaction to the Dueling Ideological Mythologists of Corporate Law Essay' (2014) 114 *Columbia Law Review* 449. However, the empirical evidence on investor short-termism is mixed. See e.g. Xuemin Yan and Zhe Zhang, 'Institutional Investors and Equity Returns: Are Short-term Institutions Better Informed?' (2007) 22 *The Review of Financial Studies* 893; Lucian A. Bebchuk, Alon Brav and Wei Jiang, 'The Long-Term Effects of Hedge Fund Activism' (2015) 185 *Columbia Law Review*, 1085–156; Martijn Cremers, Aknur Pareek, and Zacharias Sautner, 'Short-Term Investors, Long-Term Investments, and Firm Value: Evidence from Russell 2000 Index Inclusions' (2020) 66 *Management Science* 4535.

[149] Brian Bushee, 'Identifying and Attracting the "Right" Investors: Evidence on the Behavior of Institutional Investors' (2004) 16 *Journal of Applied Corporate Finance* 28 (distinguishing between 'transient', 'dedicated', and 'quasi-indexers' investors).

[150] See e.g. Lynne L. Dallas and Jordan M. Barry, 'Long-Term Shareholders and Time-Phased Voting' (2015) 40 *Delaware Journal of Corporate Law* 541; Mark J. Roe and Federico Cenzi Venezze, 'Will Loyalty Shares Do Much for Corporate Short-Termism?' (2021) 76 *Business Lawyer* 467.

[151] See e.g. Marco Becht, Yuliya Kamisarenka, and Anete Pajuste, 'Loyalty Shares with Tenure Voting: Does the Default Rule Matter? Evidence from the Loi Florange Experiment' (2020) 63 *The Journal of Law and Economics* 473 (for France) and Emanuele Bajo, Massimiliano Barbi, Marco Bigelli and Ettore Croci, 'Bolstering Family Control: Evidence from Loyalty Shares' (2020) 65 *Journal of Corporate Finance* 101755 (for Italy).

[152] Kate Burgess, 'Investors Wary of Myners' Voting Rights Idea' *Financial Times* (3 August 2009).

company founders from short-term market pressures. In December 2021, the Financial Conduct Authority (FCA) revised the Listing Rules to permit a limited form of dual-class shares within the premium segment, although strict safeguards – such as a five-year sunset clause and restrictions on enhanced voting rights – were imposed.[153] These measures aimed to balance founder control with shareholder protections but proved insufficiently attractive to issuers.[154]

In response, a broader regulatory overhaul followed in July 2024, merging the standard and premium segments of the Main Market and introducing a more permissive dual-class framework.[155] While the primary objective of these reforms was to enhance the competitiveness of the UK capital market, they also indirectly responded to concerns about the destabilising influence of transient investors but at the cost of potentially entrenching management and increasing risk of value extraction through related-party transactions, especially after the relaxation of disclosure and shareholder approval requirements.[156]

Both loyalty and dual class shares reflect an underlying belief that greater long-term commitment among key corporate actors supports sustainable value creation. However, an alternative perspective questions whether shareholder empowerment alone – whether through engagement, loyalty incentives, or founder insulation – truly guarantees corporate resilience. Advocates of this view argue for a corporate governance model that extends beyond shareholder primacy to incorporate a broader range of stakeholders.[157] This approach seeks to balance shareholder influence with corporate sustainability objectives, preventing governance mechanisms from disproportionately amplifying shareholder interests at the expense

153 FCA, *Primary Market Effectiveness Review. Feedback and Final Changes to the Listing Rules 9–15* (Policy Statement PS21/22, 2021). Listing Rules 9.2.22B and 9.2.22C in force until 28 July 2024.

154 For a critical view on these rules, see Bobby V. Reddy, 'The UK and Dual-Class Stock-Lite – Is It Really Even Better than the Real Thing?' (2024) 25 *Theoretical Inquiries in Law* 77.

155 Listing Rules 6.2.31–6.2.33.

156 Listing Rule 8.2.1. See, further, Bobby V. Reddy, 'The UK and Dual-Class Shares: From Dual-Class Shares Lite to Full Fat' (2025) 22 *European Company Law* 86.

157 The literature is too voluminous to be cited in full. See e.g. Gavin Kelly and John Parkinson, 'The Conceptual Foundations of the Company: A Pluralist Approach' (1998) 2 *Company, Financial and Insolvency Law Review* 174; Andrew Keay, 'Stakeholder Theory in Corporate Law: Has It Got what It Takes' (2010) 9 *Richmond Journal of Global Law and Business* 249. On the term 'stakeholder', see R. Edward Freeman and David L. Reed, 'Stockholders and Stakeholders: A New Perspective on Corporate Governance' (1983) 25 *California Management Review* 88.

of other stakeholders – such as employees, consumers, communities, and the environment.[158] At its core, this debate underscores a critical tension in corporate governance: whether shareholder-driven monitoring mechanisms truly serve long-term corporate resilience or merely entrench the power of certain actors while sidelining other stakeholders.[159]

3.6 Conclusion: Reframing Shareholder Activism in the Age of Shareholder Stewardship

The trajectory of institutional shareholder activism reveals deep tensions at the heart of modern corporate governance. While the Engaged Shareholder model has advanced the ideal of institutional investors as active monitors, its limitations were laid bare during moments of systemic crisis – most notably the global financial crisis of 2007–09. In contrast, the rise of hedge-fund-led activism has sparked anxieties over short-termism and value extraction, fuelling the emergence of the Transient Shareholder narrative and prompting regulatory experimentation with mechanisms such as loyalty shares and dual-class structures.

Yet neither archetype – Engaged nor Transient – fully captures the complexity of institutional investor behaviour in contemporary markets. As institutional ownership has become increasingly intermediated and diversified, the limitations of shareholder-centric governance have become more apparent. While shareholder activism has primarily highlighted the disconnection between ownership and control, shareholder stewardship shifts the focus to a different question: to whom should the power-wielder be accountable?

This conceptual turn marks the emergence of a third image of the institutional investor: the Shareholder Steward. Framing institutional investors as shareholder stewards shifts the conversation from tactical intervention to long-term responsibility. It reorients attention from shareholder primacy to broader accountability – extending not only to proximate clients and beneficiaries but also to end-investors, investee companies, and society at large. Stewardship emphasises the alignment of investment decisions with sustainable value creation and the recognition of systemic impacts arising from capital allocation.

[158] See e.g. UK Corporate Governance Code 2024, Provision 5. On how employees can be included in UK corporate governance, see e.g. Andreas Kokkinis and Konstantinos Sergakis, 'A Flexible Model for Efficient Employee Participation in UK Companies' (2020) 20 *Journal of Corporate Law Studies* 453.

[159] See also Section 1.1.

As Chapter 4 will demonstrate, this evolution is not merely a theoretical rebranding of shareholder activism. Rather, it reflects a deeper transformation in the normative and institutional expectations surrounding shareholder power. Understanding shareholder – and more broadly, investor – stewardship as a distinct governance logic, grounded in accountability, legitimacy, and responsibility, is essential to reimagining the future role of institutional investors.

4

The Anatomy of Investor Stewardship

4.1 Introduction

This chapter examines the evolving concept of investor stewardship by unpacking its intellectual foundations and exploring its practical manifestations across the modern investment ecosystem. Building on the discussion of shareholder activism in Chapter 3, it shifts the focus from *how* and *why* institutional investors intervene in corporate governance to questions of *on whose behalf they act*, and *with what responsibilities*. It asks not only how influence is exercised, but also for whom, to what end, and under what expectations.

Investor stewardship – particularly in the form of *shareholder stewardship* – has often been narrowly defined in terms of voting and engagement practices by institutional investors holding equity stakes in public companies. In this view, shareholder stewards are typically asset managers or asset owners with direct, minority shareholdings, expected to engage with portfolio companies to protect or enhance long-term value. Yet such a framing overlooks the complex and evolving architecture of accountability that now characterises institutional investment. Drawing on insights from law, management studies, political economy, and ethics, this chapter repositions stewardship as a broader and more contested concept. It reframes institutional investors not simply as agents acting on behalf of principals but as actors embedded in overlapping systems of trust, accountability, and influence.[1]

To illuminate this complexity, the chapter introduces a tripartite framework that defines investor stewardship as: (1) the exercise of

[1] This is a normative observation rather than a positive one. Whether institutional investors act as stewards rather than agents and the extent to which they act for others are empirical questions that future work should address. Chapter 6 contributes to this inquiry through an empirical analysis of stewardship disclosures under the UK Stewardship Code.

power, (2) on behalf of others, and (3) for the benefit of others. This framework clarifies the distinction between *stewards* and *agents*, while also highlighting the often-competing demands placed on institutional investors – not only by their proximate clients and beneficiaries but also by investee companies, regulators, and society more broadly.

To deepen this analysis, the discussion introduces the investment chain as a heuristic for mapping the multiple relationships through which investor stewardship unfolds. It distinguishes four interrelated forms of stewardship: (1) *client stewardship*, (2) *end-investor stewardship*, (3) *asset stewardship*, and (4) *sustainability stewardship*. These dimensions reflect the diverse roles institutional investors play within a complex, interdependent flow-of-funds system. Some responsibilities are defined by legal or contractual obligations, while others arise from evolving public expectations, soft-law frameworks, and systemic challenges, including climate change, inequality, and financial instability.

At the heart of this discussion lies the concept of the *enlightened investor steward*. Unlike a conventional agent with a fixed mandate, the enlightened steward must navigate a plural and often conflicting set of obligations – balancing financial and non-financial goals, reconciling short-term mandates with long-term risks, and mediating between private duties and public accountability. *Enlightened investor stewardship* is not about performing every stewardship role simultaneously, but about recognising and managing the tensions that arise across these interlinked relationships.

In this sense, enlightened investor stewardship is an adaptive, deliberative exercise – one in which institutional investors must reason through competing interests, including those of future beneficiaries and affected non-beneficiaries. Sustainability is not treated as a deviation from fiduciary obligation, but as integral to it: a necessary response to the deeply interconnected nature of today's financial, ecological, and social systems. This model rests on justificatory reasoning that legitimises investor decisions within a landscape of overlapping and plural accountabilities.

Ultimately, investor stewardship is not merely a technical function or regulatory add-on to existing investor duties. It is a normative undertaking – one that redefines the role of institutional investors in the twenty-first century and reshapes expectations of accountability, legitimacy, and long-term responsibility in capital markets.

4.2 Conceptual Roots and Evolving Interpretations of Stewardship

4.2.1 The Many Faces of Stewardship: From Medieval Origins to Modern Perspectives

The term 'investor stewardship' is relatively recent, though its underlying concept can be traced back to the Middle Ages. It conveys notions of supervision and management undertaken on behalf of another, coupled with notions of 'responsibility' and 'a sense of commitment to doing'.[2] Etymologically, stewardship originates from the Anglo-Saxon word 'stiweard' or 'stigweard', meaning 'house keeper' or 'house guardian', derived from 'stig' (house or a part of a house) and 'weard' (keeper).[3] Historically, as Block notes, stewardship referred to protecting a kingdom in the absence of rightful ruler or governing on behalf of an underage king.[4] Over time, the term has evolved across scholarly literature, taking on varied meanings and applications.

For accounting scholars, stewardship primarily refers to management's responsibilities in overseeing corporate resources and performance. In her seminal article, Chen identifies two core stewardship responsibilities of the manager as an 'agent': a (social) stewardship responsibility to society and a (financial) stewardship responsibility to the 'owner' (shareholder) and argues that the concept of stewardship has evolved over time in response to prevailing business ideologies.[5] Medieval notions of 'communal stewardship' were rooted in Christian theological views of man as 'steward of the God' to the early twentieth-century emphasis on financial stewardship, referred to as 'classical stewardship', and then to the mid twentieth-century 'managerial stewardship', which framed management as a 'public steward' responsible for attaining broader social objectives.[6]

Other accounting scholars identify stewardship similarly, aligning its evolution with the development of the modern corporation and situating it

[2] Massimo Contrafatto and Jan Bebbington, 'Developing Techniques for Stewardship: A Scottish Study' in Laurie Mook (ed.), *Accounting for Social Value* (University of Toronto Press 2013), 40–4.

[3] 'steward, n'. *OED Online*. Oxford University Press, December 2022. Web. 24 January 2023.

[4] Peter Block, *Stewardship: Choosing Service over Self-Interest* (Berrett-Koehler Publishers 1993), Preface, xx.

[5] Rosita S. Chen, 'Social and Financial Stewardship' (1975) 50 *The Accounting Review* 533, 535. But for a critical view of shareholders as 'owners', see Section 2.6.1.

[6] Ibid.

within the principal–agent relationship of the time.[7] They emphasise that stewardship involves those entrusted with authority to act in the interest *of others*, making the steward functionally comparable to an agent in contractarian terms. From this perspective, stewardship in accounting primarily addresses managerial control issues, particularly the separation of ownership and control in large corporations. This focus has led to the concept of 'stewardship demand', where shareholders and potential investors require both backward- and forward-looking financial information to monitor managerial performance.[8] In this sense, 'stewardship accounting' is closely linked to accountability reporting, ensuring transparency for both internal and external stakeholders while mitigating agency problems.[9]

However, this conceptualisation of stewardship by accounting scholars – rooted in the law and economics agency framework – differs significantly from how the term is understood in other academic disciplines. Scholars in management, ethics, and leadership studies conceptualise stewardship not as a subset of agency theory but as an alternative (or complementary) model to both agency and stakeholder models of governance.[10] This research strand builds upon and extends the pioneering stewardship theory of management developed by Davis, Schoorman and Donaldson.[11]

Unlike agency theory, which assumes managers are self-interested actors requiring oversight, the stewardship theory of management – drawing from psychology and sociology – posits that service to others is the defining feature of stewardship. While both agents and stewards exercise power on behalf of others, stewardship theory emphasises a fundamental shift in focus from self-interest to a commitment to '*others*'.

[7] Jacob G. Birnberg, 'The Role of Accounting in Financial Disclosure' (1980) 5 *Accounting, Organizations and Society* 71 (discussing four stages of stewardship accounting: 'the pure custodial period', 'the traditional custodial period', 'the asset utilization period', and the 'open ended period').

[8] Frøystein Gjesdal, 'Accounting for Stewardship' (1981) 19 *Journal of Accounting Research* 208. See also Birnberg, 'The Role of Accounting in Financial Disclosure', 74–5 (introducing the concept of 'strategic stewardship', which emphasises on the need for the disclosure of future-oriented data).

[9] Vincent O'Connell, 'Reflections on Stewardship Reporting' (2007) 21 *Accounting Horizons* 215, 217, 220.

[10] On a critical analysis of the stakeholder theory from a corporate social responsibility (CSR) lens, see Marianne M. Jennings and Stephen Happel, 'The Post-Enron Era for Stakeholder Theory: A New Look at Corporate Governance and the Coase Theorem' (2003) 54 *Mercer Law Review* 873.

[11] James H. Davis, F. David Schoorman, and Lex Donaldson, 'Toward a Stewardship Theory of Management' (1997) 22 *The Academy of Management Review* 20.

The stewardship theory of management contrasts sharply with agency theory's reliance on the economic 'model of man' (*homo economicus*), which assumes individuals are purely rational and self-serving.[12] While still rational, stewards are inherently pro-organisational and other-serving, but most importantly, 'self-actualizing' – deriving higher utility from advancing collective goals than from pursuing personal gain.[13] Rather than being driven by external control mechanisms, stewards operate on trust, intrinsic motivation, and a long-term commitment to serve both the corporation and the wider community.[14] Drawing on the concept of 'psychological ownership', stewardship is understood as 'an ongoing sense of obligation or duty to others', reinforcing the idea that managerial behaviour is shaped by collective responsibility rather than compliance with external constraints.[15] This perspective contrasts sharply with agency theory's emphasis on contractual oversight, reframing managerial behaviour as grounded in commitment rather than compliance.

Ethicists and leadership scholars further expand the 'for-others' aspect of stewardship to include a *duty* to create 'covenantal relationships' based on trust and virtue. This perspective introduces the concept of 'ethical stewardship', which frames stewardship as the responsible exercise of power aimed at creating long-term wealth in the best interests of the principals, various stakeholders, and society at large.[16] Social accounting and accountability research align with this broader perspective, viewing stewardship as a 'plus form' of *social accountability* – one that extends the time frame, scope, and focus of analysis, while fostering an ethos of 'nurturing, respecting and preserving'.[17] This expanded conception of stewardship, frequently

12 Michael C. Jensen and William H Meckling, 'Theory of the Firm: Managerial Behavior, Agency Costs and Ownership Structure' (1976) *Journal of Financial Economics* 305.

13 Davis *et al.*, 'Toward a Stewardship Theory of Management', 57.

14 Block, *Stewardship: Choosing Service over Self-Interest*, 6, 41; Morela Hernandez, 'Promoting Stewardship Behavior in Organizations: A Leadership Model' (2008) 80 *Journal of Business Ethics* 121, 122–3.

15 Morela Hernandez, 'Toward an Understanding of the Psychology of Stewardship' (2012) 37 *Academy of Management Review* 172, 174, 177–8. For a thorough analysis of 'psychological ownership', see Jon L. Pierce, Tatiana Kostova, and Kurt T. Dirks, 'Toward a Theory of Psychological Ownership in Organizations' (2001) 26 *Academy of Management Review* 298.

16 Cam Caldwell and Ranjan Karri, 'Organizational Governance and Ethical Systems: A Covenantal Approach to Building Trust' (2005) 58 *Journal of Business Ethics* 249; Cam Caldwell, Linda A. Hayes, Patricia Bernal, and Ranjan Karri, 'Ethical Stewardship: Implications for Leadership and Trust' (2008) 78 *Journal of Business Ethics* 153, 157–9.

17 Massimo Contrafatto, 'Stewardship Theory: Approaches and Perspectives' in Michele Andreaus, Ericka Costa, and Lee D. Parker (eds.), *Accountability and Social Accounting for Social and Non-Profit Organizations*, vol 17 (Emerald Group Publishing Limited 2014), 177, 189.

embodied in stewardship-based organisations, aligns closely with the principles of sustainable development.[18]

More recently, ecological scholars have introduced the concept of '*corporate biosphere stewardship*', describing an adaptive, knowledge-based, and collaborative process that encompasses both social and environmental dimensions. This framework is built around the principles of 'caring for, looking after and cultivating a sense of belonging'.[19] The notion of corporate biosphere stewardship also finds resonance on theological scholarship, where stewardship is interpreted in its broadest sense as the 'duty for taking care, nurturing and conservation of resources'.[20] This interpretation provides a normative foundation for corporate environmental responsibility, reinforcing the ethical imperative for corporate actors to act as stewards of both society and the natural environment.

4.2.2 *From Managerial Stewards to Shareholder Principals: Rethinking the Corporate Governance Frame*

Within corporate governance discourse, stewardship has traditionally been narrowly defined. Until recently, it primarily referred to the role of managers – broadly encompassing both senior executives and board directors – as pro-organisational, collectivist stewards rather than individualistic, self-serving agents. While often attributed to the stewardship theory of management developed in the 1990s, this conceptualisation of *managers as stewards* has existed in corporate thought and practice since the early twentieth century, albeit in less explicitly theorised terms.[21]

Dodd's portrayal of managers as 'trustees' who accept 'social responsibility' and serve broader societal interests closely aligns with the principles that

[18] Contrafatto and Bebbington, 51.

[19] Carl Folke, Henrik Österblom, Jean-Baptiste Jouffray *et al.*, 'Transnational Corporations and the Challenge of Biosphere Stewardship' (2019) 3 *Nature Ecology & Evolution* 1396; Henrik Österblom, Jan Bebbington, Robert Blasiak, Madlen Sobkowiak, and Carl Folke, 'Transnational Corporations, Biosphere Stewardship, and Sustainable Futures' (2022) 47 *Annual Review of Environment and Resources* 609, 610.

[20] Contrafatto, 'Stewardship Theory: Approaches and Perspectives', 183–5.

[21] For an early reference to managerial stewardship, see George W. Perkins, 'Corporations in Modern Business' (1908) 187 *The North American Review* 388, 394 ('It is not sufficient in corporate management to do the best one can from day to day. Corporate responsibility extends beyond to-day. The foresight, the planning ahead, the putting the house in order for the storms of the future, are the true measure of the best and highest *stewardship*, as well as of the highest order of managerial ability').

later shaped the stewardship theory of management.[22] Similarly, post-war narratives of the 'heroic' corporate manager, who governs in the collective interest rather than for personal financial gain, anticipate the 1990s construct of the manager-steward.[23] This perspective is echoed in the work of many managerialists, such as Child and Crossland in the UK and Kaysen and Drucker in the US – as well as Berle in his later writings from 1950s – who emphasise managers' social motivations over purely economic incentives. Even when they did not explicitly use the term 'steward', managers were widely perceived – and often perceived themselves – as conducting corporate affairs in a way that served a broad set of others, broadly defined to include shareholders, employees, customers, and the public.[24]

The stewardship theory of management, formalised in the 1990s, made a significant contribution to corporate governance research by offering an alternative to agency theory's assumption that managers act primarily out of self-interest.[25] Unlike agency theory, which assumes that managers require external constraints to align with shareholder objectives, stewardship theory posits that they are intrinsically motivated to act in the best interests of the organisation. Whether a manager behaves as an agent or a steward depends on psychological and situational factors.[26] More recent research, however, moves beyond a strict dichotomy, instead viewing stewardship and agency as opposite ends of a continuum – where self-interest and other-interest can coexist rather than being strictly opposed.[27]

From a legal perspective, ongoing debate persists over whether managers should be classified as agents or stewards. Many legal scholars argue that labelling managers as agents is legally inaccurate, as a defining element of agency – the principal's 'continuous control' over the agent – is often absent

22 E. Merrick Dodd Jr, 'For Whom are Corporate Managers Trustees' (1931) 45 *Harvard Law Review* 1145, 1155.

23 Harwell Wells, 'Corporation Law is Dead: Heroic Managerialism, Legal Change, and the Puzzle of Corporation Law at the Height of the American Century' (2012) 15 *University of Pennsylvania Journal of Business Law* 305.

24 Edward S. Mason, 'Introduction' in Edward S. Mason (ed.), *The Corporation and Modern Society* (Atheneum 1959), 11 (viewing managers as maintaining an 'equitable sharing of corporate gains among owners, workers, suppliers, and customers').

25 However, management scholars developed a positive rather than normative model of stewardship, examining how managers behave as stewards rather than prescribing how they should act.

26 Davis *et al.*, 'Toward a Stewardship Theory of Management', 27–38.

27 Hernandez, 'Toward an Understanding of the Psychology of Stewardship', 185; James J. Chrisman, 'Stewardship Theory: Realism, Relevance, and Family Firm Governance' (2019) 43 *Entrepreneurship Theory and Practice* 1051, 1052.

in the manager–shareholder relation.[28] Consequently, the agent–principal analogy risks conflating contractual relationships with 'true agency relationships'.[29]

By contrast, viewing managers as stewards aligns more closely with the loyalty and fiduciary responsibilities inherent in their role.[30] This is particularly relevant for company directors, whose duties derive from fiduciary obligations and the duty of care owed to the company.[31] While English courts rarely refer to directors as stewards, when they do, it is typically in relation to fiduciary duties,[32] or liability as constructive trustees.[33] Therefore, in legal discourse, stewardship is more closely associated with fiduciary principles rather than purely economic or contractual notions.

Unlike managers, shareholders have received limited attention within the stewardship theory of management – except in the case of family (controlling) shareholders, who are often depicted as loyal, self-actualised stewards committed to long-term value creation.[34] However, even this depiction is

[28] Lynne L. Dallas, 'Two Models of Corporate Governance' (1988) 22 *University of Michigan Journal of Law Reform* 19, 34–6; Arthur R. Pinto, 'Corporate Governance: Monitoring the Board of Directors in American Corporations' (1998) 46 *American Journal of Comparative Law Supplement* 317, 324.

[29] Dallas, 'Two Models of Corporate Governance', 34.

[30] For example, Lynn A. Stout, 'On the Rise of Shareholder Primacy, Signs of its Fall, and the Return of Managerialism (in the Closet) Berle IV: The Future of Financial and Securities Markets' (2012) 36 *Seattle University Law Review* 1169, 1171 (speaking of 'corporate directors and professional executives' as seeing themselves as 'stewards or trustees charged with guiding a vital social and economic institution in the interests of a wide range of beneficiaries' rather than 'as mere agents of shareholders').

[31] In the UK, the duty of care is not, as it is in the US, a fiduciary duty. For an in depth comparative analysis of the origins and nature of the directors' duty of care in the UK and the US, see David Kershaw, *The Foundations of Anglo-American Corporate Fiduciary Law* (Cambridge University Press 2018), Chapters 7 and 8.

[32] *In Plus Group Ltd & Ors v Pyke* [2002] EWCA Civ 370, [2003] BCC 332, 349: 'A directorship brings with it not only voting rights and emoluments but responsibilities of stewardship and honesty, and those who cannot discharge them should not become or remain directors'); *Mitchell v Al Jaber* [2024] EWCA Civ 423 (affirming previous dicta that a director acts as a 'fiduciary steward' for company property even post-liquidation). On company directors as fiduciaries, see generally *Regal (Hastings) Ltd v Gulliver* [1942] UKHL 1. On the circumstances under which fiduciary duties arise, see *Bristol and West Building Society v Mothew* [1998] Ch 1 (C.A.); *Al Nehayan v Kent* [2018] EWHC 333 (Comm).

[33] *Williams v Central Bank of Nigeria* [2014] AC 1189; *Burnden Holdings (UK) Ltd v Fielding* [2018] AC 857. But on why a director is not a trustee in the full legal sense, see Len S. Sealy, 'The Director as Trustee' (1967) 25 *The Cambridge Law Journal* 83; Anthony I. Ogus, 'The Trust as Governance Structure' (1986) 36 *The University of Toronto Law Journal* 186, 191–2.

[34] Isabelle Le Breton-Miller and Danny Miller, 'Agency vs. Stewardship in Public Family Firms: A Social Embeddedness Reconciliation' (2009) 33 *Entrepreneurship Theory and Practice* 1169.

increasingly contested. Scholars in family business and entrepreneurship studies challenge the theory's assumptions, pointing to the complexities of family control, entrenchment, and potential conflicts of interests.[35]

This limited treatment of shareholders within the stewardship framework stems from a deeper conceptual tension. While stewardship theorists posit that principals can act as stewards under certain situational, structural, and psychological conditions, the application of this logic to the manager–shareholder relationship remains debated.[36] As a result, corporate governance research has largely retained the agency-based dyad, casting shareholders as principals and managers as their agents.[37]

However, the rise of institutional investors as dominant shareholders disrupts this binary. It blurs the traditional boundaries between principal and agent and gives rise to more complex, multi-layered relationships that challenge the assumptions of both agency and stewardship models.

4.2.3 Beyond the Principal–Agent Dyad: Investment Management and the Realities of Delegation

While institutional investors occupy a distinct position in modern corporate governance, they have not escaped the logic of the principal–agent framework. When holding public equity, institutional investors operate in dual roles: they act as *agents* for their proximate clients and beneficiaries – such as mutual fund investors or pensioners (the principals) – and as *principals* in their relationship with company management, who act as their agents. This layered agency structure has given rise to a rich body of theoretical work that reframes the classical separation of ownership and control into a more nuanced separation: between the ownership of shares, corporate control, and the nominal shareholders on whose behalf investments are made.[38]

[35] Ibid. 1171; Jonathan D. Arthurs and Lowell W. Busenitz, 'The Boundaries and Limitations of Agency Theory and Stewardship Theory in the Venture Capitalist/Entrepreneur Relationship' (2003) 28 *Entrepreneurship Theory and Practice* 145; Chrisman, 'Stewardship Theory: Realism, Relevance, and Family Firm Governance', 1059–61.

[36] Chrisman, 'Stewardship Theory: Realism, Relevance, and Family Firm Governance', 1057–8 (arguing that the managerial stewardship theory seems to be more applicable to relationships 'among managers at different levels and between managers and nonmanagerial employees rather than relationships between owners and managers').

[37] Catherine M. Daily, Dan R. Dalton, and Albert A. Cannella, Jr, 'Corporate Governance: Decades of Dialogue and Data' (2003) 28 *The Academy of Management Review* 371, 371–2. On a critical account of the conceptualisation of shareholders as principals, see Eva Micheler, *Company Law: A Real Entity Theory* (Oxford Academic, Oxford University Press 2021), 235.

[38] On the classic problem of separation of ownership from control, see Section 2.2.2.

In their influential 2013 article, Gilson and Gordon coined the term 'the agency costs of agency capitalism' to capture the inefficiencies and incentive misalignments that arise when institutional investors act on behalf of dispersed beneficiaries.[39] These problems are compounded by familiar agency-related challenges, including free rider issues and the potential divergence between the interests of institutional investors and those on behalf of whom they are acting.[40]

However, while theoretical literature has primarily focused on dual-layered agency relationships, modern delegated portfolio management is far more complex.[41] Consider the pension fund industry as an example. When a pension fund (an asset owner) delegates portfolio management to an asset manager, it acts as the principal in its relationship with the asset manager while simultaneously serving as the agent for its proximate clients and beneficiaries (typically pension scheme members), as illustrated on the left side of Figure 4.1. When investing in public equity, it is the asset manager – not the pension fund – who formally holds shareholder status and possesses shareholder rights.[42] This positions the asset manager in a dual role: as principal in its dealings with corporate management and as agent managing the pension fund's assets (right side of Figure 4.1). Each additional link in the investment chain adds another layer of agency relationships.[43]

These multi-layered agency relationships – between institutional investors (who are the record owners) and corporate managers, as well as between record owners and beneficial owners (clients/beneficiaries) – fundamentally alter the monitoring incentives of institutional investors, challenging the conventional agency theory model of a profit-maximising agent. Beyond the familiar challenges of conflicts of interest and information asymmetries between shareholders and managers,[44] the agency costs arising from the

39 Ronald J. Gilson and Jeffrey N. Gordon, 'The Agency Costs of Agency Capitalism: Activist Investors and the Reevaluation of Governance Rights' (2013) 113 *Columbia Law Review* 863.

40 Lucian A. Bebchuk, Alma Cohen, and Scott Hirst, 'The Agency Problems of Institutional Investors' (2017) 31 *The Journal of Economic Perspectives* 89.

41 For a literature review, see Livio Stracca, 'Delegated Portfolio Management: A Survey of the Theoretical Literature' (2006) 20 *Journal of Economic Surveys* 823.

42 But see Ewan McGaughey, 'Does Corporate Governance Exclude the Ultimate Investor?' (2016) 16 *Journal of Corporate Law Studies* 221 (arguing in favour of legal changes to empower the end-investors).

43 For instance, the relationship between a consultant (agent) and the pension fund (principal), or between a proxy service advisor (agent) and an asset manager (principal), introduces additional agency relationships. Additionally, when a nominee company acts as the record owner instead of the institutional investor, another agency layer is created.

44 Jensen and Meckling, 'Theory of the Firm: Managerial Behavior, Agency Costs and Ownership Structure', 308.

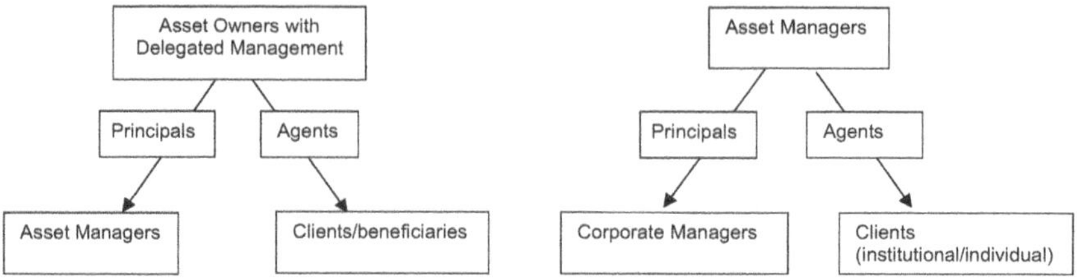

Figure 4.1 Roles of institutional investors in delegated management within the agency framework.

separation between record owners and beneficial owners undermine the incentives and competence of both asset owners and asset managers to effectively monitor their investee companies.[45] This separation results in reduced accountability and engagement, weakening overall governance and oversight mechanisms.[46]

Economists have long recognised that agency problems in delegated portfolio management differ significantly from standard agency conflicts, leading to critiques of traditional agency theory for failing to fully capture the unique challenges faced by equity-holding institutional investors, who act as both agents and principals within the investment chain.[47] For instance, agency theory typically expects asset owners to focus on selecting skilled asset managers and evaluating their performance against benchmarks.[48] However, this emphasis on monitoring often results in short-term solutions to agency costs, exposing inherent limitations in the traditional agency model.[49]

Furthermore, research in social financial and business ethics has demonstrated that the relationship between asset managers and asset owners is more complex than a straightforward principal–agent approach. There is neither a 'uniform' nor a 'unitary' principal, as participants in the

[45] One factor contributing to diminishing monitoring is that the prevailing investment model prioritises increasing assets under management through superior relative performance.

[46] For the legal and operational complexities of custody chains, see Eva Micheler, 'Custody Chains and Asset Values: Why Crypto-Securities Are Worth Contemplating' (2015) 74 *The Cambridge Law Journal* 505.

[47] Andrew Ang, *Asset Management: A Systematic Approach to Factor Investing* (Oxford University Press 2014), 498.

[48] For a critical account of this approach, see Diane-Laure Arjaliès, Philip Grant, Iain Hardie, Donald A. Mackenzie, and Ekaterina Svetlova, *Chains of Finance: How Investment Management is Shaped* (Oxford University Press 2017), 47–8, 67.

[49] See Sections 2.4.2 and 2.4.3.

investment chain frequently operate in multiple roles.[50] For example, asset owners may act as agents on behalf of their proximate clients and beneficiaries while simultaneously serving as principals in their interactions with asset managers or corporate managers, depending on whether investment management is delegated.

Adding to this complexity is the heterogeneity of institutional investors.[51] They differ in terms of investment models, time horizons, incentives, and objectives, such as prioritising liability matching versus maximising returns, as well as in their size and influence. These variations create investment chains of varying lengths, complexity, and different agency problems.[52] Furthermore, influence within these investment chains is not unidirectional; it flows both ways (from and to both the principal and agent) and can foster interactive, 'cooperative' relationships rather than relationships based solely on monitoring and control.[53]

While agency theory provides valuable insights into dyadic conflicts of interests, it struggles to address situations involving multiple principals with divergent interests.[54] Agents within the investment chain face the challenge of weighing the diverse interests of multiple principals and determining how best to serve them *all.* Unlike dyadic principal–agent models, modern investment structures are fluid, context-dependent, and shaped by overlapping roles and responsibilities. Although a full exploration of the investment chain's implications for corporate governance lies beyond the scope of this book, it is evident that modern investment management influences corporate governance in ways that agency theory alone cannot fully

[50] See Arjaliès *et al.*, *Chains of Finance: How Investment Management Is Shaped*, 48 and Guido Palazzo and Lena Rethel, 'Conflicts of Interest in Financial Intermediation' (2008) 81 *Journal of Business Ethics* 193, 194, respectively.

[51] For example, Robert E. Hoskisson, Michael A. Hitt, Richard A. Johnson, and Wayne Grossman, 'Conflicting Voices: The Effects of Institutional Ownership Heterogeneity and Internal Governance on Corporate Innovation Strategies' (2002) 45 *The Academy of Management Journal* 697.

[52] For instance, principal–agent problems are more pronounced when investors seek to maximise returns rather than hedge liabilities because, in the former case, asset managers enjoy greater freedom. Arjaliès *et al.*, *Chains of Finance: How Investment Management Is Shaped*, 67.

[53] Ibid., 51, 68 (showing how larger pension funds have the power to constrain their agents (asset managers), and how asset managers can reshape the relationships with their clients influencing them to align their goals with those of the asset managers).

[54] But see contributions to multiple agency theory in the context of IPOs: Jonathan D. Arthurs, Robert E. Hoskisson, Lowell W. Busenitz, and Richard A. Johnson, 'Managerial Agents Watching Other Agents: Multiple Agency Conflicts Regarding Underpricing in IPO Firms' (2008) 51 *Academy of Management Journal* 277.

explain.[55] A stewardship-based perspective offers a more expansive and adaptable framework for understanding the multifaceted roles of institutional investors. By capturing overlapping incentives, varying degrees of influence, and complex interdependencies within the investment chain, a theory of investor stewardship offers a more nuanced account of how institutional investors engage with and influence corporate governance.

4.3 Towards a Theory of Investor Stewardship: Power, Purpose, and Plural Accountability

4.3.1 Stewardship in Three Dimensions: A Conceptual Framework

The preceding discussion lays the foundation for a 'middle-range theory'[56] of investor stewardship, one that is specific enough to capture the complexities of institutional investors' governance roles while remaining broadly anchored in established theoretical frameworks. While stewardship lacks a universal understanding across disciplines and remains legally undefined, its essence can be distilled into three core elements: the exercise of *power* by a steward, acting *on behalf of others*, and acting *for* the benefit of *others*.

A useful analytical lens for understanding this tripartite model of investor stewardship comes from Fukuyama's theory of political order. Fukuyama argues that a stable and effective political system rests on three fundamental pillars: a strong state, the rule of law, and an accountable government.[57] While the state accumulates and exercises power, legal frameworks and accountability mechanisms exist to constrain and direct that power.[58] A similar structure applies to investor stewardship (Figure 4.2). Investor stewards, much like states, wield significant power and influence, yet their power is shaped and constrained by both formal legal obligations and broader normative expectations.

[55] For early attempts to revamp this understanding, see Iris H. Y. Chiu, 'Institutional Shareholders as Stewards: Toward a New Conception of Corporate Governance' (2011) 6 *Brooklyn Journal of Corporate, Financial, & Commercial Law* 387; Dionysia Katelouzou, 'Shareholder Stewardship: A Case for (Re)Embedding the Institutional Investors and the Corporation?' in Beate Sjåfjell and Christopher M. Bruner (eds.), *The Cambridge Handbook of Corporate Law, Corporate Governance and Sustainability* (Cambridge University Press 2019), 581–595.

[56] Raymond Boudon, 'What Middle-Range Theories Are' (1991) 20 *Contemporary Sociology* 519.

[57] Francis Fukuyama, *The Origins of Political Order* (Profile Books 2011). Francis Fukuyama, *Political Order and Political Decay* (Profile Books 2014).

[58] Fukuyama, *The Origins of Political Order*, 16.

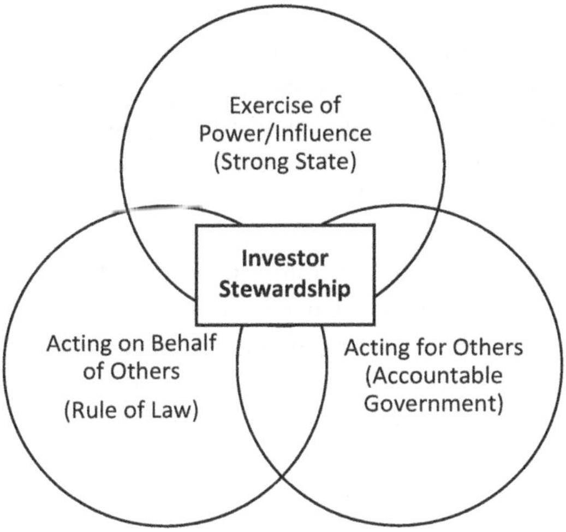

Figure 4.2 The tripartite model of investor stewardship in light of Fukuyama's political order.

Consider *shareholder stewardship*, which refers to the responsible and long-term-oriented oversight and engagement of institutional investors with the companies in which they invest. As shareholder stewards, institutional investors exert considerable influence over corporate governance through monitoring, engagement, and voting. Unlike classical agency models, which assume shareholder passivity,[59] investor stewardship recognises and supports a more active, accountable investor role in shaping corporate behaviour and enhancing accountability.

However, this monitoring role operates within a structured legal and regulatory framework – comprising both hard and soft law – that both constrains and guides institutional investors' decisions, oversight responsibilities, and engagement strategies.[60] Legal constraints ensure that institutional investors act *on behalf of* their proximate clients and beneficiaries, while broader accountability mechanisms encourage consideration *of* a wider set of stakeholders. This distinction is vital: whereas investor duties require that investors act primarily in the interests of their proximate clients and beneficiaries, accountable stewardship aspires to a broader public orientation, resisting short-term financial pressures in favour of sustainable value creation.

[59] Section 2.4.

[60] See Section 4.3.2.2 and Chapter 5.

This gives rise to a middle-range, tripartite theory of investor stewardship – a framework that bridges abstract governance theory and practical realities. Unlike macro-level political or economic theories that explain systemic shifts, or micro-level studies of isolated stewardship practices, this approach examines how institutional investors mediate competing interests and fulfil layered responsibilities across the investment chain. It challenges the conventional agency framework, which reduces corporate governance to binary relationships between principals and self-interested agents. Instead, it draws on stewardship theory in management, which posits that actors can be intrinsically motivated to act in others' interests under the right conditions.[61]

Applied to institutional investors, this theory reframes them not merely as agents bound by fiduciary duty, but as stewards committed to long-term value, trust, and sustainability. Institutionalising this model of stewardship requires effective accountability mechanisms – such as stewardship codes and disclosure frameworks – that reinforce expectations of responsible engagement, even as investors retain primary duties to their proximate clients and beneficiaries.[62]

Investor stewards thus do more than allocate capital. Through ongoing engagement, transparency, and responsiveness, they shape corporate behaviour and help govern in the public interest. Moving beyond the narrow logic of financial intermediation, they integrate broader concerns into their decision-making – embodying, in a modern sense, Aristotle's ideal of the common good. In this role, investor stewards emerge not only as economic actors but also as participants in the collective project of sustainable corporate governance.

4.3.2 *Shareholder Stewardship under the Microscope*

4.3.2.1 The Complexity and Dynamics of Institutional Shareholder Power

In any stewardship relationship, the steward exercises power, but within an organisational context the nature and extent of this power can be complex. Consider the case of a *shareholder steward* – an institutional investor, whether an asset manager or asset owner, holding a direct, minority ownership stake in a public company.[63] The central question

[61] Section 4.2.2.

[62] See Chapter 8.

[63] In the case of shareholder stewardship, it is the asset manager or the asset owner (when stewardship is not delegated) who exercises power as a shareholder (including the voting rights), and not the end-investor. But see McGaughey, 'Does Corporate Governance

is: what kind of power – defined as the 'discretion' to make choices with 'significant effects'[64] – does a shareholder steward wield over corporate affairs?

A useful starting point for this analysis is the division of power between shareholders and management. UK company law follows a 'shareholders as monitors' model, whereby shareholders are not typically direct decision-makers but instead exercise oversight functions. While they retain important rights – such as electing directors, receiving dividends, and voting on major corporate decisions, including mergers, significant transactions, and amendments to the company's constitutional documents – their involvement in day-to-day management is limited.[65] As a result, shareholder power is best characterised as partial and 'shared': it relies less on direct control and more on the capacity to monitor influence, and hold management accountable.[66]

Formally, shareholder decision-making power derives from voting rights.[67] Where a single shareholder or coalition holds a majority stake, decision-making authority effectively resides with them.[68] In contrast, under dispersed ownership, minority shareholders may still exert decision-making power – but typically jointly with management and

Exclude the Ultimate Investor?' (arguing in favour of legal changes to empower the end-investors).

[64] John E. Parkinson, *Corporate Power and Responsibility: Issues in the Theory of Company Law* (Oxford University Press 1995), 10. This definition of power differs from the Weberian understanding of power which relies on coercion and direct control over others. On the latter, see John Kenneth Galbraith, *The Anatomy of Power* (Houghton Mifflin 1983), 2. For shareholder power in general, see Lucian Arye Bebchuk, 'The Case for Increasing Shareholder Power' (2005) 118 *Harvard Law Review* 833; Marcel Kahan and Edward Rock, 'Embattled CEOs' (2010) 88 *Texas Law Review* 987; Harwell Wells, 'A Long View of Shareholder Power: From the Antebellum Corporation to the Twenty-First Century' (2015) 67 *Florida Law Review* 1033.

[65] See generally Paul L. Davies, *Gower and Davies' Principles of Modern Company Law* (9th ed., Sweet & Maxwell 2012), 435 and Sections 3.4.2 and 3.5.1.

[66] The term 'shared' power is borrowed by Edward S. Herman, *Corporate Control, Corporate Power: A Twentieth Century Fund Study* (Cambridge University Press 1981), 23. For Herman, shareholder power is shared with management. In the context of this book, shareholder power is not only shared with management but also dispersed among diverse constellations of shareholders.

[67] For voting as the most powerful tool of governance, see Chris Mallin, 'Institutional Investors: The Vote As a Tool of Governance' (2012) 16 *Journal of Management Governance*, 177–96.

[68] In contractarian terms, a controlling shareholder is both a principal vis-à-vis the managers and an agent vis-à-vis the minority shareholders.

other shareholders, through collective decision-making. In these cases, the degree of influence depends not on a fixed ownership threshold, but on the cost–benefit analysis of engagement that takes into account the ownership structure and the likelihood that engagement will be effective.[69]

Under UK company law, institutional investors are not legally required to exercise shareholder decision-making power, including voting, unless their ownership stake is substantial enough to confer complete or substantial control over the company.[70] Nevertheless, the exercise of shareholder power by institutional investors has given rise to a rich body of literature on shareholder engagement and activism.[71]

Although there is no consensus – and limited hard data – on the precise extent and nature of shareholder power exercised by different types of institutional investors (active, activist, and passive), recent developments have reinforced their influence.[72] Key trends include firm-specific institutional shareholder activism, particularly hedge-fund-style activism; constellations between hedge-fund-style activists and intermediary institutional investors; and portfolio-level shareholder activism, especially on sustainability issues, often coordinated by third parties.[73] These trends highlight the growing influence of institutional investors and underscore the importance of their stewardship roles in shaping corporate behaviour and promoting sustainable business practices.

The concept of shareholder stewardship has been so closely linked with shareholder power and engagement that, in the early stages of stewardship policy development, the two terms were often used interchangeably.[74] In

[69] See Section 3.2.2.

[70] See *Bartlett v Barclays Bank Trust Co Ltd* [1980] Ch 515 at 532 (applying to pension trustees); The Law Commission, *Fiduciary Duties of Investment Intermediaries* (Law Com No 350, 2014) 3.85–3.88 and 5.96–5.97. The situation is different in the US, where both advisers to private pension funds and mutual fund managers owe a duty to vote. See Interpretive Bulletins Relating to the ERISA of 1974, 59 Fed. Reg. 38,860, 38,863 (1994) (codified at 29 C.F.R. pt.2509.94–2 (1994) and 17 C.F.R. § 275.206(4)-6 (2022).

[71] Sections 3.2 and 3.3.

[72] See also John C. Coates, 'Thirty Years of Evolution in the Roles of Institutional Investors in Corporate Governance' in Jennifer G. Hill and Randall S. Thomas (eds.), *Research Handbook on Shareholder Power* (Edward Elgar 2015), 93 (confirming the growing power of institutional investors based on qualitative evidence).

[73] Sections 3.2.3 and 3.3.

[74] Dionysia Katelouzou, 'Something Old, Something New: Cultivating Institutional Investor Engagement through Shareholder Stewardship' in Luca Enriques and Giovanni Strampelli (eds.), *Board-Shareholder Dialogue: Policy Debate, Legal Constraints and Best Practices* (Oxford University Press 2024), 185, 201–2.

contrast, the second and third elements of the tripartite framework of investor stewardship – acting on behalf of others and for the benefit of others – have not garnered as much attention. These two crucial aspects of investor stewardship will be analysed in detail in the following subsections.

4.3.2.2 Acting on Behalf of Others: Clients and Beneficiaries

The core of any investor stewardship relationship lies in the principles of substitution and delegation of power. What sets institutional investors apart from other minority shareholders is their intermediary role: they exercise power over corporate affairs *on behalf of others*. This distinguishing feature is fundamental to stewardship relationship but generally absent in the exercise of decision-making power by other minority shareholders.[75] The case of individual (retail) investors is illustrative. Even if they become more active in monitoring and engaging with the companies they invest in, they do so in pursuit of their own interests, not on behalf of others.[76] As such, their actions do not constitute stewardship *stricto sensu*, as they do not involve delegated authority or responsibility for managing others' capital.

Under UK company law, shareholder voting rights are not typically viewed as being granted to act in the best interests of others.[77] Although certain limitations apply to the rights of controlling shareholders, shareholder power is treated as an incident of share ownership – rather than a delegated responsibility.[78] As a result, unlike company directors, shareholders are not typically bound by fiduciary duties to the company or fellow shareholders.[79] With few exceptions, they may exercise their

[75] It is a different question whether majority shareholders can fit the steward construct. On this, see Dan W. Puchniak, 'The False Hope of Stewardship in the Context of Controlling Shareholders: Making Sense Out of the Global Transplant of a Legal Misfit' (2024) 72 *The American Journal of Comparative Law* 109.

[76] On the governance role of retail investors, see Sergio Alberto Ricci and Christina M. Sautter, 'Corporate Governance Gaming: The Collective Power of Retail Investors' (2021) 22 *Nevada Law Journal* 51; Jill E. Fisch, 'Gamestop and the Reemergence of the Retail Investor' (2022) 102 *Boston University Law Review* 1799.

[77] Davies, *Gower and Davies' Principles of Modern Company Law*, 692; *Eclairs Group Ltd v JKX Oil & Gas plc Glengary Overseas Ltd v JKX Oil & Gas plc* [2015] UKSC 71, [40].

[78] See *Allen v Gold Reefs of W. Africa Ltd* [1900] 1 Ch 656; *Brown v. British Abrasive Wheel Co* [1919] 1 Ch 290; *Dafen Tinplate Co Ltd. v Llanelli Steel Co* [1920] 2 Ch 124; *Northern Counties Securities Ltd v Jackson & Steeples Ltd* [1974] 1 WLR 1133; *Arbuthnott v Bonnyman & 18 Ors* [2015] EWCA Civ 536. See also *Ebrahimi v Westbourne Galleries Ltd* 2 All E.R. 492, 500 (HL 1972) and Companies Act 2006, section 994.

[79] This is in marked contrast with the US legal regime, which imposes fiduciary duties on majority controlling shareholders particularly in cases of mismanagement of corporate property by controlling shareholders and in closely held private companies. See generally

voting rights in pursuit of self-interest, even when doing so may adversely affect other parties.[80]

For years, the fundamental distinction between directors' duties and shareholders' rights, which underpins the traditional view of shareholders as principals and directors as agents, left little space for the concept of shareholder stewardship. However, the rise of institutional investors has prompted a growing debate over whether this shareholder-centric framework, now often interpreted as asset manager-centric, remains tenable. Legal scholars have increasingly questioned whether minority institutional shareholders should bear company law duties similar to those imposed on controlling shareholders, given their expanding influence and the public interest implications of their corporate governance role.[81] This debate is particularly acute in the context of hedge fund activism.[82] Nonetheless, under current English law, institutional shareholders are not subject to any such duties unless they can be shown to exercise control.[83]

Jerry B. Helwig, 'The Fiduciary Duty of Controlling Shareholders Note' (1955) 7 *Western Reserve Law Review* 467. But see Paula J. Dalley, 'The Misguided Doctrine of Stockholder Fiduciary Duties' (2004) 33 *Hofstra Law Review* 175; Jens Dammann, 'The Controlling Shareholder's General Duty of Care: A Dogma that Should Be Abandoned' (2015) 2015 *University of Illinois Law Review* 479.

80 However, when the company is a charity, a member may be fiduciary to the objects of the charity (not the company): see *Lehtimäki v Cooper* [2020] UKSC 33, [2022] AC 155, [2021] 1 All ER 809, [35] and [50]. Even in non-charitable companies, shareholders' duties can be imposed contractually. See Jennifer Payne, 'Contractual Aspects of Shareholders' Duties' in Hanne S. Birkmose (ed.), *Shareholders' Duties* (Wolters Kluwer 2017), 107. In addition, a range of disclosure duties aimed at transparency are imposed to shareholders of listed companies (via securities regulation). See Karsten Engsig Sørensen, 'Shareholders' Duty to Disclose' in Hanne S. Birkmose (ed.), *Shareholders' Duties* (Wolters Kluwer 2017), 307. Finally, for an argument in favour of a reasonableness test of shareholder voting, see John Lowry and Ernest Lim, 'Reconsidering the Rule on Shareholders' Exercise of Voting Powers' (2020) *Journal of Business Law* 345.

81 Roberta S. Karmel, 'Should a Duty to the Corporation Be Imposed on Institutional Shareholders?' (2004) 60 *Business Lawyer* 1 (for the US); Iris H-Y Chiu and Dionysia Katelouzou, 'Making a Case for Regulating Institutional Shareholders' Corporate Governance Roles' (2018) *Journal of Business Law* 67 (for the UK); Ernest Lim, *A Case for Shareholders' Fiduciary Duties in Common Law Asia* (Cambridge University Press 2019), Chapter 3D (for Asia).

82 Iman Anabtawi and Lynn A. Stout, 'Fiduciary Duties for Activist Shareholders' (2008) 60 *Stanford Law Review* 1255.

83 It has been argued, however, that activist (minority) shareholders may be subject to directors' duties if categorised as shadow directors. See David W. Giattino, 'Curbing Rent-Seeking by Activist Shareholders: The British Approach Notes and Comments' (2011) 25 *Temple International & Comparative Law Journal* 103, 120–2. On shadow directors, see UK Companies Act, s 251, *Re Hydrodan (Corby) Ltd* [1994] B.C.C. 161; *Ultraframe (UK) Ltd. v. Fielding* [2005] All E.R. (D) 397 (Ch.).

But this does not settle the matter. Outside the narrow confines of company law, institutional shareholders clearly exercise decision-making power over corporate affairs on behalf of *others*. This substitution and delegation of power does not stem from company law but instead arises from a broader legal and regulatory framework governing investment management – comprising statutory regulation, case law, and agreements between the parties (contracts and trust deeds).

There is a well-established academic and judicial view that the undertaking to act on behalf of others in good faith and for proper purposes is the hallmark of a fiduciary relationship.[84] English case law identifies a fiduciary as someone who acts for another, creating 'a relationship of trust and confidence',[85] and who is required to 'act unselfishly' in the best interests of the principal.[86] It is this element of self-denial – placing the interests of another above one's own – that distinguishes fiduciaries from other power-holders, who may only be required to act in good faith and for proper purposes.[87]

When it comes to institutional investors, the meaning and scope of the term 'fiduciary' have long been contested.[88] The client agreement (such as between an asset owner and an asset manager) typically establishes an agency relationship in law.[89] While not all institutional investors owe fiduciary duties under UK law, they are nonetheless subject to other legal obligations, such as common law duties of care, when managing assets for others. Most UK institutional investors operate under contractual arrangements rather than formal legal trustee status. For example, UK pension funds investing in public equity, whether directly or indirectly via asset managers,[90] do so on behalf of scheme participants. In trust-based pension

[84] Len S. Sealy, 'Fiduciary Relationships' (1962) 20 *The Cambridge Law Journal* 69, 72–9.

[85] *Bristol and West Building Society v Mothew* [1998] Ch. 1 (C.A.), 18 per Lord Millett.

[86] *Al Nehayan v Kent* [2018] EWHC 333 (Comm), [2018] 1 C.L.C. 216, at [159] (Q.B.). See also *Lehtimäki v Cooper* [2020] UKSC 33, at [44]–[46] (Lady Arden) ('[t]he key principle is that a fiduciary acts for and only for another . . . he cannot exercise any power so as to benefit himself').

[87] Sarah Worthington, 'Fiduciaries Then and Now' (2021) 80 *The Cambridge Law Journal* S154, 156–7.

[88] See e.g. contributions in James P. Hawley, Andreas G. F. Hoepner, Keith L. Johnson, Joakim Sandberg, and Edward J. Waltzer (eds.), *Cambridge Handbook of Institutional Investment and Fiduciary Duty* (Cambridge University Press 2014).

[89] On investment firms as agents in law, see Lodewijk Van Setten, *The Law of Financial Advice, Investment Management, and Trading* (Oxford University Press 2019), 20–30.

[90] On the distinction between direct and indirect stewardship, see Chapter 7. It is noteworthy that trust-based pension contribution–benefit schemes dominate the private pension landscape in the UK. For data see, The Pensions Regulator, *Occupational defined*

schemes, trustees owe fiduciary duties and duties to act in the best interests of their beneficiaries, under both pensions legislation and established case law.[91] In contrast, contract-based schemes fall under the regulatory purview of the Financial Conduct Authority (FCA), which requires them to act in the best interests of their clients.[92] In both cases, the legal framework shapes the expectations placed on pension funds as stewards of retirement assets.

Asset managers investing in public equity exercise voting rights and manage assets on behalf of either intermediary institutions (such as pension funds or insurance companies) or individual (retail) investors. Where the client is an institutional investor, assets are often managed through separately managed accounts; for retail investors, the typical structure is collective investment schemes. The stewardship role of asset managers is shaped by a mix of regulatory rules and private law obligations. These include common law duties of care, and in some instances, fiduciary duties towards their clients.[93]

When pension trustees delegate investment authority to asset managers, the latter assume additional responsibilities under pension legislation, alongside obligations set out by the FCA.[94] Where asset managers invest through pooled vehicles, their legal duties are governed primarily by contract. However, these responsibilities – while significant – do not automatically confer fiduciary status. Fiduciary obligations only arise where they are explicitly established by the relationship or the governing contractual terms.[95]

contribution landscape in the UK, www.thepensionsregulator.gov.uk/en/document-library/research-and-analysis/occupational-defined-contribution-landscape-2024

91 Occupational Pension Schemes (Investment) regulations 2005 (SI 2005/3378), Regulation 4. Occupational and Personal Pension Schemes (Disclosure of Information) Regulations 2013 (SI 2013/2734), regs 6, 8–22, 24 and 25 (pension trustees).

92 COBS 2.1.1. For a comprehensive analysis, see The Law Commission, *Fiduciary Duties of Investment Intermediaries*, Chapter 8.

93 *Diamantides v JP Morgan Chase Bank* [2005] EWCA Civ 1612; *FM Capital Partners Ltd v Marino and another* [2018] EWHC 1768 (Comm) at [472]. But see *Första Ap-Fonden v Bank of New York Mellon Sa/Nv and others* [2013] EWHC 3127 (Comm) at [175]–[185] (rejecting the plaintiff's claims as 'negligence claims dressed up in fiduciary garb'). See also The Law Commission, paras. 3.17–3.24 (identifying three key indicators of a fiduciary relationship: 'discretion', 'power to act', and 'vulnerability').

94 Pensions Act 1995, section 36(1).

95 *Första Ap-Fonden v Bank of New York Mellon Sa/Nv and others* [2013] EWHC 3127 (Comm) at [175]–[185] (rejecting the plaintiff's claims as 'negligence claims dressed up in fiduciary garb'). See also The Law Commission, *Fiduciary Duties of Investment Intermediaries*, paras. 3.17–3.24 (identifying three key indicators of a fiduciary relationship: 'discretion', 'power to act', and 'vulnerability').

Under English law, an asset manager's legal duties extend only to the immediate contracting party, not to beneficiaries or end-investors further down the investment chain.[96] This reflects a foundational feature of the investment system: the structural separation between fund managers and ultimate asset holders, which narrows accountability and confines stewardship obligations to the proximate client.[97]

In conclusion, while institutional investors are not legally bound to the companies they invest in – or to other shareholders – they do bear responsibilities to those on whose behalf they act. These responsibilities are defined by a complex framework of legal and regulatory rules. Yet focusing solely on this client-facing, compliance-driven role risks missing a deeper distinction: that between the agent and the steward.

Both agents and stewards act on behalf of others, but they differ in motivation and scope. The agent is typically self-interested, seeking to maximise profit within the limits of their mandate. The steward, by contrast, is other-regarding and intrinsically motivated. Moreover, the steward's responsibility extends beyond immediate principals to a wider set of stakeholders.

It is this broader, other-regarding dimension that distinguishes stewardship not only from agency but also from legal fiduciary duty. While fiduciaries are bound to act loyally in the interest of their principal, stewards are expected to act for the benefit of others even absent formal legal obligations. This third analytical component – acting for the benefit of others – marks a shift in our understanding of stewardship. It is to this dimension that the analysis now turns.

4.3.2.3 Acting for the 'Unseen' Others: Broadening the Scope of Stewardship Accountability

While institutional investors, in their role as shareholders, exercise power *on behalf of* their proximate clients and beneficiaries, a central question looms: *whom should this power ultimately serve*? To address this, it is useful to

[96] *Seymour v Caroline Ockwell & Co* [2005] EWHC 1137, at [142] and [143] (rejecting that those who give advice to professional clients owe duties of care beyond their proximate clients). Of course, the asset managers' duties are subject to the investment mandate and English courts have confirmed that fiduciary duties are subject to modification by contract. See e.g. *Fiduciary Duties of Investment Intermediaries*, paras. 10.24, 10.49, 10.51.

[97] John Morley, 'The Separation of Funds and Managers: A Theory of Investment Fund Structure and Regulation' (2013) 123 *Yale Law Journal* 1228. For a critical analysis of the implications of this structure on governance, see Roger M. Barker and Iris H-Y Chiu, *Corporate Governance and Investment Management: The Promises and Limitations of the New Financial Economy* (Edward Elgar Publishing 2017), 67–78.

revisit the concept of psychological ownership, originally introduced by stewardship theorists to distinguish stewards from agents. Unlike legal ownership,[98] psychological ownership is not defined by formal rights but by a selective state in which the individual feels a sense of possession and identification with the 'ownable'.[99] Initially, this concept was applied to explain stewardship behaviours among managers and employees.[100]

Attempts to extend psychological ownership to institutional shareholders, however, remain fragmented and underdeveloped. Sikavica and Hillman applied the concept to develop a behavioural theory of shareholder activism,[101] arguing that a shareholder's willingness to engage in firm-specific activism depends on the strength of their psychological ownership. Shareholders with weak psychological ownership are more likely to exit, while those with a strong sense of identification – yet lacking control – are more inclined to use voice mechanisms.[102] Still, their model does not fully account for the different types of activist shareholders, the varying forms of activism, or the broader market and institutional conditions that influence these behaviours.[103]

A more systematic application of psychological ownership to institutional shareholders comes from management scholars McNulty and Nordberg, who link stewardship theory with the concept of 'universal' ownership.[104] They distinguish what they term 'active ownership' from mere trading, asserting that institutional investors acting as active owners

[98] 'Legal ownership' is traced to the theory of property rights and is commonly referred to the bundle of rights provided to shareholders by company law. On the property-right-account of ownership, see John Armour and Michael J. Whincop, 'The Proprietary Foundations of Corporate Law' (2007) 27 *Oxford Journal of Legal Studies* 429, 437–8. On legal ownership, generally see Antony M. Honoré, 'Ownership' in Antony Gordon Guest (ed.), *Oxford Essays in Jurisprudence: A Collaborative Work* (Oxford University Press 1961).

[99] Pierce *et al.*, 'Toward a Theory of Phychological Ownership in Organizations', 299.

[100] Hernandez, 'Toward an Understanding of the Psychology of Stewardship', 153.

[101] Kate Sikavica and Amy Hillman, 'Towards a Behavioural Theory of Corporate Ownership and Shareholder Activism' (2008) 2008 *Academy of Management Annual Meeting Proceedings* 1. It should be noted, however, that they define 'shareholder activism' very broadly as including voice, exit, and loyalty.

[102] Ibid., 5.

[103] See e.g. Ruth V. Aguilera and Gregory Jackson, 'The Cross-National Diversity of Corporate Governance: Dimensions and Determinants' (2003) 28 *The Academy of Management Review* 447.

[104] Terry McNulty and Donald Nordberg, 'Ownership, Activism and Engagement: Institutional Investors as Active Owners' (2016) 24 *Corporate Governance: An International Review* 346.

possess both psychological and legal ownership.[105] Active ownership, in this view, involves continuous engagement with a long-term orientation, extending beyond episodic shareholder activism. Their model rests on two key propositions. Firstly, unlike psychological ownership among employees or customers, active ownership cannot exist independently of legal ownership. Secondly, like psychological ownership, active ownership is a 'cognitive-affective' construct – shaped by the interaction between market structures and institutional norms.[106] When these forces – such as financial incentives, investment strategies, and formal rights – favour rational calculation over emotional connection to investable assets, institutional investors are more likely to exit than to remain loyal.[107]

However, substituting the term 'psychological' with 'active' in the context of stewardship is problematic. Both terms are anchored in the notion of 'ownership', which is conceptually misaligned with the legal and practical role of shareholders in companies.[108] Framing stewardship in terms of ownership risks conflating the steward's role with property rights and can obscure the relational and delegated nature of stewardship. For example, the 'feeling' of responsibility that psychological ownership entails is difficult to apply to institutional investors who hold highly diversified, minority stakes and often lack a deep connection to individual companies.[109]

The term 'active ownership' also introduces ambiguity. In portfolio management, 'active' typically refers to the strategy of selecting securities to outperform a benchmark, in contrast to passive strategies that replicate index performance. Consequently, the term 'active ownership' may unintentionally exclude stewardship by passive funds, even though such funds often engage at the portfolio level on systemic issues.[110] Moreover, anchoring 'active ownership' in legal ownership limits the scope of stewardship to formal fiduciary relationships, thereby overlooking the broader array of

[105] Ibid., 351.

[106] Ibid., 349–51.

[107] Ibid., 352. For an indirect path that supports investor stewardship via changes in the articles of association rather than in law, see Donald Nordberg, 'Governing corporations with "strangers": Earning membership through investor stewardship' (2023) *Philosophy of Management* (online).

[108] See Sections 2.2.1 and 2.2.2.

[109] Pierce *et al.*, 'Toward a Theory of Phychological Ownership in Organizations', 303.

[110] It is also argued that if one examines all the aspects of passive investing it is 'actually very active' from index construction to portfolio management and engagement with companies. See Eric Balchunas, 'Five Ways 'Passive' Investing Is Actually Quite Active' *Bloomberg* (3 March 2017).

others – such as end-investors or stakeholders in portfolio companies – for whom investor stewards arguably act.

Finally, both terms – 'psychological' and 'active' ownership – fail to capture stewardship beyond equity holdings, making them inadequate for articulating stewardship in fixed income or alternative asset classes.[111]

For these reasons, the enduring core of investor stewardship is best understood not in terms of ownership, but as a commitment to *act for others.* While institutional investors' formal obligations are directed towards their proximate clients and beneficiaries, their actions often affect a diverse range of 'others'.[112] This extended sense of responsibility – distinguishing a steward from a profit-maximising agent – is the hallmark of investor stewardship. A steward is not necessarily altruistic, but they are *other-serving*, demonstrating a deliberate and 'calculated' attentiveness to the interests of multiple parties.[113] Acting for others, therefore, encompasses both intrinsic motivations and calculated, extrinsically motivated behaviours shaped by social, regulatory, and market forces.[114]

As Fisch and Schwartz observe in their analysis of public pension funds in the US, multi-layered accountability is most visible in institutions where the separation between those exercising investment discretion and those whose capital is at stake is most acute.[115] Public pension funds, with their vast pools of capital and diffuse beneficiary base, exemplify the 'stewardship ideal': institutions acting on behalf of 'unseen' others whose voices are rarely heard in corporate decision-making, yet whose economic futures are deeply intertwined with the investment system. However, the other-regarding function of stewardship is not confined to public pension funds; it also arises in commercial settings shaped by fee maximisation, client segmentation, and market competition. In these contexts, the notion

111 Section 7.4.

112 Whether societal benefits from investment management are collateral outcomes or primary mandates is beyond this article's scope. Except for impact investing, where generating societal benefits is a primary goal, aligning investment strategies with societal goals is pursued within fiduciary duty and prudent investment management, recognising potential collateral benefits.

113 Oliver E. Williamson, 'Calculativeness, Trust, and Economic Organization' (1993) 36 *The Journal of Law and Economics* 453, 485–6 (considering calculativeness in the context of trust). Cf. the notion of 'internalized trust' in Margaret M. Blair and Lynn A. Stout, 'Trust, Trustworthiness, and the Behavioral Foundations of Corporate Law' (2001) 149 *University of Pennsylvania Law Review* 1735, 1750–1.

114 On the complexity of motivations, see Bruno S. Frey, *Not Just for the Money* (Edward Elgar Publishing 1997), 14.

115 Jill Fisch and Jeff Schwartz, 'The Singular Role of Public Pension Funds in Corporate Governance' (2025) 104 *Texas Law Review* 735.

of acting for others is mediated by business models that frequently prioritise the interests of intermediaries over those of ultimate beneficiaries. This misalignment makes the role of stewardship frameworks even more vital, as they provide the normative and procedural scaffolding through which delegated responsibility might be made more transparent, accountable, and socially attuned. From this tension emerges a normative 'golden thread' of stewardship – one that binds institutional actors not only to their contractual clients but also to the ultimate interests of those whose savings underpin the financial system.[116] This thread is not purely legal; it is also ethical, relational, and systemic. It signals an evolving understanding of institutional investors' role in society – not merely as fiduciaries acting within a narrow legal frame, but as governance actors embedded in a wider network of trust-based expectations and public responsibilities.

In this respect, the other-regarding function of investor stewardship is conceptually aligned with the trusteeship model of the board, where the board's role is to promote the long-term interests of the company as a whole.[117] Analogously, acting for others within the stewardship framework can be viewed as a form of 'self-actualizing' *trusteeship* – a mode of governance that seeks to benefit both the steward and those they serve.[118] While an extensive literature on trust and trusteeship lies beyond the scope of this discussion,[119] the key point is that within the investment chain, institutional investors are embedded in a mix of formal legal obligations and trust-based, relational expectations.[120]

This conceptual alignment between investor stewardship and trusteeship highlights the evolving nature of institutional investors' responsibilities – not only as fiduciaries bound by legal obligations, but as relational actors

[116] Ong Boon Hwee and Mark Goyder, *Entrusted: Stewardship for Responsible Wealth Creation* (World Scientific and Stewardship Asia 2020), 129–30 (adopting a much broader concept of stewardship as including stewardship by companies' boards and the state).

[117] See also Section 8.3.2.

[118] But see Colin Mayer, 'Ownership, Agency, and Trusteeship: An Assessment' (2020) 36 *Oxford Review of Economic Policy* 223, 235 (adopting a narrower view equating stewardship with 'enlightened self-interest' as opposed to a broader notion of trusteeship which is concerned 'with the interests of others').

[119] See e.g. Surendra Arjoon, 'Corporate Governance: An Ethical Perspective' (2005) 61 *Journal of Business Ethics* 343; Rene Reich-Graefe, 'Deconstructing Corporate Governance: The Mechanics of Trusting' (2013) 38 *Delaware Journal of Corporate Law* 103.

[120] The emphasis on 'relationships based on trust and respect' across the investment chain is evident in the Kay Review: John Kay, *The Kay Review of UK Equity Markets and Long-Term Decision Making* (July 2012), 44–8.

embedded in a wider system of trust and accountability. As these responsibilities expand beyond narrow financial mandates, a crucial question arises: under what conditions is investor stewardship not only normatively desirable but also economically rational?

4.3.3 The Economics of Investor Stewardship: Incentives, Costs, and Portfolio-Level Justification

The tripartite structure of investor stewardship – power, acting on behalf of others, and acting for others – helps define the conditions under which institutional investors allocate resources to stewardship activities, including shareholder engagement. Power determines their capacity to influence corporate decisions, acting on behalf of others ensures alignment with the interests of proximate clients and beneficiaries, and acting for others introduces an accountability dimension, ensuring that stewardship extends beyond long-term financial returns to broader stakeholder considerations.

To illustrate the economic rationale behind investor stewardship, consider the case of asset managers exercising *micro-level shareholder stewardship*, that is, firm-specific monitoring and engagement with investee companies.[121] Like shareholder activism, stewardship is only rational when its benefits outweigh its costs.[122] However, asset managers differ from activist hedge funds in their financial incentives. While hedge funds are directly rewarded from enhancing individual company performance, asset managers earn fees as a fraction (α) of Assets under Management (AUM) rather than through direct performance-based compensation.[123] Their primary financial incentive lies in attracting and retaining investors rather than generating excess returns on individual investments. As a result, firm-specific engagement is a lower financial priority for asset managers, since asset managers focus on relative performance rather than absolute returns.[124] This structural dynamic fundamentally shapes their approach to stewardship.

[121] See further Section 7.2.1.

[122] On a cost-benefit analysis of shareholder activism, see Section 3.2.2.

[123] On this incentive structure, see also Bebchuk *et al.*, 'The Agency Problems of Institutional Investors', 96.

[124] Gilson and Gordon, 'The Agency Costs of Agency Capitalism: Activist Investors and the Reevaluation of Governance Rights', 890. For a theoretical model of when mutual funds should vote on behalf of their investors, see Sean J. Griffith, 'Opt-In Stewardship: Toward an Optimal Delegation of Mutual Fund Voting' (2020) 98 *Texas Law Review* 983.

From an economic perspective, micro-level shareholder stewardship is financially viable only if the expected increase in portfolio value justifies its costs. Since asset managers' fees are tied to AUM, stewardship must generate enough value to compensate for its direct costs (C):

$$\alpha \text{ x } \Delta V_p > \text{ C}, \tag{4.1}$$

where ΔV_p represents the portfolio-wide value created through stewardship activities.

This condition (*portfolio-level stewardship viability condition*) ensures that shareholder stewardship aligns with the asset manager's business model. If engagement fails to generate sufficient value, asset managers have little financial incentive to pursue it. Additionally, constrained cost structures – particularly in low-fee passive strategies – limit the resources available for meaningful engagement.[125]

However, stewardship extends beyond financial returns to encompass broader interests, including those of clients, beneficiaries, portfolio companies, communities, and the environment. To account for these non-financial benefits, an additional component (B) is introduced into Equation 4.1 to represent intangible value, including customer trust, enhanced corporate reputation, stronger sustainability practices, risk mitigation, and positive social impact. Incorporating these broader benefits, the expanded portfolio-level viability condition for stewardship becomes:

$$\alpha \text{ x } \Delta V_p + B > C. \tag{4.2}$$

This adjustment acknowledges that while stewardship activities may not always yield immediate financial gains, they contribute to long-term value beyond traditional cost–benefit calculations. However, quantifying these non-financial benefits remains challenging due to complex interdependencies among stakeholders, investable assets, the environment, and broader communities. The scarcity of reliable data further complicates measurement efforts, while the uneven distribution of these benefits can create conflicts of interest, making it difficult to align stakeholder priorities.[126] Additionally, the temporal misalignment between incurred costs and realised gains

[125] Dominic O'Connell, 'Active fund managers face extinction as investors turn more passive' *The Times* (3 January 2025) (reporting that passive tracker funds charge annual fees as low as 0.07 per cent, whereas actively managed funds typically cost around 0.8 per cent).

[126] Sakis Kotsantonis and George Serafeim, 'Four Things No One Will Tell You about ESG Data' (2019) 31 *Journal of Applied Corporate Finance* 50; Bjorg Jonsdottir, Throstur Olaf Sigurjonsson, Lara Johannsdottir, and Stefan Wendt, 'Barriers to Using ESG Data

presents a significant challenge for investor stewards operating under short-term performance pressures.

Beyond an asset manager's private incentives, shareholder stewardship is only justified from the perspective of the company being engaged if it yields a net positive impact. However, even when firm-specific engagement does not generate sufficient value ($\Delta V_C < C$), asset managers may still pursue it for other reasons, such as reputational benefits, strategic signalling, or compliance with stewardship codes.

Unlike hedge-fund-style activists, asset managers typically hold more diversified portfolios and do not engage across all holdings. Instead, they focus their stewardship efforts on selected companies, which means the effectiveness of stewardship must be assessed in aggregate rather than on a firm-by-firm basis. The overall economic justification for micro-level shareholder stewardship, therefore, hinges on the cumulative impact of firm-specific engagements across the portfolio. From a corporate governance perspective, the total weighted value created across all engaged firms should exceed the associated costs:

$$\sum\nolimits_{i=1}^{n} (\Delta V_{C_i} \text{ x } w_i) > C, \tag{4.3}$$

where ΔV_{C_i} represents the change in value of firm i due to engagement, w_i is the weighting of the firm i in the portfolio, and n represents all firms engaged by the asset manager.

This *aggregate firm-level condition* (Equation 4.3) highlights that the economic justification for stewardship depends on its collective impact across multiple firms rather than the outcome of any single engagement. While individual engagements may not yield direct financial gains, the aggregate effect across all engagements must be net positive to support the case for micro-level shareholder stewardship. Moreover, firm-level engagement can generate spillover effects, shaping governance norms, industry practices, and broader market efficiency. These wider benefits enhance value across multiple holdings, reinforcing the economic rationale for stewardship even when firm-specific benefits alone do not outweigh the costs.[127]

In summary, micro-level shareholder stewardship must be economically rational both within the asset manager's business model and, in aggregate, at the firm level. However, because asset managers prioritise portfolio-wide

for Investment Decisions' (2022) 14 *Sustainability* 5157; Chris Newlands, 'Data shortfall undermines ESG investment, asset managers warn' *Financial Times* (9 December 2024).

127 Scott Hirst and Lucian Bebchuk, 'Big Three Power, and Why It Matters' (2022) 102 *Boston University Law Review* 1547, 1586–8.

value creation over the performance of individual firms, the firm-level condition should be evaluated in aggregate rather than on a case-by-case basis. Even if some engagements fall short of the firm-level value thresholds, they may still be justified if they contribute to broader portfolio objectives – such as risk mitigation, regulatory compliance, or long-term market efficiency.

Importantly, the economic incentives for stewardship differ between active and passive managers. For active managers, the aggregate firm-level condition is particularly relevant, as they tend to engage selectively with companies where governance improvements are expected to generate excess returns. In contrast, passive managers – who cannot divest from index constituents – are more likely to engage at the portfolio level. Their stewardship activities focus on addressing systemic risks, improving governance standards, and promoting sustainability practices that support long-term value across their entire holdings.

Ultimately, for both active and passive managers, the economic justification for stewardship lies in its portfolio-wide impact. However, this does not diminish the role of firm-specific engagement. For active managers, it remains a central mechanism for delivering value; for passive managers, it serves as a tool to influence market norms and mitigate broader risks. Whether through targeted company interventions or portfolio-wide strategies, the viability of shareholder stewardship depends on its capacity to generate long-term value while balancing costs, incentives, and regulatory expectations.

4.4 The Multi-layered Relationships of Investor Stewardship

4.4.1 From Delegation to Accountability: Stewardship across the Investment Chain

Understanding the costs and benefits of investor stewardship becomes more complex when financial intermediation gives rise to multiple, overlapping responsibilities within the asset management ecosystem. Rather than operating through a single, direct relationship, investor stewardship unfolds across a web of interconnected roles and responsibilities. A central link in this network is the relationship between asset owners and asset managers – particularly when asset owners outsource fund management due to limited internal capacity. In such delegated structures, four interrelated stewardship relationships emerge: (1)

client stewardship, (2) *end-investor stewardship*, (3) *asset stewardship*, and (4) *sustainability stewardship*.[128]

Each of these relationships is oriented towards a specific group of 'others' whose interests the investor steward is expected to serve. These relationships can be visualised through a simplified flow-of-funds framework (Figure 4.3),[129] tracing the journey of capital from individual savers (end-investors), through financial intermediaries, to investable assets, and, ultimately, to real economic activity. Crucially, the origins of this capital are embedded in human, natural, and social systems – underscoring that markets do not exist in isolation but rely on broader societal and ecological foundations.[130]

The flow of funds is intermediated by assets owners, asset managers, and other market actors (omitted from Figure 4.3 for simplicity).[131] Notably, only client stewardship is governed by hard law. The other stewardship relationships – end-investor, asset, and sustainability stewardship – are primarily shaped by soft law, informal norms, and public expectations. In Figure 4.3, this distinction is visually expressed through solid and dotted lines, with dotted lines denoting stewardship responsibilities that are often contested, negotiated, and evolving.

Asset owners who delegate stewardship to asset managers nonetheless retain stewardship responsibilities.[132] As *client stewards* (1), they exercise power on behalf of, and for the benefit of, their clients, or where applicable, beneficiaries, as defined by contracts, mandates, or trust deeds.[133] When appointing asset managers, they maintain stewardship *indirectly* by setting the terms of investment mandates and monitoring

[128] To simplify the terminology, I do not consider other actors of the intermediated securities chain, including brokers and custodians, even though they may impact asset stewardship. For an analysis of intermediated securities in the UK, see The Law Commission, *Intermediated Securities: Who Owns Your Shares? A Scoping Paper* (11 November 2020) and contributions to Louise Gullifer and Jennifer Payne (eds.), *Intermediation and Beyond* (Hart 2019). Also, I do not account for stewardship in relation to 'secondary financial assets' owned through collective investment schemes.

[129] The circles in Figure 4.3 represent the parties that may benefit from the investor stewardship exercised by the asset manager when stewardship is delegated.

[130] Section 1.1.

[131] For the more complex set of 'buy-side' and 'sell-side' intermediaries that 'sit between' savers and capital markets, see Arjaliès *et al.*, *Chains of Finance: How Investment Management is Shaped*, 4–9.

[132] To maintain simplicity in our terminology, we do not account for the potential stewardship role played by service providers, such as investment consultants and proxy advisors. For the relationship between trustees and investment consultants, see ibid., 70–5.

[133] Section 4.3.2.2.

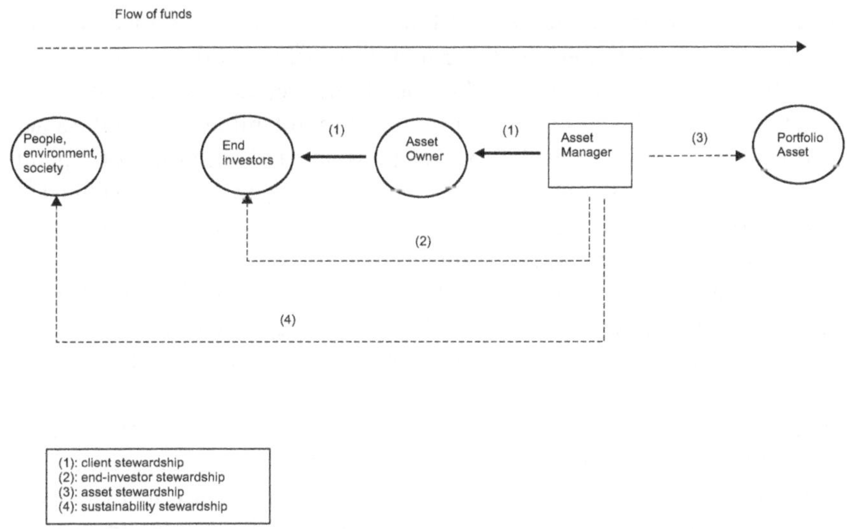

Figure 4.3 Multiple relationships of investor stewardship in the context of asset management.

compliance.[134] Their role extends beyond oversight; they are expected to guide investment managers to align with the long-term interests of clients and end-investors.[135]

Asset managers, in turn, act as *client stewards* (1) for asset owners – such as pension funds and insurance companies – who themselves serve as stewards for their own clients or beneficiaries. This arrangement creates a multi-layered structure of stewardship responsibilities distributed across the investment chain. Alignment across these layers, however, is not automatic. Incentive misalignments frequently emerge when fee structures, performance benchmarks, and industry norms privilege short-term relative performance over long-term absolute value.[136] This short-term orientation – shaped by regulatory pressures, compensation models, and competitive

[134] The UK Stewardship Code 2020 formalises indirect stewardship by asking from asset owners to monitor the stewardship activities of their asset managers and investment consultants. Financial Reporting Council, *The UK Stewardship Code 2020* (2019), Principle 8 (Principles for Asset Owners and Asset Managers).

[135] For empirical evidence on the degree of alignment in the voting of asset owners and asset managers, see Andreas G. F. Hoepner, *UK Asset Owner Stewardship Review 2023: Understanding the Degree & Distribution of Asset Manager Voting Alignment* (2023).

[136] For taxonomies of the conflicts of interest in financial intermediation, see John R. Boatright, 'Conflicts of Interest in Financial Services' (2000) 105 *Business and Society Review* 201; Palazzo and Rethel, 'Conflicts of Interest in Financial Intermediation', 201.

dynamics – can fragment stewardship efforts, as each intermediary may optimise for its own interests rather than those of the end-investor.[137]

At the same time, despite the rhetoric of financial democratisation, most beneficiaries remain disconnected from meaningful influence over the assets held in their name. The aspiration for 'pension fund socialism' or a genuinely participatory shareholder economy has largely gone unfulfilled.[138] These structural limitations expose the insufficiency of relying on client stewardship alone to secure accountability to ultimate savers.

It is in response to these gaps that a second layer – *end-investor stewardship* (2) – becomes critical. Represented by a dotted line in Figure 4.3, this layer lacks formal legal grounding but is normatively significant. It is oriented not toward intermediate contractual or legal duties, but reflects obligations to end-investors as the ultimate bearers of investment outcomes over time, and seeks to ensure that stewardship ultimately serves those whose capital is at stake. The Kay Review gave early voice to this vision, advocating fiduciary-like responsibilities across the entire investment chain.[139] While client stewardship may implicitly encompass end-investors, end-investor stewardship makes that accountability explicit, helping to reconnect savers – the 'true owners' of capital – with the influence that has been delegated on their behalf.[140]

Both client and end-investor stewardship concern the *internal* governance of the stewardship function. They focus on chains of accountability within investment management, linking institutional investors to their clients and beneficiaries, while differing in how far that accountability is extended toward the ultimate bearers of investment outcomes.

Asset stewardship (3), by contrast, relates to the *external* governance dimension: how institutional investors influence the companies or assets in which they invest.[141] Here, the investor acts as an *asset steward* (3),

[137] Kay Review, 40–3.

[138] Ronald B. Davis, *Democratizing Pension Funds: Corporate Governance and Accountability* (UBC Press, Vancouver, 2008); Jill E. Fisch, 'Securities Intermediaries and the Separation of Ownership from Control' (2010) 33 *Seattle University Law Review*, 877–88.

[139] Kay Review, Recommendation 7 and para 9.9. See also Department for Business Innovation and Skills, *Ensuring Equity Markets Support Long-Term Growth, The Government Response to the Kay Review* (2012), para 2.8 (suggesting that all participants in the investment chain 'should act in the best long-term interests of their clients or beneficiaries').

[140] Kay Review, 10 (concluding that '[t]he growth of intermediation has led to increased costs for investors, an increased potential for misaligned incentives and a tendency to view market effectiveness through the eyes of intermediaries rather than companies or end investors').

[141] This is the 'sell-side' of the investment chain which involves various intermediaries, such as brokers or dealers, which are however omitted from the analysis for simplicity purposes.

exercising power over its holdings, such as companies in the case of shareholder stewardship.[142] In the case of public equity, this corresponds to the *corporate governance aspect* of investor stewardship.

This includes both formal and informal modes of engagement, such as dialogue, voting, and, when necessary, divestment – all aimed at influencing corporate behaviour and driving long-term value creation.[143] In the UK, *asset stewardship* in public equities is embedded in policy initiatives that encourage institutional shareholder engagement. These policies – reflecting the 'Engaged Shareholder' image – are premised on the belief that institutional investors are uniquely placed to hold corporate management accountable and curb short-termism through firm-specific monitoring and engagement.[144] This vision lies at the heart of first-generation stewardship codes, which called on institutional shareholders to contribute to long-term value creation through firm-specific oversight.[145]

4.4.2 Sustainability Stewardship: Expanding the Stewardship Mandate

While the preceding section mapped stewardship relationships rooted in the investment chain, a fourth dimension – sustainability stewardship – extends the investor's responsibilities outwards, towards systemic challenges and the public interest. This section explores the motivations, expectations, and implications of this expanded stewardship mandate.

This broader perspective prompts a foundational question: 'What is the purpose of asset management?' Fundamentally, asset management exists to serve those who entrust their funds (clients and beneficiaries)

[142] The term *asset stewardship* does not suggest that an asset, such as a company, is merely a passive object. From a sociological perspective, an asset can be viewed as a subject with its own agency and governance challenges. However, while this dynamic is central to the shareholder–management relationship, this book does not explore it in depth.

[143] On exit as stewardship, see e.g. Marco Becht, Anete Pajuste, and Anna Toniolo, 'Voice through Divestment' European Corporate Governance Institute – Finance Working Paper No 900 <https://ssrn.com/abstract=4386469>. For a critical analysis of divestment as an effective form of engagement, especially when carbon-intensive assets are in stake, see Alperen Afşin Gözlügöl and Wolf Georg Ringe, 'Net-Zero Transition and Divestments of Carbon-Intensive Assets' (2023) 56 *UC Davis Law Review* 1963. See also Theodor F. Cojoianu, Francisco Ascui, Gordon L. Clark, Andreas G. F. Hoepner, and Dariusz Wójcik, 'Does the Fossil Fuel Divestment Movement Impact New Oil and Gas Fundraising?' (2020) 21 *Journal of Economic Geography* 141 (raising concerns about the limits of exit as a systemic stewardship strategy).

[144] Section 3.5.1.

[145] Section 5.3.1.

and, in doing so, to serve the interests of end-investors as the ultimate bearers of investment outcomes over time. At the same time, it plays a broader economic role by reallocating capital from individual savers (end-investors) to investment opportunities with greater potential.[146]

This dual purpose encompasses both private and public dimensions. From a private perspective, asset management aims to mitigate risk and generate returns for investors who provide capital, aligning with client and end-investor stewardship. From a public perspective, it contributes to the real economy and society by facilitating capital intermediation and allocation, central to asset stewardship.[147] Enhancing the long-term performance of investable assets benefits not only investors – through improved risk-adjusted portfolio returns – but also other stakeholders directly connected to these assets, including fellow shareholders, bondholders, or employees.

Assuming the role of a sustainability steward (relationship 4 in Figure 4.3) requires institutional investors to engage with a more complex and less clearly defined set of responsibilities. This involves accounting for the interests of a wider range of stakeholders – many of whom are only loosely connected to, or entirely external to, the investable asset. Traditionally, systemic risks and efforts to improve environmental, social, and economic conditions have been treated as externalities, lying outside the formal remit of business actors.[148] While institutional investors do not have a monopoly on efforts to mitigate such externalities, their substantial size and market influence make their involvement in 'sustainable development' essential.[149]

Sustainability stewardship reflects this shift. It involves fostering long-term sustainable value that extends beyond narrow financial

[146] James Hawley and Jon Lukomnik, *The Purpose of Asset Management* (2018). For a broad consideration of 'others' in the fiduciary context, see Neil Stuart Eccles, 'Remarks on Lydenberg's "Reason, Rationality and Fiduciary Duty"' (2018) 151 *Journal of Business Ethics* 55, 57–60.

[147] For the public aspects of shareholder stewardship, see Dionysia Katelouzou, 'Reflections on the Nature of the Public Corporation in an Era of Shareholder Activism and Stewardship' in Barnali Choudhury and Martin Petrin (eds.), *Understanding the Company: Corporate Governance and Theory* (Cambridge University Press 2017), 117–44.

[148] Luca Enriques, Henry Hansmann, Reinier Kraakman, and Mariana Pargendler, 'The Basic Governance Structure: Minority Shareholders and Non-Shareholder Constituencies' in Reinier Kraakman, John Armour, Paul Davies, *et al.* (eds.), *The Anatomy of Corporate Law* (3rd ed., Oxford University Press 2017), 93.

[149] *Report of the World Commission on Environment and Development: Our Common Future* (October 1987) <https://sustainabledevelopment.un.org/content/documents/5987our-common-future.pdf>.

performance and embraces broader public purposes. While sustainability stewards continue to act on behalf of clients and beneficiaries, they also advocate for issues like climate action, labour rights, and responsible corporate behaviour – thereby positioning stewardship as a driver of systemic change.

The motivations for sustainability stewardship may be intrinsic, extrinsic, or both. Intrinsically motivated stewards are driven by ethical convictions and a sense of responsibility for the societal and environmental impacts of their investment decisions.[150] These actors – further explored in Chapter 7 as sustainability-oriented stewards – demonstrate a convergence between motivation and relationship: they act both for systemic stakeholders and because of a values-based conviction.[151] This alignment is often evident in the public stewardship statements of large asset managers and other institutional investors, who tie sustainability principles to fiduciary commitments.[152]

Extrinsic motivations, by contrast, are shaped by evolving regulatory, contractual, and reputational pressures. These include compliance with stewardship codes and sustainability disclosure regulations, adherence to client mandates, and growing expectations from stakeholders and civil society.[153] In addition, risk mitigation and the identification of long-term market opportunities further incentivise sustainability-oriented behaviour.[154] Regardless of what drives them, sustainability stewards direct their efforts outward – seeking to shape real-world outcomes consistent with broader public interest.

[150] However, sustainability stewardship is not synonymous with impact investing which typically targets specific positive environmental or social outcomes with a high degree of both intentionality and additionality.

[151] Section 7.5.

[152] Section 6.6.3.1.

[153] For instance, within the EU, the Sustainable Finance Disclosure Regulation (SFDR) and the Taxonomy Regulation impose mandatory disclosure requirements on institutional investors. See Regulation (EU) 2019/2088 of the European Parliament and of the Council of 27 November 2019 on sustainability-related disclosures in the financial services sector, Official Journal of the European Union no. L 317 of 12 December 2019, p. 1 and Regulation (EU) 2020/852 of the European Parliament and of the Council of 18 June 2020 on the establishment of a framework to facilitate sustainable investment, and amending Regulation (EU) 2019/2088, Official Journal, No. L 198 of June 22nd 2020, p. 13.

[154] Generally on the demand side of the market for stewardship, see Dionysia Katelouzou and Eva Micheler, 'Investor Capitalism, Sustainable Investment and the Role of Tax Relief' (2022) 23 *European Business Organization Law Review* 217.

4.4.3 The Enlightened Investor Steward: Navigating Plural Accountability

The four stewardship relationships – client, end-investor, asset, and sustainability – are not isolated or sequential. They intersect, overlap, and at times compete, generating tensions, trade-offs, and ambiguities in how institutional investors understand and discharge their responsibilities. Asset managers, particularly those acting on behalf of asset owners in delegated structures, frequently operate across all four dimensions. In doing so, they position themselves as *enlightened investor stewards* – actors who must navigate a pluralistic landscape of accountability.

Enlightened investor stewardship is not defined by the simultaneous or uniform performance of all roles. Rather, it entails the capacity to recognise, balance, and mediate between overlapping responsibilities – guided as much by 'values' as by 'value'.[155] In delegated relationships, this means prioritising the interests of proximate clients and beneficiaries, thereby fulfilling the role of a *client steward*, while also attending to the interests of *end-investors* beyond the immediate relationship. At the same time, it entails safeguarding the long-term resilience and performance of investable assets as an *asset steward*, while remaining responsive to systemic environmental, social, and economic risks that engage *sustainability stewardship*.

Crucially, enlightened investor stewardship does not require systemic concerns to override mandated responsibilities – whether fiduciary, contractual, or regulatory – or financial performance metrics. Instead, it calls for a more principled deliberation of competing interests and temporal claims. Here, Licht's reconceptualisation of the fiduciary duty of impartiality becomes instructive. Traditionally seen as a requirement to treat multiple legal beneficiaries fairly, Licht extends this idea to encompass not only present but also future beneficiaries, and to consider fairness across dimensions of time and interest.[156]

Applied to the stewardship context, this expanded understanding of impartiality offers a useful normative lens. Although end-investors, investee assets, and broader societal stakeholders are not formal legal beneficiaries of institutional investors, their interests are increasingly affected by investment

[155] On the difference between 'values' and 'value', see Laura T. Starks, 'Presidential Address: Sustainable Finance and ESG Issues – Value versus Values' (2023) 78 *The Journal of Finance* 1837.

[156] Amir N. Licht, 'Stakeholder Impartiality: A New Classic Approach for the Objectives of the Corporation' in Arthur B. Laby and Jacob Hale Russell (eds.), *Fiduciary Obligations in Business* (Cambridge University Press 2021), 301–17.

decisions. Enlightened investor stewardship, then, requires institutional investors to deliberate upon and justify how they weigh these competing interests – even if only some hold legal standing. This is not merely a technical balancing act but also a reasoned process of prioritisation and justification in which investor stewards must demonstrate how their decisions reflect the layered and interdependent responsibilities they hold.

For example, addressing climate change may involve active engagement with high-emission firms – even at the expense of short-term returns – if such engagement helps mitigate systemic risks and preserve long-term portfolio value.[157] Similarly, promoting governance reform or social equity may not align with immediate financial benchmarks but can yield enduring benefits for portfolios and stakeholders alike. These choices demand justificatory reasoning that reflects stewardship's multi-relational nature.

This deliberative approach also aligns with the universal owner thesis, which holds that large, diversified investors – whose financial performance is tied to the long-term health of the global economy – have incentives to internalise systemic risks that cannot be diversified away.[158] From this perspective, investor stewardship is not only a fiduciary function but also a public responsibility: a means of preserving financial system stability and long-term societal well-being.

Importantly, enlightened investor stewardship does not reject investor duties. Instead, it reinterprets them in light of twenty-first century realities. It acknowledges that short-term financial imperatives and long-term sustainability goals are often in tension – but insists that these tensions must be actively negotiated rather than ignored. The enlightened investor steward meets this challenge by embedding sustainability within core investment practices while maintaining accountability to proximate clients and beneficiaries.

[157] For empirical evidence supporting engagement as a mechanism to improve long-term performance over the long-term even if short-term returns are sacrificed, see Robert G. Eccles, Michael P. Krzus, Jean Rogers, and George Serafeim, 'The Need for Sector-Specific Materiality and Sustainability Reporting Standards' (2012) 24 *Journal of Applied Corporate Finance* 65; Elroy Dimson, Oğuzhan Karakaş, and Xi Li, 'Active Ownership' (2015) 28 *The Review of Financial Studies* 3225.

[158] James Hawley and Andrew Williams, 'The Emergence of Fiduciary Capitalism' (1997) 5 *Corporate Governance: An International Review* 206; Ellen Quigley, *Universal Ownership in the Anthropocene* (2019) <https://ssrn.com/abstract=3457205>, 31 (favouring a 'duty of expansion', that is 'the duty of Universal Owners to extend participation to communities and regions of the world currently underrepresented among large institutional investors'). For a criticism of the theory of universal owners, see Benjamin J. Richardson and Maziar Peihani, 'Universal Investors and Socially Responsible Finance: A Critique of a Premature Theory' (2015) 30 *Banking & Finance Law Review* 405.

In operational terms, enlightened investor stewardship reflects the dual purpose of institutional investors: they must deliver financial returns while also serving as allocators of capital in ways that shape environmental and social outcomes. Whether articulated through sustainability mandates, systemic risk oversight, fiduciary reform, or rights-based approaches, these evolving orientations converge on a common goal: to embed broader accountability within the institutional architecture of investment.

What ultimately defines the enlightened investor steward is not the exhaustive fulfilment of every stewardship function, but the judgement, deliberative capacity, and flexibility required to reconcile multiple, and sometimes conflicting, imperatives – reaffirming stewardship as both a strategic practice and a normative commitment.

4.5 Conclusion: Towards an Enlightened Investor Stewardship Ecosystem

This chapter has demonstrated that investor stewardship cannot be reduced to a simple agent–principal dyad or confined to a single set of legal or regulatory duties. Instead, it unfolds within a multi-layered ecosystem composed of distinct but interconnected stewardship relationships – client, end-investor, asset, and sustainability stewardship. Each layer carries its own expectations, accountability frameworks, and normative underpinnings, shaped by a mix of legal, contractual, and informal obligations. These relationships frequently intersect, and sometimes conflict, producing a governance terrain marked by structural complexity and normative pluralism.[159]

To navigate this fragmented and dynamic landscape, the chapter introduced the concept of the *enlightened investor steward* – a pluralistic figure who balances competing responsibilities with contextual judgement. Enlightened investor stewardship does not require the simultaneous fulfilment of all stewardship roles, but rather the capacity to reconcile tensions across them: acting in the best interests of proximate clients and beneficiaries, preserving the long-term value of investable assets, and responding to systemic risks that implicate the broader economy, environment, and society.

[159] See generally Colin Scott, 'Regulation in the Age of Governance: The Rise of the Post-Regulatory State' in Jacint Jordana and David Levi-Faur (eds.), *The Politics of Regulation* (Edward Elgar 2004), 145–74; Julia Black, 'Constructing and Contesting Legitimacy and Accountability in Polycentric Regulatory Regimes' (2008) 2 *Regulation & Governance* 137; Ralf Michaels, 'Global Legal Pluralism' (2009) 5 *Annual Review of Law & Social Science* 1.

This broader vision resonates with earlier insights from public policy and regulatory debates. For instance, the UK's Wilson Committee in the 1980 observed that institutional investors – due to the broad base of their policyholders – are 'inescapably tied to the economy as a whole'.[160] Such recognition has gradually begun to influence regulatory thinking. The Final Report of the Company Law Review Steering Group called for enhanced institutional investor oversight, improved transparency, and stronger mechanisms of accountability – arguing that shareholder influence must serve, rather than undermine, the public interest and sustainable corporate governance.[161]

In the aftermath of the global financial crisis of 2007–09, this agenda gained renewed urgency. The crisis exposed the fragility of financialised capitalism and underscored the risks of short-termism embedded within intermediary-led investment chains. In response, new discourses around responsible investment, ESG integration, and impact investing emerged.[162] In this evolving paradigm, investor stewardship becomes more than a mechanism of shareholder oversight; it offers a way to embed broader accountability into the institutional architecture of finance. Institutional investors are no longer viewed solely as agents of private wealth but increasingly as stewards of shared economic, social, and ecological futures.

The next chapter turns to the regulatory infrastructures – especially the UK Stewardship Code – that seek to institutionalise these evolving responsibilities. It examines how the normative foundations of investor stewardship are being constructed, contested, and operationalised within national and transnational regulatory spaces.

[160] Committee to Review the Functioning of Financial Institutions (Wilson Committee), *Report* (Cmnd 7937, 1980), para 12.39.

[161] The Company Law Review Steering Group, *Modern Company Law for a Competitive Economy: Final Report* (2001), paras. 1.57, 3.53 and 3.54.

[162] Steve Lydenberg, 'Reason, Rationality, and Fiduciary Duty' (2014) 119 *Journal of Business Ethics* 365, 369–71.

5

Regulating Stewardship The UK Stewardship Code and the Expansion of Normative Ambitions

5.1 Introduction

The UK has long played a pioneering role in the global evolution of shareholder – and more broadly, investor – stewardship. This leadership did not arise from grassroots shareholder activism, but from a distinctive model of financial intermediation in which institutional investors act on behalf of pensioners, savers, and other ultimate beneficiaries of investment capital. It was further shaped by a supportive regulatory environment, a tradition of soft-law governance, and public policy debates that positioned institutional investors as stewards of both financial and societal outcomes. Although this model is not unique to the UK, the British approach stands out for how it has been formalised through stewardship codes and increasingly robust regulatory oversight. In this context, institutional investors have supplanted individual shareholders as the primary agents of corporate influence, operating within a governance system defined by intricate chains of delegation and evolving norms of accountability. This transformation was propelled by broader political and economic shifts, including the expansion of shareholder democracy – as promoted through Thatcher-era privatisations and mass share ownership schemes – and the consolidation of institutional ownership in the decades that followed.[1]

Before public regulators became formally involved, stewardship in the UK was largely a product of investor-led initiatives – most notably the efforts of the Institutional Shareholders' Committee (ISC). Throughout the 1990s and 2000s, the ISC issued a series of best-practice statements that played a foundational role in articulating institutional investor responsibilities and developing the stewardship lexicon later adopted by regulators.

This chapter traces the formative role of the ISC in shaping the UK's stewardship framework and examines its institutional legacy in

[1] Sections 1.1 and 2.5.

the first-generation UK Stewardship Code (1G UK Code), introduced by the Financial Reporting Council (FRC) in 2010 and revised in 2012.[2] It explores the transition from market-led self-regulation to regulator-led oversight, and follows the conceptual evolution of stewardship: from activism to engagement, from engagement to stewardship, and most recently, from client-centric stewardship to an expanded model of other-regarding accountability.

This normative trajectory reaches its most ambitious expression in the second-generation UK Stewardship Code (2G UK Code), introduced in 2020.[3] Representing a decisive shift in both scope and purpose, the 2G UK Code redefines stewardship as the responsible allocation, management, and oversight of capital to create sustainable value for clients and beneficiaries, while also generating positive outcomes for the economy, environment, and society. Extending its remit beyond equities to all asset classes, the 2G UK Code places integration, systemic risk, and public purpose at the core of stewardship, and replaces the earlier comply-or-explain model with a more rigorous, apply-and-explain regime focused on demonstrable outcomes.

Finally, the chapter reflects on the global diffusion of the UK model – particularly the widespread adoption of the 1G UK Code's 'seven principles' across more than 20 jurisdictions. Frequently hailed as the international 'gold standard', the 1G UK Code has catalysed the transnationalisation of stewardship norms, transforming investor responsibility into a cornerstone of global financial governance. While the 2G UK Code signals a bold new direction, the foundational architecture built by the ISC and institutionalised in the 1G UK Code continues to shape how stewardship is understood, institutionalised, and exported around the world.

5.2 Early Investor-Led Stewardship: The Legacy of the Institutional Shareholders' Committee

5.2.1 *From Proprietors to Stewards: The 1991 ISC Statement in the Shadow of Cadbury*

The shift from viewing shareholders as proprietors to recognising them as stewards began to take shape through a series of investor-led initiatives in

[2] Financial Reporting Council, *The UK Stewardship Code 2010* (2010) [UK Code 2010]; Financial Reporting Council, *The UK Stewardship Code 2012* (2012) [UK Code 2012].

[3] Financial Reporting Council, *The UK Stewardship Code 2020* (2019) [UK Code 2020].

the 1990s.[4] These efforts sought to strengthen the relationship between shareholders and public companies and laid the groundwork for what later evolved into formal stewardship codes.[5] The original aim was to promote more effective shareholder engagement as a means of improving long-term returns and supporting the efficient functioning of capital markets.

The origins of UK shareholder stewardship policy can be traced back to the early 1990s – although the concept was then framed in different terms. A pivotal role in these early developments was played by the now-defunct ISC, established in 1972 at the behest of the Bank of England following the bankruptcy and nationalisation of Rolls-Royce. This initiative reflected the government's broader aim to strengthen institutional investor relationships with public companies.[6] The ISC was supported by the four major UK institutional investors' associations of the time: the National Association of Pension Funds and the associations (then separate) representing investment trusts, unit trusts, and insurers.[7]

The ISC's founding mission was 'to co-ordinate and extend existing investment protection activities of institutional investors with a view, where this is judged necessary, to stimulating action by industrial and commercial companies to improve efficiency'.[8] However, during the 1970s, the ISC's impact was limited. UK institutional investors remained largely reluctant to engage directly with company management, and stewardship – as it is now understood – has not yet taken root.[9] Nonetheless, by the 1980s and into the 1990s, the ISC gradually evolved into a key platform for the early development of shareholder governance practices. Its growing influence laid the foundation for what would later become the UK's robust and codified stewardship regime.

[4] See also Sections 2.6 and 3.6.

[5] On the distinction between preliminary stewardship initiatives and stewardship codes, see Dionysia Katelouzou and Mathias Siems, 'The Global Diffusion of Stewardship Codes' in Dan W. Puchniak and Dionysia Katelouzou (eds.), *Global Shareholder Stewardship* (Cambridge University Press 2022), 634–5.

[6] On the creation of the ISC, see Aled Davies, *The City of London and Social Democracy: The Political Economy of Finance in Britain, 1959 – 1979* (Oxford Academic, Oxford University Press 2017), 45–52.

[7] The Investment Management Association (IMA) originated in 1993 from the merger of the Association of Trusts and Investment Funds and the Fund Managers Association. Later, in 2014 the Association of British Insurers' Investment Affairs Division merged into the IMA, which in 2015 rebranded as The Investment Association.

[8] Davies, *The City of London and Social Democracy: The Political Economy of Finance in Britain*, 1959–1979, 50.

[9] Ibid., 51. On the passivity of UK institutional investors over this period, see Section 2.3.

In 1991 – one year prior to the publication of the landmark Cadbury Report – the ISC issued a statement setting out non-binding best practices for the responsibilities of institutional shareholders.[10] Though less detailed than the stewardship codes that would follow, the 1991 ISC Statement marked a turning point. It articulated the role of institutional shareholders in corporate governance and urged them to act as 'true proprietors' by using their influence to promote sound corporate governance in their investee companies.[11] In doing so, the 1991 ISC Statement revived long-standing, ownership-based justifications for shareholder governance, reflecting the image of the 'Engaged Shareholder'.[12] This early articulation laid important conceptual foundations for the later formalisation of stewardship codes in the UK.

The statement set out nine principles aimed at strengthening corporate governance through more engaged and responsible shareholding. Its focus was squarely on improving board accountability by encouraging institutional investors to promote dialogue with company directors, exercise voting rights, influence board composition, scrutinise executive remuneration, and assess takeover offers with care and independence. By placing shareholder engagement at the centre of institutional investors' responsibilities, the 1991 ISC Statement aligned closely with the objectives of the forthcoming Cadbury Report, which similarly sought to enhance the effectiveness and accountability of corporate boards. The Cadbury Committee explicitly endorsed the ISC's approach, and the two documents together laid the conceptual and normative foundations for the UK's subsequent corporate governance and stewardship codes – each helping to clarify and institutionalise the respective roles of boards and shareholders in the governance of listed companies.[13]

At the same time, the 1991 ISC Statement acknowledged that institutional investors must prioritise their 'fiduciary responsibility to those on whose behalf they are investing'.[14] While it did not specify who exactly constituted this group, the language suggests an early awareness of what this book has referred to as *client stewardship* – the idea that stewardship involves not only

[10] 'Appendix: "The Responsibilities of Institutional Shareholders in the UK"' (1992) 1 *Business Ethics: A European Review* 199 (hereinafter the 1991 ISC Statement).

[11] Ibid.

[12] Section 3.5.1.

[13] The Committee on the Financial Aspects of Corporate Governance, *Report of the Committee on the Financial Aspects of Corporate Governance* (1992) 4.59, 6.11, 6.12, and 6.16.

[14] Appendix: 'The Responsibilities of Institutional Shareholders in the UK', 201.

monitoring corporate governance but also serving the long-term interests of the proximate clients and beneficiaries.[15] Although the primary emphasis was on firm-level monitoring, this fiduciary framing embedded shareholder engagement within a broader architecture of accountability across the investment chain. This dual orientation – towards corporate governance and fiduciary responsibility – would become a defining feature of the UK's evolving stewardship regime in the decades that followed.

5.2.2 *From Activism to Engagement: The 2002–2007 ISC Principles*

In 2002 – just over a decade later after its initial statement – the ISC revised its guidelines in response to mounting regulatory scrutiny and market pressures, spurred by corporate failures such as the Enron scandal.[16] One key driver behind this revision was the 2001 Myners Review, which recommended imposing a statutory duty on asset managers to intervene in companies through voting or other engagement mechanisms.[17] This suggestion likely spurred institutional investors to reinforce self-regulatory efforts in a bid to pre-empt formal regulation.[18]

The 2002 ISC Statement – followed by largely unchanged updates in 2005 and 2007 – set out five core principles delineating the responsibilities of both 'institutional shareholders' and their 'agents'. At the time, 'institutional shareholders' was the preferred term, broadly defined to include pension funds, insurance companies, investment trusts, and other collective investment vehicles. Their 'agents' referred to investment managers to whom stewardship responsibilities were commonly delegated.[19] This framing reflected the double agency framework, which emphasises the accountability of investment managers (as agents) to their institutional clients for implementing engagement strategies.[20]

[15] Section 4.3.2.2.

[16] On the regulatory responses in the US, UK, and EU following Enron, see contributions to John Armour and Joseph A. McCahery (eds.), *After Enron: Improving Corporate Law and Modernising Securities Regulation in Europe and the US* (Hart 2006).

[17] Paul Myners, *Institutional Investment in the United Kingdom: A Review* (2001), 14 and 93.

[18] On self-regulation in general, see Robert Baldwin, Martin Cave and Martin Lodge, *Understanding Regulation: Theory, Strategy, and Practice* (Oxford Academic, Oxford University Press 2011), Chapter 8.

[19] Institutional Shareholders' Committee, *The Responsibilities of Institutional Shareholders and Agents – Statement of Principles* (2002), 1; Institutional Shareholders' Committee, *The Responsibilities of Institutional Shareholders and Agents – Statement of Principles* (2005), 1; Institutional Shareholders' Committee, *The Responsibilities of Institutional Shareholders and Agents – Statement of Principles* (2007), 1.

[20] Section 4.2.3.

Yet, the terminology of 'institutional shareholders' was conceptually imprecise. Under UK company law, it is generally the investment managers – not the asset owners – who are the legal shareholders, vested with voting rights and the ability to engage with investee companies. This disjunction exposed a structural tension: those labelled 'shareholders' may neither hold legal title to shares nor exercise shareholder rights directly. Still, the ISC's use of this term signalled an emerging recognition of stewardship as a layered and delegated function – one shaped by the complex relationships between asset owners, their agents, and investee firms.

The first principle called for the establishment of a publicly available policy outlining the institutional investor's approach to engagement.[21] This policy was to include mechanisms for monitoring investee companies, initiating and sustaining dialogue, managing conflicts of interest, deciding when to intervene, and exercising voting rights. Regular review and ongoing monitoring of investee companies' performance were emphasised, with a particular focus on early issue identification and effective dialogue as tools to protect and enhance shareholder value.[22]

Where concerns emerged – whether strategic, operational, or governance-related – the ISC principles emphasised that institutional shareholders and/or their agents, acting in the best financial interests of their beneficiaries or clients, should be prepared to intervene.[23] Such intervention was to be informed and supported by clearly defined escalation procedures, and not contingent on investment style or portfolio weightings; even those with a passive approach or underweight positions were expected to act where necessary. Potential triggers for intervention included issues such as weak corporate strategy, underperformance, acquisition or disposal decisions, failures in board oversight or internal controls, inadequate succession planning, excessive executive remuneration, or deficient approaches to corporate social responsibility.

A tiered approach to intervention was encouraged, beginning with private engagement – such as additional meetings with management or with the chair, senior independent director, or all independent directors. If concerns persisted, shareholders were expected to escalate action by engaging collaboratively with other investors, expressing concern through the company's advisers, or making public statements ahead of shareholder

[21] Section 2 of the ISC Statements of 2002, 2005 and 2007.
[22] Section 3 of the ISC Statements of 2002, 2005 and 2007.
[23] Section 4 of the ISC Statements of 2002, 2005 and 2007.

meetings. More assertive steps could include submitting shareholder resolutions or requisitioning an extraordinary general meeting to initiate governance changes. Crucially, institutional shareholders and/or their agents were expected to vote all shares held on behalf of clients wherever possible and to withhold support for the board if dialogue failed to yield satisfactory results. In such cases, best practice entailed informing the company of the intended vote and the reasons behind it. Furthermore, they were expected to assess and report on the outcomes of their engagement, balancing transparency with confidentiality to ensure constructive outcomes.[24]

A notable linguistic shift occurred between the 2002 ISC Statement and its 2005 and 2007 iterations: the term *activism* – used in the 2002 version – was replaced by the term *engagement*. In the context of the 2002 statement, activism did not carry the adversarial connotations typically associated with hedge-fund-style interventions.[25] Instead, it was presented as a responsible, fiduciary-driven process grounded in ongoing monitoring and the expectation to intervene where necessary. This conception of activism encompassed a graduated spectrum of actions, from informal oversight and dialogue to more formal mechanisms such as voting, public signalling, and shareholder resolutions. The legitimacy of this approach was reinforced by the Higgs Review, which endorsed the ISC's 'code of activism' and recommended its inclusion in the Combined Code on Corporate Governance, lending further institutional support to activism as a constructive element of shareholder oversight.[26]

The later adoption of the term engagement signalled a strategic reframing rather than a substantive shift in expectations. While the underlying principles remained largely consistent, engagement conveyed a more collaborative and less confrontational tone, aligning more closely with the relational ethos of emerging stewardship discourse. This shift in language also served to broaden the appeal of the ISC principles, making them more accessible to a wider range of institutional investors, including those with passive strategies or more traditional governance philosophies. By presenting stewardship as a spectrum of constructive practices rather than a narrowly activist role, the ISC created space for a more inclusive and adaptable stewardship framework.

Despite the change in terminology, the five core principles remained largely consistent across the 2002, 2005, and 2007 ISC Statements,

[24] Section 5 of the ISC Statements of 2002, 2005 and 2007.

[25] Section 3.2.2.

[26] Derek Higgs, *Review of the Role and Effectiveness of Non-executive Directors* (2003), para 15.24.

indicating that the shift from activism to engagement was more rhetorical than substantive. Interestingly, neither the 1991 ISC Statement nor its later iterations explicitly used the term *stewardship*, even though each set out best practices for institutional investors acting as shareholders of UK-listed companies. All four statements explicitly acknowledged the duty of institutional shareholders and their agents to prioritise the interests of their proximate clients and beneficiaries, stating unambiguously that "[t]he duty of institutional shareholders and agents is to end beneficiaries and not to the wider public".[27] This framing underscores the narrow client-centric orientation of early UK stewardship thinking, with little reference to broader, public-oriented or other-regarding notions of stewardship.

The ISC statements placed strong emphasis on shareholder oversight and company-level engagement, anticipating key elements of what would later be formalised as asset stewardship.[28] This focus reflected the investor-led nature of the ISC initiatives, which prioritised the role of institutional investors in monitoring corporate governance and holding boards to account. Their primary concern was to ensure that institutional investors discharged their responsibilities as stewards of clients' capital – within a framework shaped by fiduciary and contractual duties – not to advance broader social or environmental goals. The underlying orientation was resolutely shareholder-centric, guided by prevailing legal and market norms. Yet, in consistently affirming the outward-facing responsibilities of institutional investors in relation to investee companies, the ISC laid important conceptual foundations for the more structured, code-based approach to stewardship that would emerge in the following decade.

5.2.3 The ISC Code 2009: From Shareholder Engagement to Stewardship

In 2009, the ISC's guidance – previously issued under the title '*The Responsibilities of Institutional Shareholders and Agents – Statement of Principles*' – underwent a significant transformation in both form and substance. It was rebranded as the '*Code on the Responsibilities of Institutional Investors*' and adopted the well-established *comply-or-explain* framework, mirroring the approach used in the UK Corporate Governance Code.[29] Under this model, institutional investors were expected either to

[27] 2002 ISC Statement, 2; 2005 ISC Statement, 2; 2007 ISC Statement, 2.

[28] Section 4.4.1.

[29] The ISC Code on the Responsibilities of Institutional Investors (hereinafter ISC Code 2009) is available as Appendix B at Financial Reporting Council, *Consultation on*

adhere to the Code's principles or to provide a public explanation for any deviations, thereby promoting transparency and accountability.[30] By framing the document as a 'code' and aligning it with the comply-or-explain approach, the ISC signalled a more formalised and structured commitment to good governance, aiming to demonstrate proactive self-regulation and forestall more prescriptive regulatory interventions.

A further shift in terminology saw the emergence of *institutional investors* as an umbrella term encompassing both 'institutional shareholders' (such as pension funds, insurers, investment trusts, and other collective investment vehicles) and their appointed 'agents'.[31] While this linguistic consolidation aimed to streamline the regulatory audience under a single label, it did not resolve the underlying conceptual and legal distinctions between asset owners and their delegates. On the one hand, the adoption of the term institutional investors signals a shift towards collective accountability, acknowledging the interdependent roles of asset owners and managers in fulfilling stewardship functions. On the other hand, the continued use of institutional shareholders and agents – terms that are legally imprecise – reaffirms the principal–agent logic at the heart of fiduciary relationships, in which investment managers act on behalf of clients and beneficiaries. This dual usage thus reflects a deeper conceptual tension: between evolving normative expectations of shared responsibility and the legal and operational realities of delegation that characterise the modern investment chain.

Content-wise, the ISC Code 2009 marked a significant conceptual evolution with the formal adoption of the term stewardship, replacing the earlier language of engagement (used in the 2002, 2005, and 2007 ISC Statements) and activism (used in the 2002 version). This shift in terminology was likely intentional, signalling a broader and more integrated view of institutional investors' responsibilities. Whereas engagement and activism typically referred to direct interactions with company management – ranging from dialogue to more assertive interventions – stewardship evoked the idea of long-term,

a Stewardship Code for Institutional Investors (January 2010), www.frc.org.uk/documents/6299/Consultation_on_a_Stewardship_Code_for_Institutional_Investors.pdf.

30 Ibid., 25. For a critical discussion of the limitations of the comply-or-explain model, see Iain MacNeil and Xiao Li, '"Comply or Explain": market discipline and non-compliance with the Combined Code' (2006) 14 *Corporate Governance: An International Review* 486; John Roberts, Paul Sanderson and David Seidl, 'The UK Corporate Governance Code Principle of "Comply or Explain": Understanding Code Compliance as "Subjection"' (2020) 56 *Abacus* 602.

31 ISC Code 2009, Introduction & Scope.

responsible oversight, encompassing both corporate governance relationships and the careful management of entrusted capital on behalf of others.

The ISC Code 2009 articulated seven principles designed to guide institutional investors in fulfilling their stewardship responsibilities. Several of these principles echoed prior ISC statements – for example, public disclosure of stewardship policies (Principle 1), ongoing monitoring of investee companies (Principle 3), the escalation of concerns (Principle 4), and periodic reporting on stewardship activities (Principle 7). However, the ISC Code 2009 also introduced new provisions in response to shifting regulatory expectations. These included the requirement to develop and disclose a policy on managing conflicts of interest (Principle 2), a strengthened emphasis on collective engagement (Principle 5), and clearer guidance on voting policy and the disclosure of voting records (Principle 6).

The inclusion of a separate principle on conflicts of interest is particularly noteworthy and resonates with the emerging adoption of the stewardship concept. It reflects the dual expectations placed on institutional investors: on the one hand, to act in the best interests of their proximate clients and beneficiaries (client stewardship), and on the other, to exercise informed and responsible oversight of investee companies (asset stewardship). Nonetheless, as with its predecessors, the ISC Code 2009 reaffirms that the primary duty of institutional investors remains owed to their proximate clients and beneficiaries, rather than to the broader public – thereby reasserting the continued primacy of fiduciary and other legal obligations within the stewardship framework.[32]

Together, these developments represented a meaningful broadening and formalisation of institutional investor responsibilities, laying important groundwork for what would become the UK Stewardship Code. The ISC Code 2009 reflects a more developed understanding of stewardship as encompassing both *outward-facing* responsibilities towards corporate governance and *inward-facing* obligations to proximate clients and beneficiaries. Traditional tools of shareholder oversight – such as monitoring, escalation, and voting – are positioned alongside principles addressing conflicts of interest and transparency. In this way, the ISC Code 2009 implicitly affirms the dual character of investor stewardship: as both a mechanism for promoting effective corporate governance and a framework for fulfilling the legal, contractual, and regulatory responsibilities that institutional investors owe within the investment chain.

[32] See also Section 4.3.2.2.

Yet despite this expanded framework, the fundamental logic of the earlier ISC statements remained intact. These early-stage, investor-led frameworks shared a common aim: to rouse institutional investors from a historically passive stance and position them as vigilant 'monitors' in their role as shareholders. In this context, monitoring did not imply micro-managing investee companies or eliminating the option to divest but rather promoted informed oversight and responsible use of shareholder rights.

In line with this approach, the ISC Code 2009 reaffirmed that the core purpose of stewardship was to protect and enhance shareholder value. Principle 3, which focused on monitoring, encouraged early identification of risks to preserve shareholder value, while Principle 4 explicitly described escalation as 'a method of protecting and enhancing shareholder value'. Thus, stewardship – as framed in the ISC Codes – was not conceived as a public interest mandate, but as a mechanism for safeguarding the financial interests of clients and beneficiaries.

This orientation was emblematic of the ISC's broader regulatory posture throughout the 2000s – a model of 'regulated autonomy' that sought to fortify investor-led standards in response to growing external pressures.[33] Like the 2002 revisions, the ISC Code 2009 aimed to demonstrate institutional accountability and promote effective shareholder engagement through a voluntary, principles-based structure designed to forestall more prescriptive legal interventions.

5.3 Regulator-Led Stewardship: The FRC and the Two Generations of the UK Stewardship Code

5.3.1 The First-Generation UK Stewardship Code (2010/12): Building a Market for Engagement

The turning point in the evolution of UK stewardship policy came with the 2009 Walker Review on corporate governance in UK banks, which criticised institutional investors for their passive response during the global financial crisis of 2007–09. Highlighting a failure of shareholder oversight, the review called for a cultural shift – from disengaged ownership to active stewardship – and recommended the establishment of 'a code of shareholder stewardship'.[34] This recommendation catalysed the

[33] John Holland, 'Self-regulation and the financial aspects of corporate governance' (1996) *Journal of Business Law* 127, 129.

[34] David Walker, *A Review of Corporate Governance in UK Banks and Other Financial Industry Entities: Final Recommendations* (2009) 707, 17, 70.

transition from industry-led to regulator-led stewardship, culminating in the launch of the UK Stewardship Code by the FRC in July 2010.[35]

Rooted in the ISC Code 2009, the UK Stewardship Code 2010 (UK Code 2010) built directly on investor-driven principles while placing them under formal public oversight.[36] In line with the Walker Review's recommendations, the FRC assumed responsibility for the Code – signalling a shift in the UK's regulatory architecture and marking a move towards more structured and transparent stewardship expectations of institutional investors.

Reflecting the UK's long-standing preference for 'market-invoking' regulation,[37] particularly in financial services, the UK Code 2010 retained close alignment with market norms regarding the role of institutional investors. Its transformation from the ISC's voluntary principles into a soft-law instrument overseen by a public regulator exemplifies 'enforced self-regulation',[38] otherwise referred to as 'meta-regulation'[39] – a defining feature of the UK's evolving, market-oriented governance landscape and its long-standing reliance on soft corporate governance codes.

Faithful to the spirit of both the ISC's earlier principles and its 2009 Code, the UK Code 2010 framed shareholder stewardship as a means to 'enhance the quality of engagement between institutional investors and companies to help improve long-term returns to shareholders and the efficient exercise of governance responsibilities'.[40] It translated this vision into seven high-level principles – substantively carried over from the ISC Code 2009 – with

35 Financial Reporting Council, *The UK Stewardship Code* (July 2010) [UK Code 2010], <www.frc.org.uk/getattachment/e223e152-5515-4cdc-a951-da33e093eb28/UK-Stewardship-Code-July-2010.pdf>.

36 In its consultation preceding the introduction of the UK Stewardship Code, the FRC recognised the ISC 2009 Code as a 'good starting point' for the UK Code and included it in Appendix B. See Financial Reporting Council, *Consultation on a Stewardship Code for Institutional Investors* 5, 25–30.

37 But this market-invoking, principles-based corporate governance regulation is not the norm everywhere, such as in the US. See e.g. Dionysia Katelouzou and Peer Zumbansen, 'The Transnationalization of Corporate Governance; Law, Institutional Arrangements, & Corporate Power' (2021) 38 *Arizona Journal of International and Comparative Law* 1 (arguing that private ordering in corporate governance must be seen in the context of the fundamental transformation of the political economy brought about by the last twenty or more years of globalisation).

38 John Braithwaite, 'Enforced Self-Regulation: A New Strategy for Corporate Crime Control' (1981) 80 *Michigan Law Review* 1466.

39 Cary Coglianese and Evan Mendelson, 'Meta-Regulation and Self-Regulation' in Robert Baldwin, Martin Cave and Martin Lodge (eds.), *The Oxford Handbook of Regulation* (Oxford Academic, Oxford University Press 2010), 146–168.

40 UK Code 2010, 1.

modest refinements in language and framing. These principles addressed the public disclosure of stewardship policies (Principle 1); management of conflicts of interest (Principle 2); monitoring of investee companies (Principle 3); escalation of concerns (Principle 4); collective engagement (Principle 5); voting policies and disclosure of voting activity (Principle 6); and periodic reporting on stewardship and voting outcomes (Principle 7).

Although the UK Code 2010 also addressed aspects of transparency within internal investment processes and business models,[41] its central objective – consistent with the ISC's earlier approach – was to enhance the effectiveness of institutional investor engagement with investee companies. In doing so, it aimed to counter concerns about market short-termism and to respond to critiques, emerging in the aftermath of the global financial crisis of 2007–09, that institutional investors had failed to hold corporate boards accountable. More broadly, it reflected a regulatory effort to safeguard shareholder rights from erosion – particularly by demonstrating that those rights could be exercised responsibly and effectively, as underscored by the FRC's leadership at the time.[42] At the core of this approach was a broad conception of shareholder engagement, as encompassing 'purposeful dialogue on strategy, performance and the management of risk, as well as on issues that are the immediate subject of votes at general meetings'.[43]

However, this formulation of stewardship – centred on shareholder rights and firm-level engagement – soon came under pressure. The UK Stewardship Code 2010 had a relatively short lifespan, as growing concerns about the broader dynamics of the investment chain prompted calls for reform. Chief among these was the Kay Review, which offered a trenchant critique of prevailing investment practices and called for a more embedded stewardship culture across the equity investment system.[44] The Review argued that the structure of the investment chain encouraged fragmentation and short-term behaviours, impeding effective oversight.[45] Among others, it highlighted the weak transmission of

[41] See e.g. UK Code 2010, Principle 2.

[42] Lady Hogg, the then-FRC chairman, stated in 2010: 'If we don't protect shareholder rights the ultimate danger is the drying-up of equity capital and to prevent these rights being overridden by international regulators, shareholders need to be able to demonstrate they're used responsibly and effectively.' Kate Burgess and Miles Johnson, 'FRC Offers Blueprint for Investor Engagement', *Financial Times* (1 July 2010).

[43] UK Code 2010, 1.

[44] John Kay, *The Kay Review of UK Equity Markets and Long-Term Decision Making* (July 2012) 28.

[45] Ibid., 14–21.

stewardship expectations from asset owners to asset managers – especially in cases where asset owners lacked the capacity, expertise, or incentives to hold their agents to account. This accountability gap, it warned, threatened to marginalise the long-term interests of end-investors.

In response, the FRC issued a revised version of the Code in 2012.[46] While the UK Stewardship Code 2012 (UK Code 2012) retained the original seven high-level principles, it significantly expanded the Preface to clarify the content, application, and expectations associated with these principles.[47] Notably, it articulated stewardship as a means not just to improve corporate behaviour but also as a mechanism to enhance 'the functioning of the market for investment mandates' with the ultimate aim of 'enhancing and protecting the value of the ultimate beneficiary or client'.[48] In doing so, the UK Code 2012 sought to foster a more efficient 'market for stewardship', underpinned by the regulatory assumption that asset owners, acting in the interests of their beneficiaries, would demand high-quality stewardship, and that asset managers would, in turn, compete for mandates on the basis of the quality of their stewardship practices.[49]

Despite this expanded conceptual framing, the 2012 Code retained the structural core and substantive emphasis of its 2010 predecessor. Its primary focus remained on corporate governance engagement, and it offered only limited guidance on the internal governance challenges within investment institutions. In this sense, the shift from the 2010 to the 2012 Code was evolutionary rather than transformative. Accordingly, this account treats the two versions as a cohesive whole – referred to here as the 'first-generation' UK Stewardship Code, or simply the 1G UK Code.[50]

Addressed primarily to 'institutional investors' with equity holdings in UK-listed companies,[51] the 1G UK Code distinguishes between two main categories of actors: 'asset owners' – defined as pension funds, insurance companies, investment trusts, and other collective investment vehicles – and

46 Financial Reporting Council, *The UK Stewardship Code* (September 2012) [UK Code 2012], www.frc.org.uk/documents/1528/UK_Stewardship_Code_September_2012.pdf.

47 UK Code 2012, 2–4.

48 UK Code 2012, 2 and Principle 1.

49 See Dionysia Katelouzou and Eva Micheler, 'Investor Capitalism, Sustainable Investment and the Role of Tax Relief' (2022) 23 *European Business Organization Law Review* 217.

50 See also Paul Davies, 'The UK Stewardship Code 2010–2020: From Saving the Company to Saving the Planet?' in Dionysia Katelouzou and Dan W. Puchniak (eds.), *Global Shareholder Stewardship* (Cambridge University Press 2022), 44 (referring to the 2010 and 2012 versions together as the 'first version' of the UK Stewardship Code).

51 UK Code 2012, 2.

'asset managers', who carry out day-to-day investment decisions.[52] Although asset managers play an essential role in operationalising stewardship, the Code makes clear that the responsibility does not lie with them alone. Asset owners are expected to 'set the tone for stewardship' and to hold their managers accountable for the quality and effectiveness of their stewardship activities.[53] Even where stewardship is outsourced – whether to asset managers or third-party providers – asset owners 'remain responsible for ensuring those activities are carried out in a manner consistent with their own approach to stewardship'.[54] In this spirit, the 1G UK Code also extends its expectations to service providers, such as proxy advisors and investment consultants, urging alignment with its principles where relevant.[55]

This formulation built on a terminological shift already evident in the ISC Code 2009, which had adopted 'institutional investors' as an umbrella term encompassing both 'institutional shareholders' and their 'agents'. The 1G UK Code retained the broader framing of institutional investors but replaced the more ambiguous term 'agents' with 'asset managers' to better reflect the legal and functional realities of the investment chain. Similarly, it replaced 'institutional shareholders' with 'asset owners' to clarify that share ownership is typically indirect and mediated through delegated investment relationships. In doing so, the Code emphasised the interdependence of asset owners and asset managers in delivering effective stewardship and signalled a shift towards shared responsibility and collective accountability across the institutional investment ecosystem.

While the Code's primary focus remained on equity stewardship in listed companies, the 2012 revision encouraged – though did not require – signatories to disclose how their stewardship approach applies across other asset classes.[56]

At its core, however, the overarching aim of the 1G UK Code was to prompt rationally 'apathetic' institutional investors to adopt a more

52 UK Code 2012, 1. Note that retail investors (asset owners) who invest in asset managers are not under any onus under the UK Stewardship Code.

53 UK Code 2012, 2–3. But see Anna Tilba and Arad Reisberg, 'Fiduciary Duty under the Microscope: Stewardship and the Spectrum of Pension Fund Engagement' (2019) 82 *The Modern Law Review* 456, 486 (highlighting the limits that interpretations of fiduciary duties pose on pension funds' approaches to stewardship). For a similar discussion in the US, see Bernard S. Sharfman, 'The Conflict between BlackRock's Shareholder Activism and ERISA's Fiduciary Duties' (2020) 71 *Case Western Reserve Law Review* 1241.

54 UK Code 2012, 2.

55 UK Code 2012, 2.

56 UK Code 2012, para 10.

engaged, long-term approach to shareholding – one designed to mitigate excessive risk-taking and short-termism at the company level. Often described as an 'Engagement Code',[57] it placed meaningful shareholder engagement at the centre of its stewardship vision, encouraging activity that goes beyond box-ticking exercises and narrow performance metrics. The 2012 revision, in particular, urged institutional investors to pursue constructive dialogue with corporate boards and management across a broad range of issues, including 'strategy, performance, risk, capital structure, and corporate governance, including culture and remuneration'.[58]

Engagement, as envisioned by the 1G UK Code, encompassed a range of formal and informal practices, including the exercise of voting rights, ongoing dialogue outside the general meeting context (Principle 4), and collective engagement among investors (Principle 5).[59] Crucially, it involved listening as well as speaking – particularly when companies depart from the UK Corporate Governance Code and offer explanations under the 'comply or explain' framework.[60] While the Code prioritised relationship-building over confrontational tactics, it acknowledged escalation as a legitimate means of protecting and enhancing shareholder value.[61] Recommended actions ranged from private meetings with directors to public statements, shareholder resolutions, or even requisitioning general meetings.[62]

In this way, the 1G UK Code framed engagement as a continuous, relationship-based process – embedded within broader systems of institutional accountability and corporate governance. Its ambition was to reorient institutional investment towards long-term value creation by countering short-termist behaviours – not through formal legal obligations, but by promoting a culture of responsible ownership. The 1G UK Code marked a decisive step in the institutionalisation of investor stewardship in the UK – translating the ISC's market-driven ethos into a publicly overseen framework designed to reshape shareholder behaviour. In doing so, it laid the conceptual and regulatory foundations for the more expansive vision of stewardship that would take shape in the next iteration of the Code.

[57] Davies, 'The UK Stewardship Code 2010–2020: From Saving the Company to Saving the Planet?', 47.
[58] UK Code 2012, 1.
[59] Ibid., 6.
[60] Ibid., 7.
[61] Ibid., 8.
[62] Ibid.

5.3.2 *Stewardship Reimagined: The Second-Generation UK Code (2020)*

By the late 2010s, however, it had become increasingly apparent that the 1G stewardship framework had not gone far enough. Despite its success in formalising expectations around shareholder engagement, the Code struggled to foster a robust culture of long-term stewardship in practice. This was due in part to structural changes in equity ownership – domestic institutional investors, the Code's primary audience held a shrinking share of UK equities – alongside persistent misalignments between stewardship responsibilities and commercial incentives.[63] Many institutional investors lacked the capacity, expertise, or motivation to deliver the kind of firm-specific monitoring and engagement the Code envisioned.[64]

Critiques of the 1G UK Code extended beyond issues of participation and capacity. Some commentators questioned whether firm-level shareholder engagement, on its own, could meaningfully address the deeper structural challenges of poor corporate governance and short-termism that the Code sought to resolve. On this view, stewardship needed to evolve beyond narrow governance metrics to reflect a broader set of accountability relationships, including those to stakeholders and society at large.[65] Moreover, soft-law instruments like the UK Stewardship Code, grounded in voluntary adherence and process-based disclosures, were increasingly viewed as inadequate to meet these growing demands.[66] What was needed, critics argued, was not only stronger regulatory underpinning but also a decisive shift from procedural compliance to demonstrable outcome-based accountability.

These concerns were compounded by persistent weaknesses in reporting practices. Stewardship disclosures were often superficial and lacked meaningful detail – particularly in relation to conflicts of interest, voting

[63] For early critique, see Brian R. Cheffins, 'The Stewardship Code's Achilles' Heel' (2010) 73 *The Modern Law Review* 1004; Lee Roach, 'The UK Stewardship Code' (2011) 11 *Journal of Corporate Law Studies* 463; Arad Reisberg, 'The UK Stewardship Code: On the Road to Nowhere?' (2015) 15 *Journal of Corporate Law Studies* 217. For data on the increase of foreign ownership in UK public equities, see Section 2.5.2.

[64] See also Section 4.3.3.

[65] See e.g. Janet Williamson, 'The Emperor's New Clothes – Enlightened Shareholder Value and the UK Stewardship Code' in Sigurt Vitols and Johannes Heuschmid (eds.), *European Company Law and the Sustainable Company: a Stakeholder Approach*, vol II (ETUI 2013), 260.

[66] For a critical discussion of the coerciveness of the UK Code 2012 and the limits of private regulation in ensuring effective stewardship and corporate governance practices, see Dionysia Katelouzou and Peer Zumbansen, 'The New Geographies of Corporate Governance' (2020) 42 *University of Pennsylvania Journal of International Law* 1130.

behaviour, and collective engagement – raising doubts about whether formal signatory status translated into meaningful stewardship practice.[67] The 2018 Kingman Review crystallised these criticisms, concluding that the Code was 'not effective in practice' and risked entrenching a culture of box-ticking rather than genuine accountability.[68]

It was against this backdrop of growing criticism and reform momentum that the FRC launched a major overhaul of the UK Stewardship Code. The result was the 2020 iteration – referred to in this account as the second-generation or '2G' UK Code – which marked a decisive departure from its predecessors. The 2G UK Code embraced a broader, more ambitious, outcome-oriented vision of stewardship: one that was inclusive of a wider range of asset classes, organisational models, and investment strategies.

Structurally, the 2G UK Code is organised around four thematic areas: organisational purpose and governance; the investment approach, including ESG integration; engagement with investee companies; and the exercise of rights and responsibilities, particularly voting. Unlike the 2012 Code, which applied a single set of principles to all signatories, the 2020 version introduces differentiated expectations: twelve principles are directed at asset owners and asset managers, while a distinct set of six additional principles is tailored specifically to service providers, such as proxy advisors and investment consultants.

Although the same twelve principles apply to both asset owners and asset managers, the Code differentiates their reporting expectations where appropriate. For example, asset owners may report on the expectations they set for third-party asset managers and investment consultants tasked with implementing stewardship activities on their behalf.[69] More broadly, the 2G UK Code recognises that signatories vary in size, structure, and investment approach. It does not require fund-by-fund or strategy-specific disclosure, but it does expect signatories to provide a clear, proportionate account of how stewardship is undertaken across different funds, asset classes, and geographies.[70] This flexible model reinforces the Code's shift from uniform procedural compliance towards more context-sensitive, outcome-oriented accountability.

The scope of the 2G Code is also markedly broader. Stewardship expectations now extend beyond public equities to include other asset classes such

67 See also Section 6.6.2.

68 John Kingman, *Independent Review of the Financial Reporting Council* (December 2018), 8.

69 UK Code 2020, Principle 8.

70 Ibid., 6.

as fixed income, infrastructure, and private markets.[71] The Code explicitly accommodates both active and passive investment strategies, acknowledging that large, diversified asset managers may shape outcomes at the systemic level even when intensive firm-level engagement is not feasible. Crucially, stewardship is no longer defined solely by reference to shareholder engagement. Instead, it is framed as the 'responsible allocation, management and oversight of capital to create long-term value for clients and beneficiaries leading to sustainable benefits for the economy, the environment and society'.[72] This expanded definition signals a conceptual shift – positioning stewardship as a multidimensional responsibility that connects financial decision-making to long-term value creation and broader societal goals.

In line with this broader functional remit, the aims of stewardship under the 2G UK Code have also evolved. The Code moves decisively beyond firm-specific monitoring to embrace a broader, multi-level vision of stewardship – encompassing micro-, portfolio-, system- and macro-level stewardship.[73] Institutional investors are no longer viewed solely as monitors of corporate governance, but increasingly as 'guardians of market integrity' – actors with the capacity to engage with systemic risks through collaboration with regulators, industry bodies, and civil society organisations.[74] This expanded vision of stewardship brings with it a heightened focus on sustainability and long-term value creation across the financial system.

A central feature of this redefinition is the integration of ESG objectives into the heart of the stewardship agenda.[75] Whereas the UK Code 2010 omitted ESG considerations, and the 2012 version mentioned them only in passing, the 2G UK Code embeds them explicitly in Principle 7. This requires signatories to 'systematically integrate stewardship and investment, including material environmental, social and governance issues, and climate change, to fulfil their responsibilities'. The Code acknowledges that ESG

[71] Ibid., 4 and 21.
[72] UK Code 2020, 4. While the Code does not explicitly define what constitutes broader environmental and societal interests, references to 'people, the environment and society' tend to be interpreted within the confines of agency theory as those 'directly affected' by corporate activity. See Beate Sjåfjell, 'Sustainability and Law and Economics: An Interdisciplinary Redefinition of Agency Theory' in Beate Sjåfjell, Roseanne Russell and Maja van der Velden (eds.), *Interdisciplinary Research for Sustainable Business: Perspectives of Women Business Scholars* (Springer 2022), 81–109.
[73] See further Section 7.2.
[74] UK Code 2020, 4 and Principle 4.
[75] UK Code 2020, Principle 7.

factors – especially climate change, social inequality, and governance failures – are no longer peripheral concerns but material financial and systemic risks that institutional investors must actively address. As Paul Davies aptly notes, the 2G UK Code represents a shift 'from saving the company to saving the planet'.[76]

Equally significant is the evolution in stewardship techniques. While engagement remains a central tool, the 2G UK Code makes clear that it is only one of several methods available to institutional investors. Stewardship now encompasses a broad array of practices, including capital allocation, investment decision-making, oversight of service providers, collaborative initiatives, and public policy advocacy.[77] Buy and sell decisions are placed on an equal footing with voting and dialogue, reinforcing the idea that stewardship must span the full investment life cycle. This broader, systemic orientation is particularly suited to the diversified portfolios of large institutional investors, who increasingly pursue forms of 'beta activism' aimed at addressing market-wide challenges – such as climate risk, labour standards, and board diversity – rather than solely focusing on firm-specific governance or performance issues.[78]

Taken together, these changes mark a significant evolution in the UK's stewardship framework – both conceptually and operationally. By broadening the scope of stewardship across asset classes, market participants, and modes of influence; deepening its foundations to encompass sustainability and systemic risk; and strengthening accountability through outcome-based reporting, the 2G UK Code aspires to embed stewardship more fully within the operational and cultural fabric of institutional investment. It reflects an ambitious effort to re-embed investment practices within structures of long-term value creation and societal accountability.[79] Crucially, however, this ambition has not been pursued through statutory enforcement, but through the deployment of disclosure-based mechanisms that operate within a system of reputational incentives and market-driven discipline.

[76] Davies, 'The UK Stewardship Code 2010–2020: From Saving the Company to Saving the Planet?', 44.
[77] UK Code 2020, 4 and 7.
[78] Section 3.2.3.
[79] Section 5.4.

5.3.3 *Soft Law with Teeth: Reinforcing the Market for Stewardship*

5.3.3.1 Disclosure as Governance: How Market Logic Shapes Stewardship Compliance

Although conceived as a voluntary initiative, the UK Stewardship Code quickly acquired a quasi-mandatory character. Mirroring the UK Corporate Governance Code, the 1G UK Code adopted a 'comply-or-explain' model.[80] Institutional investors were not legally obliged to become signatories, but those who did were expected to publicly disclose their stewardship policies, report on their adherence to the Code's principles, and explain any areas of non-compliance.

The 2G UK Code raised the bar by replacing this model with an 'apply-and-explain' approach.[81] While signatory status remains voluntary, those who commit to the Code are now expected to implement its principles and provide a reasoned explanation of *how* they have done so in practice. This marks a subtle but important shift: rather than merely stating whether they comply, signatories must now demonstrate the rationale and effectiveness of their chosen approach. In doing so, the Code advances a more substantive model of accountability – one that places implementation and impact, rather than intent alone, at the centre of stewardship reporting.

Most notably, the 2G UK Code redirects the focus from policy articulation to practical outcomes.[82] Instead of a one-off statement of commitment, signatories are required to publish an annual stewardship report detailing how the principles have been applied. This outcome-oriented model was designed to close the persistent gap between formal compliance and meaningful execution – a gap that had significantly limited the effectiveness of the 1G UK Code.

This tightening of expectations was reinforced by the Code's regulatory architecture, which – though formally voluntary – has exerted growing coercive pressure in practice. Nowhere is this more evident than in the case of asset managers authorised by the Financial Conduct Authority (FCA). Although the Code itself is not legally binding, the FCA (then the Financial Services Authority) introduced in December 2010 a requirement for all firms authorised to manage funds on behalf of clients to disclose whether, and to what extent, they complied with the Code, and to explain

[80] UK Code 2012, 2.
[81] Ibid., 4.
[82] Ibid., 6.

any deviations.[83] This created a form of enforced self-regulation: firms could opt out of the Code, but not out of transparency. Non-compliance did not attract formal sanctions, but it could trigger reputational risks or regulatory scrutiny.

A similar dynamic unfolded in the public sector. Since 2016, all Local Government Pension Scheme (LGPS) funds in England and Wales have been required to publish an Investment Strategy Statement (ISS), which must set out, among other things, the administering authority's policy on the exercise of rights – such as voting rights – attached to investments.[84] While the Department for Communities and Local Government stopped short of mandating adoption of the UK Stewardship Code, its 2016 guidance strongly encouraged LGPS funds to become signatories and report on their adherence using a comply-or-explain approach.[85] Signing the Code was presented as the clearest way to demonstrate compliance with ISS stewardship obligations.

This quasi-mandatory trajectory continued with the implementation of the revised Shareholder Rights Directive (SRD II) in May 2019, which requires UK asset managers, insurers and reinsurers to develop and explain how they have implemented an engagement policy for their listed equity investments.[86] This includes how they monitor investee companies, exercise voting rights, and use proxy advisors.[87]

Further statutory reinforcement followed in October 2019. Trustees of occupational pension schemes – both Defined Benefit (DB) and Defined Contribution (DC) – with 100 or more members became legally required to include in their Statement of Investment Principles (SIP) a policy on the

[83] UK Code 2012, 4; Financial Conduct Authority, Conduct of Business Sourcebook 2.2.3R, www.handbook.fca.org.uk/handbook/cobs2.

[84] The Local Government Pension Scheme (Management and Investment of Funds) Regulations 2016, Regulation 7(2)(f).

[85] Department for Communities and Local Government, *Local Government Pension Scheme: Guidance on Preparing and Maintaining an Investment Strategy Statement* (July 2017) 10 ('Administering authorities should become Signatories to the Code and state how they implement the seven principles and guidance of the Code, which apply on a "comply or explain" basis').

[86] Directive (EU) 2017/828 of the European Parliament and of the Council of 17 May 2017 amending Directive 2007/36/EC as regards the encouragement of long-term shareholder engagement [2017] OJ L132/1 [SRD II]. See also Section 5.5.

[87] For UK asset managers – defined to include, among others, MiFID investment firms, UCITS management companies, and AIFMs – see Financial Conduct Authority, COBS 2.2B SRD requirements, www.handbook.fca.org.uk/handbook/cobs2. For UK insurers and reinsurers, see Financial Conduct Authority, Senior Management Arrangements, Systems and Controls (SYSC) 3.4 SRD requirements, www.handbook.fca.org.uk/hand book/sysc3/sysc3s4 .

exercise of rights and engagement with investee companies.[88] Although the SIP regime does not compel alignment with the UK Stewardship Code, it closely tracks its principles, reinforcing the Code's role as the prevailing benchmark for best practice in investor stewardship.

Taken together, these developments illustrate how the UK Stewardship Code has evolved from a soft-law initiative into a form of quasi-mandatory governance – particularly for FCA-regulated asset managers. While the Code's principles apply broadly across the investment chain, only asset managers are formally required to disclose whether they apply the Code and to justify any deviations. No equivalent obligation applies to asset owners or service providers. This asymmetry places the regulatory burden of transparency and justification most squarely on asset managers, blurring the line between voluntary adherence and regulatory expectation.

However, this quasi-coercive effect has not extended to overseas institutional investors – who now represent a significant and growing portion of UK equity ownership.[89] To accommodate these actors without imposing duplicative or burdensome obligations, the 1G UK Code introduced a flexible approach: overseas investors who adhere to other national or international stewardship standards may rely on disclosures made under those regimes to demonstrate compliance with the UK Code.[90] This flexibility was preserved in the 2G UK Code, which explicitly allows signatories to align their UK stewardship reporting with the requirements of other relevant international standards.[91]

In doing so, the 2G UK Code positions itself not only as a domestic benchmark but also as a globally adaptable soft-law instrument – capable of responding to the realities of cross-border investment and international regulatory pluralism. This flexible posture reflects the Code's broader evolution: one that increasingly balances normative ambition with institutional pragmatism. Nowhere is this balancing act more evident than in the patterns of uptake and withdrawal among Code signatories – trends that reveal how market dynamics, regulatory nudges, and reputational incentives have shaped participation over time.

[88] See The Occupational Pension Schemes (Investment and Disclosure) (Amendment) Regulations 2019 (SI 2019/982), which amended the Occupational Pension Schemes (Investment) Regulations 2005 (SI 2005/3378).

[89] Section 2.5.2 (reporting that the proportion of UK domiciled companies quoted shares owned by non-UK investors stood at 56.3 per cent by the end of 2020).

[90] UK Code 2012, 3. On non-UK stewardship frameworks, see Section 5.5.

[91] UK Code 2020, 30.

5.3.3.2 Charting Commitment: The Rise, Fall, and Renewal of Signatories

Figure 5.1 illustrates the evolving uptake of the UK Stewardship Code. In the five years following its introduction in 2010, the number of signatories rose steadily, reaching a record high of 321 in 2015. This initial momentum was interrupted in 2016, likely due to the introduction of the FRC's tiered reporting system – a reputational enforcement mechanism aimed at improving the quality of stewardship reporting, promoting transparency, and enhancing the market for investment mandates.[92]

Under the tiering framework, signatories were assessed and categorised into different tiers based on the substance and clarity of their stewardship disclosures. The intent was to distinguish genuinely engaged institutions from those offering superficial or boilerplate compliance. The first assessment, published in November 2016, led to the voluntary withdrawal of twenty signatories, while twenty-eight asset managers were placed in Tier 3 – the lowest category. These firms were given six months to improve their reporting or risk removal from the signatory list. In August 2017, a second

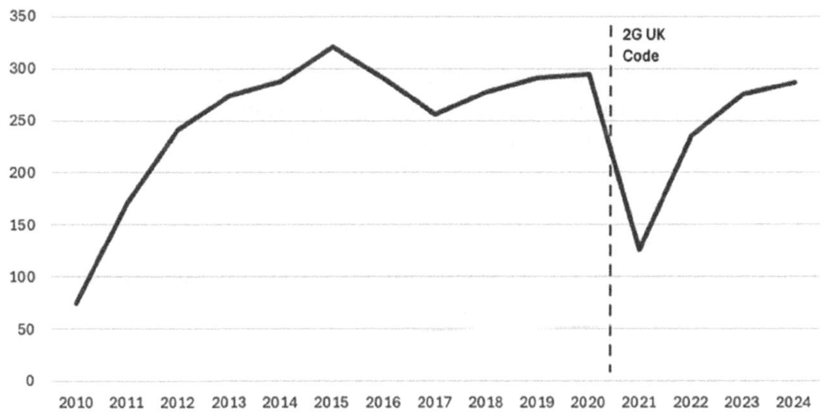

Figure 5.1 Number of stewardship signatories, 2010–2024.

[92] Financial Reporting Council, *FRC Promotes Improved Reporting by Signatories to the Stewardship Code* (14 December 2015) <www.frc.org.uk/news-and-events/news/2015/12/frc-promotes-improved-reporting-by-signatories-to-the-stewardship-code/>. On tiering as a distinctive form of membership and adherence sanction within an established stewardship network, see Dionysia Katelouzou and Konstantinos Sergakis, 'Shareholder Stewardship Enforcement' in Dan W. Puchniak and Dionysia Katelouzou (eds.), *Global Shareholder Stewardship* (Cambridge University Press 2022), 572–98.

assessment showed that 256 signatories remained.[93] The FRC discontinued Tier 3, as some firms had improved their reports and others had opted to withdraw rather than revise.

According to the FRC, the exercise resulted in notable improvements: approximately eighty Tier 2 signatories upgraded their disclosures to meet Tier 1 standard. The FRC saw the reduction in signatories not as a setback but as a positive refinement – arguing that organisations for whom stewardship is irrelevant should not be using the Code as a compliance tool. In its view, withdrawal under these circumstances was not only acceptable but also appropriate.[94]

From 2018 onward, signatory numbers began to recover, reaching 295 by 2020.[95] This resurgence was driven by growing uptake among asset managers and a broader shift in market expectations around stewardship. Investors increasingly recognised the reputational and strategic value of aligning with stewardship norms, especially amid rising public and regulatory scrutiny.

However, this upward trajectory was sharply disrupted in 2021, when the number of signatories fell to 126 – less than half the previous year's total. This abrupt drop coincided with the introduction of the 2G UK Stewardship Code, which came into force in January 2020. The 2G UK Code introduced an expanded notion of stewardship and replaced the earlier comply-or-explain model with a more demanding 'apply-and-explain' framework, requiring signatories to submit annual Stewardship Reports demonstrating not only their policies but also how they had implemented the Code's principles in practice.[96]

The FRC's first assessment under the 2G UK Code in 2021 received 189 applications, but only 125 organisations – roughly two-thirds – were accepted as signatories. The remainder were invited to reapply after addressing shortcomings in their reports.[97] Since then, participation has

93 Financial Conduct Authority, *FRC Removes Tier 3 Categorisation for Stewardship Code Signatories* (3 August 2017) <www.frc.org.uk/news-and-events/news/2017/08/frc-removes-tier-3-categorisation-for-stewardship-code-signatories/>.

94 Financial Reporting Council, *Developments in Corporate Governance and Stewardship 2016* (January 2017), 26 ('[s]ignatories assessed as Tier 1 do not necessarily provide a "perfect" statement, but provide a good overview of their approach to stewardship').

95 Of these, 178 were asset managers, 105 asset owners, and 12 service providers. Data as of May 2020, on file with author.

96 Sections 5.3.1 and 5.3.2.

97 Financial Reporting Council, *FRC Lists Successful Signatories to the UK Stewardship Code* (6 September 2021), https://www.frc.org.uk/news-and-events/news/2021/09/frc-lists-successful-signatories-to-the-uk-stewardship-code/.

steadily rebounded: 235 signatories were listed in 2022, 275 in 2023, and 287 in 2024. Although the total has yet to match the 2015 high, the upward trend signals growing adaptation to the new expectations. More importantly, it suggests that the 2G UK Code is fostering a more robust and committed stewardship community – one aligned not only with the formal requirements of the Code but also with its evolving normative aspirations.

Taken together, these fluctuations chart the evolution of the UK Stewardship Code from a broad-based, lightly enforced standard into a more selective and rigorous benchmark. Viewed in this light, the enforcement mechanisms surrounding the Code – though formally non-binding and ranging from reporting thresholds and reputational tiering to regulatory nudges – have strengthened the market-based logic underpinning the UK Stewardship Code. Rather than imposing binding legal requirements, they enhance reputational differentiation and signal quality, allowing asset owners to identify credible stewards and incentivising asset managers to compete on substantive performance.[98]

Supporting this model is a broader institutional infrastructure – including the Investor Forum[99] and the Investment Association's Public Register[100] – which promotes a system of 'dynamic accountability' across the investment chain. In line with what Sabel and Zeitlin term 'experimentalist governance', this architecture enables iterative learning, benchmarking, and peer oversight, rather than relying on rigid top-down enforcement.[101] Within this evolving framework, the UK Stewardship

98 See also Section 5.3.3.1.

99 The Investor Forum was established in 2014 as a direct response to the recommendations of the 2012 Kay Review, with the aim of promoting long-term, collaborative engagement between institutional investors and UK-listed companies. It serves as a collective engagement mechanism and a platform for investor dialogue with issuers. Further information on its role and activities is available at www.investorforum.org.uk/. In 2024, the Investor & Issuer Forum was launched as a complementary initiative, offering a neutral space for structured dialogue between company boards and institutional investors outside the context of specific engagements. More information is available at www.investorandissuerforum.org.uk.

100 The Investment Association launched the Public Register in December 2017 at the request of the UK Government, following the 2017 Green Paper on Corporate Governance Reform. The Register records significant shareholder dissent – defined as 20 per cent or more of votes cast against a board-endorsed resolution – promoting transparency and accountability in listed companies. In parallel with the introduction of a new reporting requirement under the 2018 UK Corporate Governance Code, the Investment Association also issued guidance on long-term reporting for companies appearing on the Register. Further information is available at www.theia.org/public-register.

101 Michael C. Dorf and Charles F. Sabel, 'A Constitution of Democratic Experimentalism' (1998) 98 *Columbia Law Review* 267; Charles F. Sabel and Jonathan Zeitlin, 'Learning

Code functions not merely as a set of principles but also as a reputational and institutional scaffold – one that reshapes investor conduct and aligns financial intermediation with long-term value creation.

5.4 The Expanding Normative Purpose of Stewardship: From Shareholder Oversight to Other-Regarding Responsibility

Investor stewardship has undergone a profound transformation – from a primarily investor-driven tool for corporate governance to a regulator-shaped framework infused with broader societal objectives. Originally conceived as a mechanism to improve corporate governance through firm-level engagement and shareholder accountability, stewardship is now increasingly framed as a vehicle for promoting long-term value, addressing systemic risks – such as climate change, inequality, and financial instability – and aligning capital with the interests of both end-investors and society at large.

The 1991 ISC Statement articulated a clear objective: to encourage institutional investors to exercise ownership rights in support of sound corporate governance. Central to this vision was the 'Engaged Shareholder', premised on the economic logic that active shareholder oversight could curb managerial opportunism and enhance firm performance.[102] The (rebuttable) assumption was that such monitoring not only improves the governance and performance of investee companies but also enhances market efficiency. The ISC Code 2009 codified this rationale, retaining a narrow, client-focused orientation while laying the groundwork for the FRC's formal codification of stewardship.

The UK Stewardship Code 2010 built on this foundation, seeking to legitimise shareholder engagement that supports long-term value creation. Like its predecessor, it promoted normative expectations of appropriate shareholder behaviour, particularly in times of corporate and economic distress. Principle 5, for example, encouraged collective action, implicitly framing stewardship as a stabilising force distinct from short-term, value-extractive activism often associated with hedge funds. The Code thus

from Difference: The New Architecture of Experimentalist Governance in the EU' (2008) 14 *European Law Journal* 271.

102 Section 3.5.1. See also Iris H-Y Chiu, 'Turning Institutional Investors into "Stewards": Exploring the Meaning and Objectives of "Stewardship"' (2013) 66 *Current Legal Problems* 443, 457.

functioned not only as a guide to best practice but also as a *normative gatekeeping mechanism* – legitimising certain forms of investor influence (such as long-term engagement) while implicitly discouraging short-term, extractive strategies.[103]

Even in its early forms, stewardship recognised dual responsibilities: to investee companies (asset stewardship) and to proximate clients and beneficiaries (client stewardship). This duality was embedded in the 1G UK Code and formalised a more relational understanding of the investor's role.

The 2012 revision marked a conceptual pivot. While retaining the oversight function, it shifted emphasis away from engagement – which appeared with similar frequency in the ISC Code 2009 and the UK Code 2010 – and toward stewardship as the organising framework. As Table 5.1 shows, references to 'stewardship' in the 2012 version significantly outnumbered those to 'engagement' – rising to 1.96 per cent of total words compared to just 0.30 per cent – signalling both a rhetorical and substantive reorientation.

This rhetorical shift signalled a broader normative ambition. The UK Code 2012 explicitly framed stewardship as a means of improving 'the functioning of the market for investment mandates', thereby extending its scope beyond corporate governance to encompass the governance of

Table 5.1 *Shifting terminology in UK stewardship framerowkrs: From engagement to stewardship.*

		Engage/Engagement		Stewardship	
Code	Length of Text in Words	Times Appearing	Frequency (%)	Times Appearing	Frequency (%)
ISC Code 2009	1504	10	0.66	6	0.40
UK Code 2010	1997	14	0.70	13	0.65
UK Code 2012	2954	9	0.30	58	1.96

103 On the role of stewardship codes as norm entrepreneurs and soft-law gatekeepers of appropriate investor conduct, see Section 8.2.1.

institutional investors themselves.[104] It placed greater emphasis on internal organisational structures, asset owner–manager relationships, and the role of disclosure in fostering alignment and accountability throughout the investment chain. Under this expanded framing, engagement was no longer confined to corporate oversight; it became an instrument of fiduciary risk management, oriented towards the long-term interests of both clients and the ultimate owners of capital.

In doing so, the Code laid the foundations for what this book refers to as *end-investor stewardship* – a stewardship relationship that emphasises responsibility not just to proximate clients and beneficiaries but also to -end-investors dispersed across complex chains of financial intermediation and across time.[105] Institutional shareholding was reconceived not as a set of entitlements, but as a series of layered obligations embedded within the broader architecture of investment governance. Principles 1, 2, 6, and 7 extended these responsibilities to areas such as disclosure, conflict-of-interest management, and voting – all aimed at enhancing transparency and strengthening accountability throughout the investment chain. This reconceptualisation also laid the groundwork for the distinction between direct and indirect stewardship, with asset owners expected to set the tone and hold delegated stewards – such as asset managers – accountable.[106]

The 2012 revision also deepened the normative foundations of stewardship by anchoring it in a broader conception of social legitimacy. As the Walker Review observed, large institutional shareholders occupy a 'highly influential position' in the financial system and must 'earn and be accorded an at least implicit social legitimacy'.[107] On this view, the exercise of shareholder rights is accompanied by a reciprocal obligation: institutional investors – particularly large fund managers – are expected to demonstrate long-term attentiveness not only to investee company performance but also to the interests of their proximate clients and beneficiaries, end-investors, and the wider market.[108]

[104] UK Code 2012, 2. Further on the market for stewardship, see Dionysia Katelouzou and Eva Micheler, 'The Market for Stewardship and the Role of the Government' in Dan W. Puchniak and Dionysia Katelouzou (eds.), *Global Shareholder Stewardship* (Cambridge University Press 2022), 67–90.

[105] See Section 4.4.1.

[106] UK Code 2012, para 6. On the distinction between direct and indirect stewardship, see further Section 7.3.

[107] Walker, *A Review of Corporate Governance in UK Banks and Other Financial Industry Entities*, 70.

[108] Ibid., para 5.7 (proposing a 'duty of stewardship'). See further Iris H-Y Chiu and Dionysia Katelouzou, 'From Shareholder Stewardship to Shareholder Duties: Is the

The opening paragraph of the 2012 Code made this explicit, asserting that 'effective stewardship benefits companies, investors and the economy *as a whole*'.[109] This language signals a shift from an agency-centric model to a broader conception of stewardship as a public good. Rather than expanding shareholder power, the 1G UK Code aimed to clarify investor responsibilities – towards clients and beneficiaries, investee companies, and the wider economy. This ethos echoed earlier UK governance reforms, such as the Cadbury Report, which emphasised transparency and accountability as pillars of good governance.[110]

The 1G UK Code explicitly linked investor stewardship with board accountability under the UK Corporate Governance Code, positioning stewardship as integral to the UK's comply-or-explain model and relying on engaged shareholders to uphold governance standards.[111] This dual role – enhancing accountability both within companies and across the investment chain – was embedded in a broader regulatory trajectory. From the Cadbury Review's endorsement of the 1991 ISC Statement to the Higgs Review's support for the ISC's 2002 principles, and the promotion of board–shareholder dialogue through the Combined Code and its successors, the UK governance model came to rest on a *dual-code architecture.*[112] The 2018 UK Corporate Governance Code continued this tradition, explicitly referencing the UK Stewardship Code and encouraging institutional investors to 'engage constructively and discuss with the company any departures from recommended practice'.[113] Together, the two Codes were designed to strengthen the comply-or-explain model and uphold high standards of corporate accountability across UK capital markets.

Time Ripe?' in Hanne S. Birkmose (ed.), *Shareholders' Duties* (Wolter Kluwer 2017), 131–52 (asserting that the Principles of the UK Stewardship Code can evolve into concrete institutional shareholder duties).

109 UK Code 2012, 1 (emphasis added).

110 Cadbury Report, paras. 7.4–7.5. ('The way forward is through clear definitions of responsibility and an acceptance by all involved that the highest standards of efficiency and integrity are expected of them. . . . This will involve a sharper sense of accountability and responsibility all round – accountability by boards to their shareholders, responsibility on the part of all shareholders to the companies they own and, accountability by professional officers and advisers to those who rely on their judgment.')

111 UK Code 2010, 1; UK Code 2012, 1.

112 Cadbury Report, para 4.59; Higgs Review, 10. See also Section 5.2.2.

113 Financial Reporting Council, UK Corporate Governance Code 2018, www.frc.org.uk/documents/5167/UK_Corporate_Governance_Code_2018.pdf, 2.

In recent revisions, however, this alignment has begun to unravel. The 2G UK Code no longer emphasises shared responsibility or investor oversight of comply-or-explain deviations. Similarly, the 2024 revision of the UK Corporate Governance Code adopts a more muted stance on the role of institutional investors in monitoring deviations from corporate governance norms,[114] as stewardship is repositioned as a more autonomous and normatively expansive framework – less tied to corporate governance enforcement and more concerned with investment management and broader environmental, social, and systemic outcomes.

Yet this evolution introduces a conceptual and legal tension: institutional investors remain subject to private fiduciary law, with duties owed primarily to clients and beneficiaries. And it is mainly through the soft-law framework of the Stewardship Code that these obligations are extended – first to investee firms, then to the wider public.[115] The 2020 revision of the UK Stewardship Code marked the most ambitious step in this reorientation. By tying stewardship to sustainable outcomes for the economy, environment, and society, the Code broadened the legitimacy of investment beyond financial performance.[116] The integration of ESG factors within this framework reinforces this shift: ESG is no longer framed solely as a means to optimise risk-adjusted returns, but as a vehicle for aligning capital with wider societal and ecological priorities – such as climate resilience, equity, and responsible governance.[117] In doing so, the 2G UK Code affirms its broader regulatory ambition: to re-socialise financial markets around shared societal goals and ground investment practices in a framework of other-regarding responsibility.

Viewed through a Polanyian lens, this shift is part of a wider 'double movement': a reassertion of social norms and regulatory constraints in

[114] Financial Reporting Council, UK Corporate Governance Code 2024, www.frc.org.uk/documents/6709/UK_Corporate_Governance_Code_2024_a2hmQmY.pdf, 3.

[115] See further Section 8.2.1 on the crowding-in function of stewardship codes. In the case of climate-related stewardship, expectations have acquired more concrete regulatory footing through the UK's implementation of the Taskforce on Climate-Related Financial Disclosures (TCFD), which requires FCA-regulated asset managers and asset owners to report on climate-related risks across all asset classes they manage or administer. See FCA Handbook, ESG 2.2.1 on the annual TCFD entity report. For the scope of this rule, see Financial Conduct Authority, *Enhancing climate-related disclosures by asset managers, life insurers and FCA-regulated pension providers* (Policy Statement PS21/24, December 2021), paras. 1.08–1.12.

[116] Section 5.3.2.

[117] This shift in the focus of shareholder – and more broadly, investor – stewardship from firm-level governance concerns to broader societal and systemic challenges – reflects a wider reorientation of corporate purpose beyond shareholder primacy. See also Section 1.1.

response to the disembedding effects of unregulated markets.[118] The 2020 UK Code embraces this re-embedding, calling on institutional investors not merely to monitor corporate behaviour but to also act as market shapers through engagement, capital allocation, and even policy advocacy.[119] The result is a more expansive conception of stewardship – one that ties investor duties to the long-term resilience of companies, the stability of markets, and the well-being of society. In this way, the 2G UK Code reframes stewardship as a mechanism not only for shareholder oversight but also for the responsible governance of capital itself. Yet caution is warranted. A persistent disconnect remains between the ambitious regulatory goals of long-term, other-regarding stewardship and the mechanisms currently used to achieve them – namely, soft-law, market-led frameworks with limited enforcement power. This regulatory disjuncture, and the challenges it poses for embedding systemic accountability into investor practice, will be examined in greater depth in Chapter 8.

5.5 The 'Gold Standard' and Its Global Reach: The UK Code as Global Reference Point

Against the backdrop of the UK's ambitious – but contested – stewardship reforms, the UK model, particularly the 1G UK Code, has gained global traction. What began as a market-led initiative has become a regulatory reference point, catalysing the proliferation of stewardship codes across diverse jurisdictions and institutional contexts. Within less than fifteen years, stewardship codes – largely modelled on the UK's 1G Code, widely regarded as the 'gold standard' – have emerged in twenty-four jurisdictions beyond the UK.[120] At the same time, supranational frameworks at the EU and international levels have embedded stewardship principles into broader

[118] Karl Polanyi, *The Great Transformation: The Political and Economic Origins of Our Time* (Beacon Press 1944), 79.

[119] Dionysia Katelouzou, 'Shareholder Stewardship: A case for (Re)Embedding the Institutional Investors and the Corporation?' in Beate Sjåfjell and Christopher M. Bruner (eds.), *The Cambridge Handbook of Corporate Law, Corporate Governance and Sustainability* (Cambridge University Press 2019), 581–95. But see Lorraine E. Talbot, 'Polanyi's Embeddedness and Shareholder Stewardship: A Contextual Analysis of Current Anglo-American Perspectives on Corporate Governance' (2011) 62 *Northern Ireland Legal Quarterly* 451.

[120] These are Australia, Brazil, Canada, Denmark, Germany, Hong Kong, India, Italy, Japan, New Zealand, Kenya, Korea, Malaysia, the Netherlands, Norway, Russia, Singapore, South Africa, Spain, Switzerland, Taiwan, Thailand, Turkey, and the US.

corporate governance agendas,[121] transforming investor stewardship into a truly international corporate law phenomenon.[122]

In a co-authored study with Professor Siems, we define a stewardship code broadly as:

> a non-binding set of principles, standards or best practices that is accompanied by recommendations and suggestions directed to institutional investors (mainly asset owners and asset managers) and in some case to service providers or lawmakers, issued by public or private bodies, and relating to the oversight role of institutional investors to create long-term value for clients and beneficiaries and promote corporate sustainability, including engagement and monitoring of investee companies (corporate governance aspects) as well as their responsibilities towards their clients and end-beneficiaries, avoiding conflicts of interests and reporting duties (investment management aspects).[123]

This broad yet precise definition captures the diversity of stewardship frameworks that have emerged worldwide. Many of these developments are documented in *Global Shareholder Stewardship*, a volume I co-edited with Professor Dan Puchniak, which provides the first comprehensive, comparative, and empirical analysis of stewardship codes across jurisdictions.[124] The book examines forty-four codes – thirty-eight of

[121] The most important transnational stewardship codes include the ones developed by the European Fund and Asset Management Association (EFAMA) and International Corporate Governance Network (ICGN). The SRD II also incorporates aspects of shareholder stewardship usually found in stewardship codes in its Articles 3g (engagement policy), 3h (investment strategy of institutional investors and arrangements with asset managers), 3i (transparency of asset managers. On transposition of the stewardship provisions of the SRD II by Member States, see Dionysia Katelouzou and Konstantinos Sergakis, 'When Harmonization Is Not Enough: Shareholder Stewardship in the European Union' (2021) 22 *European Business Organization Law Review* 203.

[122] Mariana Pargendler, 'The Rise of International Corporate Law' (2020) 98 *Washington University Law Review* 1765.

[123] Katelouzou and Siems, 'The Global Diffusion of Stewardship Codes', 632–4. This broad definition of stewardship codes includes 'preliminary initiatives', like the one in Norway, defined as 'a set of principles, standards or best practices relating to the stewardship role of institutional investors, but which is limited in its scope (e.g. it applies to a specific group of institutional), in its content (e.g. it refers only to voting rights), or in its drafting style (e.g. it is drafted as a policy statement or has no guidance even though it adopts a principle-based approach)'. See ibid. 638.

[124] Dionysia Katelouzou and Dan W. Puchniak (eds.), *Global Shareholder Stewardship* (Cambridge University Press 2022). It is noteworthy that in addition to the forty-five codes addressed to institutional investors there is one stewardship code, that is, the Singapore Family Code, which aims to incentivize family controllers (and not institutional investors) to use their controlling power to steward the company for the benefit of

which were introduced after the launch of the UK Stewardship Code in 2010.[125] Since its publication, eleven additional codes have emerged, bringing the total to fifty-five.[126] Of these, fifty are jurisdiction-specific, spanning twenty-five jurisdictions across six continents (twenty in Europe, seventeen in Asia, five in North America, three in Africa, three in Oceania, and two in South America), while the remaining five are regional or international in scope.

The global diffusion of stewardship codes has generated growing interest from both scholars and policymakers. Academic debate has focused on the drivers, authorship, content, and enforcement of these codes, while policy discussions have increasingly turned to the challenges of implementation, regulatory coherence, and the risk of superficial or boilerplate reporting.

A key area of divergence concerns the identity of the code issuers. The evolution of the UK Stewardship Code itself illustrates a clear progression from 'pure' self-regulation to a more structured form of public–private co-regulation. The earliest statement, issued in 1991 by the ISC, was entirely private in origin. The 1G UK Code, introduced by the FRC, largely adopted the ISC's principles but shifted the model towards 'facilitated' self-regulation, where market-led standards are supported by public endorsement and oversight.[127] The 2020 revision continued this trajectory, reinforcing the FRC's role as a hybrid regulator operating at the intersection of state authority and industry practice.

all stakeholders. See Stewardship Asia Centre, Stewardship Principles for Family Businesses (2018), www.stewardshipasia.com.sg/sites/default/files/2020-09/SPFB-brochure-0913.pdf.

125 For a list, see Katelouzou and Siems, 'The Global Diffusion of Stewardship Codes', 634.

126 These are the DVFA German Stewardship Guidelines (2020); the Recommendations for the Implementation of the Principles of Responsible Investment (Russia 2020); the Brazilian Code of Stewardship (2021); the ICGN Global Stewardship Principles (2020); Malaysian Code for Institutional Investors (2022), www.iicm.org.my/malaysian-code-for-institutional-investors-2022/; Stewardship Code Aotearoa New Zealand (September 2022) www.stewardshipcode.nz; the Second Code for Responsible Investing in South Africa 2022 (CRISA 2), www.crisa2.co.za/crisa2code/; Singapore Stewardship Principles for Responsible Investors 2.0 (March 2022) www.stewardshipasia.com.sg/docs/saclibraries/default-document-library/ssp_for-20responsible-20investor-202-0-1-.pdf?sfvrsn=82133969_3; Spanish Stewardship Code (2023), www.cnmv.es/docportal/Buenas-practicas/CBPinversores.pdf; Stewardship Principles for Institutional Investors (Taiwan 2023); and the Principles for Responsible Management 60/1696 (Turkey 2024).

127 On the differences between self-regulation and co-regulation, see generally Ian Bartle and Peter Vass, *Self-Regulation and the Regulatory State: A Survey of Policy and Practice* (2005).

Outside the UK, stewardship codes exhibit significant heterogeneity in both institutional design and regulatory intensity. As of 2020, nineteen codes across eleven jurisdictions have been issued by governmental or quasi-governmental bodies, while twenty-one codes in nine jurisdictions originated from private organisations – typically, industry associations or institutional investor groups.[128] Publicly issued codes generally adopt a comply-or-explain or apply-or-explain model, but only the UK embeds a quasi-mandatory element: though framed as voluntary, compliance with the UK Stewardship Code is effectively required for key institutional investors due to regulatory expectations, oversight by the FRC, and broader market pressures.[129] Among privately issued codes, five adopt similar disclosure-based mechanisms,[130] while the remaining codes remain entirely voluntary – lacking formal enforcement and functioning primarily as aspirational frameworks.[131]

Patterns of regulatory evolution vary as well. In nine non-UK jurisdictions – Brazil, Canada, India, Italy, Japan, the Netherlands, Norway, South Africa, and Taiwan – amended versions of inaugural stewardship codes have been introduced, with the original issuers remaining in place.[132] This continuity suggests a state of *institutional stasis* – or near-stasis – in global stewardship frameworks. Such inertia may prove especially limiting where codes are privately issued and lack robust mechanisms for monitoring, enforcement, or revision.[133]

Despite significant variation in formal design, authorship, enforcement mechanisms, and institutional context, the vast majority of stewardship codes share a common normative aim: to 'awaken' institutional investors and promote shareholder engagement as a mechanism for improving corporate governance.[134] This shared objective reflects a widely held belief

[128] See the combined findings of Dionysia Katelouzou and Dan W. Puchniak, 'Global Shareholder Stewardship: Complexities, Challenges and Possibilities' in Dan W. Puchniak and Dionysia Katelouzou (eds.), *Global Shareholder Stewardship* (Cambridge University Press 2022), 19 and Katelouzou and Siems, 'The Global Diffusion of Stewardship Codes', 653.

[129] Section 5.3.3.1.

[130] These are the codes in Australia, Italy, South Africa, Switzerland, and South Korea.

[131] These are the codes in Brazil, Canada, Singapore, and the US.

[132] Data on file with the author.

[133] However, the preservation of pure self-regulation may also be interpreted as a successful pre-emption of public actors issuing a code. See e.g. Georgy Egorov and Bård Harstad, 'Private Politics and Public Regulation' (2017) 84 *The Review of Economic Studies* 1652.

[134] An exception here is the Singapore Family Code, which aims to incentivise family controllers (and not institutional investors) to use their controlling power to steward the company for the benefit of all stakeholders. For a critical analysis of this code, see Dan

that institutional investor involvement – particularly through monitoring and dialogue – can play a critical role in enhancing corporate accountability. However, beneath this shared aspiration, stewardship codes diverge significantly in purpose. Some adopt a narrow focus on protecting shareholder value, while others embrace a more expansive vision that links stewardship to stakeholder interests and long-term sustainability. For example, the initial version of the Japanese Stewardship Code prioritised the interests of shareholders over those of ultimate beneficiaries or broader stakeholders.[135]

Empirical research confirms this overall pattern of convergence around the UK model. Of the thirty-five jurisdiction-specific stewardship codes published between 2010 and 2020, twenty-nine are closely modelled on the 1G UK Code. These codes adopt a corporate governance–centric conception of stewardship, encouraging institutional investors to engage with individual public companies in which they typically hold minority stakes but collectively often wield significant influence.[136] This diffusion of UK-style micro-level shareholder stewardship reinforces the UK's standing as a leading *exporter of corporate governance* norms – a position already established through the earlier global proliferation of corporate governance codes.[137]

Although the 1G UK Code did acknowledge aspects of investment management – such as how fund managers align their strategies with client interests, manage conflicts of interest, and demonstrate accountability across the investment chain – these elements remained relatively underdeveloped. Principles 2 and 7, which address conflicts of interest and transparency, have been widely replicated in other codes,[138] yet the broader obligations that institutional investors owe *upstream* to their

W. Puchniak and Samantha S. Tang, 'Singapore's Embrace of Shareholder Stewardship: A Puzzling Success' in Dan W. Puchniak and Dionysia Katelouzou (eds.), *Global Shareholder Stewardship* (Cambridge University Press 2022), 297–315.

135 For a detailed comparative analysis of the UK and Japanese Stewardship Codes, see Gen Goto, 'The Logic and Limits of Stewardship Code: The Case of Japan' (2019) 15 *Berkeley Business Law Review* 365.

136 Katelouzou and Puchniak, 'Global Shareholder Stewardship: Complexities, Challenges and Possibilities', 13. That institutional investors are collective majorities is recognised by both Principle 4 of the 1G UK Code, which suggests 'intervening jointly with other institutions on particular issues' as a strategy for escalation and Principle 5 on collective action. On how these principles travelled around the word, see Katelouzou and Siems, 'The Global Diffusion of Stewardship Codes', 651–2.

137 See e.g. Brian R. Cheffins, 'Corporate Governance Reform: Britain as an Exporter' (2000) 8 *Hume Papers on Public Policy* 10.

138 Katelouzou and Siems, 'The Global Diffusion of Stewardship Codes', 650.

clients and beneficiaries have remained largely peripheral in both global policy development and academic discourse.

Only a small subset of pre-2020 stewardship codes meaningfully departed from the UK model in this regard. Notably, just four placed greater emphasis on the investment management dimension of stewardship, shifting the focus away from engagement with investee companies and towards the fiduciary responsibilities that institutional investors bear as financial intermediaries.[139]

Another significant exception is the South Africa's Code for Responsible Investing (CRISA) – first issued in 2011 (CRISA) and revised in 2022 (CRISA 2) – which stands out for its explicit emphasis on sustainable investment and ESG considerations.[140] Closely aligned with the ethos of the UN-supported Principles for Responsible Investment (PRI),[141] the South African framework extends stewardship beyond both micro-level shareholder engagement and the protection of beneficiary assets.[142] It defines stewardship as encompassing responsibilities to all those affected by institutional investors' power – ranging from internal and external stakeholders to society and the environment.[143]

While the idea that stewardship should address sustainability concerns predated 2020, most early codes, including the 1G UK Code, treated ESG considerations as secondary to traditional corporate governance concerns. ESG factors were typically framed within a narrow model of micro-level shareholder stewardship, instrumentalised primarily to protect long-term

[139] These are: The FSC Standard 23: Principles of Internal Governance and Asset Stewardship (Australian Code 2017), both versions of the Industry Recommendation for the Members of the Norwegian Fund and Asset Management Association: Exercise of Ownership Rights (Norway 2012 and 2019), and the Guidelines for institutional investors governing the exercising of participation rights in public limited companies (Swiss Code 2013). See Katelouzou and Puchniak, 'Global Shareholder Stewardship: Complexities, Challenges and Possibilities', 8 and 38–43.

[140] For a comprehensive analysis of the 2011 version of CRISA, see Natania Locke, 'Encouraging Sustainable Investment in South Africa: CRISA and Beyond' in Dan W. Puchniak and Dionysia Katelouzou (eds.), *Global Shareholder Stewardship* (Cambridge University Press 2022), 471–89.

[141] Further on the PRI, see 'What are the Principles for Responsible Investment?', www.unpri.org/about-us/what-are-the-principles-for-responsible-investment

[142] Locke, 'Encouraging Sustainable Investment in South Africa: CRISA and beyond', 473–4.

[143] CRISA 2, 7 (defining the outcomes of investor stewardship as 'realising benefits to society, the environment and/or other stakeholders alongside financial return'). Internal stakeholders are defined as those 'directly affiliated with the organisation', including 'its governing body, management, employees and shareholders'. External stakeholders include 'trade unions, civil society organisations, government, consumers and customers'. See CRISA 2, 18.

shareholder value rather than embraced as part of a broader sustainability or public-interest mandate.[144] There were, however, notable variations in emphasis: the International Corporate Governance Network (ICGN) Global Stewardship Principles of 2016, for example, placed comparatively greater weight on ESG integration, signalling a more forward-looking approach.[145] Nonetheless, across earlier frameworks, references to ESG fell short of a substantive reconceptualisation of stewardship's normative purpose.

The broader trend, therefore, remains one of convergence around a UK-inspired model of micro-level shareholder stewardship. The seven principles of the 1G UK Code – often referred to as the 'UK's Seven Magic Principles'[146] – have had a profound global influence. Research indicates that the vast majority of non-UK stewardship codes have adopted all, or nearly all, of these principles.[147] Automated textual analysis of a sample of forty-one UK and non-UK codes further reinforces the UK's status as a global 'stewardship norm exporter'.[148] The 2012 iteration of the UK Code, in particular, has emerged as the most influential version, serving as a key reference point for stewardship frameworks – especially in Asian common law jurisdictions.[149]

At the same time, the diffusion of stewardship norms has been multidimensional. Intra-jurisdictional codes such as those issued by European Fund and Asset Management Association (EFAMA) and ICGN have also shaped the global stewardship landscape, while regional clusters – such as those between Korea and Japan – have contributed to distinctive local adaptations.[150] Although computational analysis captures key patterns of textual alignment, it may underestimate the UK Code's full normative

144 See also Section 6.6.2.5.

145 ICGN Global Stewardship Principles 2016, Preamble, at 5 and Principle 6.

146 Dionysia Katelouzou and Henning Jacobsen, *Global Shareholder Stewardship: A Conference Report* (2020), 24, https://ssrn.com/abstract=3610792 ('[w]hat all the jurisdictional panels have demonstrated is that ostensibly "seven" is the "magic number" in terms of stewardship principles').

147 See Katelouzou and Puchniak, 'Global Shareholder Stewardship: Complexities, Challenges and Possibilities', 13 (reporting that 77.29 per cent of all the Non-UK codes studied have adopted all seven principles – with 91.43 per cent of the codes adopting five or more principles) and Katelouzou and Siems, 'The Global Diffusion of Stewardship Codes', 649–52 (finding on the basis of the text of the codes that the principles of the G1 UK Code relating to escalation activities and collective action have travelled less successfully compared to the other principles).

148 Katelouzou and Siems, 'The Global Diffusion of Stewardship Codes', 632.

149 Ibid., 643–8.

150 Ibid.

impact. Core principles and concepts are often expressed in different languages tailored to local legal, market, and cultural conditions, or diluted in translation where codes are issued in non-English languages.[151] As such, the influence of the 1G UK Code likely exceeds what automated analysis alone can detect, reinforcing its reputation as the international 'gold standard' of stewardship.[152]

At the regional level, the EU has moved to institutionalise stewardship principles by embedding and extending many of the norms developed in national codes – particularly those established by the 1G UK Code. The revised SRD II draws heavily on it, incorporating its emphasis on monitoring, dialogue, voting, and conflict-of-interest management into a harmonised EU framework. Article 3g requires institutional investors and asset managers to develop and publicly disclose engagement policies, while also linking stewardship to both financial and non-financial performance – explicitly mandating attention to environmental and social risks. It further requires engagement with key stakeholders, notably employees, thereby embedding a more stakeholder-oriented logic absent from the UK Code's more investor-centric framing.[153] Articles 3h and 3i reinforce this shift by imposing additional reporting obligations, intended to enhance transparency and promote long-term alignment between investment strategies and beneficiary interests. In this way, SRD II both builds upon and transcends the UK model – broadening stewardship's normative scope to include public interest objectives and systemic accountability.

At the same time, Article 3g of SRD II formally adopts a comply-or-explain approach. Yet, as has been elsewhere argued, this framework effectively imposes a *de facto duty to engage* – or a 'duty to demonstrate engagement'.[154] While institutional investors and asset managers are permitted to explain why they do not pursue an engagement strategy, the accompanying disclosure requirements under Articles 3h and 3i – to report

[151] For instance, the Malaysian Code 2014 does not mention even once the term 'escalat-e/ion' but in substantive terms has an equivalent principle on intervention which resembles too closely Principle 4 of the 2G UK Code. Similarly, the Canadian Code does not make any reference to the word 'collect-ive' but it includes a principle on collaborative action which draws heavily on Principle 5 of the 2G UK Code. See further Katelouzou and Puchniak, 'Global Shareholder Stewardship: Complexities, Challenges and Possibilities', 14.

[152] This is confirmed by policy research. See Financial Reporting Council, *The influence of the UK Stewardship Code 2020 on practice and reporting* (July 2022), 71–2.

[153] SRD II, Recital 14 and Article 3g.

[154] Chiu and Katelouzou, 'From Shareholder Stewardship to Shareholder Duties: Is the Time Ripe?', 143.

on how engagement policies are implemented and the outcomes achieved – create regulatory pressure to act. In practice, the need to report on engagement conduct implies that some form of engagement must occur in order for the disclosure to be meaningful. Through this disclosure-driven logic, SRD II contributes to the juridification of stewardship, embedding a functional duty to engage as part of a broader effort to re-regulate capital markets in the post-GFC era.[155]

5.6 Conclusion: Institutionalising Principles, Encountering Practice

Taken together, the developments traced in this chapter underscore the remarkable normative reach of the UK's stewardship model – especially the 1G UK Code – as both a conceptual benchmark and a regulatory reference point. Much like the earlier proliferation of corporate governance codes, the diffusion of stewardship norms demonstrates how soft-law travels: not only through formal legal transplants but also via regulatory imitation, strategic adaptation, and discursive alignment. This process reflects the continuing interplay – and occasional tension – between private ordering and public regulation in the governance of capital markets.

Yet the UK model has not been transplanted wholesale. While many jurisdictions have drawn on its core principles and institutional architecture, others have adapted its framework to fit their own legal traditions, market structures, and political economies. In this respect, the UK Stewardship Code has not simply been exported; it has helped catalyse a broader global debate about the nature, purpose, and scope of investor responsibility in the twenty-first century.

However, most scholarly and policy attention has focused on the international uptake of the UK Code, with far less scrutiny of how stewardship has been interpreted, operationalised, or contested within the UK itself. This raises a critical and underexplored question: to what extent have UK institutional investors embraced, internalised, or resisted the very stewardship principles they helped to promote abroad?

155 The reference of Article 3g to engagement policies, including stakeholder concerns and the reduction of social and environmental risks and cooperation with stakeholders, also reflect such position. For a critical approach, see Alessio M. Pacces, 'Shareholder Activism in the CMU' in Danny Busch, Emilios Avgouleas, and Guido Ferrarini (eds.), *Capital Markets Union in Europe* (Oxford University Press 2018), 507–525.

The next chapter turns to this domestic dimension. Drawing on a systematic analysis of the disclosures submitted under the 2012 and 2020 iterations of the UK Stewardship Code, it investigates how stewardship is articulated, practiced, and transformed in the UK context. Through textual and computational methods, the chapter offers new insights into how a globally influential regulatory model is negotiated in practice – shedding light on the lived realities behind an increasingly institutionalised ideal.

6

Empirical Insights into UK Stewardship Reporting

A Textual and Computational Analysis

6.1 Introduction

This chapter investigates how the UK Stewardship Code has been interpreted and operationalised by institutional investors through their public disclosures. While the UK stewardship model has been widely exported and hailed as a 'gold standard', comparatively little empirical attention has been paid to how the Code functions in practice within the UK itself. Addressing this gap, the chapter examines how signatories to the 2012 and 2020 iterations of the UK Stewardship Code have internalised, reframed, or resisted its principles – particularly as the regulatory focus has shifted from box-ticking compliance to outcome-oriented, values-driven stewardship.[1]

Although formally non-binding, stewardship statements function as both regulatory artefacts and instruments of strategic communication. They are addressed to multiple audiences: the Financial Reporting Council (FRC), which oversees the Code; institutional clients, whose allocation decisions increasingly turn on perceptions of stewardship credibility; and broader stakeholders, including pension beneficiaries and the public. Situated at the intersection of soft law, market accountability, and reputational signalling, these disclosures provide a distinctive empirical lens for examining how institutional investors narrate and enact stewardship in practice.

To analyse these dynamics, the chapter applies a multi-method Natural Language Processing (NLP) framework that combines socio-legal inquiry with measures of disclosure complexity, readability assessment, lexical frequency, and topic modelling. This approach enables

[1] See Financial Reporting Council, *The UK Stewardship Code 2012* (2012) [UK Code 2012] and Financial Reporting Council, *The UK Stewardship Code 2020* (2019) [UK Code 2020], respectively.

a systematic investigation not only of *what* is disclosed but also of *how* stewardship is narratively framed, and *why* those narratives diverge across investor types, geographies, and organisational characteristics. In doing so, the chapter contributes to two intersecting literatures: the methodological field of computational text analysis[2] and the growing body of empirical research on responsible investment.[3] It also sheds light on the evolving nature of stewardship as both a regulatory technology and a field of institutional narration – and explores the extent to which emerging 'other-regarding' narratives are beginning to reshape the normative core of stewardship in the UK.

6.2 Research Design and Methodological Framework

6.2.1 A Multi-method Approach to Analysing Stewardship Disclosures

Natural Language Processing (NLP) has evolved significantly since its origins in the late 1940s, when early efforts focused on rule-based machine translation. It is now a dynamic, interdisciplinary field that brings together insights from artificial intelligence, linguistics, cognitive science, and computer science.[4] Initially dominated by symbolic and linguistically informed models, NLP has undergone a profound transformation since the late 1990s, driven by the increasing availability of digital corpora, advances in machine learning, and greater computational power.

Contemporary NLP encompasses a wide range of computational techniques for analysing, interpreting, and representing human language in ways that enable machines to perform tasks such as text classification, information retrieval, and summarisation.[5] At its core, NLP seeks to transform potentially ambiguous natural language into structured,

[2] See e.g. Justin Grimmer and Brandon M. Stewart, 'Text as Data: The Promise and Pitfalls of Automatic Content Analysis Methods for Political Texts' (2013) 21 *Political Analysis* 267; Matthew Gentzkow, Bryan Kelly and Matt Daddy, 'Text as Data' (2019) 57 *Journal of Economic Literature* 535.

[3] See e.g. Philipp Krueger, Zacharias Sautner and Laura T. Starks, 'The Importance of Climate Risks for Institutional Investors' (2020) 33 *The Review of Financial Studies* 1067; Rob Bauer, Tobias Ruof and Paul Smeets, 'Get Real! Individuals Prefer More Sustainable Investments' (2021) 34 *The Review of Financial Studies* 3976.

[4] Diksha Khurana, Aditya Koli, Kiran Khatter and Sukhdev Singh, 'Natural Language Processing: State of the Art, Current Trends and Challenges' (2023) 82 *Multimedia Tools and Applications* 3713.

[5] Elizabeth D. Liddy, 'Natural Language Processing' in Miriam A. Drake (ed.), *Encyclopedia of Library and Information Science*, vol 1 (2nd ed., Marcel Dekker Inc. 2001), 2126.

machine-interpretable representations. Addressing such ambiguity requires a mix of linguistic theory, probabilistic inference, and increasingly, deep learning architectures.[6] Techniques such as stemming, lemmatisation, and morphological parsing help to normalise linguistic variation, while collocation analysis and syntactic parsing identify patterns of word co-occurrence and structural dependency.[7] These features form the basis of semantic clustering, which underpins topic modelling and other approaches to automated content classification.

A defining development in modern NLP has been the rise of statistical and corpus-based methods, which have opened the door for its broader adoption across a wide range of research fields. In particular, NLP now offers scalable and replicable alternatives to traditional content analysis, which is often constrained by subjectivity and limited reproducibility.[8] Whereas conventional qualitative content analysis involves coding texts against abstract, theory-driven categories, NLP-based methods such as topic modelling detect recurrent patterns of co-occurrence and infer latent semantic structures, thereby reducing reliance on manual interpretation.

This chapter applies these methods to the empirical analysis of stewardship disclosures under the UK Stewardship Code. Issued by institutional investors, these statements occupy a unique space at the intersection of regulation and strategic communication. While formally non-binding, they are publicly disclosed and addressed to multiple audiences: the FRC, which oversees the Code's implementation; institutional clients, whose capital allocation decisions are shaped by perceptions of stewardship credibility; and, indirectly, end-beneficiaries such as retail investors and pension holders, as well as stakeholders connected to investable assets. This layered audience structure, combined with the Code's hybrid regulatory status, renders stewardship disclosures particularly rich material for textual analysis.

To examine how stewardship is framed in practice, the chapter adopts a multi-method NLP-based framework applied to disclosures from the two key iterations of the UK Stewardship Code – 2012 and 2020.[9] The analysis unfolds in four stages: (1) measuring disclosure length and reporting complexity; (2) assessing linguistic readability and textual

6 Gobinda G. Chowdhury, 'Natural Language Processing' (2003) 37 *Annual Review of Information Science and Technology* 51.

7 Amelie Kutter and Cathleen Kantner, 'Corpus-Based Content Analysis: A Method for Investigating News Coverage on War and Intervention', International Relations Online Working Paper, 2012/01.

8 Ibid.

9 See further Section 5.3.

similarity; (3) using relative frequency analysis to map dominant concepts and reporting priorities; and (4) applying STM to uncover latent themes and examine variation across signatories.

This framework enables a systematic and scalable analysis of stewardship discourse, identifying not only which themes emerge across disclosures but also how they vary across institutional types and reporting contexts. To apply this approach meaningfully, however, it must be grounded in a carefully curated and representative textual corpus. The next subsection outlines how this corpus was constructed, detailing the criteria for inclusion, the composition of the 2012 and 2020 samples, and key attributes of the signatories involved.

6.2.2 *Stewardship Statements as Empirical Data: Sample Construction and Corpus*

The data collection process spanned from January 2021 to August 2023 and involved multiple steps to curate separate textual samples for stewardship disclosures under the 2012 and 2020 versions of the UK Stewardship Code. The analysis focuses on asset managers and asset owners, excluding service providers from the sample.[10] As defined in the UK Code 2012, asset owners are institutional investors such as pension funds and insurance companies that own assets and typically delegate investment management, while asset managers are firms appointed by asset owners to manage investments on their behalf, often exercising stewardship responsibilities through engagement and voting.[11]

For the textual sample to the UK Code 2012 (hereinafter 2012 sample), determining the number of signatories presented certain challenges, as signatory figures fluctuated over time before stabilising just below 300 after 2019.[12] Using the FRC's signatory list as of December 2019,[13] a preliminary sample of 283 signatories was identified. The most recent stewardship statement for each signatory was then retrieved, primarily

[10] This exclusion reflects the analytical focus of the study: service providers, such as proxy advisors and ESG data vendors, are not direct stewards of capital but rather act as intermediaries supporting stewardship activities. As such, including them would have introduced significant variation in organisational purpose, reporting practices, and accountability structures, complicating the analysis of how institutional investors themselves interpret and implement stewardship under the UK Stewardship Code.

[11] UK Code 2012, para 6.

[12] Section 5.3.3.2.

[13] The list is available on the FRC's website: https://media.frc.org.uk/documents/Stewardship_Code_2012_Signatory_list.pdf.

from the FRC's website, supplemented by extensive searches of signatories' own webpages and direct email communications. In total, stewardship statements for 275 signatories were successfully collected.[14] Following a familiarisation phase and initial review for data quality and categorisation, six statements exhibiting over 97 per cent textual similarity and one non-compliance explanation were excluded.[15] The final 2012 sample thus comprises stewardship statements from 268 signatories, classified by investor type into 174 asset managers and 94 asset owners.

A similar process was followed to construct the 2020 sample. Based on the FRC's signatory list as of May 2023, stewardship statements were collected for 244 signatories, all available through the FRC's online repository.[16] The resulting 2020 sample comprises 186 asset managers and 58 asset owners – reflecting a notable decline in asset owner participation relative to the 1G UK Code.[17] This decline likely stems from structural developments, including the consolidation of stewardship activities through asset pooling (particularly among public pension schemes) and the increasing delegation of stewardship responsibilities to asset managers.[18] Together these shifts may have reduced the need for many asset owners to produce stand-alone disclosures.

Combined, the two textual samples comprise a total of 346 unique institutional investors: 235 asset managers and 111 asset owners. Of these,

[14] The statements of the following signatories were unable to be identified: Aberdeen Japan Investment Trust plc, Aberdeen New Dawn Investment Trust plc, Aberdeen UK Tracker Trust plc, Jaguar Land Rover Pension Trustees Ltd, J. Stern & Co, London Borough of Hackney, Mirova, and Murray Income Fund.

[15] The following statements were removed due to over 97 per cent similarities with other statements in the sample: Epworth Investment Management Limited; Hermes EOS; NFU Mutual Investment Services Ltd. (MISCO); Premier Portfolio Managers Ltd; Pension and Assurance Scheme for Lay Employees of the Methodist Church; and Strategic Equity Capital. In addition, the statement of Hansa Trust plc was removed due to its nature as an explanation of non-compliance to the UK Code 2012.

[16] www.frc.org.uk/library/standards-codes-policy/stewardship/uk-stewardship-code-signatories/.

[17] The sample excludes the statements of Cardano and Tower Willis who are both asset managers and service providers.

[18] However, asset pooling within UK public pension schemes has not been without challenges. On recent resistance to consolidation efforts, see Mary McDougall and Stephanie Stacey, 'Council pension "pools" in England and Wales reject government push to merge' *Financial Times* (1 March 2025). On the delegation of stewardship and investment functions by asset owners, see The Investment Association, *Investment Relationships for Sustainable Value Creation: Alignment Between Asset Owners and Investment Managers* (June 2022) (reporting, among others, that '[t]he majority of UK based pension schemes delegate investment activity in this way, with some notable exceptions, particularly larger asset owners who have their own in-house investment management teams').

165 (124 asset managers and 41 asset owners) are signatories to both the 2012 and 2020 Codes.[19] In contrast, 102 are solely signatories to the UK Code 2012 (49 asset managers and 53 asset owners), and 79 investors are exclusive signatories to the UK Code 2020 (63 asset managers and 16 asset owners).

The majority of signatories are well-established investors, with 62.65 per cent founded before 2000 and a median founding year of 1993. Signatories vary widely in size, with assets under management ranging from USD19 million to USD8,478.70 billion. The average size is USD202.07 billion, while the median is USD14.34 billion, reflecting the broader dispersion among the largest signatories compared to the smallest ones.[20] As expected, asset managers tend to be larger than asset owners.[21]

Most signatories (72.25 per cent) are headquartered in the UK. Although this may be inconsistent with the ownership structure of UK-listed companies – where foreign ownership is predominant[22] – it reflects the strong compliance-drive incentives for both FCA-authorised asset managers and UK pension funds to become signatories to the Code.[23] By investor type, UK domiciliation is even more pronounced among asset owners, 92.79 per cent of whom are UK-based compared to 62.55 per cent of asset managers. This pattern likely stems from the inherently domestic orientation of asset owners, such as public and private pension funds, which manage assets on behalf of local beneficiaries and are therefore more deeply embedded in national regulatory and market contexts.[24] By contrast, asset managers – particularly larger firms – tend to operate across multiple jurisdictions and serve a global client base, thereby rendering their stewardship commitments more contingent on the regulatory environment and reputational expectations prevailing in each market.[25]

19 This overlap allows for comparisons of reporting patterns across the two Code iterations among institutional investors that remained signatories in both periods. See Section 6.6.

20 Across the two samples, the average and median AUM of signatories are £229.12 billion and £14.40 billion, respectively, in the 2012 sample, compared to £268.45 billion and £23.49 billion in the 2020 sample.

21 The average and median size of asset managers is USD334.27 billion and USD26.16 billion, respectively, while asset owners have on average USD29.27 billion assets under management (the median is USD9.48 billion).

22 Section 2.5.2.

23 Section 5.3.3.1.

24 On the broader trend whereby asset owners are encouraged or mandated to support national economic objectives through their investment choices, see Mary McDougall, 'Pensions minister says schemes must invest more in UK' *Financial Times* (5 March 2025).

25 See e.g. Harriet Agnew and Brooke Masters, 'The relentless advance of American asset managers in Europe' *Financial Times* (17 December 2024).

Of the signatories to the UK Code 2012, 192 (118 asset managers and 74 asset owners) were assessed by the FRC as Tier 1 signatories, while the remaining 75 (55 asset managers and 20 asset owners) were classified as Tier 2. Notably, 75.52 per cent of Tier 1 signatories transitioned to the UK Code 2020, compared to only 41.33 per cent of Tier 2 signatories. This disparity suggests that Tier 2 signatories were less committed to, or less capable of meeting, the enhanced standards of stewardship introduced under the second-generation (2G) UK Code.

Finally, with respect to engagement approach, 71 signatories (64 asset managers and 7 asset owners) pursue shareholder activism strategies, based on data collected from Diligent Market Intelligence, a private database tracking activist campaigns since 2006.[26]

Having established the composition and characteristics of the two textual samples, the following sections turn to the empirical analysis. Drawing on the aforementioned NLP methods, the chapter examines how stewardship is communicated across disclosures – beginning with surface-level attributes such as disclosure length and readability, and progressing towards more interpretive techniques that uncover deeper thematic structures and rhetorical variation.

6.3 Evaluating the Depth and Readability of Stewardship Disclosures

6.3.1 *Measuring Scale and Structural Variation in Stewardship Reporting*

To assess how the scale and structure of stewardship reporting evolved between the two iterations of the UK Stewardship Code, this section

[26] Diligent Market Intelligence defines shareholder activism broadly as '[t]he advocacy by minority shareholders that various strategic levers are pulled by a public company in a bid to create shareholder value, which is broadly achieved by improving underlying operational performance, exploring strategic alternatives, lifting governance standards, and returning capital to shareholders'. Diligent Market Intelligence classifies activist investors into five different categories based on their focus: (1) primary focus activists for whom proactive and systematic activist investing forms a significant majority of their investment portfolios; (2) partial focus activists who employ proactive and systematic activist investing only for a part of their assets; (3) occasional focus activists for whom activist investing is often reactive rather than proactive in nature and employed only infrequently; (4) engagement focus activists for whom shareholder activism is an escalation of their investment stewardship responsibilities; and (5) concerned shareholders who collectively attempt to enforce change at a single company. Diligent Market Intelligence is subscription-based database, available here: www.insightia.com.

begins with a quantitative analysis of disclosure volume. The text was first standardised – converted to British English and stripped of non-core content such as tables of contents, forewords, appendices, glossaries, and disclaimers. This process yielded a total corpus of 7,518,292 words, comprising 668,610 from the 2012 sample and 6,849,682 from the 2020 sample. Statement length varied widely, ranging from 252 words to 93,135 words. The average word count was 14,684, while the median was 4,973 words, indicating significant dispersion and skewness.

Table 6.1 presents descriptive statistics, including total word counts, average and median statement lengths, and standard deviation by investor type and Code iteration. The data reveal a dramatic expansion in statement length under the 2020 Code. Total word counts increased more than tenfold, with substantial rises in both average and median lengths. This trend reflects the broader scope of the revised Code and a corresponding increase in the level of detail provided by signatories. The higher standard deviation in the 2020 sample also suggests divergent interpretations of the Code's requirements and disparities in organisational capacity, reporting strategy, and resources.

Under the UK Code 2012, statements from both asset managers and asset owners were relatively similar in length and much shorter than those produced under the 2020 Code. By contrast, the 2020 disclosures show greater variability, particularly among asset managers, who produced longer and more diverse reports. As illustrated in Figure 6.1, asset manager statements span a wider range, with higher medians, and noticeable outliers – indicating diverse approaches to reporting. While asset owners also increased the length and variability of their statements, their disclosures tend to be shorter and display fewer extremes.

This shift towards lengthier and more detailed reporting reflects the 2020 Code's heightened demands – particularly its focus on outcomes, systemic stewardship, and illustrative case studies.[27] The variability in word counts – particularly among asset managers – reflects differing interpretations of the Code's requirements as well as variation in organisational capacity, reporting strategy, and resourcing.

Building on the observed expansion in disclosure length under the UK Code 2020, further analysis examines how reporting scale varies with institutional size. Figure 6.2 highlights a clear trend when analysing report lengths by investor size. Larger institutional investors, measured by assets under management (natural logarithm), tend to produce longer stewardship statements. This trend is observed for both asset managers

[27] Section 5.3.2.

Table 6.1 *Descriptive statistics for the corpus of stewardship statements*

	2012 UK Code				2020 UK Code			
	Total	Average	Median	St. Dev.	Total	Average	Median	St. Dev.
Asset Managers	507,248	2,915	2,691	1,352	5,459,560	29,352	26,470	14,650
Asset Owners	161,362	1,716	1,614	872	1,390,122	23,967	20,961	11,865
All	668,610	2,495	2,247	1,334	6,849,682	28,072	25,547	14,202

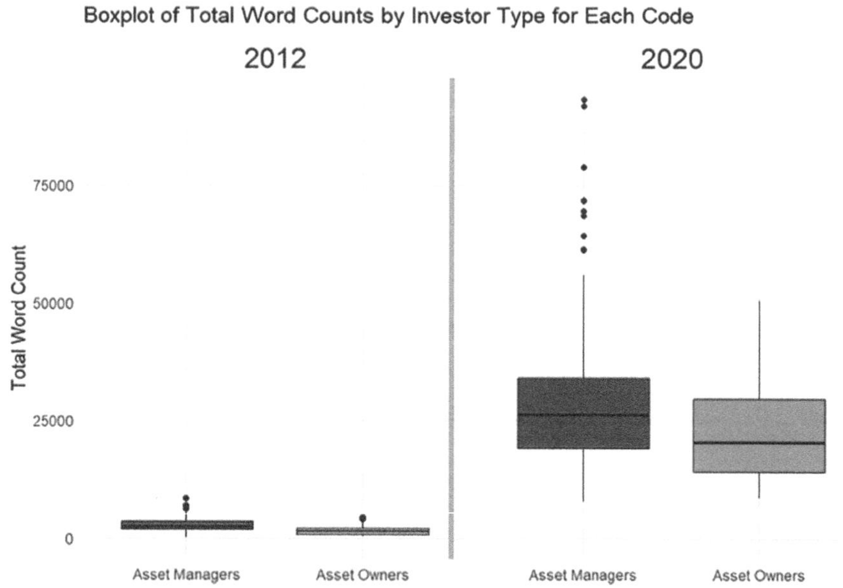

Figure 6.1 Comparison of stewardship statement lengths by investor type under the 2012 and 2020 UK Stewardship Codes.

(dark grey) and asset owners (light grey). The relationship between size and word count is stronger for asset managers, as evidenced by R^2 values of 13 per cent and 17 per cent in the 2012 and 2020 samples, respectively. Larger asset managers also produce the longest statements, as shown in the upper-right region of the two scatterplots. While a positive correlation is absent for asset owners in the 2012 sample, the 2020 data reveal a notable shift, with larger asset owners producing longer statements and an R^2 value of 11 per cent. This suggests some convergence in reporting patterns between asset managers and asset owners under the 2020 Code.

Additionally, both investor types exhibit variability in statement length for a given size, with this variability being more pronounced at higher AUM levels, particularly for asset managers. The findings indicate that larger asset managers are more likely to allocate resources towards producing longer and potentially more detailed statements. Although asset owners show a similar trend under the 2020 Code, the relationship is less pronounced, suggesting differences in priorities, resources, or reporting practices between the two investor types.

Overall, the findings highlight a shift towards more comprehensive and detailed stewardship reporting under the 2G UK Code. However, an increase in length does not necessarily equate to greater clarity. Longer

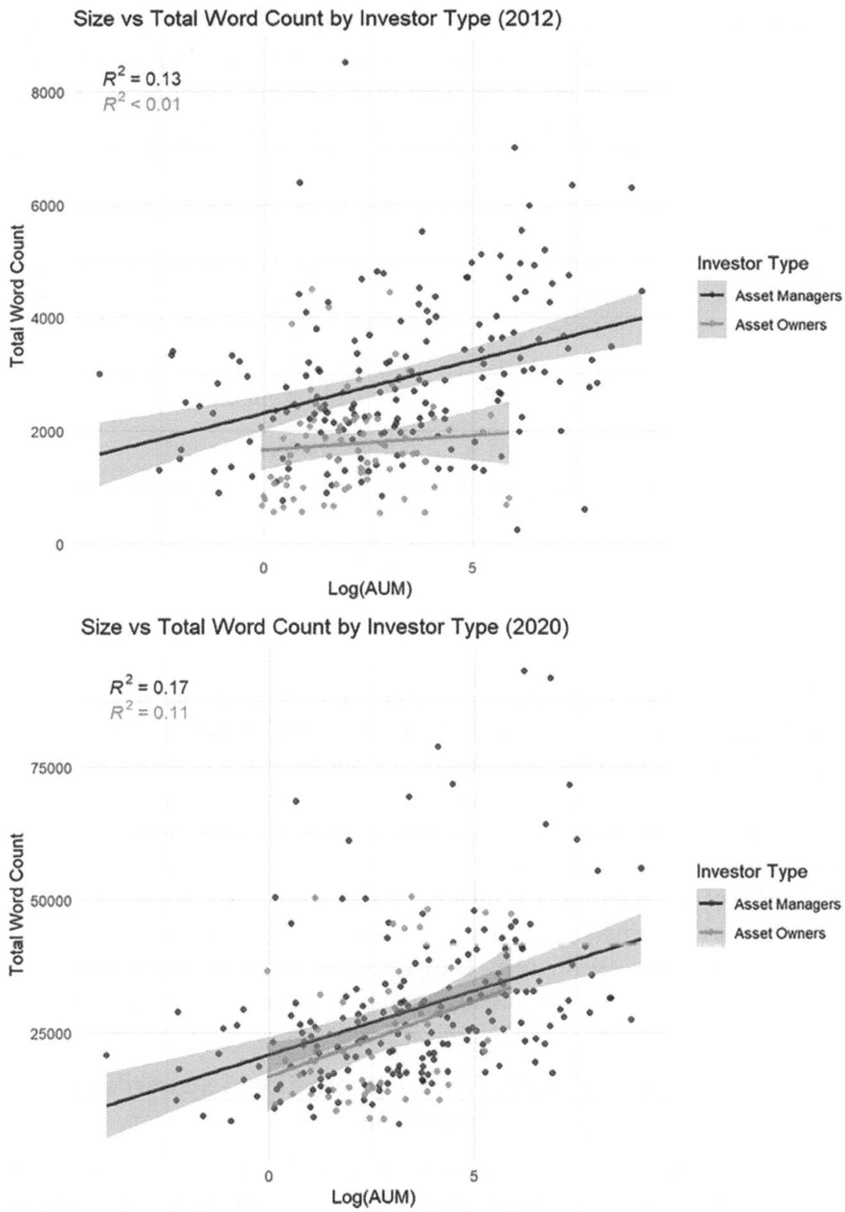

Figure 6.2 Stewardship statement lengths by investor type and investor size under the 2012 and 2020 UK Stewardship Codes.

statements may enhance transparency and depth, but they can also introduce complexity, making disclosures more difficult to interpret. The next section assesses this balance by examining whether the expanded statements improved readability or contributed to disclosure complexity.

6.3.2 *Assessing Readability and Linguistic Complexity*

To evaluate the readability and linguistic clarity of stewardship disclosures, Gunning's Fog Index was calculated for each signatory statement. The Fog Index quantifies text complexity by analysing sentence length and the proportion of complex words – defined as those containing three or more syllables. The formula for the index is:

$$\text{Fog Index} = 0.4 \times (\text{Average sentence length} + \text{Percentage of complex words}).$$

This score represents the estimated number of years of formal education required to read and comprehend a given document.[28] Higher scores indicate greater complexity, suggesting that the text may be more difficult to understand.

Table 6.2 presents the Fog Index statistics for stewardship statements in the 2012 (Panel A) and 2020 (Panel B) samples, both overall and by investor type. The results indicate only minor variations in readability complexity across the full distribution, with the median stewardship statement requiring approximately twenty-one years of formal education to be fully understood – a level comparable to other financial reports.[29] Notably, despite the increasing length of statements following the introduction of the UK Code 2020, Fog Index scores remained stable. This suggests that the additional content did not necessarily increase linguistic complexity but instead enhanced the depth of reporting without making disclosures significantly harder to comprehend.

6.4 Patterns of Similarity and Originality in Stewardship Reporting

To build on the analysis of statement length and readability, the next step examines the extent of textual similarity across stewardship disclosures.

[28] For an application in 10-K filings, see Travis Dyer, Mark H. Lang and Lorien Stice-Lawrence, 'The Evolution of 10-K Textual Disclosure: Evidence from Latent Dirichlet Allocation' (2017) 64 *Journal of Accounting and Economics* 221, 225.

[29] Ibid., 225 (reporting an average Fog index score of 21.34 for 10-K disclosures in the US).

Table 6.2 *Fog index scores for stewardship statements under the UK Stewardship Codes (2012 and 2012)*

Panel A: UK Code 2012							
Investor Type	Minimum	First Quartile	Median	Mean	Third Quartile	Maximum	St dev
All	16.920	20.320	21.380	21.510	22.490	27.770	1.837
Asset Managers	16.925	20.155	21.288	21.311	22.472	27.774	1.702
Asset Owners	17.842	20.523	21.522	21.891	22.589	27.124	2.018
Panel B: UK Code 2020							
Investor Type	Minimum	First Quartile	Median	Mean	Third Quartile	Maximum	St dev
All	16.680	20.480	21.500	21.680	22.650	32.930	1.809
Asset Managers	17.927	20.346	21.453	21.602	22.532	32.932	1.866
Asset Owners	16.682	21.110	21.690	21.944	22.858	26.183	1.602

While the Fog Index assesses linguistic complexity, it does not indicate whether statements are highly standardised or exhibit diversity in reporting practices. To address this, textual similarity analysis is applied to identify patterns of repetition, drafting conventions, and the presence of boilerplate language across signatory statements. This section employs two complementary methods – WCopyfind and cosine similarity – to assess the degree of textual overlap among statements, both across signatories and over time. These analyses provide a clearer picture of whether the UK Code 2020 led to more differentiated and tailored disclosures or whether elements of standardisation persist in stewardship reporting.

6.4.1 *Phrase-Level Overlap: Insights from WCopyfind Analysis*

To identify similarities among the signatories' statements, the open-source plagiarism detection software WCopyfind 4.1.1 was used.[30] This tool has been previously applied in empirical legal studies to investigate textual borrowing, including in court opinions and trade agreements, policy dissemination and rulemaking, and the global diffusion of stewardship codes.[31] WCopyfind detects 'matches', both exact and approximate, between two or more text documents. It quantifies shared phrases by calculating a similarity score, calculated as the ratio of matched words to total words.

For this analysis, the 268 statements to the UK Code 2012 and the 244 statements to the UK Code 2020 were uploaded into the software separately. Within each sample, statements were systematically compared with all others using the software's default settings to identify identical text

[30] Available at <https://plagiarism.bloomfieldmedia.com/software/wcopyfind/>.

[31] See e.g. Paul M. Collins Jr, Pamela C. Corley, and Jesse Hamner, 'The Influence of Amicus Curiae Briefs on US Supreme Court Opinion Content' (2015) 49 *Law & Society Review* 917; Adam Feldman, 'Counting on Quality: The Effects of Merits brief Quality on Supreme Court Decisions' (2016) 94 *Denver University Law Review* 43; Rachael K. Hinkle, 'Into the Words: Using Statutory Text to Explore the Impact of Federal Courts on State Policy Diffusion' (2015) 59 *American Journal of Political Science* 1002; Todd Allee and Manfred Elsig, 'Are the Contents of International Treaties Copied and Pasted? Evidence from Preferential Trade Agreements' (2019) 63 *International Studies Quarterly* 603. For a similar example, see Joshua M. Jansa, Eric R. Hansen, and Virginia H. Grey, 'Copy and Paste Lawmaking: Legislative Professionalism and Policy Reinvention in the States' (2019) 47 *American Politics Research* 739; Dionysia Katelouzou and Mathias Siems, 'The Global Diffusion of Stewardship Codes' in Dan W. Puchniak and Dionysia Katelouzou (eds.), *Global Shareholder Stewardship* (Cambridge University Press 2022), 631, 641–4; Maraam A. Dwidar, 'Diverse Lobbying Coalitions and Influence in Notice-and-Comment Rulemaking' (2022) 50 *Policy Studies Journal* 199.

strings. The default configuration excluded matching phrases shorter than six words and applied a minimum match threshold of 80 per cent to account for minor linguistic variations while ensuring comparability. The software also permitted up to two nonmatching words ('imperfections') within otherwise identical phrasing. Additionally, letter case, numbers, outer punctuation, and nonwords were ignored to standardise comparisons.

WCopyfind identified seventy-eight matching pairs in the 2012 sample and thirty in the 2020 sample. Overlap was measured by calculating the total word count of all common strings (perfectly matching phrases) for each pair as a percentage of the total word count. Given that stewardship statements vary significantly in length, differences in size often influence the extent of overlap between pairs. To account for this, Tables 6.3 and 6.4 report the ten most closely matched pairs, presenting the percentage of perfectly matching phrases for each pair in the 2012 and 2020 samples, respectively. Both percentages – the overlap in the older statement and the overlap in the newer statement – are essential for accurately interpreting the data. While the influence of the older statement on the newer one is discernible, the overlap in the older statement provides additional context. For example, if a newer statement fully incorporates an older statement but also adds substantial new content, making it ten times longer, the overlap in the newer statement would appear as only 10 per cent. However, knowing that the overlap in the older statement is 100 per cent reveals that the original text was fully retained. Without this additional information, the extent of textual borrowing could be overestimated.

Table 6.3 reveals significant overlaps in the 2012 sample, particularly among asset owner pairs, which exhibit high levels of similarity. For instance, Wiltshire and Worcestershire (Rank 1), Pilkington and Whitbread (Rank 2), MNPOF and Whitbread (Rank 4), and Pilkington and Cummins (Rank 5) all show overlaps exceeding 70 per cent. These high percentages suggest a strong degree of standardisation in asset owners' stewardship statements, likely driven by adherence to predefined formats, shared templates, or reliance on common drafters such as investment consultants.[32] Additionally, some asset owners may belong

[32] On the influential role investment consultants play in shaping how asset owners assess and engage on stewardship, see PRI, *Working towards a Sustainable Financial System: Investment Consultant Services Review* (2017). For example, the Investment Consultants Sustainability Working Group (ICSWG), comprising seventeen consulting firms, has issued targeted guidance to improve stewardship reporting. This includes tools such as targeted engagement metrics and case study formats to assist asset owners in evaluating

Table 6.3 *Most similar pairs of 2012 stewardship statements by common strings*

Rank	Older Statement	Newer Statement	Common Strings (in Words)	All Words in Older Statement	All Words in Newer Statement	Overlap in Older Statement	Overlap in Newer Statement
1	Wiltshire (Sep 16)	Worchestershire (Apr 19)	2,112	2,725	2,481	75.50%	85.13%
2	Pilkington (Aug 16)	Whitbread (Sep 16)	1,303	1,858	1,531	70.13%	85.11%
3	Alvento (Jan 17)	Adelphi (Dec 18)	1,863	2,203	2,404	84.57%	77.50%
4	MNOPF (Aug 16)	Whitbread (Sep 16)	1,158	2,390	1,531	48.45%	75.64%
5	Pilkington (Aug 16)	Cummins (Sep 16)	1,707	1,858	2,438	91.87%	70.02%
6	WHEB (Jun 2016)	Menhaden (Mar 17)	1,001	2,836	1,499	35.30%	66.78%
7	MNOPF (Aug 16)	Cummins (Sep 16)	1,570	2,390	2,438	65.69%	64.40%
8	Pilkington (Aug 16)	MNFOP (Aug 16)	1,530	1,858	2,390	82.35%	64.02%
9	Staffordshire (Aug 18)	Shropshire (Mar 20)	1,352	1,833	2,135	73.76%	63.33%
10	CIC Capital Fund (May 16)	HSBC (Jul 20)	1,852	2,661	3,096	69.60%	59.82%

Table 6.4 *Most similar pairs of 2020 stewardship statements by common strings*

Rank	Older Statement	Newer Statement	Common Strings (in Words)	All Words in Older Statement	All Words in Newer Statement	Overlap in Older Statement	Overlap in Newer Statement
1	Mineworkers (N/A)	British Coal (N/A)	12,785	15,553	15,200	82.20%	84.11%
2	Cumbria (N/A)	Scottish Borders (N/A)	3,047	25,572	11,539	11.92%	26.41%
3	M&G (Apr 2022)	M&G AO (Apr 2022)	4,800	44,980	30,769	10.67%	15.60%
4	River and Mercantile (Apr 2022)	Downing (Oct 2022)	2,071	22,374	17,373	9.26%	11.92%
5	Cumbria (N/A)	Lincolnshire (N/A)	1,577	25,572	13,409	6.17%	11.76%
6	DWS (Apr 2022)	CCLA (N/A)	1,304	64,331	12,415	2.03%	10.50%
7	Epoch (Oct 2022)	CCLA (N/A)	1,233	26,450	12,415	4.66%	9.93%
8	Herald (Spring 2022)	CCLA (N/A)	1,180	24,949	12,415	4.73%	9.50%
9	Kempen (N/A)	CCLA (N/A)	1,171	28,430	12,415	4.12%	9.43%
10	Edinburgh Partners (Mar 2021)	CCLA (N/A)	1,168	14,137	12,415	8.26%	9.41%

to the same organisation or network, such as the Local Authority Pension Fund Forum (LAPFF), further contributing to textual similarities.

By contrast, asset managers demonstrate greater variability in overlap percentages, suggesting a more tailored approach to stewardship reporting. The notable exception is Alvento and Adelphi Capital (Rank 3), whose statements exhibit high overlap percentages (84.57 per cent in the older statement and 77.50 per cent in the newer statement).[33] However, beyond this pair, overlap percentages among asset managers drop sharply from these levels, indicating a greater degree of content variability compared to asset owners.

A consistent trend across most pairs is that overlap percentages are higher in older statements than in newer ones. This suggests that newer statements are more likely to incorporate additional content or reflect substantive updates to stewardship practices, potentially in response to evolving regulatory standards or shifting market expectations. Additionally, smaller statements tend to exhibit higher overlap percentages relative to their total length (e.g. the Wiltshire–Worcestershire pair), underscoring a greater reliance on standardised templates for shorter disclosures.

The decline in textual overlap between statements in the 2020 sample, as shown in Table 6.4, reinforces the broader shift towards more distinct and context-specific stewardship reporting. With the notable exception of the Mineworkers-British Coal pair (Rank 1), which stands out with exceptionally high overlap percentages (82.20 per cent and 84.11 per cent, respectively), most 2020 statements exhibit only moderate to low levels of textual similarity. This contrasts sharply with the 2012 statements, where overlap percentages were significantly higher, particularly among asset owner pairs.

their managers' stewardship. See ICSWG, *Engagement Reporting Guide* (Original November 2021, latest update November 2024).

33 For instance, the following passage appears in both statements: 'Institutional investors should have a robust policy on managing conflicts of interest in relation to stewardship and this policy should be publicly disclosed. It is our policy and duty to act in the best interest of our clients. Where possible, we seek to organise our business activities to avoid conflicts of interest. For example, we do not have any financial affiliates (e.g. connected brokerage facilities), we do not have any direct investments (all our investing is conducted through the funds we manage), and we do not hold client money. Where conflicts are unavoidable, we develop both formal and informal procedures for their management. These include the maintenance of an inventory of all potential and actual conflicts of interest, the key risks and how we actively manage them. Such procedures are designed to ensure that the management of the conflict takes place in such a way that the firm or its employees are not advantaged and that no client is disadvantaged'.

While shared drafting practices, investment consultants, and industry networks likely influenced both sets of disclosures, the 2020 Code's emphasis on outcomes-focused reporting may have encouraged signatories to provide more substantive, narrative-driven accounts of their stewardship activities, reducing textual uniformity.[34] As a result, signatories appear to have tailored their statements more explicitly to reflect their investment practices, governance priorities, evolving regulatory requirements, and heightened client or beneficiary expectations.

Additionally, the increased length of the 2020 statements contributes to the lower overlap percentages.[35] Longer statements inherently contain more unique content, which dilutes the proportion of identical text between pairs. This trend is evident in cases such as CCLA's statement, which, despite overlapping with several other statements, shows low relative overlap percentages (4.12 per cent to 10.50 percent) due to its overall length.

Together, these findings suggest an evolution in stewardship reporting between the 2012 and 2020 iterations of the UK Stewardship Code, marked by a shift from standardised, template-driven approaches to more tailored, detailed, and context-sensitive narratives. However, the analysis of exact textual overlap does not fully capture the semantic similarities and conceptual coherence between disclosures. Both 'false positives', where word matches are coincidental, and 'false negatives', where similar ideas are conveyed using different wording and go undetected, may arise.

To address these limitations, cosine similarity offers a more context-sensitive approach, assessing the structural and thematic alignment of statements beyond exact phrasing. By supplementing exact phrase matching with cosine similarity, the next section evaluates whether the decline in textual overlap reflects a genuine shift in reporting practices rather or simply linguistic rewording.

6.4.2 Lexical Similarity and Boilerplate Language: A Cosine Similarity Analysis

The observed decline in textual overlap suggests a shift in reporting practices, potentially reflecting a move away from repetitive language in stewardship disclosures. However, this also raises broader concerns

[34] See Section 5.3.3.1.

[35] Section 6.3.1.

about standardisation – specifically the challenge of ensuring consistency without sacrificing transparency and substantive engagement. This issue ties to the ongoing debate on 'disclosure overload', where both mandatory and voluntary disclosures become excessively lengthy and difficult to interpret.[36] The use of boilerplate disclosures, which has been extensively scrutinised across contracts, consumer protection documents, and financial reports, often undermines the goal of informed decision-making by relying on vague, non-specific language.[37] In the context of investor stewardship, such disclosures risk becoming compliance-driven tick-box exercises, diminishing their credibility as governance tools.

To assess this issue empirically, recent work – including computational text analysis – has examined boilerplate across corporate communications such as risk factor disclosures,[38] proxy statements,[39] and mutual fund disclosures.[40] Building on these methods, this study uses cosine similarity based on 5-grams – a method that quantifies textual similarity by comparing the frequency of contiguous five-word sequences – to measure textual repetition in stewardship disclosures.[41] Higher cosine similarity values, ranging from zero to one, indicate greater textual similarity, suggesting a stronger reliance on standardised language. By quantifying the prevalence of formulaic language, the analysis provides insight into how disclosure practices have evolved under the 2020 Code and whether they reflect more authentic, differentiated reporting.

Table 6.5 presents the highest ten pairwise similarity scores, along with their corresponding frequency values, for both the 2012 and 2020

[36] Troy A. Paredes, 'Blinded by the Light: Information Overload and Its Consequences' (2003) 81 *Washington University Law Quarterly* 417; Virginia Harper Ho, 'Disclosure Overload? Lessons for Risk Disclosure & ESG Reporting Reform from the Regulation S-K Concept Release' (2020) 65 *Villanova Law Review* 67.

[37] See e.g. Margaret Jane Radin, *Boilerplate: The Fine Print, Vanishing Rights, and the Rule of Law* (Princeton University Press 2013); Ian Ayres and Alan Schwartz, 'The No-Reading Problem in Consumer Contract Law' (2014) 66 *Stanford Law Review* 545.

[38] Dyer *et al.*, 'The Evolution of 10-K Textual Disclosure: Evidence from Latent Dirichlet Allocation', 229–36; Richard A. Cazier, Jeff L. McMullin and John S. Treu, 'Are Lengthy and Boilerplate Risk Factor Disclosures Inadequate? An Examination of Judicial and Regulatory Assessments of Risk Factor Language' (2021) 96 *The Accounting Review* 131.

[39] Sudipta Basu, Alice Lee and Todd Schifeling, 'Rhetorical Contests in Environmental and Social Proposals in Proxy Statements (2023)' <https://ssrn.com/abstract=4407413>.

[40] Susan Smelcer, Anne M. Tucker and Yusen Xia, 'Copy, Paste, Disclose: The Informative Value of Boilerplate in Mutual Fund Disclosures' (2024) <https://ssrn.com/abstract=4753030>.

[41] For a similar methodological approach, see ibid., 26–8. Additional analysis using 4-grams yielded no substantive differences in the results.

Table 6.5 *Top ten most textually similar stewardship statements in the 2012 and 2020 samples*

Rank	2012 Sample Investor Pair		Freq	2020 Sample Investor Pair		Freq
1	Pilkington	Cummins	0.85	Mineworkers	British Coal	0.87
2	Mineworkers	British Coal	0.84	Darwin Property	Darwin Alternative	0.64
3	Whitbread	Pilkington	0.84	Worcestershire	LGPS	0.50
4	Whitbread	Cummins	0.78	West Midlands	LGPS	0.27
5	Worcestershire	Wiltshire	0.69	Worcestershire	West Midlands	0.25
6	Alvento	Adelphi Capital	0.67	Cornwall Pension	Brunel	0.13
7	BAT	BASF	0.64	Scottish Borders	Cumbria	0.12
8	Pilkington	MNOPF	0.64	M&G AO	M&G	0.11
9	Towers Watson	Siemens	0.63	Schroders	Legal & General	0.10
10	MNOPF	Cummins	0.61	Lodbrok	AGF	0.09

samples. In the 2012 sample, several asset owner pairs exhibit high similarity scores, with Pilkington and Cummins showing the highest match (0.85), followed closely by Mineworkers and British Coal (0.84) and Whitbread and Pilkington (0.84). In contrast, in the top ten most similar pairs only one involves asset managers – Alvento and Adelphi Capital (0.67). This suggests that boilerplate language is far more prevalent among asset owners, who likely rely on common templates or third-party common drafters, whereas asset managers tend to produce more distinct and customised stewardship statements.

Turning to the 2020 sample, the cosine similarity scores highlight notable differences in textual overlap compared to the 2012 sample. The highest similarity score (0.87) is observed between Mineworkers and British Coal, both asset owners. Beyond this pair, however, the similarity scores drop significantly. The second-highest similarity score (0.64) is between Darwin Property Investment Management (Guernsey) Limited and Darwin Alternative Investment Management (Guernsey) Limited, indicating that some investment entities maintain highly consistent wording across statements issued by different fund managers.

Unlike reporting to the UK Code 2012, where multiple asset owner pairs had scores above 0.80, the 2020 sample exhibits a marked decline in similarity. Few pairs exceed a similarity score of 0.50, with most asset owner pairs ranging between 0.10 and 0.30, highlighting a shift away from standardised language. This trend aligns with the 2G UK Code's transition from policy-based reporting to outcomes-focused reporting, which encourages signatories to provide more specific, context-driven narratives rather than relying on standardised disclosures.

These findings are consistent with the textual similarity analysis based on exact phrase matching, reinforcing that the 2G UK Code has encouraged more meaningful and context-specific disclosures for stakeholders. While the combination of exact phrase matching detection and cosine similarity analysis provides a robust framework for evaluating the formal and structural characteristics of stewardship disclosures, these metrics alone cannot fully capture their qualitative substance, necessitating complementary analysis. Given that the Fog Index analysis reveals no significant changes in readability, it becomes critical to examine whether the observed increase in statement length reflects genuine shifts in content or instead amounts to expanded but formulaic reporting.

6.5 Shifting Emphases: A Frequency Analysis of Key Concepts

Relative frequency analysis provides a valuable starting point for identifying dominant reporting patterns and tracking shifts in disclosure priorities over time. Quantifying how often key terms appear offers an empirical foundation for assessing how the language of stewardship has evolved across the 2012 and 2020 iterations of the UK Stewardship Code. To systematically examine how signatories to the two Codes conceptualise stewardship, the analysis begins by calculating the relative frequency of unigrams (single-word tokens) and 2-grams (two-word phrases) in each statement. Each word's absolute frequency was divided by the total word count of the document and standardised per 1,000 words, a conventional approach for comparing documents of varying lengths.[42]

To ensure consistency, standard preprocessing steps were applied. Stopwords were removed, and all text was tokenised, with words reduced to their base or root forms through stemming or lemmatisation. This process avoids inflating frequency counts by consolidating lexical variants (e.g. 'invest', 'investment', and 'investing' were reduced to 'invest'). Plural forms were also standardised (e.g. 'companies' → 'company') to ensure conceptual rather than grammatical comparisons. Two-word phrases were similarly extracted from the tokenised text to detect recurring patterns and thematic emphases in stewardship discourse.

This quantitative approach not only highlights the most frequently used terms but also reveals differences in emphasis between asset managers and asset owners. It enables comparative analysis of how reporting priorities have shifted over time, particularly in response to evolving regulatory expectations and broader market trends. The following sections present these findings in turn, beginning with the dominant themes and reporting patterns in the 2012 sample, and then examining the transformations evident in the 2020 disclosures.

[42] Frequency word lists have long been part of the standard methodology for analysing corpora linguistics. For a review of the relevant literature, see Alistair Baron, Paul Rayson and Dawn Archer, 'Word Frequency and Key Word Statistics in Historical Corpus Linguistics' (2009) 20 *Anglistik: International Journal of English Studies* 41.

6.5.1 *The 2012 Sample: Micro-level Stewardship through Voting and Engagement*

Table 6.6 presents the thirty most frequently used individual words (unigrams) and word pairings (2-grams) across the entire 2012 sample and separately within subsets categorised by investor type. Across all investors, the most frequently used words include 'vote', 'manage', 'invest', 'company', and 'engage'. This suggests that stewardship reporting under the 2012 Code was primarily centred on firm-specific voting and engagement, aligning with the micro-level shareholder stewardship model.[43] However, beyond these shared terms, clear distinctions emerge in how asset managers and asset owners conceptualise and implement shareholder stewardship.

While voting remains central to both groups – consistent with Principle 4 of the UK Code 2012 – their approach and rationale differ. Asset managers closely link voting with investment decision-making and engagement with investee companies, as reflected in frequently used terms like 'proxy', 'engage', and 'active'. This suggests that voting is part of a broader strategy of direct corporate engagement, often exercised through proxy voting and shareholder resolutions.[44] Beyond formal voting mechanisms, stewardship extends to informal engagement, such as meetings and dialogue with board directors, as indicated by the frequent use of 'meeting', 'shareholder(s)', and 'corporate/ion(s)'. The two-word phrase (2-gram) analysis reinforces this, with phrases like 'proxy voting', 'engage company/ies', 'vote policy/(ies)', and 'general meeting(s)' frequently appearing in asset manager statements.

In contrast, asset owners do not frequently mention 'proxy' in their stewardship disclosures, despite 'vote' remaining prominent. This likely reflects they usually exercise stewardship indirectly,[45] focusing instead on governance-related terms such as 'stewardship', 'policy', 'principle', 'govern', and 'monitor', suggesting that voting is framed within a broader fiduciary and oversight role rather than as an engagement tool. The 2-gram

[43] See also Section 7.2.1.

[44] On the role of proxy advisors, see e.g. Andrew F. Tuch, 'Proxy Advisor Influence in a Comparative Light' (2019) 99 *Boston University Law Review* 1459; Andrey Malenko, Nadya Malenko and Chester Spatt, 'Creating Controversy in Proxy Voting Advice' (2025) 80 *The Journal of Finance* 2303. But see Arnoud Boot, Jan Krahnen, Lemma Senbet and Chester Spatt, 'The Controversy over Proxy Voting: The Role of Fund Managers and Proxy Advisors' (2023) 79 *Financial Analysts Journal* 8 (suggesting that the Big Three are more influential in voting than ISS over time).

[45] On indirect stewardship, see Section 7.3.

Table 6.6 *Most frequently occurring unigrams and 2-grams in 2012 stewardship statements*

ALL		Asset Managers		Asset Owners	
Unigrams	2-grams	Unigrams	2-grams	Unigrams	2-grams
vote	institut_investor	vote	institut_investor	manag	invest_manag
manag	conflict_interest	compani	proxi_vot	invest	institut_investor
invest	investe_compani	manag	conflict_interest	fund	principl_institut
compani	proxi_vot	invest	investe_compani	vote	conflict_interest
engag	invest_manag	client	corpor_govern	compani	stewardship_cod
stewardship	corpor_govern	engag	principl_institut	stewardship	pension_fund
investor	principl_institut	will	stewardship_cod	activ	vote_activ
will	stewardship_cod	stewardship	vote_activ	engag	respons_invest
polici	vote_activ	investor	interest_cli	polici	corpor_govern
client	respons_invest	interest	invest_manag	investor	investe_compani
activ	asset_manag	polici	best_interest	respons	fund_manag
interest	fund_manag	activ	respons_invest	principl	asset_manag
fund	stewardship_activ	conflict	asset_manag	report	stewardship_activ
principl	interest_cli	proxi	fund_manag	will	engag_activ
respons	public_disclo	govern	engag_compani	institut	public_disclo
conflict	engag_compani	principl	manag_conflict	interest	monitor_invest
govern	best_interest	respons	public_disclo	pension	engag_compani

Table 6.6 (*cont.*)

ALL		Asset Managers		Asset Owners	
Unigrams	2-grams	Unigrams	2-grams	Unigrams	2-grams
report	manag_conflict	issu	vote_polici	code	stewardship_respon
institut	stewardship_respon	sharehold	stewardship_activ	govern	manag_conflict
issu	vote_polici	institut	portfolio_manag	monitor	environment_soci
sharehold	monitor_invest	meet	invest_process	truste	herm_eo
proxi	engag_activ	report	invest_team	includ	stewardship_vot
meet	potenti_conflict	includ	stewardship_respon	asset	vote_right
code	invest_process	corpor	potenti_conflict	conflict	day_day
includ	compani_invest	code	compani_invest	sharehold	vote_engag
corpor	sharehold_valu	investe	compani_manag	issu	best_pract
monitor	portfolio_manag	fund	sharehold_valu	meet	pension_committ
investe	environment_soci	esg	monitor_invest	corpor	discharg_stewardship
process	invest_team	process	vote_deci	public	extern_invest
provid	pension_fund	inform	general_meet	statement	annual_report

analysis supports this interpretation, highlighting phrases such as 'corporate governance', 'voting activity', 'stewardship responsibility/ies', and 'monitoring investment(s)'. This suggests asset owners concentrate on overseeing external asset managers rather than engaging directly with investee companies, reflecting their role in setting high-level governance expectations.

The presence of terms such as 'client' and 'interest' in asset manager statements reflects a deliberate emphasis on aligning stewardship activities with the priorities and expectations of proximate clients.[46] Moreover, the frequent references to 'conflict interest' and the need to 'manage conflict(s)' reveal an acute awareness of the tensions that can arise between different stakeholder groups – particularly in the context of shareholder voting. These formulations highlight the investment management dimension of stewardship, where institutional investors must navigate the complexities of acting as fiduciaries of other people's money while upholding their stewardship responsibilities.[47]

For asset owners, stewardship efforts appear more governance-driven. The exclusive presence of terms like 'trustee' and 'pension' highlights their fiduciary responsibilities, particularly in overseeing external asset managers to ensure alignment with long-term investment goals. The frequent mention of 'public', 'statement', and 'report' in asset owner statements underscores their emphasis on transparency and broader accountability. The 2-gram analysis supports this finding, with 'public disclosure(s)' appearing frequently, reinforcing the asset owners' role as high-level governance overseers rather than hands-on micro-level stewards.

Finally, 'ESG' appears exclusively among the top thirty terms in asset manager statements, suggesting that some had already begun voluntarily integrating ESG language into their stewardship disclosures – even though the UK Code 2012 made little reference to ESG.[48] This early

[46] For instance, Aberdeen Standard Investments states: 'We believe that it is mutually beneficial for companies and long-term investors to have a relationship based on accountability, engagement and trust. Such a relationship helps to ensure that each has a good understanding of the other's views and expectations. It also enables us to exercise constructive influence as and when appropriate. We believe *this serves to enhance the long-term value of our clients' investments and to protect their interests when necessary*'. (emphasis added). See Aberdeen Standard Investments, *The UK Stewardship Code Overview* (July 2019) (on file with the author).

[47] Section 4.3.

[48] On how often ESG is referred by the stewardship codes themselves, see Dionysia Katelouzou and Alice Klettner, 'Sustainable Finance and Stewardship: Unlocking Stewardship's Sustainability Potential' in Dionysia Katelouzou and Dan

inclusion may reflect client mandates requiring ESG integration, efforts at competitive differentiation, or alignment with emerging global norms around responsible investing.[49] By contrast, asset owners did not explicitly frame their stewardship activities through an ESG lens. However, references to 'environmental and social' factors imply that ESG considerations were implicitly embedded within broader fiduciary obligations.[50] Supporting this interpretation, the concept of responsibility features prominently in stewardship reporting. The token 'responsibility/responsible' ranks fifteenth in frequency across the full sample, underscoring the view that stewardship is regarded as a core responsibility of institutional investors – not only to their clients and beneficiaries but also to wider stakeholders as public equity 'owners'.[51] Similarly, the bigram 'responsible investment' ranks tenth overall, twelfth among asset managers, and eighth among asset owners, reinforcing existing research on the role of shareholder stewardship in operationalising responsible investment.[52]

Taken together, the 2012 disclosures reflect a predominantly micro-level conception of stewardship, centred on proxy voting and firm-level oversight. Yet, even at this early stage, signs of institutional role differentiation and nascent ESG integration were evident – foreshadowing the deeper shifts that would be formalised in the 2020 Code.

W. Puchniak (eds.), *Global Shareholder Stewardship* (Cambridge University Press 2022), 549, 561–5.

[49] See e.g. Quinn Curtis, Jill Fisch and Andriana Z. Robertson, 'Do ESG Mutual Funds Deliver on Their Promises?' (2021) 120 *Michigan Law Review* 393 (providing an empirical overview of the rise of ESG mutual funds in the US).

[50] See e.g. PRI and others *Fiduciary Duty in the 21st Century* (2015), 9 <www.unpri.org/download?ac=1378> (supporting a positive obligation on investors to integrate ESG issues).

[51] For example, Hermes Fund Managers explicitly frame stewardship as a responsibility that extends beyond responsible investing to responsible ownership: 'our duty extends beyond being *responsible investors* to acting as responsible owners of the companies and assets in which we have invested. … We believe that effective and constructive dialogue with boards and management by investors should contribute to better management of companies and ultimately support their long-term success. This, in turn, should lead to *wider benefits to society and for our clients' beneficiaries*' (emphasis added). Hermes Fund Managers 2017 (on file with the author).

[52] Katelouzou and Klettner, 'Sustainable Finance and Stewardship: Unlocking Stewardship's Sustainability Potential', 656–571.

6.5.2 *The 2020 Sample: The Shift Away from Micro-level Stewardship and the Rise of ESG*

A notable shift in the 2020 sample, as revealed by Table 6.7, which lists the thirty most frequently occurring unigrams and 2-grams for the full sample and by investor type, is the greater emphasis on sustainability and long-term risk management, as reflected in the frequent use of 'ESG', 'sustain', and 'climate', alongside phrases such as 'long-term', 'climate change', and 'net zero' across all investor groups. These terms indicate that stewardship reporting has expanded beyond firm-specific engagement to address broader, systemic concerns, particularly climate-related risks and long-term value creation.

As in the 2012 statements, asset managers and asset owners frame stewardship differently. The emergence of 'ESG' as the fifth most frequently used term across both the full 2020 sample and the asset manager subsample – compared to twenty-seventh in the 2012 asset manager subsample – demonstrates the growing prominence of ESG stewardship, particularly among asset managers.[53] In contrast, asset owners continue to place comparatively less emphasis on 'ESG' as a stand-alone term, instead of using terms such as 'climate' and 'responsibility'.

The bigram analysis highlights these distinctions further. Asset managers frequently reference 'ESG risk', 'ESG integration', and 'ESG factor', signalling a risk-based approach where ESG is integrated into investment decision-making. This suggests that signatory asset managers increasingly treat ESG as a matter of financial and portfolio management, reinforcing its role in risk mitigation and value creation. In contrast, asset owners prioritise bigrams such as 'climate change', 'climate risk', 'human rights', and 'due diligence', reflecting a stronger focus on long-term sustainability risks and responsible investment practices. Their emphasis on governance frameworks, regulatory alignment, and fiduciary responsibilities points to a more structured and oversight-oriented approach to ESG – one concerned with setting expectations and monitoring implementation, rather than exercising direct investment influence.

The increased prominence of 'risk' across all investor categories further suggests that stewardship reporting under the UK Code 2020 has become more closely linked to risk oversight, particularly concerning market-wide and systemic risks.[54] The bigram analysis reinforces this shift, highlighting frequent references to 'risk management', 'climate

[53] See also Section 7.5.
[54] UK Code 2020, Principle 4.

Table 6.7 *Most frequently occurring unigrams and 2-grams in 2020 stewardship statements*

ALL		Asset Managers		Asset Owners	
Unigrams	2-grams	Unigrams	2-grams	Unigrams	2-grams
invest	long_term	invest	long_term	invest	climat_chang
manag	climat_chang	compani	invest_team	manag	invest_manag
compani	respons_invest	manag	climat_chang	fund	respons_invest
engag	asset_manag	engag	respons_invest	engag	long_term
esg	invest_team	esg	proxi_vot	compani	net_zero
risk	net_zero	risk	asset_manag	risk	asset_manag
vote	conflict_interest	vote	conflict_interest	asset	pension_fund
client	proxi_vot	client	net_zero	vote	fund_manag
report	invest_manag	sustain	portfolio_manag	climat	conflict_interest
sustain	engag_compani	team	fix_incom	report	asset_class
fund	asset_class	report	engag_compani	esg	invest_strategi
team	fix_incom	provid	invest_process	stewardship	engag_compani
climat	portfolio_manag	includ	invest_manag	polici	case_studi
asset	case_studi	stewardship	third_parti	includ	climat_risk
stewardship	invest_process	polici	asset_class	respons	asset_own
includ	risk_manag	climat	case_studi	activ	human_right
polici	servic_provid	respons	risk_manag	pension	climat_relat

provid	third_parti	asset	servic_provid	provid	stewardship_activ
respons	esg_risk	activ	corpor_govern	will	risk_manag
activ	esg_integr	portfolio	esg_integr	member	stewardship_cod
will	corpor_govern	will	sustain_invest	chang	esg_risk
portfolio	fund_manag	issu	esg_risk	govern	decis_mak
govern	sustain_invest	fund	investe_compani	review	servic_provid
issu	stewardship_activ	govern	environment_soci	committe	best_pract
process	investe_compani	process	esg_factor	meet	extern_manag
chang	environment_soci	investor	stewardship_activ	issu	invest_team
investor	esg_factor	market	esg_issu	year	pension_schem
strategi	human_right	busi	due_dilig	strategi	engag_activ
market	esg_issu	strategi	best_pract	sustain	esg_issu
relat	best_pract	relat	risk_opportun	relat	due_dilig

risk', and 'ESG risk', indicating that stewardship is increasingly framed as a tool for managing financial and non-financial risks, rather than solely as an exercise in shareholder rights or corporate governance.

However, the framing of risk differs by investor type. Asset managers embed risk considerations within investment decision-making and long-term portfolio oversight, as evidenced by frequent references to terms such as 'portfolio management', 'investment process', and 'risk management'. Asset owners, by contrast, emphasise governance and oversight, using stewardship to set expectations, monitor external managers, and ensure long-term risk mitigation, as reflected in terms such as 'committee', 'review', and 'governance'. This differentiation aligns with survey evidence showing that investors use ESG information for diverse reasons – from risk management and performance enhancement to ethical alignment – depending on strategy, mandate, and client preferences.[55]

At the same time, although voting remains a key stewardship activity, the unigram analysis indicates a relative decline in emphasis on proxy voting, with 'vote' appearing less frequently than 'engage'. This suggests a growing preference for dialogue and informal engagement strategies, particularly across multiple asset classes, rather than a focus solely on shareholder voting in equity markets. The absence of 'proxy' from the top thirty most frequently used words in the 2020 sample further supports this shift.

Yet the bigram analysis provides a more nuanced perspective. While 'proxy vote' was among the most frequently referenced stewardship tools under the UK Code 2012, it remains notable under the UK Code 2020, particularly among asset managers. This suggests that proxy voting continues to play an important role but is now one component of a broader engagement strategy rather than the primary mechanism of stewardship. Compared with reporting under the UK Code 2012, disclosures under the UK Code 2020 indicate a repositioning of stewardship towards direct engagement, multi-asset stewardship, and influence through dialogue, rather than relying primarily on formal voting mechanisms.

Asset managers frequently reference 'engage company' and 'investment strategy', highlighting their role in active corporate engagement and portfolio-level stewardship. Asset owners, by contrast, emphasise 'monitor investment' and 'stewardship responsibility', reinforcing their position as indirect stewards tasked with oversight rather than direct engagement.

[55] See Amir Amel-Zadeh and George Serafeim, 'Why and How Investors Use ESG Information: Evidence from a Global Survey' (2018) 74 *Financial Analysts Journal* 87.

A further notable trend is the explicit reference to 'fixed income', signalling a widening of stewardship beyond equity holdings to include additional asset classes. This broadening reflects the growing importance of bondholder engagement and fixed-income stewardship strategies in influencing corporate behaviour. Likewise, the frequent mention of 'service provider' points to growing reliance on third-party providers, such as proxy advisors, ESG rating agencies, and engagement specialists, in supporting the implementation of stewardship practices.

The 2020 disclosures also reveal a marked shift in tone and emphasis, reflecting the 2G UK Code's outcomes-focused approach. Compared to the more principles-based framing of disclosures under the UK Code 2012, the frequent use of terms such as 'report', 'process', 'change', and 'strategy' highlights a greater concern with demonstrating implementation, effectiveness, and accountability.

Taken together, these high-frequency terms offer a useful entry point into understanding how stewardship is narrated and prioritised by different signatories. To move beyond surface-level patterns and gain deeper insight into the thematic content of stewardship reporting, the following section turns to topic modelling. This approach helps uncover the latent structures within the disclosures, offering a more systematic understanding of how stewardship narratives have evolved and diversified across the 2012 and 2020 iterations of the UK Stewardship Code.

6.6 Mapping Stewardship Themes: Structural Topic Modelling

6.6.1 *Topic Modelling Design: Preprocessing, Estimation, and Model Selection*

To examine how stewardship is thematically framed in the disclosures submitted under the two iterations of the UK Stewardship Code, an *unsupervised* machine learning–based approach has been employed. Unlike supervised methods, which rely on predefined labels, unsupervised techniques are particularly well-suited for analysing large text corpora, as they detect latent patterns and thematic structures without prior assumptions – making them especially effective for uncovering meaning in unstructured textual data.[56]

[56] David M. Blei, 'Probabilistic Topic Models' (2012) 55 *Communication of the ACM* 77; Grimmer and Stewart, 'Text as Data: The Promise and Pitfalls of Automatic Content Analysis Methods for Political Texts', 281.

The technique used is Structural Topic Modelling (STM), a probabilistic text-mining method designed to detect co-occurring word patterns and infer latent thematic structures across a corpus. STM extends standard topic modelling frameworks such as Latent Dirichlet Allocation (LDA) by allowing researchers to incorporate document-level metadata.[57] Each topic is represented as a distribution over words, and each document is modelled as a mixture of topics, based on the relative frequency and co-occurrence of terms. Like other generative models, STM treats documents as 'bags of words', disregarding syntax and word order in favour of identifying underlying semantic patterns.

What distinguishes STM from earlier topic models is its ability to estimate how topic prevalence (the extent to which a topic appears in a document) and topic content (the specific language used) vary systematically across document-level covariates.[58] This makes it particularly suitable for analysing stewardship disclosures, which are shaped by differing strategic priorities, institutional capacities, and regulatory environments. Rather than analysing documents in isolation, STM allows researchers to examine how stewardship narratives diverge or converge across institutional characteristics and over time.

Although STM has gained traction in disciplines such as political science[59] and criminology,[60] it remains underutilised in legal and corporate governance research.[61] Yet its scalability, replicability, and sensitivity to heterogeneity make it a valuable tool for analysing regulatory and legal texts – especially in domains such as stewardship, where narratives are evolving and shaped by a diverse array of institutional actors and contexts.

The analysis was conducted using the *stm* software package for R programming language, which enables both automated topic estimation

57 David M. Blei, Andrew Y. Ng and Michael I. Jordan, 'Latent Dirichlet Allocation' (2003) 3 *Journal of Machine Learning Research* 993.

58 Margaret E. Roberts, Brandon M. Stewart, and Edoardo M. Airoldi, 'A Model of Text for Experimentation in the Social Sciences' (2016) 111 *Journal of the American Statistical Association* 988.

59 Margaret E. Roberts, Brandon M. Stewart, Dustin Tingley *et al.*, 'Structural Topic Models for Open-Ended Survey Responses' (2014) 58 *American Journal of Political Science* 1064.

60 Scott M. Mourtgos and Ian T. Adams, 'The Rhetoric of De-policing: Evaluating Open-Ended Survey Responses from Police Officers with Machine Learning-Based Structural Topic Modeling' (2019) 64 *Journal of Criminal Justice* 61.

61 For an early application of STM in legal research, see Dionysia Katelouzou, 'The Rhetoric of Activist Shareholder Stewards' (2021) 18 *New York University Journal of Law & Business* 665.

and visualisation of topic distributions.[62] Prior to modelling, the text was preprocessed using the *quanteda* toolkit for NLP.[63] This included normalisation of spelling and grammar, removal of stopwords, numerals, and words shorter than three characters, tokenisation (splitting text into individual words or tokens), and stemming via Porter's algorithm to reduce inflected word forms to their base stems.[64] To enhance topic coherence and minimise noise, terms appearing in fewer than ten documents were removed, as were ubiquitous words – such as 'stewardship' and 'code' – which risked dominating the model and distorting topic estimation.[65]

The final processed corpus consisted of 93,551 tokens and 1,466 terms (unique tokens) for the 2012 sample, and 319,028 tokens and 4,079 unique terms for the 2020 sample. To improve robustness and ensure replicability, a spectral initialisation algorithm was used in the estimation process, reducing the model's sensitivity to random starting values – a known limitation in mixed-membership models such as STM.[66]

The next step involved selecting the number of topics (K) to estimate – each corresponding to a distinct, latent theme. There is no universally 'correct' number of topics, and scholars generally agree that no definitive statistical test can determine the optimal K or the overall quality of a topic model. A model with too few topics risks producing overly broad themes lacking analytical specificity, while too many topics may overfit the data, fragmenting coherent themes into multiple overlapping topics and reducing interpretability.[67] To identify a balanced solution, a range of models ($K = 2$ to 20) were evaluated using diagnostic criteria such as held-out likelihood, residual analysis, and semantic coherence (i.e., the frequency with which the most probable words in a topic appear together in

62 Margaret E. Roberts, Brandson M. Stewart and Dustin Tingley, 'stm: An R Package for Structural Topic Models' (2019) 91 *Journal of Statistical Software* 1. For a list of studies utilising the *stm* package, see STM, <www.structuraltopicmodel.com/>.

63 See generally Kenneth Benoit, Kohei Watanabe, Haiyan Wang, *et al.*, 'quanteda: An R Package for the Quantitative Analysis of Textual Data' (2018) 30 *Journal of Open Source Software* 774.

64 M. F. Porter, 'An algorithm for suffix stripping' (1980) 14 *Program* 130.

65 For a similar methodological approach, see Dyer *et al.*, 'The Evolution of 10-K Textual Disclosure: Evidence from Latent Dirichlet Allocation', 244.

66 Roberts *et al.*, 'stm: An R Package for Structural Topic Models', 10.

67 Paul DiMaggio, Manish Nag and David Blei, 'Exploiting Affinities between Topic Modeling and the Sociological Perspective on Culture: Application to Newspaper Coverage of U.S. Government Arts Funding' (2013) 41 *Poetics* 570.

documents).[68] For both the 2012 and 2020 samples, a six-topic model ($K = 6$) was selected as providing the most analytically useful representation of the stewardship discourse.[69]

Together, this modelling framework provides the basis for the analysis that follows, enabling a structured interpretation of the six topics identified in the 2012 and 2020 samples and permitting variation in their prevalence to be examined across institutional characteristics and signatory experience.

6.6.2 *Topic Clusters in the 2012 Stewardship Disclosures*

The *stm* package identifies latent topics by analysing patterns of word co-occurrence across a corpus of documents. However, while the algorithm provides statistical clustering, the interpretation of these topics is an inherently qualitative task, requiring the researcher to assign meaning based on the coherence, frequency, and exclusivity of the words associated with each topic. This interpretive process combines statistical outputs with domain expertise, ensuring that patterns in language are meaningfully contextualised.

Figure 6.3 presents the estimated proportion of the corpus associated with each of the six topics. Topic 1 emerges as the most prevalent, signalling its rhetorical dominance across the 2012 disclosures, while Topic 4 ranks lowest, suggesting it represents a more marginal but still analytically important strand of the stewardship discourse.

While the list of highest probability words offers an initial indication of a topic's semantic core (see Figure 6.3), a more comprehensive interpretation draws on four word profiles generated by the *stm* package: the most frequent terms within a topic, used to assess semantic coherence (*highest probability*); terms that are both frequent and exclusive to a topic, indicating distinctiveness (*FREX*); words that appear significantly less often in other topics, enhancing differentiation (*Lift*); and terms whose salience is calculated as the ratio of their log frequency in a given topic to their log frequency across the rest of the corpus (*Score*).[70]

These metrics were supplemented by word clouds and manual examination of keywords, with particular attention paid to semantic coherence,

[68] See, further, Roberts *et al.*, 'stm: An R Package for Structural Topic Models', 11–13.

[69] A manual examination of semantic coherence and word exclusivity was also conducted to determine the number of topics with the strongest explanatory power.

[70] For the technical details, see Roberts *et al.*, 'stm: An R Package for Structural Topic Models', 14.

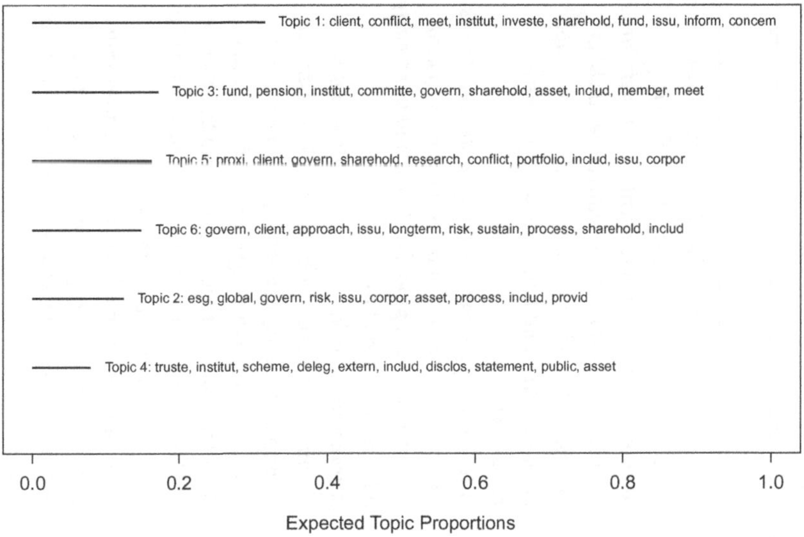

Figure 6.3 Distribution of estimated topics in the 2012 corpus.

interpretive clarity, and how each topic relates to broader patterns of stewardship discourse under the 1G UK Code. As expected, commonly used tokens, such as '*institut*', '*client*', '*sharehold*', and '*asset*', appear across multiple topics, reflecting their centrality to the rhetorical and language employed by signatories to the UK Code 2012. However, notable differences in the frequency and exclusivity of certain terms across the six topics indicate that signatories articulate and interpret the concept of stewardship in diverse and context-specific ways.

To provide an interpretive structure for this analysis, Table 6.8 offers a typology of the six identified stewardship narratives, summarising their thematic emphasis, institutional positioning, and rhetorical function. Each topic is discussed in the following sections in order of prevalence, drawing on both quantitative and qualitative features of the model.

6.6.2.1 Orthodox Shareholder Stewardship (Topic 1)

The most dominant topic, Topic 1, captures a traditional model of shareholder stewardship, defined by institutional investors' dual accountability: to investee companies through engagement (*asset stewardship*) and to clients and beneficiaries whose capital they manage

Table 6.8 *Typology of stewardship narratives in disclosures under the UK Stewardship Code 2012, ranked by prevalence*

Topic	Label	Core Features	Conceptual Framing
Topic 1	Orthodox Shareholder Stewardship	Corporate governance-focused, board-level engagement; voting; executive pay; shareholder meetings; fiduciary duty; conflicts of interest	*A micro-level model of shareholder stewardship rooted in governance oversight and fiduciary alignment with proximate clients and beneficiaries*
Topic 3	Collective Stewardship by Public Asset Owners	LAPFF and LGPS participation; committee oversight; public sector ethics; alert systems and joint voting mechanisms	*A coalition-based model of indirect stewardship expressed through structured collaboration, public accountability, and long-term administrative responsibility*
Topic 5	Stewardship Infrastructure and Advisory Processes	Proxy voting execution; analyst research; proxy advisor influence (e.g. ISS, Glass Lewis); procedural consistency	*A technical-operational framing of stewardship as an embedded process in investment management, reliant on internal procedural tools and third-party advisory infrastructure*
Topic 6	Emerging Enlightened Shareholder Stewardship	Long-term value creation; sustainability integration; client alignment; trust-based relationships	*A transitional, values-driven narrative that blends commercial purpose with responsible investment principles, framing stewardship as a normative commitment to other-regarding responsibilities*
Topic 2	Early ESG-Informed Stewardship	ESG metrics and scoring; global norms (PRI, SRI); early climate and social risk disclosures	*A tentative and externally driven model in which ESG begins to inform stewardship, often framed in terms of alignment and legitimacy*
Topic 4	Trustee-Oriented Indirect Stewardship	Pension trusteeship; manager delegation; internal monitoring; beneficiary alignment	*An inward-facing model of indirect stewardship grounded in fiduciary governance, focused on oversight, delegation, and safeguarding beneficiary interests*

(*client stewardship*).[71] This 'orthodox' approach reflects the core practices associated with first-generation stewardship, namely board-level dialogue, proxy voting, and governance risk oversight.[72]

The frequent appearance of terms such as '*meet*' and '*sharehold*' underscores the centrality of engagement meetings as a primary channel for raising concerns directly with company boards and executives.[73] Meanwhile, the prominence of '*remuneration*' points to a continued focus on executive pay – long a staple of governance scrutiny.[74] At the same time, references to '*client*', '*conflict*', and '*fund*' highlight the intermediary role of signatories, who must balance engagement with investee companies against the expectations and fiduciary interests of the clients and beneficiaries they represent.[75]

Taken together, these patterns reveal a stewardship model centred on micro-level shareholder engagement and investor accountability to proximate clients and beneficiaries. The dual emphasis on influence

[71] On the four relationships of investor stewardship, see Section 4.4.

[72] A similar emphasis on 'orthodox stewardship' is evident among activist shareholder stewards, suggesting that traditional governance-focused engagement practices continue to shape stewardship strategies even in more assertive investor contexts. See Katelouzou, 'The Rhetoric of Activist Shareholder Stewards', 732.

[73] For example, Oxburgh Partners highlight that 'continued monitoring of the company and corporate governance through face-to-face meetings continues for as long as we hold the investment', reflecting a long-term, relationship-based approach. Saltus likewise emphasises engagement as integral to its investment process, noting that it 'seeks to maintain open communications with the management of investee companies through regular meetings and updates'. Revera describes its engagement strategy as involving 'direct verbal or written communication with the company' and expresses a willingness to 'act either individually or in conjunction with other investors to effect change by voting at a meeting of the company concerned'. See Oxburgh Partners LLP, *The Stewardship Code* (on file with the author), Saltus, *Stewardship Code* (on file with the author), and Revera Asset Management, *The Stewardship Code* (on file with the author), respectively.

[74] For instance, Slater emphasises that encourage 'executive remuneration policies that align directors' and shareholders' interests. We pay particular attention to schemes that create excessive equity dilution'. See Slater Investments, *Slater Investment Limited's approach to its responsibility as an Institutional Shareholder* (on file with the author).

[75] This is echoed in Dalton's framing of stewardship as a way to 'deliver consistent outperformance whilst ensuring that both client interests remain paramount'. See Dalton Strategic Partnership LLP, *Stewardship Policy* (December 2017) (on file with the author). In a similar vein, Seneca states that '[a]ctive engagement is appropriate to ensure our investee companies are conducting themselves in a manner that gives value to our clients and that of the wider community. . . . If we are in a position to influence behaviour, by means of the size of our investment, then we will seek to do so. However, the level of engagement has to be considered in terms of what is likely to be achievable and what benefit and value will be achieved for our investors'. See Seneca Investment Managers, *Statement of Compliance with the Stewardship Code* (on file with the author).

and obligation reinforces the view that effective shareholder stewardship operates at the intersection of governance oversight and fiduciary alignment, positioning institutional investors not only as allocators of capital but also as custodians of corporate governance standards.[76]

6.6.2.2 Collective Stewardship by Public Asset Owners (Topic 3)

The second most prevalent topic in the 2012 sample highlights a model of collective, institutionally coordinated stewardship, led primarily by Local Government Pension Schemes (LGPS) and other public or quasi-public asset owners. The prominence of terms such as *'pension'*, *'fund'*, *'local'*, and *'authority'* reflects a stewardship discourse grounded in public accountability, shared governance structures, and a long-term orientation aligned with the interests of scheme beneficiaries.

These disclosures highlight a model of *indirect stewardship*, in which strategic direction is retained in-house, even as day-to-day execution of engagement is delegated to external managers.[77] Oversight is typically exercised through pension committees or local boards, which are tasked with setting engagement priorities, monitoring manager performance, and ensuring alignment with the scheme's broader fiduciary objectives.[78]

A central feature of this model is participation in collective initiatives – most notably the LAPFF – which is consistently highlighted across disclosures as a key platform for coordinated engagement with investee companies and the promotion of corporate governance reform.[79] Proxy

[76] Section 4.3.

[77] Section 7.3.

[78] For instance, Staffordshire Pension Fund emphasises that 'much of the day-to-day responsibility for implementing stewardship is delegated', but notes that oversight remains with the Fund, supported by the Pensions Panel and Committee. See Staffordshire Pension Fund, *Statement of Compliance with UK Stewardship Code* (August 2018) (on file with the author).

[79] For example, Wiltshire Pension Fund describes LAPFF as a vehicle 'to promote the investment interests of local authority pension funds ... while promoting social responsibility and corporate governance'. See Wiltshire Pension Fund, *Statement of Compliance with Stewardship Code* (2016) (on file with the author). The role played by the LAPFF alert system in identifying issues of concern and initiating targeted engagement is also emphasised in several statements, including that of the Gwynedd Pension Fund. See Gwynedd Pension Fund, *Stewardship Code Statement* (on file with the author). For further details on LAPFF's structure and collaborative engagement model, see https://lapfforum.org.

voting, meanwhile, is frequently conducted in accordance with LAPFF recommendations and implemented in collaboration with PIRC, a specialist proxy advisory and research provider.[80]

What emerges from these disclosures is a coalitional model of indirect shareholder stewardship – one that enables smaller asset owners to amplify their influence by coordinating their voice and actions. Particularly where individual holdings are modest, this collective approach allows public sector funds to exert meaningful pressure on governance outcomes while preserving internal oversight and strategic coherence.[81]

6.6.2.3 Stewardship Infrastructure and Advisory Processes (Topic 5)

This theme captures the procedural architecture of shareholder stewardship, focusing on how proxy voting is structured, informed, and operationalised within institutional investment organisations. The prominence of terms such as *'proxi'*, *'research'*, *'analyst'*, and *'recommend'* reflects the widespread reliance on proxy advisors like ISS and Glass Lewis, in combination with in-house analysis.[82]

Disclosures associated with this topic reveal underlying tensions between third-party inputs and internal oversight – illustrating how asset managers attempt to balance the efficiency of external research with the need to exercise fiduciary judgement. This balancing act is especially visible in the use of internal proxy committees, escalation protocols, and periodic voting policy reviews designed to ensure that decisions remain aligned with investor mandates.[83]

[80] See e.g. Cumbria Local Government Pension Scheme, *Statement of Compliance with the UK Stewardship Code*, Principle 3 (on file with the author).

[81] See Wiltshire Pension Fund, *Statement of Compliance with Stewardship Code* (2016) (on file with the author) stating that '[c]ollective engagement through LAPFF enables us to maximise our influence'.

[82] See e.g. Harding Loevener, *The UK Stewardship Code* (on file with the author).

[83] For instance, GMO delegates much of the operational handling of proxy voting to ISS yet retains discretion to override standard recommendations when investment professionals deem it appropriate, especially in cases of conflict of interest or material divergence from client interests. See Grantham, Mayo, Van Otterloo & Co. LLC, *Statement Regarding Support of the UK Stewardship Code* (on file with the author). Franklin Templeton likewise leverages ISS, Glass Lewis, and Egan-Jones, but clearly states that its investment managers exercise independent judgement when deciding final votes. See Franklin Templeton, *Statement of Compliance with the UK Stewardship Code* (June 2019) (on file with the author).

Terms like *'procedur'*, *'propos'*, and *'compens'* point to a strong emphasis on standardised and transparent decision-making, particularly around contentious governance issues such as executive pay and board appointments.[84] At the same time, the appearance of terms such as *'conflict'*, *'vendor'*, and *'inconsist'* signals growing scrutiny of proxy advisory firms – especially when recommendations appear misaligned with investor mandates or lack contextual specificity.[85]

Taken together, this topic reflects the routinisation of stewardship within large investment institutions, where proxy voting is increasingly integrated into institutional processes and supported by a layered governance infrastructure. Yet it also highlights broader debates surrounding reliance on third-party service providers – raising questions about procedural soundness, the appropriate calibration between standardisation and discretion in stewardship practice, and accountability.[86]

6.6.2.4 Emerging Enlightened Shareholder Stewardship (Topic 6)

Topic 6 captures a values-driven model of shareholder stewardship, grounded in principles of long-termism, sustainability integration, and an ethic of other-regarding responsibility.[87] It aligns with the concept

[84] Harding Loevener explicitly supports remuneration policies that align executive pay with shareholder returns and documents instances where they have opposed management proposals on compensation grounds. See Harding Loevener, *The UK Stewardship Code* (on file with the author).

[85] For instance, Dimensional Fund Advisors note that their 'Proxy Voting Policies have been formulated to encourage our portfolio companies to adopt and maintain corporate governance policies that are consistent with our clients' best interests and the preservation of the value of their investments.' See Dimensional Fund Advisors Ltd., *Stewardship Code* (on file with the author). Morgan Stanley, meanwhile, reports that it conducts annual due diligence on its retained proxy advisors to ensure competency and impartiality, signalling the importance of oversight, even within delegated frameworks. See Morgan Stanley, *Morgan Stanley Investment Management Ltd.'s Statement on compliance with the UK Stewardship Code* (September 2018) (on file with the author).

[86] See e.g. Florian Berg, Kornelia Fabisik and Zacharias Sautner, 'Is History Repeating Itself? The (Un)Predictable Past of ESG Ratings' European Corporate Governance Institute – Finance Working Paper 708/2020 <https://ssrn.com/abstract=3722087>.

[87] For instance, Hermes Investment Management states that '[w]e believe this purpose includes a duty to deliver holistic returns – outcomes for our clients that go far beyond the financial and consider the impact our decisions have on society, the environment and the wider world. ... We have a duty therefore to act as responsible owners of those companies in which we have invested and the assets that we manage to the advantage of society as a whole'. See Hermes Investment Management, *Approach to stewardship* (December 2017) (on file with the author).

of *enlightened shareholder* – and more broadly, *enlightened investor – stewardship*, where stewardship is not merely a tool for managing risk but a vehicle for aligning capital with broader economic, environmental, and social outcomes.[88]

Terms such as '*client*', '*longterm*', '*govern*', '*risk*', and '*return*' signal a gradual shift away from compliance-driven or reactive approaches towards a more strategic, forward-looking conception of stewardship, where investment strategy and stewardship are closely intertwined.[89] Normative and sustainability-related language is central to this topic. The recurring use of '*sustain*', along with terms like '*trust*' and '*responsibility*', reveals a deeper ethical framing – one in which engagement is not only about mitigating downside risk but also about proactively shaping corporate behaviour to support long-term planetary and societal goals.[90]

This topic also underscores the dual orientation of institutional stewardship. Outward-facing engagement with investee companies is paired with an internal commitment to aligning investment strategies with clients' values and long-term objectives. References to client stewardship underscore the idea that ESG integration serves not just financial outcomes but also ethical alignment with beneficiary priorities.[91]

Taken together, disclosures associated with this topic reveal a distinctive stewardship rhetoric, one built on trust-based relationships, purpose-driven capital allocation, and a systemic view of engagement that extends beyond individual issues to include market and societal structures. This broader perspective was, in many ways, ahead of its time, given that the 1G UK Code largely emphasised firm-specific engagement and did not explicitly mandate consideration of systemic risks or externalities. The approach captured in this topic reflects an early articulation of an

88 Section 4.4.3.

89 This orientation is exemplified by statements such as Merian's view that 'stewardship is simply good investment practice', and Coutts' integration of responsible ownership into the 'core part of how we think about investment'. See Merian Global Investors, *Our Approach to Stewardship* (on file with the author) and Coutts, *Statement on compliance with the UK Stewardship Code* (on file with the author).

90 For instance, British Coal's collaboration with Hermes EOS involves a milestone system for engagement, tracking companies' responses to long-term concerns and facilitating accountability beyond the AGM cycle. See British Coal Staff Superannuation Scheme Trustees Limited, *UK Stewardship Code Compliance Statement* (on file with the author).

91 For instance, Investec Asset Management states that '[t]he integration of material ESG factors into our investment process and decision making is an important element of preserving and growing our client capital over the long-term'. See Investec (91), *UK Stewardship Code Statement* (July 2016) (on file with the author).

enlightened, other-regarding conception of stewardship – one that would gain increasing traction under the 2G UK Code.[92]

6.6.2.5 Early ESG-Informed Stewardship (Topic 2)

Though less prevalent in the 2012 sample, Topic 2 marks the entry of ESG (Environmental, Social, and Governance) considerations into the stewardship discourse. Terms such as *'ESG'*, *'global'*, *'climat'*, *'govern'*, and *'risk'* suggest that engagement with sustainability issues was taking shape.[93] In some cases, ESG was not merely an investment lens but part of the organisation's identity.[94] The recurring use of *'score'* indicates growing reliance on ESG metrics and scoring systems as tools for evaluating sustainability risks and opportunities.[95] Other keywords – such as *'SRI'*, *'footprint'*, *'gender'*, and *'emiss'* – point to an expanded definition of materiality – one that extends beyond traditional financial indicators to include social and environmental externalities.[96]

Disclosures linked to this topic frequently reference global sustainability frameworks such as the Principles for Responsible Investment (PRI) and the United Nations Global Compact, reflecting efforts to align with emerging international standards.[97] However, despite the breadth of ESG-

92 Section 6.6.3.1.

93 For instance, Robeco states that 'companies with sustainable business practices have a competitive advantage and are more successful in the long term', and links its stewardship policy directly to value-oriented ESG engagement strategies. See Robeco Institutional Asset Management, *Stewardship Policy* (on file with the author).

94 Candriam, for example, defines stewardship as 'a means to promote sustainable business models' and explicitly references gender, emissions, and social outcomes as areas of focus. The Church of England Pensions Board, although more values-driven, also ties ESG integration to fiduciary duty and theological ethics, framing ESG engagement not as a trend but as 'essential' to fulfilling long-term obligations. See Candriam Investors Group, *Candriam Statement regarding the UK Stewardship Code* (December 2016) (on file with the author) and Church of England Pensions Board, *Stewardship Implementation Framework* (on file with the author).

95 Candriam provides one of the most detailed examples of ESG scoring. Their funds are assessed using a two-tiered scoring system: a *Micro-score*, which evaluates how well a company incorporates stakeholder interests into strategy, and a *Macro-score*, which scores exposure to six sustainable development challenges (e.g. climate change, health, and wellness). These scores are visualised and benchmarked, with results publicly available on their website. See further Candrian Investors Group, *Candriam Statement regarding the UK Stewardship Code* December (2016) (on file with the author).

96 See e.g. Candrian Investors Group, *Candriam Statement Regarding the UK Stewardship Code* (December 2016) (on file with the author) and TOBAM, *UK Stewardship Code Statement* (December 2018) (on file with the author).

97 For instance, Kempen notes its adherence to over 100 international initiatives, including the OECD Principles of Corporate Governance, the International Corporate

related language, Topic 2's relatively modest weight (ranking fifth out of six) underscores its tentative and externally motivated character at the time. Under the 1G UK Code, ESG integration remained largely voluntary – more often framed as a response to client demand, reputational concerns, or alignment with emerging global trends, rather than as a fully operationalised component of investment strategy. While some signatories had begun to adopt ESG practices through screening, engagement, or impact initiatives, many disclosures reveal a cautious or symbolic uptake.

Topic 2 thus reflects an incipient but uneven shift in stewardship practice. Some signatories appear to anticipate the future institutionalisation of ESG as a stewardship norm, while others adopt it in more instrumental terms – framing it as a way to meet client expectations or enhance legitimacy.

While both Topic 2 and Topic 6 reference environmental and social considerations, their framing and function differ markedly. In Topic 2, ESG is positioned as a set of external standards – something to acknowledge, report on, or align with.[98] This indicates a reactive, compliance-oriented stance, where ESG is deployed as a means of reputational risk management.[99] In Topic 6, by contrast, ESG is internalised as part of a purpose-led institutional identity, embedded in long-term strategy and driven by a normative vision of market transformation. Here, stewardship becomes a vehicle for shaping corporate and systemic behaviour in pursuit of shared sustainability goals.[100]

Even the notion of client stewardship is articulated differently across these topics. In Topic 2, it typically signals responsiveness to external

Governance Network (ICGN) Governance principles, the United Nations Guiding Principles on Business and Human Rights, and the Task Force on Climate-related Financial Disclosures (TCFD), and identifies ESG as a core screening and monitoring tool across all in-house and external portfolios. See Kempen, *UK Stewardship Statement* (September 2018) (on file with the author).

98 For instance, signatories such as Kempen and Robeco describe their adherence to dozens of international initiatives and use ESG criteria to screen investments. See Kempen, *UK Stewardship Statement* (September 2018) (on file with the author) and Robeco Institutional Asset Management, *Stewardship Policy* (on file with the author).

99 For instance, Candriam and TOBAM link ESG to responsible investing outcomes but present it in procedural terms – through scoring systems, exclusions, or alignment with global codes. See Candrian Investors Group, *Candriam Statement Regarding the UK Stewardship Code* (December 2016) (on file with the author) and TOBAM, *UK Stewardship Code Statement* (December 2018) (on file with the author).

100 For instance, Hermes Investment Manager speaks of long-term engagement milestones and systemic impact across ESG dimensions, while the Mineworkers pension scheme defines its stewardship approach as enabling 'beneficial and sustained change', linking fiduciary responsibility directly to environmental and social outcomes. See Hermes Investment Manager, *Approach to stewardship* (December 2017) (on file with the author) and Mineworkers Pension Scheme Limited, *UK Stewardship Code* (on file with the author), respectively.

expectations – whether from clients, beneficiaries, or the broader public – reflecting a more reactive, compliance-oriented posture. In Topic 6, by contrast, client stewardship is grounded in value alignment, trust-based relationships, and a long-term sense of responsibility, highlighting a more relational and purpose-driven model.[101]

Ultimately, while both topics recognise the relevance of ESG, they differ in depth, tone, and underlying purpose. Topic 2 reflects an ESG-informed model, in which ESG is present, but often peripheral, shaped by external norms and not yet systematically embedded within investment practice. Topic 6, by contrast, presents a vision of *enlightened shareholder* – and more broadly, *enlightened investor* – stewardship, grounded in a recognition of the interdependence between institutional investors, investee companies, and the broader social and ecological systems in which they operate. This distinction prefigures the trajectory of the 2G UK Code, which would go on to elevate ESG from a peripheral concern to a central pillar in stewardship practice and disclosure.

6.6.2.6 Trustee-Oriented Indirect Stewardship (Topic 4)

The least prevalent topic centres on the internal governance of pension schemes, particularly private occupational schemes, and the role of trustees as central actors in the stewardship ecosystem. This topic highlights a distinct model of indirect stewardship, where trustees are primarily responsible not for engaging directly with investee companies, but for setting expectations, selecting and monitoring asset managers, and safeguarding the integrity of stewardship processes through robust oversight.[102]

The prominence of terms such as '*trustee*', '*scheme*', '*deleg*', and '*beneficiary*' reflects this governance-oriented approach. Trustees are positioned not simply as fiduciaries, but as *gatekeepers of stewardship standards*, responsible for maintaining alignment between outsourced stewardship activity and the interests of scheme members.[103] Even where day-to-day engagement and

[101] Coutts, for example, explicitly notes that ESG is embedded in how it selects and reviews third-party managers to ensure consistency with its values. See Coutts, *Statement on compliance with the UK stewardship code* (on file with the author).

[102] As the Siemens Benefits Scheme explains, 'the Trustee has delegated responsibility for the selection, retention and realisation of investments to external investment managers and in so doing it has also delegated day-to-day implementation of its stewardship activity'. See Siemens Benefits Scheme, *Stewardship Statement* (July 2013) (on file with the author). See also Section 7.3.

[103] For instance, Merchant Navy Officers Pension Fund (MNOPF) describes working through a Delegated CIO to facilitate effective stewardship 'in the best interests of the

proxy voting are delegated, disclosures reveal a strong emphasis on *chain-of-responsibility oversight*, supported by terms such as '*disclos*', '*question*', and '*extern*' – highlighting a strong focus on transparency, scrutiny, and accountability in the monitoring of external managers.[104]

What distinguishes this indirect stewardship model from the collaborative model of indirect stewardship involving public-sector asset owners highlighted in Topic 3 is its focus on scheme-level governance and the contractual management of delegation, rather than on collective influence or coalition-based engagement. The trustees' role is centred on defining investment beliefs, setting stewardship expectations, and integrating ESG principles into manager selection and review processes.

Notably, Topic 4 also captures an aspirational dimension in the trustee discourse. Terms like '*encourag*', '*pursuit*', '*readi*', and '*compat*' suggest that trustees are increasingly expected to uphold broader values, including ESG alignment and long-term sustainability.[105] In several statements, stewardship is framed not merely as a fiduciary duty but as a component of broader scheme governance, woven into investment beliefs, manager mandates, and communication with scheme members.[106]

Taken together, these patterns reflect a model of trustee-oriented indirect stewardship, where oversight, alignment, and accountability form the backbone of responsible investment practice. Rather than engaging companies directly, trustees shape the stewardship landscape

ultimate beneficiaries'. See Merchant Navy Officers Pension Fund, *Statement of commitment to the UK Stewardship Code* (on file with the author).

104 For instance, the Cummins UK Pension Plan details how it 'meets with the Plan's equity managers on an annual basis to review corporate governance and stewardship' and 'oversees its investment consultant's process' to assess and improve manager performance. See Cummins UK Pension Plan, *UK Stewardship Code Statement* (September 2016) (on file with the author).

105 For instance, the Pilkington Superannuation Scheme outlines how stewardship is 'framed in the context' of long-term fiduciary responsibility, and highlights efforts to maintain 'awareness of key industry developments' and to oversee stewardship not only through reporting but also through ongoing training and belief reaffirmation. See Pilkington Superannuation Scheme, *UK Stewardship Code Statement* (August 2016) (on file with the author). The Whitbread Group Pension Fund echoes this approach, stating that it aims to remain aligned with best practice and supports 'the work of industry groups such as the Pensions and Lifetime Savings Association (PLSA)'. See Whitbread Group Pension Fund, *UK Stewardship Code Statement* (September 2016) (on file with the author).

106 The MNOPF, for example, reports that ESG integration and stewardship practices are part of the criteria used in selecting and monitoring investment managers, and that its Delegated CIO is expected to 'encourage asset owners and asset managers to adhere to the letter and spirit of applicable best practice standards'. See Merchant Navy Officers Pension Fund (MNOPF), *Statement of commitment to the UK Stewardship Code* (on file with the author).

through delegation with direction – ensuring that external managers execute stewardship in a manner that reflects the scheme's values, obligations, and long-term goals.

6.6.2.7 Concluding Reflections: The Plural Foundations of Reform

The typology presented in Table 6.8 brings analytical clarity to the six topics identified through the STM analysis, mapping the diverse conceptual terrain of stewardship as articulated in the UK Code 2012 disclosures. It reveals that, even prior to the codification of ESG in the 2G UK Code, stewardship was far from uniform. Across the corpus, institutional investors framed stewardship in varied and sometimes conflicting ways – ranging from traditional governance engagement to procedurally routinised practices to emerging commitments to sustainability and public accountability.

This heterogeneity reflects the plural institutional logics that shaped how stewardship was understood and operationalised in practice: some narratives centred on shareholder oversight and fiduciary alignment (Topic 1), others emphasised collaboration and public sector leadership (Topic 3), trustee-oriented forms of indirect stewardship (Topic 4), procedural standardisation (Topic 5), or emerging values-driven approaches (Topic 6). Meanwhile, ESG appeared both as a tentative point of alignment (Topic 2) and as a forward-looking, normative commitment (Topic 6).

Taken together, these distinctions foreshadow the differentiated evolution of stewardship practices in the years that followed. The insights from the 2012 disclosures anticipate the broader transformations formalised under the 2G UK Code – where ESG, systemic thinking, and stakeholder accountability would move from the periphery to the centre of the stewardship agenda.

6.6.3 Topic Clusters in the 2020 Stewardship Disclosures

The UK Code 2020 marked a pivotal moment in the institutionalisation of stewardship. It significantly expanded the levels, assets, and mechanisms through which stewardship is expected to operate – embedding ESG considerations, system-level thinking, and broader stakeholder accountability at the heart of stewardship practices. In contrast to the more fragmented and tentative narratives observed in the 2012 disclosures, the 2020 sample reflects a landscape in which stewardship is both normatively ambitious and operationally formalised.

Building on the same STM methodology applied to the 2012 sample, this section identifies and interprets the dominant themes that shape the language and logic of stewardship under the 2G UK Code. Figure 6.4 presents the estimated proportion of the 2020 corpus attributed to each of the six topics, along with the highest-probability words associated with each topic, with Topic 6 emerging as the most dominant and Topic 2 as the least prevalent.

The analysis examines how signatories responded to the revised Code's expectations – particularly its emphasis on purpose-driven stewardship, real-world outcomes, and systemic impact. It traces both continuities and notable shifts in disclosure practices across signatories. To anchor the discussion, Table 6.9 presents a typology of the six thematic narratives identified through topic modelling of the 2020 disclosures, summarising their substantive focus, institutional associations, and rhetorical function. Each topic is discussed below in order of prevalence, drawing on both quantitative and qualitative features of the model.

6.6.3.1 Other-Regarding Stewardship: The Normative Turn (Topic 6)

Topic 6, the most prevalent theme in the 2020 sample, reflects the institutional mainstreaming of other-regarding – primarily climate-related – stewardship and marks a decisive departure from the tentative

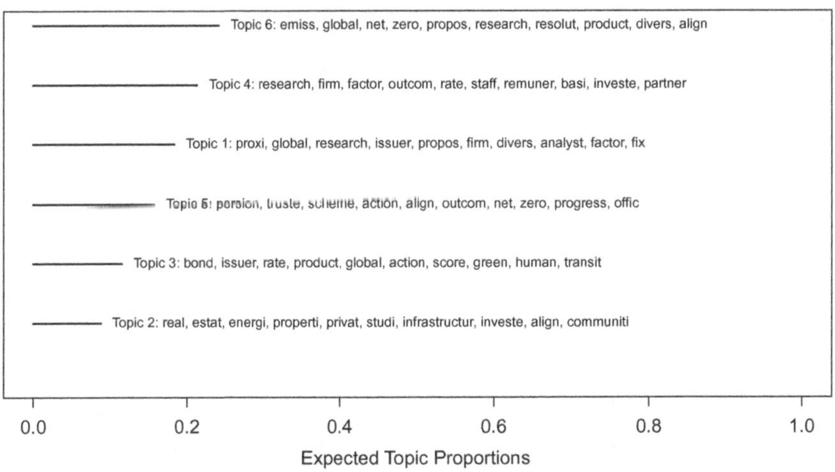

Figure 6.4 Distribution of estimated topics in the 2020 corpus.

Table 6.9 *Typology of stewardship narratives in the disclosures under the UK Stewardship Code 2020, ranked by prevalence*

Topic	Label	Core Features	Conceptual Framing
Topic 6	Other-Regarding Stewardship: The Normative Turn	Net-zero alignment; emissions targets; shareholder resolutions; integration of climate goals into governance (e.g. executive pay, board oversight)	*A values-driven, normatively anchored model of stewardship that repositions climate action as a central fiduciary responsibility. Engagement strategies focus not only on corporate governance reform but also on shaping market behaviour to align with global sustainability goals. Reflects the institutional mainstreaming of other-regarding stewardship under the 2G UK Code*
Topic 4	Bottom-Up Fundamental Stewardship	Research-intensive engagement; small- and mid-cap focus; financial fundamentals; executive pay; capital allocation	*A pragmatic, manager-led approach grounded in fundamental analysis and firm-specific engagement, prioritising governance outcomes and financial performance*
Topic 1	Governing Stewardship from Within: Infrastructure, Intermediation, and Internal Control	Proxy voting frameworks; third-party advisory input; procedural oversight; ESG integration through internal controls and committees	*A procedural model of stewardship embedded in investment operations, balancing external advisory inputs with internal accountability and strategic governance*

Topic 5	Trustee-Led Stewardship: From Delegation to Direction	LGPS and asset owner initiatives; collective influence (e.g. LAPFF); net-zero commitments; pooled vehicles; board-level oversight	*A trustee-led, impact-oriented model emphasising intergenerational responsibility, collaborative engagement, and system-level sustainability objectives*
Topic 3	Stewardship in Debt Capital Markets	ESG-labelled bonds; sovereign and corporate engagement; biodiversity and deforestation risks; data-driven due diligence; life cycle monitoring	*A multi-asset extension of stewardship where bondholders engage across the debt life cycle to influence sustainable capital allocation and systemic resilience*
Topic 2	Stewardship in Real Assets and Private Markets	Real estate, infrastructure, private markets; site-level engagement; tenant well-being; environmental compliance; bespoke ESG strategies	*An emergent but uneven stewardship narrative applied to illiquid assets, reflecting innovation in applying ESG principles beyond listed equities*

and marginal ESG references characteristic of the 2012 disclosures. Whereas earlier mentions of climate were often externally motivated and framed as tangential to financial performance, the 2020 disclosures captured by this topic articulate a markedly more assertive and integrated model – one that embeds climate-related objectives across both shareholder engagement and investment management.

At its core, this theme positions stewardship as a mechanism for achieving net-zero alignment, emissions reduction, and the systemic decarbonisation of business models.[107] The prominence of terms such as '*emiss*', '*net*', '*zero*', '*resolut*', '*propos*', and '*AGM*' reflects a discourse grounded in measurable transition outcomes and formal shareholder mechanisms. These disclosures reveal a model of investor stewardship where escalation mechanisms, particularly shareholder resolutions and proxy voting at AGMs, play a central role in pressing companies to enhance climate-related disclosures, adopt science-based targets, and ensure board-level oversight of sustainability strategies.[108]

A defining feature of Topic 6 is the integration of environmental aims with corporate governance levers. Climate targets are frequently tied to executive pay structures ('*pay*'), indicating a move away from siloed ESG analysis towards strategically aligned interventions that embed climate responsibility into core corporate performance structures.[109]

While frequent references to '*plc*' reaffirm the centrality of UK-listed equities, the scope of concern extends well beyond domestic regulatory compliance. Instead, the stewardship narratives articulated in this topic align with global decarbonisation pathways and fiduciary logics that

[107] For instance, Brewin Dolphin explicitly frames its stewardship strategy around net-zero alignment, stating its commitment to 'engage constructively with companies and funds to encourage them to disclose climate risks, set targets and make progress towards these targets', as part of its membership in the Net Zero Asset Managers (NZAM) initiative. See Brewin Dolphin, *Stewardship & Engagement Report For the year to 31 December 2021* (April 2022) (on file with the author).

[108] For instance, Evenlode highlights escalation practices as a key component of its climate stewardship strategy, particularly in cases of carbon non-disclosure or inadequate climate commitments. See Evenlode Investment, *Annual Responsible Investment Report 2021* (on file with the author).

[109] For instance, Genesis Investment Management illustrates the integration of climate engagement into its core fiduciary mandate, with a stated ambition to set portfolio-level targets. Through engagement with companies such as Bidcorp, the international foodservice group, Genesis leveraged its influence to advocate for the integration of emissions targets into executive incentive schemes and supported the capital allocation towards low-carbon investments. See Genesis Investment Management, *Annual Stewardship Report 2021* (on file with the author).

increasingly view climate engagement as essential to long-term value preservation.[110] In this sense, the climate discourse in Topic 6 is locally embedded but globally oriented.

In this respect, Topic 6's discursive profile closely mirrors the ideal of other-regarding stewardship.[111] It reflects a more normatively anchored conception of stewardship – grounded in the transformative ethos of the 2G UK Code – and demonstrates how climate-related engagement has evolved from a supplementary concern to a central pillar of institutional investor responsibility.

6.6.3.2 Bottom-Up Fundamental Stewardship (Topic 4)

Topic 4, the second most prevalent theme in the 2020 sample, reflects a bottom-up, research-intensive model of investor stewardship. It is firmly grounded in traditional investment analysis and prioritises financial fundamentals, firm-specific performance, and governance outcomes.[112] This theme illustrates how shareholder engagement – particularly at the firm-specific level – remains closely linked to the practices of active portfolio management, especially within small- and mid-cap equity markets.[113]

The prominence of terms such as '*research*', '*firm*', '*rate*', '*staff*', '*stock*', and '*remuner*' points to a stewardship strategy centred on financial

[110] For instance, Generation frames climate stewardship not simply as risk mitigation but as a fiduciary duty to 'contribute to the long-term stability of financial systems and real economies'. Its approach – operationalised through the creation of *Just Climate*, active membership in coalitions such as NZAM and the Institutional Investors Group on Climate Change (IIGCC), and proprietary engagement frameworks – demonstrates how climate considerations are embedded across the firm's portfolio management, escalation practices, and voting strategies. See Generation, *Stewardship Report 2021* (on file with the author).

[111] As articulated in Martin Currie's 2022 stewardship statement, this vision of stewardship is explicitly tied to systemic sustainability outcomes: 'Effective stewardship is not just a means of protecting long-term value creation – it is a tool for delivering real-world positive outcomes.' See Martin Currie, *Stewardship Annual Report 2022* (on file with the author).

[112] For instance, Teviot frames engagement as an extension of deep fundamental analysis in a niche, under-researched segment of the market. As they explain: 'Teviot's investment universe encompasses many companies that are poorly researched, often leading to mispriced investment opportunities. . . . Deep knowledge of the individual companies leads to a sounder understanding of both the risks and opportunities, enabling Teviot to engage with the benefit of knowledge that has a greater chance of resonating with companies'. See Teviot Partners Investment Managers, *Submission to the Financial Reporting Council (FRC) under the Stewardship Code 2020* (on file with the author).

[113] See e.g. Herald Investment Management Limited, *2021 Stewardship Code Report* (Spring 2022) (on file with the author).

valuation, corporate structure, and executive pay.[114] Engagements under this model are typically selective and diagnostic, often targeting long-term improvements in governance efficiency or addressing perceived underperformance.[115] Mentions of '*dividend*', '*broker*', and '*trade*' reinforce the theme's orientation towards capital allocation and investor returns, while references to smaller firms suggest that many of these engagements occur outside the large-cap index-tracked space.

Compared to 2012 disclosures – where governance engagement was frequently framed in terms of general board dialogue and proxy voting – Topic 4 reflects a more data-informed and diagnostic approach, consistent with institutional investors' rising expectations for transparency, accountability, and performance attribution. Yet, unlike the policy-led or macro-level stewardship models found in other topics, this theme embodies a pragmatic, asset manager-led framework, grounded in investment conviction, managerial discretion, and direct company knowledge.

Ultimately, Topic 4 underscores the enduring relevance of qualitative judgement and fundamental company research within stewardship practice. Even amid rising pressures to address systemic risks and global sustainability goals, many investors continue to pursue a firm-specific, bottom-up style of engagement – one premised on the belief that effective stewardship begins with a deep understanding of the business itself.

6.6.3.3 Governing Stewardship from Within: Infrastructure, Intermediation, and Internal Control (Topic 1)

Topic 1, the third most prevalent theme in the 2020 sample, centres on the governance infrastructure of stewardship, reflecting a procedural and systematised model in which proxy voting, third-party research integration, and internal oversight are embedded within the operational routines of investment organisations. The frequent appearance of terms such as '*proxy*', '*vendor*', '*analyst*', '*issuer*', and '*research*' underscores the role of external service providers – such as proxy advisors, ESG data vendors,

[114] Aberforth positions valuation as the 'primary consideration' in any investment decision, with engagement – particularly around governance and capital allocation – serving as a tool for enhancing client returns. The firm notes that 'discreet engagement with the boards of investee companies ... can improve investment returns, to the benefit of clients'. Aberforth, *Compliance with the UK Stewardship Code* (on file with the author).

[115] As Marathon explains, 'making an investment with the intention of holding it for around a decade ... one is incentivised to take an interest in ensuring that the business is managed to do well over a longer time frame'. See Marathon, *Report on Marathon's Compliance with the UK Stewardship Code for the Year 2021* (on file with the author).

and analytics platforms – in shaping voting decisions, contextualising corporate information, and facilitating coordinated shareholder responses.

Yet stewardship in this context is not reducible to outsourcing. Rather, it reflects a governance model mediated through intermediation: a carefully managed interplay between external inputs and internal accountability mechanisms.[116] While stewardship functions are often distributed across ESG-dedicated personnel, cross-functional committees, and escalation pathways, ultimate authority remains with the asset manager – even as operational processes become increasingly reliant on standardised tools and advisory infrastructure.[117]

Investment teams typically operate within internally governed but externally benchmarked frameworks, drawing on third-party research for issue tracking and comparative analysis, while adhering to firm-wide voting policies and escalation protocols. This approach facilitates consistency and scalability but also requires a delicate balance between operational efficiency and meaningful accountability.[118] A striking example is the challenge posed by conflicting ESG metrics. As one signatory notes, 'two different ESG measurement agencies give our portfolio two different results with significant conflicts within individual names', underscoring the difficulties of attribution and benchmarking in a landscape shaped by divergent data standards.[119] Such inconsistencies

[116] For instance, RBC Global Asset Management (GAM) states that while it 'subscribes to the proxy voting research of both ISS and Glass Lewis . . . voting authority rests solely with RBC GAM'. William Blair also highlights that while it has developed a multi-layered governance architecture for stewardship, including a dedicated Proxy Committee, an ESG Leadership Team, and an ESG Risk Working Group, proxy voting is conducted using research inputs from ISS, with final decisions remaining in house and reviewed for conflicts by the compliance team. See RBC Global Asset Management, *Commitment to the UK Stewardship Code* (2021) (on file with the author) and William Blair Investment Management, UK Stewardship Code 2021 Report (on file with the author), respectively.

[117] For instance, Dimensional Fund Advisors implements stewardship through a cross-functional framework, with an Investment Stewardship Committee overseeing proxy policies and service provider performance, while a dedicated team manages engagements and ESG controversies in line with its systematic, research-driven investment approach. See Dimensional, *2021–2022 Annual UK Stewardship Code Report* (on file with the author).

[118] For instance, AllianceBernstein highlights that effective stewardship demands 'a high level of accountability and oversight' and must be 'embedded in our investment process and aligned with our fiduciary duty'. See AllianceBernstein, *AB Global Stewardship Statement and 2021 Report* (on file with the author).

[119] Metropolis Capital, *UK Stewardship Code Report 2020* (30 April 2022), 13 (on file with the author).

highlight the indispensable role of internal oversight in interpreting, contextualising, and making informed use of ESG information.

This balancing act is as a defining feature of Topic 1. As investor stewardship becomes more routinised and expansive, firms must ensure that their internal governance – through mechanisms such as proxy committees, periodic policy reviews, and ESG oversight structures – continues to uphold both transparency and strategic intent. These systems are necessary not only for operational coordination and compliance but also for preserving the strategic purpose of stewardship amid increasing automation and external intermediation.[120]

6.6.3.4 Trustee-Led Stewardship: From Delegation to Direction (Topic 5)

Topic 5, the fourth most prevalent theme in the 2020 sample, captures a public sector, trustee-led model of stewardship, rooted in the institutional practices of LGPS and other collective asset owner initiatives. It marks a significant evolution from the 2012 disclosures, where trustee engagement was largely compliance-oriented and delegation-based. By contrast, the 2020 sample presents a more strategic and outward-facing, other-regarding approach, in which fiduciary duty is reinterpreted through the lens of climate alignment, long-term value creation, and systemic risk mitigation.[121]

The recurrence of terms such as '*pension*', '*trustee*', '*scheme*', '*align*', '*outcome*', '*net*', and '*action*' signals the consolidation of a stewardship discourse that embeds climate considerations into core investment beliefs. Across LGPS reports, this is reflected in formalised ESG governance, enhanced transparency, and clearly articulated sustainability objectives. Investor stewardship is no longer confined to monitoring risks – it is now tied to funding mandates, transparency, and intergenerational accountability.[122] Trustees and their advisory bodies increasingly

[120] See e.g. AGF International Advisors Company Limited, *Commitment to the UK Stewardship Code* (For period January 1 – December 31, 2021) (on file with the author).

[121] For instance, Lambeth Fund presents stewardship as a leadership responsibility that involves speaking out and fostering long-term relationships, driven by clear investment beliefs that link ESG integration with fiduciary duty and systemic outcomes. See London Borough of Lambeth Pension Fund, *Stewardship Report 2021/2022* (on file with the author).

[122] For instance, the Scottish Borders Council Pension Fund articulates stewardship as a responsibility rooted in public purpose, noting its revised Responsible Investment Policy and ESG monitoring regime as critical tools for delivering 'sustainable, risk-adjusted performance'

take on a proactive role, shaping stewardship practices and outcomes rather than merely overseeing their execution.

A defining feature of this trustee-led model of stewardship is its commitment to collaborative frameworks. References to initiatives such as the LAPFF and the Transition Pathway Initiative (TPI) underscore a growing emphasis on collective influence, enabling smaller funds to participate meaningfully in high-impact engagement. Rather than acting in isolation, asset owners coordinate around shared values and data-driven tools to advance macro-level, system-wide goals.[123]

This collective orientation is reinforced by robust internal governance. Stewardship oversight is typically exercised through pensions committees, local boards, and other institutional mechanisms that ensure strategic alignment and accountability. Participation in pooling arrangements enhances access to climate-resilient investment strategies and specialised stewardship expertise, while ongoing trustee development – through training, policy reviews, and performance monitoring – supports informed and responsible decision-making.[124]

The prominence of terms like '*outcome*' and '*action*' within this topic reflects a clear pivot from risk-based to impact-oriented stewardship. These asset owners increasingly position themselves not as passive monitors of financial and non-financial risks, but as active participants in driving systemic change, seeking to align capital allocation with the net-zero transition and broader environmental and social goals. As a result, investment strategies are designed not only to deliver long-term financial returns but also to generate measurable, real-world outcomes.[125] This trustee-led model of stewardship signals a shift in

over time. See Scottish Borders Council Pension Fund, *Stewardship Report 2021* (on file with the author).

[123] Cumbria LGPS, for example, emphasises its reliance on LAPFF, BCPP (Border to Coast Pension Partnership), and an internally defined culture of 'engagement over divestment'. Its collaborative activities range from direct issuer engagement to participation in climate-related working groups and the development of net-zero metrics. See Cumbria Local Government Pension Scheme, *Stewardship Report 2021/22* (on file with the author).

[124] See e.g. Lincolnshire County Council Pension Fund, *Stewardship Code 2021/22* (on file with the author).

[125] As Westminster pension fund asserts, stewardship is no longer limited to investment performance alone but must be evaluated by 'the carbon reduction the Fund has achieved over time' and its ability to influence policy and corporate practices in the real economy. See Westminster City Council Pension Fund, *UK Stewardship Code, Application for Signatory of the Code* (on file with the author).

authority – from delegated oversight to directional influence – anchored in values-based leadership, policy innovation, and long-horizon accountability.

6.6.3.5 Stewardship in Debt Capital Markets (Topic 3)

Topic 3, the fifth most prevalent theme in the 2020 sample, captures a stewardship model oriented towards fixed income markets, marking the growing extension of stewardship practices beyond listed equities into bond markets and the wider debt capital spectrum.[126] The prominence of terms such as '*bond*', '*issuer*', '*sovereign*', '*rate*', '*product*', '*biodivers*', and '*deforest*' highlights a discourse within debt capital markets shaped by climate and nature-related risks, alongside a mounting imperative to direct capital towards sustainable outcomes.[127]

Investors associated with this theme engage not merely as lenders but also as stewards of systemic resilience, influencing issuers to ensure credible use of proceeds, enhance disclosure, and support environmental and social targets. Importantly, stewardship in this space spans the full life cycle of debt instruments: from pre-issuance framework development and due diligence to post-issuance monitoring and impact assessment.[128] To overcome the structural and informational constraints historically associated with fixed income markets, investors often rely on collaborative platforms and data-driven tools.[129]

This theme also reflects the rising importance of ESG data providers and sustainability benchmarks within fixed income investing.[130] As

[126] On sovereign stewardship, see Dionysia Katelouzou, *The Varieties of Investor Stewardship: A Conference Report* (2024) <https://ssrn.com/abstract=4986769>.

[127] For instance, as of the end of 2020, Storebrand reported that 10 per cent of its assets were directed towards solution companies aligned with the UN Sustainable Development Goals, green bonds, and other certified ESG-linked assets, and nearly 40 per cent of its portfolio was fossil-free. See Storebrand Asset Management, *UK Stewardship Code Application, Reporting period 30 September 2020–30 September 2021* (on file with the author).

[128] See e.g. Mirova, *Mirova's 2022 Stewardship Report* (on file with the author) (exemplifying how through pre-issuance dialogue, primary market analysis and post-issuance monitoring, they seek to shape the structure and integrity of green and social bond frameworks). See also Union Bancaire Priveé, *The UK Stewardship Code Report 2021*, 72–3 (on engagement with corporate and sovereign issuers and exercising rights in fixed income) (on file with the author).

[129] For instance, TOBAM strengthens its fixed income stewardship through partnerships with third-party researchers and NGOs, including ISS and Urgewald, which support its engagement priorities and exclusion strategies. See TOBAM, *UK Stewardship Code, Revised Application October 2021* (on file with the author).

[130] See e.g. ibid.

investors assess issuer credibility, evaluate alignment with sustainability targets, and measure real-world performance, tools such as ESG ratings, taxonomies, and climate risk models have become integral to both investment decision-making and engagement strategies.

Ultimately, Topic 3 illustrates the broadening reach of stewardship – from equity-based engagement to a more comprehensive, multi-asset model. As sustainability risks intensify and expectations for transparency and accountability rise, stewardship in debt markets – especially in fixed income – is increasingly recognised not as peripheral, but as a vital component of long-term, outcome-oriented responsible investment.

6.6.3.6 Stewardship in Real Assets and Private Markets (Topic 2)

Topic 2, though the least prevalent theme in the 2020 sample, captures an emergent discourse on stewardship within non-listed asset classes – particularly real estate, infrastructure, and private markets. Although marginal in overall weight, this theme marks a significant extension of stewardship principles into illiquid and physical assets, reflecting the broader ambitions of the 2G UK Code to embed responsible investment across the investment universe.

The prominence of terms such as '*real*', '*estate*', '*property*', '*infrastructure*', '*private*', and '*energy*' points to a growing focus on how investor stewardship can be exercised outside listed equity markets, where influence is exerted through ownership structures, direct asset management, and long-term project governance. In these contexts, stewardship is operationalised through tools such as board representation, planning processes, and active management strategies.[131] Stewardship is closely tied to tangible outcomes, including energy efficiency, tenant well-being, and environmental compliance – objectives that require site-specific oversight and sustained engagement throughout the life cycle of an asset.[132]

131 Arcus Infrastructure Partners, for example, articulates a model of stewardship centred on 'controlling interests in unlisted company infrastructure assets', enabling the firm to 'actively monitor governance and significantly influence the business'. See Arcus Infrastructure Partners LLP, *UK Stewardship Code Report 2021* (on file with the author).

132 See e.g. Quinbrook Infrastructure Partners, *Investment Impact and Stewardship Outcomes Report 2021* (on file with the author); Darwin Property Investment Management (Guernsey) Limited, *Stewardship Report 2022 Responsible Investing* (on file with the author); Darwin Alternative Investment Management (Guernsey) Limited, *Stewardship Report 2022 Responsible Investing* (on file with the author).

Compared to the 2012 sample – where stewardship in private and real assets was largely absent – Topic 2 reveals the beginnings of institutionalisation. Its relatively low prevalence in the 2020 disclosure sample nevertheless suggests that these practices remained nascent, concentrated among a subset of specialist investors with the governance structures and organisational capacity to integrate stewardship into non-listed investment strategies.

Ultimately, Topic 2 underscores both the expanding reach of stewardship and the uneven pace of ESG integration across asset classes.[133] While the extension of stewardship beyond listed equities is increasingly recognised as necessary, its translation into private and real assets remains a developing frontier – characterised by innovation, experimentation, and ongoing challenges in standardisation and accountability.

6.6.3.7 Concluding Reflections: Maturation and Narrative Diversification

Together, the six topics identified in the 2020 sample reveal both the institutional maturation and thematic diversification of investor stewardship under the 2G UK Code. Compared to the 2012 disclosures, the 2020 narratives are more normatively ambitious, operationally structured, and asset-class inclusive. Stewardship is no longer framed predominantly in terms of micro-level shareholder engagement and fiduciary duty to proximate clients and beneficiaries; instead, it increasingly reflects the broader relational responsibilities articulated in the framework of *enlightened investor stewardship* set out in Chapter 4. Investors express awareness of their position not only vis-à-vis proximate clients and beneficiaries or investee companies, but also in relation to end-investors, financial systems, and the wider social and especially environmental context on which long-term value depends.

While some themes – such as bottom-up engagement and internally governed stewardship practices – highlight continuity in method, others – particularly those centred on climate integration, trustee-led collective stewardship, and the extension of stewardship into debt, real assets, and private markets – mark a significant discursive and strategic shift. The rising prominence of other-regarding goals, the movement from risk monitoring to impact orientation, and the embedding of stewardship across

[133] For instance, LaSalle integrates ESG oversight into the day-to-day management of its real estate assets, reporting on initiatives such as climate risk mapping, tenant engagement, and building retrofits to reduce energy consumption and carbon emissions. See LaSalle, *UK Stewardship Code 2022 Report* (on file with the author).

organisational functions all resonate with the concept of enlightened investor stewardship as a multi-level, multi-actor practice. These patterns suggest a deepening recognition that investor stewardship involves the exercise of power both *on behalf of* and *for others*, including those 'unseen others' whose interests are shaped by institutional investment decisions.[134]

Viewed through this lens, the 2020 sample depicts a field in transition: one moving decisively beyond shareholder engagement as the core of stewardship towards a more systematic, purpose-driven model aligned with global sustainability imperatives and evolving fiduciary norms. These findings point to the institutionalisation of stewardship as a multidimensional practice – spanning proximate clients and beneficiaries, end investors, investee assets, and the wider systems that condition long-term value. In doing so, they provide empirical grounding for the framework of enlightened investor stewardship, illustrating how its core tenets are beginning to take root across narrative, organisational, and asset-class boundaries.

6.6.4 Explaining Thematic Variation

A key advantage of STM is its ability to incorporate document-level metadata – referred to as covariates – directly into the estimation process. This enables researchers to examine how both topical prevalence (the extent to which a topic is discussed) and topical content (the specific language used to express it) vary systematically with observable characteristics.

This functionality is particularly well-suited to the stewardship context, where disclosures exhibit notable variation in tone, emphasis, and rhetorical style across different types of signatories. In this analysis, covariates such as investor type and organisational size were included to capture institutional heterogeneity and explore how these features shape stewardship narratives.

6.6.4.1 Key Narrative Drivers in the 2012 Sample

To analyse the 2012 disclosures, five document-level covariates were incorporated into the STM: *Investor Type*, *Country*, *Size*, *Tier* and *Activist*. Full definitions and coding rules for these variables are provided in Table 6.10. These covariates were used to analyse variation in topical prevalence – defined as the proportion of each document devoted to

[134] See Section 4.3.2.3.

Table 6.10 *Independent variables for structural topic modelling*

Variables	Definition
Investor type	Equals 1 if the signatory is an asset manager, and 2 if the signatory is an asset owner
Country	Primary headquarters location of the signatory. Equals 1 if the primary headquarters is in the UK, and 0 otherwise. Source: Diligent Market Intelligence and the signatory's website
Activist	Equals 1 if the signatory engages in activist strategies (e.g. shareholder proposals, public campaigns), and 0 otherwise. Source: Diligent Market Intelligence and the signatory's website
Tier	Equals 1 if the signatory's statement has been assessed by the FRC as a Tier 1 statement under the UK Stewardship Code 2012, and 0 otherwise
Size	The natural logarithm of the signatory's assets under management in billion USD as of January 2024. Source: Diligent Market Intelligence and the signatory's' website
Signatory 2012	Equals 1 if the signatory to the UK Stewardship Code 2020 has already been a signatory to the 2012 iteration of the Code, and 0 otherwise

a given topic – and to identify the institutional factors most strongly associated with different stewardship themes.

To evaluate the explanatory power of each covariate, five nested regression models were estimated, with each successive model introducing an additional variable. The full model specification is expressed as follows:

$$Topic\_Proportion_K \sim Constant_K + b_1(InvestorType) + b_2(Country)$$
$$+ b_3(Size) + b_4(Tier) + b_5(Activist) + error_K$$

STM also allows for analysis of topical content – how the language used within a topic varies across groups. For example, asset managers signatories may use different terminology when discussing ESG-related topics than asset owners. However, due to the limitations of the *stm* R package, which restricts content estimation to a single covariate at a time, attempts to include multiple content covariates led to instability in topic structure and labelling.[135] As a result, content covariates were excluded from the final

[135] See also Roberts *et al.*, 'stm: An R Package for Structural Topic Models', 18–21.

STM specification. Instead, variation in terminology was explored through complementary relative frequency analysis.[136]

The five nested regression models applied to the 2012 sample revealed clear and systematic variation in how different institutional characteristics influence stewardship narratives (Table 6.11).

Investor Type emerged as the most consistently significant predictor of variation in topic prevalence. Asset managers were significantly more likely to emphasise Topic 1 (*Orthodox Shareholder Stewardship*) and Topic 2 (*Early ESG-Informed Stewardship*), reflecting their focus on board-level engagement, governance risks, and growing responsiveness to ESG-related frameworks. In contrast, asset owners were significantly more likely to reference Topic 3 (*Collective Stewardship by Public Asset Owners*) and Topic 4 (*Trustee-oriented Indirect Stewardship*). These patterns highlight a stronger emphasis among asset owners on fiduciary accountability and the delegation of stewardship responsibilities to external managers (indirect stewardship). Collective engagement, in particular, was most characteristic of public pension funds, often coordinated through platforms such as the LAPFF. While asset managers also showed a positive association with Topic 6 (*Emerging Enlightened Shareholder Stewardship*) – a values-driven narrative grounded in long-termism and sustainability – the effect was not statistically significant across all model specifications, suggesting a tentative engagement with other-regarding, purpose-led stewardship at this stage.

Country of domicile also played a significant role in shaping the content of stewardship reporting. UK-based signatories were more likely to adopt the traditional, engagement-centred narrative associated with Topic 1, characterised by board-level engagement, monitoring of governance risks, and an emphasis on fiduciary accountability to clients and beneficiaries. They also exhibited a modest positive association with Topic 6 (*Emerging Enlightened Shareholder Stewardship*), suggesting selective early engagement with values-driven language. By contrast, international signatories were significantly more likely to reference Topic 2, drawing on global responsible investment norms such as the UN Global Compact and the PRI, and demonstrating greater receptiveness to ESG metrics and sustainability disclosures. These signatories also showed a positive association with Topic 5 (*Stewardship Infrastructure and Advisory Processes*), reflecting a greater reliance on

[136] On variation in language by investor type, see Section 6.5.

Table 6.11 *Effects of institutional characteristics on topic prevalence, 2012 sample*

	Model I					
	Topic 1	Topic 2	Topic 3	Topic 4	Topic 5	Topic 6
(Intercept)	0.759***	0.230***	−0.435***	−0.160***	0.447***	0.160***
Investor Type	−0.334***	−0.081***	0.457***	0.180***	−0.215***	−0.010
	Model II					
	Topic 1	Topic 2	Topic 3	Topic 4	Topic 5	Topic 6
(Intercept)	0.643***	0.288***	−0.432***	−0.160***	0.535***	0.127***
Investor Type	−0.416***	−0.041*	0.458***	0.458***	−0.031	−0.031
Country	0.298***	−0.146***	−0.003	−0.001	0.082***	0.082**
	Model III					
	Topic 1	Topic 2	Topic 3	Topic 4	Topic 5	Topic 6
(Intercept)	0.763***	0.239***	−0.352***	−0.156***	0.443***	0.052
Investor Type	−0.427***	−0.036*	0.452***	0.181***	−0.143***	−0.024
Country	0.245***	−0.124***	−0.042	−0.003	−0.186***	0.116***
Size	−0.023***	0.010**	−0.016	−0.001	0.017***	0.014**

	Model IV					
	Topic 1	Topic 2	Topic 3	Topic 4	Topic 5	Topic 6
(Intercept)	0.693***	0.331***	−0.432***	−0.204**	0.396***	0.201***
Investor Type	−0.418***	−0.047**	0.462***	0.187***	−0.138***	−0.042*
Country	0.243***	−0.126***	−0.039	−0.003	−0.185***	0.111***
Size	−0.020***	0.006	−0.012	0.001	0.018***	0.008
Tier	0.04	−0.053**	0.044	0.028	0.029	−0.081***

	Model V					
	Topic 1	Topic 2	Topic 3	Topic 4	Topic 5	Topic 6
(Intercept)	0.683***	0.302***	−0.433***	−0.187**	0.409***	0.221***
Investor Type	−0.412***	−0.031***	0.463***	0.178***	−0.144***	−0.05*
Country	0.241***	−0.134***	−0.040	0.001	−0.182***	0.113***
Size	−0.021***	0.003	−0.012*	0.002	0.020***	0.009*
Tier	0.04	−0.047**	0.043	0.024	0.026	−0.088***
Activist	0.026	0.056**	0.004	−0.022	−0.031	−0.027

This table reports results from five nested linear regression models estimating the association between institutional characteristics and the prevalence of six stewardship topics identified through STM in the 2012 sample. The models sequentially introduce *Investor Type, Country, Size, Tier*, and *Activist Strategy* to assess their explanatory contribution. Coefficients indicate the direction and magnitude of each variable's effect on topic proportions. Statistical significance is denoted as *** $p < 0.001$, ** $p < 0.05$, and * $p < 0.10$.

formalised procedural frameworks, proxy advisory systems, and third-party research as core components of their stewardship activities.

Size, measured by total assets under management, was positively and consistently associated with Topic 5, indicating that larger institutions are more likely to formalise and disclose structured stewardship processes. These include proxy voting mechanisms, internal governance structures, and the use of external service providers – practices enabled by greater organisational capacity and operational scale. Conversely, smaller institutions were more inclined to emphasise Topic 1, suggesting a continued reliance on traditional governance-focused stewardship, likely driven by resource constraints that limit the development of more process-intensive systems.

Tier had a limited impact overall but was negatively associated with Topics 2 and 6. This indicates that Tier 2 signatories were significantly less likely to incorporate ESG-related discourse or adopt values-oriented narratives, supporting the view that these discourses were still emerging in the early stewardship landscape, particularly among signatories with less mature or transparent reporting practices. Notably, the limited explanatory power of *Tier* suggests that the FRC's decision to discontinue the tiering system under the UK Code 2020 was a step in the right direction – shifting emphasis from hierarchical labels to substantive quality and outcome-focused reporting.[137]

Finally, *Activist* showed only a limited overall effect, although a modest positive association with Topic 2 was observed. This suggests that signatories identifying with activist strategies were somewhat more likely to integrate ESG-related language into their disclosures. While the effect was not large, it signals a degree of alignment between activist stewardship and global ESG norms, especially regarding climate and social risk. Nonetheless, the relatively weak association also reflects the heterogeneity of activist practice and indicates that ESG framing was not yet a defining feature of activist strategy in this early phase of stewardship development.

Together, these findings demonstrate that institutional characteristics – particularly *Investor Type* and *Country* of origin – play a significant role in shaping the thematic contours of stewardship reporting under the UK Code 2012.

[137] See Section 5.3.3.2.

6.6.4.2 Key Narrative Drivers in the 2020 Sample

A similar analytical approach was applied to the 2020 sample. Five document-level covariates were again incorporated into the STM: *Investor Type*, *Country*, *Size*, *Activist*, and, a new variable, *Signatory 2012*, which replaced the earlier *Tier* classification. *Signatory 2012* is a binary variable coded as 1 if the organisation had already been a signatory to the 2012 iteration of the UK Stewardship Code and 0 otherwise (Table 6.10), offering an alternative measure of signatory experience and maturity. Organisations that signed the UK Code 2012 are assumed to have had earlier exposure to stewardship principles and a longer history of formal engagement practices. Including *Signatory 2012* as a document-level covariate allows for the exploration of whether experience under the earlier regime systematically shapes thematic emphasis in the 2020 stewardship disclosures.

As with the 2012 sample, document-level covariates were included to model variation in topical prevalence. The full model specification is expressed as follows:

$$Topic\_Proportion_K \sim Constant_K + b_1(InvestorType) + \ b_2(Country)$$

$$+b_3(Size) + \ b_4(Signatory2012) + b_5(Activist) + error_K$$

The nested regression models for the 2020 sample (Table 6.12) highlight how institutional characteristics systematically shape stewardship narratives under the 2G UK Code.

Investor Type emerges as a significant differentiator across multiple topics. Because *Investor Type* is coded as 1 for asset managers and 2 for asset owners, the negative coefficients for Topic 1 (*Governing Stewardship from Within: Infrastructure, Intermediation, and Internal Control*), Topic 4 (*Bottom-up Fundamental Stewardship*), and Topic 6 (*Other-Regarding Stewardship: The Normative Turn*) indicate that asset managers emphasise these themes more strongly than asset owners. Conversely, the strong positive association with Topic 5 (*Trustee-Led Stewardship: From Delegation to Direction*) suggests that asset owners – particularly public-sector pension schemes – are more engaged in trustee-led, outcome-oriented stewardship models. No significant differences appear for Topic 3 (*Stewardship in Debt Capital Markets*) or Topic 2 (*Stewardship in Real Assets and Private Markets*), implying that stewardship in these areas is still evolving and not yet strongly shaped by institutional form.

Table 6.12 *Effects of institutional characteristics on topic prevalence, 2020 sample*

	Model I					
	Topic 1	Topic 2	Topic 3	Topic 4	Topic 5	Topic 6
(Intercept)	0.446***	0.124***	0.193***	0.432***	−0.552***	0.364***
Investor Type	−0.211***	−0.029	−0.061*	−0.178***	0.574***	−0.099**
	Model II					
	Topic 1	Topic 2	Topic 3	Topic 4	Topic 5	Topic 6
(Intercept)	−0.499***	0.127***	0.217***	0.386***	−0.557***	0.327***
Investor Type	−0.092**	−0.022	−0.007	−0.274***	0.571***	−0.176***
Country	−0.291***	−0.015	−0.132	0.239***	0.013	0.189***
	Model III					
	Topic 1	Topic 2	Topic 3	Topic 4	Topic 5	Topic 6
(Intercept)	0.324***	0.189***	0.191***	0.549***	−0.514***	0.266***
Investor Type	−0.098***	−0.020	−0.008	−0.273***	0.569***	−0.174***
Country	−0.202***	−0.047	−0.119***	0.159***	−0.008	0.217***
Size	−0.023***	−0.013**	0.005	−0.033***	−0.008**	0.012**

Model IV

	Topic 1	Topic 2	Topic 3	Topic 4	Topic 5	Topic 6
(Intercept)	0.316***	0.207***	0.198***	0.560***	−0.517***	0.234***
Investor Type	−0.095***	−0.019	−0.008	0.187***	0.570***	−0.042*
Country	−0.207***	−0.034	−0.112***	0.167***	−0.007	0.194***
Size	−0.035***	−0.009	0.008	−0.031***	0.083*	0.006
Signatory 2012	0.02	−0.062**	−0.028	−0.042*	0.969	0.110***

Model V

	Topic 1	Topic 2	Topic 3	Topic 4	Topic 5	Topic 6
(Intercept)	0.322***	0.215***	0.191***	0.579***	−0.516***	0.212***
Investor Type	−0.105***	−0.024	0.003	−0.287***	0.568***	−0.155***
Country	−0.202***	−0.033	−0.119***	0.173***	−0.004	0.184***
Size	0.038***	−0.009	0.005	−0.027***	−0.007	0.001
Signatory 2012	0.028	−0.059**	−0.036	−0.034	0.002	0.100***
Activist	−0.040	−0.013	0.046*	−0.067**	−0.011	0.084**

This table reports results from five nested linear regression models estimating the association between institutional characteristics and the prevalence of six stewardship topics identified through STM in the 2020 sample. The models sequentially introduce *Investor Type, Country, Size, Signatory (2012)*, and *Activist Strategy* to assess their explanatory contribution. Coefficients indicate the direction and magnitude of each variable's effect on topic proportions. Statistical significance is denoted as *** $p < 0.001$, ** $p < 0.05$, and * $p < 0.10$.

Country effects are equally pronounced. UK-based signatories are significantly more likely to emphasise other-regarding stewardship (Topic 6) and bottom-up firm-specific engagement (Topic 4), but less likely to focus on stewardship governance (Topic 1) and stewardship in debt markets (Topic 3). These findings are consistent with the UK's leadership in climate-related financial governance and suggest a growing emphasis among UK institutions on detailed, asset-specific engagement, and other-regarding stewardship practices.

Size plays a smaller but still notable role. Larger institutions are more likely to foreground Topic 1, reflecting the capacity of large organisations to build internal stewardship infrastructures and integrate third-party advisory tools. By contrast, they are slightly less likely to emphasise Topic 4, suggesting a shift away from resource-intensive, bottom-up engagement towards scalable, policy-based stewardship strategies.

Signatory 2012 status – the indicator of prior experience under the UK Code 2012 – further shapes stewardship narratives. Experienced signatories show significantly greater engagement with other-regarding stewardship (Topic 6), consistent with the idea that organisational maturity supports the integration of systemic and normative goals into stewardship practices. Newer signatories show slightly higher emphasis on Topic 2, which may reflect efforts – particularly among smaller or niche investors – to distinguish themselves by focusing on infrastructure, real estate, and private markets. It may also reflect the broader scope of the 2G UK Code: earlier versions centred on public listed equities and therefore offered little incentive for non-equity investors to sign on.

Activist orientation reveals an important and somewhat unexpected pattern. While activist signatories show a stronger association with debt capital stewardship (Topic 3) and other-regarding stewardship (Topic 6), they are negatively associated with bottom-up, firm-specific stewardship (Topic 4). Given that activist investors traditionally specialise in concentrated, firm-specific interventions, their weaker emphasis on bottom-up stewardship is notable.[138]

Several explanations emerge. First, contemporary activist strategies increasingly extend beyond individual firm-level governance to embrace systemic stewardship tools – such as policy engagement, collaborative initiatives, and sustainability-themed campaigns – aimed at shaping broader market and regulatory structures.[139] The positive association

[138] Section 3.2.2.
[139] Sections 3.2.3, 3.3.2 and 3.3.3.

with Topic 6 suggests a normative reframing of activism, aligned with rising expectations around climate risk, inequality, and long-term value creation.

Second, although many institutional investors use disclosures as signalling instruments,[140] activists face distinct reputational pressures. Given long-standing concerns about the adversarial nature of activist interventions,[141] they may be particularly motivated to frame their disclosures in normative or system-oriented terms. By foregrounding systemic risks and public-interest goals – such as climate change, inequality, or long-term value creation – activists can reposition their strategies within a legitimacy-enhancing narrative. This rhetorical shift helps counter perceptions of short-termism and signals alignment with evolving regulatory and market expectations. While firm-level analysis remains central to many activist approaches, such granular detail is often backgrounded in disclosures that prioritise credibility, purpose, and wider systemic impact.

Taken together, these findings suggest that stewardship narratives of activist institutional investors are becoming more rhetorically ambitious and strategically multifaceted.[142] Moving beyond conventional firm-level engagement, activists increasingly operate across asset classes and public policy domains, positioning themselves as contributors to system-level change rather than merely corporate reformers.

Overall, the results for the 2020 sample underscore the maturation and diversification of stewardship practices under the 2G UK Code. No longer a uniform exercise centred solely on shareholder rights and firm-level engagement, stewardship has evolved into a complex and differentiated ecosystem. Its contours are shaped by institutional characteristics such as investor type, geography, organisational scale, signatory experience, and activist orientation. This heterogeneity marks a significant shift: from stewardship as a compliance obligation to a strategic, purpose-driven, multi-asset endeavour – one increasingly aligned with systemic risk management, global sustainability imperatives, and evolving conceptions of fiduciary responsibility.

140 See e.g. Arleta A. A. Majoch, Andreas G. F. Hoepner and Tessa Hebb, 'Sources of Stakeholder Salience in the Responsible Investment Movement: Why Do Investors Sign the Principles for Responsible Investment?' (2017) 140 *Journal of Business Ethics* 723 (providing empirical evidence that institutional investors often adopt responsible investment codes such as the PRI for reputational and legitimacy-related reasons).

141 Section 3.2.2.

142 For early empirical evidence on activist stewardship narratives under the 1G UK Code, see Katelouzou, 'The Rhetoric of Activist Shareholder Stewards', 740.

6.7 Conclusion: What Stewardship Disclosures Reveal – and Don't

This chapter has applied a multi-method NLP framework to examine how institutional investors have interpreted and operationalised the UK Stewardship Code across its two generations. The findings reveal a trajectory of growing complexity, ambition, and heterogeneity in stewardship discourse – shifting from the compliance-oriented and relatively standardised narratives under the 1G UK Code to the more differentiated, strategic, and aspirational disclosures under the 2G UK Code. STM uncovered a typology of underlying stewardship themes, while regression analysis showed how institutional characteristics – such as size, investor type, geography, activist orientation, and prior signatory experience – shape disclosure practices.

A central insight is the emergence of other-regarding stewardship: a values-driven orientation that links investment activity to long-term sustainability, systemic risk mitigation, and broader public accountability. While not yet dominant, this normative shift is most visible among large, UK-based, and experienced signatories, suggesting that regulatory embeddedness and organisational capacity enable deeper engagement with stewardship's wider purposes.

Yet for all their expanded length and rhetorical sophistication, stewardship disclosures also conceal as much as they reveal. Few statements provide clear evidence of implementation or tangible outcomes. Many remain vague about internal decision-making, escalation protocols, or how investor stewardship is integrated into investment practice. In some cases, longer disclosures appear to substitute narrative density for substantive transparency – raising the risk of *stewardship washing*, where aspirational language and formal compliance mask the absence of meaningful behavioural change.

What emerges, then, is not convergence around a single model of best practice, but a strategically diverse and narratively plural field of investor stewardship. The 2G UK Code has elevated expectations and encouraged more substantive engagement, but wide variation persists in how its principles are interpreted and enacted – particularly regarding its systemic and normative dimensions.

To make sense of this pluralism, the next chapter develops a typology of investor stewardship – mapping how investors vary in their levels, motivations, and modes of monitoring and engagement, as well as proposing an integrated framework to navigate these distinctions.

7

The Varieties of Investor Stewardship

A Typology and Framework for Reform

7.1 Introduction

The preceding chapters have traced the intellectual, regulatory, and empirical evolution of shareholder – and more broadly, investor – stewardship in the UK. From its origins in investor-led codes of best practice to its institutionalisation under the Financial Reporting Council (FRC), the UK's stewardship regime has operated both as a domestic experiment and a global reference point. It has shaped international regulatory discourse, informed normative expectations, and contributed to the diffusion of stewardship principles across diverse institutional investors and financial markets.

Yet, as Chapter 6 revealed, the practice of investor stewardship remains highly uneven. Disclosures submitted under the two generations of the UK Stewardship Code exhibit significant variation – from boilerplate, compliance-driven reporting to more substantive narratives grounded in long-term value creation, systemic risk engagement, and broader societal accountability.

This chapter builds on those empirical insights by taking an interpretive turn. It develops a typology of the *varieties of investor stewardship* that synthesises conceptual, regulatory, and narrative perspectives. While rooted in the logic of shareholder stewardship, the typology is designed to be asset-agnostic. It provides a flexible framework for understanding how stewardship responsibilities are interpreted and operationalised across asset classes – reflecting the growing heterogeneity of institutional capital, investment strategies, and fiduciary mandates.

The typology draws on close qualitative analysis of stewardship disclosures, especially those submitted under the second-generation (2G) UK Stewardship Code. Whereas the topic modelling in Chapter 6 offered a data-driven map of narrative variation, it could not fully capture the internal logics, strategic choices, and normative framings embedded in these narratives. This chapter addresses that gap by developing a set of ideal-type categories that represent distinct stewardship logics as articulated in the disclosures. These types are not intended as rigid taxonomies or exhaustive descriptions of practice. Rather, they function as heuristic tools – analytical lenses for navigating the plural, overlapping, and evolving forms of stewardship emerging in the field.

Importantly, the typology recognises that institutional investors rarely adhere to a single stewardship model. Instead, they selectively blend different forms depending on asset class, organisational structure, internal capabilities, and the expectations of clients and beneficiaries. The aim is not to impose normative uniformity, but to provide a structured way of understanding the diversity – and strategic implications – of how investor stewardship is imagined and enacted in practice.

7.2 Investor Stewardship across Four Levels

7.2.1 Levels of Investor Stewardship: Micro, Portfolio, System, and Macro

Investor stewardship can be differentiated by the level at which it is exercised – ranging from micro-level to portfolio-level, system-level, and macro-level stewardship (Figure 7.1). These levels reflect distinct scopes of influence and strategic orientation, from direct interventions with individual companies to efforts aimed at reshaping market norms, regulatory frameworks, and the structural conditions of capital markets.

Micro-level investor stewardship, also referred to as 'issuer-specific stewardship',[1] involves the exercise of influence by institutional investors over *individual* portfolio assets. In the context of public equities, this includes monitoring corporate behaviour, voting on shareholder resolutions, and engaging with company management on specific governance, environmental or performance-related issues. This form of stewardship was central to the first-generation (1G) UK Code and continues to feature prominently in stewardship disclosures, especially among UK-based asset managers.[2]

However, as already outlined, economically rational engagement at the micro-level requires alignment with the asset manager's business model

[1] Bobby V. Reddy, 'The Emperor's New Code? Time to Re-evaluate the Nature of Stewardship Engagement under the UK's Stewardship Code' (2021) 84 *The Modern Law Review* 842.

[2] Sections 5.3.1 and 6.6.4.2.

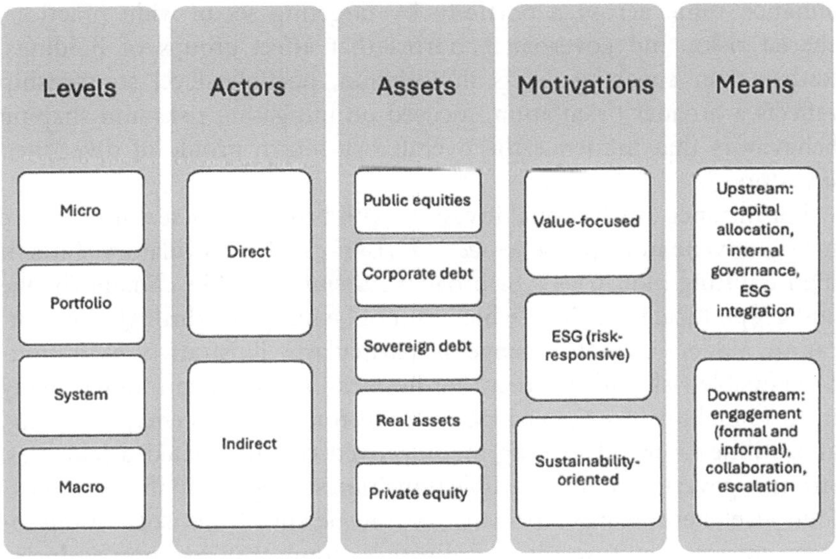

Figure 7.1 Typology of investor stewardship.

and a demonstrable capacity to generate value – what has previously been termed the portfolio-level stewardship viability condition.[3] In practice, sustained engagement with every investee company is not feasible for most institutional investors. While activist stewards and select active managers may pursue intensive issuer-specific strategies, they represent a small minority within the broader investment landscape. For the majority – particularly passive managers and those with limited internal capacity – micro-level stewardship is constrained by costs, incentive structures, and operational scale, and is therefore typically undertaken on a prioritised, discretionary basis.[4]

As a result, both policy discourse and industry practice have increasingly turned towards *portfolio-level stewardship*.[5] This approach seeks to

[3] Section 4.3.3.

[4] The practical barriers, such as resource allocation, ownership thresholds, and market structures, constraining investors' ability to engage at the firm level, are acknowledged in stewardship reporting. See e.g. James Hambro & Partners, *Stewardship Report* (2021), 76 (on file with the author) (noting that '[t]he resource-intensive nature of engagement means that we must prioritise those instances where we believe change will be most impactful. ... In practice, this means most of our engagement is focused on our direct equity investments').

[5] Others use the term 'systematic risk activism' or 'systematic stewardship' to describe institutional shareholders' monitoring and discipline aiming at enhancing the value of

enhance value across a portfolio by targeting sector-wide practices, shared risks, and governance norms that affect groups of holdings. Rather than engaging assets in isolation, portfolio-level stewardship reflects a broader orientation, focused on mitigating risks and shaping behaviours that influence the overall risk-return profile of diversified investors.

For instance, institutional investors with broad, cross-sector exposure may intervene in response to *sectoral risks* – such as regulatory shifts in high-emitting industries – or broader *systemic risks* like climate change and geopolitical instability, which cannot be mitigated through diversification alone.[6] Climate change is particularly illustrative: as a non-diversifiable risk with far-reaching implications, it has prompted many institutional investors to engage entire sectors – such as energy, mining, and utilities – by advocating for improved climate-related disclosures, stronger governance, and credible transition strategies.[7] In this way, portfolio-level stewardship represents a strategic shift from isolated micro-level engagement towards coordinated action that reshapes industry practices, mitigates systemic risks, and reinforces governance standards across the market. It also creates positive spillover effects, extending value beyond the directly targeted companies and supporting long-term risk-adjusted returns throughout the investment chain.

Building on this, many institutional investors have adopted overarching stewardship frameworks that aim to address system-wide, non-diversifiable risks – such as climate change, biodiversity loss, liquidity risk, and social challenges like diversity and indigenous rights.[8] When these high-level principles are operationalised – either through individual efforts or collaborative initiatives – they give rise to *system-level stewardship*. Unlike micro- or portfolio-level approaches, system-level stewardship targets the structural features of financial markets themselves, with the goal of mitigating beta risk – systemic factors that affect

the entire portfolio rather than the value of a specific target company; see John C. Jr. Coffee, 'The Coming Shift in Shareholder Activism: From "Firm-Specific" to "Systematic Risk" Proxy Campaigns (and How to Enable Them)' (2021) 16 *Brooklyn Journal of Corporate, Financial & Commercial Law* 45 and Jeffrey N. Gordon, 'Systematic Stewardship' (2021) 47 *Journal of Corporation Law* 627, respectively.

6 Madison Condon, 'Externalities and the Common Owner' (2020) 95 *Washington Law Review* 143–8 and 63–4. See also Section 3.3.1 on index funds and common ownership.

7 Sections 4.3.3 and 6.6.3.1.

8 See e.g. Reconciliation & Responsible Investment Initiative: www.rrii.org. See also Sections 3.3.3 and 7.2.2.

overall market performance – rather than seeking alpha through asset selection, and asset- or portfolio-specific engagement.[9]

This form of stewardship typically focuses on promoting market-wide norms, strengthening disclosure standards, and internalising externalities that threaten the resilience of the financial system. In some cases, it may involve engaging with systemically important firms or participating in cross-sector initiatives, even in the absence of direct equity or debt holdings, to influence behaviours and establish consistent expectations across the market.[10]

A further layer of stewardship has emerged from the recognition that enduring systemic change requires action beyond the confines of the financial sector. *Macro-level stewardship* involves collaboration with a wide range of external stakeholders – including governments, regulators, standard-setters, international organisations, and civil society – to shape the policy and institutional frameworks that underpin capital markets.[11] It reflects a commitment to collective action in addressing large-scale externalities that no single investor or industry body can address in isolation.

The UK Stewardship Code 2020, through Principle 4, explicitly supports both system- and macro-level stewardship.[12] It calls on signatories to identify and respond to systemic risks that transcend individual holdings, and to collaborate with a wide range of stakeholders to do so.

9 System-level stewardship has much in common with the so-called beta activism, which is designed to affect non-diversifiable systematic risks. On beta activism, see Section 3.2.3.

10 For instance, Sarasin & Partners engaged with BP on climate-related financial disclosures and Paris-aligned accounting practices, despite holding no equity or debt in the company. Sarasin justified the engagement as necessary to address market-wide mispricing of climate risk and to influence audit and reporting standards with broader systemic implications. See Sarasin & Partners, Stewardship Report, *UK Stewardship Code* (April 2022), 55 (on file with the author). Impax Asset Management similarly reports engaging collaboratively with nineteen companies it did not own as part of thematic initiatives on climate risk and food system transition. See Impax Asset Management, *UK Stewardship Code Statement* (April 2022), 30.

11 Aviva Investors explicitly use the term macro-stewardship to refer to 'engaging with regulators, governments and other entities to change the "rules of the game" in favour of business providing solutions to sustainability problems or supporting the transition to a sustainable future'. See Aviva Investors, *2021 Responsible Investment Annual Review*, 27 (on file with the author). But see Financial Conduct Authority, *Finance for Positive Sustainable Change: Governance, Incentives and Competence in Regulated Firms* (February 2023), para 3.85 (using the term 'macro' stewardship as synonymous to system-level stewardship, that is, stewardship 'influencing the functioning of financial markets').

12 Financial Reporting Council, *The UK Stewardship Code 2020* (2019) [UK Code 2020], 4 and Principle 4.

However, translating these higher-order stewardship activities into tangible outcomes remains challenging. Systemic risks such as climate change, inequality, and governance failures are characterised by diffuse, long-term impacts that resist straightforward attribution.[13] While efforts to internalise negative externalities may strengthen market resilience, the benefits to individual portfolios are typically indirect, delayed, and difficult to quantify.[14]

7.2.2 *Blended Stewardship: Cross-Level Complementarity*

While the typology of micro-, portfolio-, system-, and macro-level stewardship offers a useful framework for analysing distinct modes of investor influence, the boundaries between these categories are increasingly fluid in practice. Institutional investors rarely operate within isolated stewardship levels. Instead, many stewardship activities span firm-specific, sectoral, and systemic dimensions, reflecting the growing complexity of global challenges such as climate change, human rights, and economic inequality.[15] Addressing these issues effectively often requires cross-level coordination and integrated strategies – a pattern referred to here as *blended stewardship*. This emerging approach reflects the deliberate layering of tools, relationships, and interventions across different points in the investment

[13] The difficulty in attributing specific outcomes to investor action is acknowledged in many stewardship reports. See e.g. DWS, *UK Stewardship Code Report 2021*, 53 (on file with the author) (noting that 'even though in most cases it is not possible to achieve change in companies' or government policies and practices through the actions of a single investor', in some cases they can see a 'correlation' between their actions and the actions of the markets) and Sarasin & Partners, *Stewardship Report, UK Stewardship Code* (April 2028), 28 (on file with the author) (observing that 'there are inevitably numerous statistical challenges' in attributing ESG performance, citing limited data, short time periods, and correlation versus causation concerns).

[14] See e.g. Prudential Assurance Company, *Stewardship Report* 2021 (April 2022), 37 (on file with the author), which notes that 'engagement is a multi-year process and the criteria to determine whether engagement has been successful is not well-defined and often subjective'.

[15] Take, e.g., the 'climate engagement escalation programme' of Aviva Investors, the global asset management business of Aviva plc, targeting thirty 'systematically important carbon emitters'. This programme entails both micro-level, portfolio-, and market-level engagement, but at the same time it is supported by engagement with policymakers and governments to promote sustainability within business' strategies. See Aviva Investors, *Aviva becomes the first major insurer worldwide to target Net Zero carbon by 2024* (1 March 2021), www.aviva.com/newsroom/news-releases/2021/03/aviva-becomes-the-first-major-insurer-worldwide-to-target-Net-Zero-carbon-by-2040/

chain to manage financial risks and contribute to broader societal and market outcomes.

A growing number of collaborative investor initiatives exemplify this multi-level dynamic, operating simultaneously across micro-, portfolio-, system-, and macro-levels. Notable examples include Climate Action 100+,[16] the Coalition for Inclusive Capitalism,[17] the Institutional Investors Group on Climate Change,[18] Interfaith Center on Corporate Responsibility (ICCR),[19] the Net-Zero Asset Managers Initiative (NZAM),[20] the UN-convened Net-Zero Asset Owner Alliance,[21] the Global Sustainable Investment Alliance,[22] the FTSE Transition Pathway Initiative (TPI), and Ceres, among others.

In their stewardship disclosures, investors frequently highlight participation in initiatives such as Climate Action 100+, engaging with high-emitting companies to advocate for Paris-aligned disclosures and science-based net zero targets.[23] These are clear expressions of micro-level stewardship, focused on shaping firm-level strategy, governance, and climate accountability.

At the portfolio-level, investors rely on tools developed by initiatives such as NZAM and TPI to evaluate and manage transition risks across asset holdings.[24] These frameworks facilitate the integration of emissions metrics, sectoral decarbonisation pathways, and climate alignment data into portfolio construction and reallocation decisions – enabling investors to systematically assess and differentiate between credible and non-credible transition plans.

At the system-level, initiatives like TPI and IIGCC (Institutional Investors Group on Climate Change) support sector-wide coordination

[16] www.climateaction100.org.

[17] https://coalitionforinclusivecapitalism.com.

[18] www.iigcc.org.

[19] www.iccr.org.

[20] www.netzeroassetmanagers.org.

[21] www.unepfi.org/net-zero-alliance/.

[22] www.gsi-alliance.org.

[23] See e.g. Brandywine Global, *2021 Stewardship Report*, 48–49 (on file with the author) and Candriam, *2021 UK Stewardship Review* (April 2022), 56 (on file with the author), reporting engagement with Pemex and Rio Tinto as part of Climate 100+ collaborative initiative. Similarly, Coutts, via Hermes EOS, co-led engagement with LyondellBasell, leveraging Dutch law to prompt AGM discussions on net-zero alignment, which resulted in the company committing to a 2050 target. See Coutts, *Stewardship Policy* (2021), 52 (on file with the author).

[24] See e.g. Atlas Infrastructure, *2020 Stewardship Report*, 40 and BNP Paribas Asset Management, *2021 Sustainability Report*, 12 (on file with the author).

by offering standardised methodologies, disclosure benchmarks, and engagement templates, fostering more consistent practices across the market.[25]

At the macro-level, these collaborative platforms also contribute to shaping global policy and regulatory frameworks. Investor coalitions have jointly responded to EU regulatory consultations, supported the development of initiatives such as the Taskforce on Climate-Related Financial Disclosures (TCFD) and the Taskforce on Nature-Related Financial Disclosures, and engaged with multilateral bodies, including the UN, G20, and COP summits.[26]

A compelling illustration of blended stewardship is the Investor Mining and Tailings Safety Initiative, launched in response to the 2019 Brumadinho disaster.[27] Led by the Church of England Pensions Board and the Council on Ethics of the Swedish National Pension Funds, and supported by a coalition of over 100 investors representing more than USD20 trillion assets under management,[28] the initiative integrated multiple levels of stewardship. It combined micro-level and portfolio-level engagement through coordinated disclosure requests and board-level pressure on mining companies,[29] system-level stewardship via the development of a global standard for tailings management,[30] and macro-level collaboration with the United Nations

[25] For instance, Ardevora and Border to Coast report using TPI data to inform voting and engagement strategy, fostering consistency across institutional investors engaging in climate-related stewardship. See Ardevora, *2022 Stewardship Report*, 50 (on file with the author) and Border to Coast, *Responsible Investment and Stewardship Report*, 26 (on file with the author).

[26] See e.g. BNB Paribas Asset Management, *2021 Sustainability Report*, 51–5 (providing various examples of public policy advocacy and regulatory engagement).

[27] For the Brumadinho disaster, see Gabriel de Sá, 'Brazil's Deadly Dam Disaster May Have Been Preventable' *National Geographic* (29 January 2019).

[28] www.churchofengland.org/about/leadership-and-governance/church-england-pensions-board/pensions-board-investments/investor-1.

[29] See e.g. Church of England Pensions Board and Council on Ethics of the Swedish National Pension Funds, *Letter to Board Chairs and Chief Executive Officers of Listed Extractive Companies* (2019) <https://bit.ly/3aJH9Sq> (announcing the launch of the Investor Mining and Tailings Safety Initiative and calling for enhanced disclosure of tailings storage facilities following the Brumadinho disaster). References to the initiative also appear in stewardship reports such as Baillie Gifford, *Our Investment Stewardship Activities* (2021), 48 (on file with the author) (highlighting ongoing engagement with Vale both individually and through coordinated efforts under the Mining & Tailings Safety Initiative); BMO Global Asset Management, *Stewardship Report* (2021), 25 (on file with the author) (describing BMO's role as a founding supporter and co-lead of the initiative, including engagement on public tailings disclosures and board-level risk governance).

[30] https://globaltailingsreview.org/global-industry-standard/. See also The Church of England Pensions Board, *Stewardship Report 2021*, 21 and 38 (on file with the author),

Environment Programme (UNEP) and other public and civil society actors.[31] This initiative illustrates how investors can operate across multiple levels of stewardship simultaneously, leveraging distinct strategies to mitigate systemic risk while promoting public interest outcomes.

Another illustration is the Net Zero Standard for Oil and Gas, developed by the IIGCC with analytical support from the TPI and under the chairmanship of the Church of England Pensions Board.[32] Initially released as a draft in September 2021 and finalised in April 2023, the Standard aims to address transition risks in the oil and gas sector by providing a unified investor-led benchmark for assessing corporate alignment with net zero objectives. At the firm level, investors have used the Standard to guide engagements with companies such as BP, Shell, and TotalEnergies, focusing on emissions targets, capital expenditure, and long-term transition strategy.[33] At the portfolio level, the Standard supports asset managers in assessing the credibility of transition plans and aligning capital allocation with climate goals.[34] At the system level, it introduces consistent disclosure and performance

which details the Board's leadership in developing the *Global Industry Standard on Tailings Management (GISTM)* in collaboration with UNEP and mining industry actors, as a direct response to the systemic risks posed by tailings storage facilities. The Church of England Pensions Board explicitly identifies tailings safety as a systemic issue – given its potential for catastrophic failure, its global prevalence in supply chains, and the sector's critical role in the low-carbon transition – and frames its initiative as an effort to strengthen resilience across the mining ecosystem. The initiative is cited as an exemplar of investor response under Principle 4 of the UK Code 2020.

31 www.unep.org/news-and-stories/press-release/international-advisory-panel-support-new-global-tailings-management. See also The Church of England Pensions Board, *Stewardship Report* (2021), 21 (on file with the author), describing collaboration with UNEP and the International Council on Mining and Metals (ICMM) to develop the GISTM, alongside efforts to establish a Global Tailings Institute.

32 www.iigcc.org/media-centre/iigcc-publishes-net-zero-standard-for-oil-gas.

33 The Church of England Pensions Board, *Stewardship Report* (2021), 16 (on file with the author) (detailing engagements with BP, Shell, and TotalEnergies using the Net Zero Standard as a framework to evaluate company strategy, capital allocation, and emissions targets). See also Sarasin & Partners, *Stewardship Report, UK Stewardship Code* (2022), 54 (on file with the author), which, while not referencing the Standard explicitly, outlines engagements with the same firms focused on climate accounting, net-zero alignment, and the integration of climate risk into audited financial statements – reflecting a similar concern with credibility and systemic impact. Sarasin was a signatory to the draft Net Zero Standard from its initial release in September 2021, reaffirming its commitment to science-based transition expectations in the oil and gas sector: see https://sarasinandpartners.com/ie/stewardship-post/sarasin-a-signatory-of-net-zero-standard-for-oil-and-gas-companies/.

34 The Church of England Pensions Board, *Stewardship Report* (2021), 16 (on file with the author).

benchmarks, enhancing comparability and enabling coordinated engagement across the sector. And at the macro-level, it aligns with broader policy frameworks through engagement with global standard-setters and climate governance initiatives.

Together, these examples demonstrate how blended stewardship enables institutional investors to engage across multiple levels of influence – firm, portfolio, system, and macro. In doing so, it operationalises enlightened investor stewardship, offering a pragmatic approach to reconciling competing demands: between short-term performance and long-term stability, between fiduciary obligations and public value, between material risk and normative responsibility.[35] Blended stewardship thus offers more than a tactical strategy; it embodies a more coordinated and institutionally ambitious vision of what stewardship can – and arguably must – become in a world where capital decisions increasingly affect, and are shaped by, the interests of unseen others.

7.3 The Actors of Stewardship: Direct and Indirect Stewards across the Investment Chain

While the previous section focused on the *levels* at which stewardship is exercised, *who* performs stewardship is equally important. Investor stewardship is neither singular nor uniform – it is carried out by a wide range of actors across the investment chain, including asset owners, asset managers, consultants, proxy advisors, and other intermediaries.[36] These actors vary in their proximity to assets under management, the degree of influence they exercise, and the nature of their accountability relationships. To account for this diversity, stewardship can be broadly classified into two categories: direct and indirect stewardship (as illustrated in Figure 7.1).

Direct stewardship occurs where the institutional investor conducting stewardship is also the asset holder and engages directly with the asset. This includes asset owners, such as pension funds, that carry out stewardship activities in-house, as well as asset managers who engage directly with assets either on their own account or on behalf of retail investors.[37] The focus of direct stewardship lies in the relationship between the asset

[35] For a comprehensive analysis of the enlightened investor stewardship model, see Section 4.4.

[36] See also Section 4.4.1.

[37] In the latter case, stewardship may be said to be exercised *indirectly* on behalf of retail investors. However, because retail investors themselves do not qualify as investor

holder and the investee asset (asset stewardship). At the same time, this relationship is embedded within a broader and closely connected set of obligations between the asset holder and their proximate clients and beneficiaries (client stewardship).[38] As already explained, both dimensions are increasingly understood not only in financial terms but also in relation to sustainability objectives, reflecting growing expectations that stewards act on behalf of long-term environmental and societal goals (sustainability stewardship).[39]

Indirect stewardship refers to arrangements in which stewardship responsibilities are delegated.[40] Here, stewardship unfolds across multiple layers of accountability. Asset managers or other service providers – such as proxy advisors and environmental, social, and governance (ESG) data providers – serve as client stewards for institutional clients, such as asset owners.[41] Where asset managers are entrusted with delegated stewardship responsibilities, they exercise direct asset stewardship within an indirect governance framework, engaging with investee assets on behalf of asset owners. In doing so, asset managers must both exercise influence across different asset classes and justify their stewardship decisions to the delegating party. When they also incorporate long-term environmental and societal objectives into these practices, they assume the role of sustainability stewards, aligning fiduciary (or contractual) responsibilities with broader public interest goals.

Indirect stewardship brings into focus a further dimension: end-investor stewardship. This refers to the relationship between those exercising delegated stewardship – such as asset managers – and the ultimate beneficiaries

stewards, these instances constitute *direct stewardship* by intermediaries. For a discussion of why retail investors are not considered investor stewards, see Section 4.3.2.2.

38 Section 4.4.1.

39 Section 4.4.2.

40 This is the case even though investment decisions are outsourced within the parameters of the investment mandate.

41 While forms of indirect stewardship over proxy advisors and data providers fall outside this book, several stewardship reports in the 2020 sample illustrate meaningful oversight and engagement in these areas. See e.g. Sarasin & Partners, *Stewardship Report, UK Stewardship Code* (April 2022), 52 (on file with the author) and Columbia Threadneedle Investments, *Stewardship Report 2021*, 55 (on file with the author), detailing proxy advisor oversight, including formal quality review and the use of quarterly 'report cards'. On engagement with ESG data providers, see e.g. Comgest, *UK Stewardship Code 2021, Annual Report*, (October 2022), 41–2 (on file with the author), which describes an instance in which the firm corrected a provider's erroneous taxonomy classification through direct engagement. On stewardship by service providers, including investment consultants, proxy advisors, and data and research providers, see UK Code 2020, Principles 1–6 for Service Providers.

of capital, including current and future beneficiaries, such as pension savers, insurance policyholders, and retail investors.[42] While often implicit in contractual structures, this relationship is increasingly acknowledged in stewardship reporting, often framed in terms of beneficiary engagement, client responsiveness, or alignment with member values.[43]

At the same time, asset owners who delegate stewardship responsibilities remain stewards in an indirect but influential sense. Through mandate design, monitoring, and oversight, they continue to act as client stewards for their beneficiaries, holding asset managers accountable for how stewardship is executed. The UK Code 2020 formally recognises this model of oversight, placing explicit responsibility on asset owners to oversee the stewardship practices of their investment managers and consultants.[44] In parallel, recent UK regulations require asset owners to assess whether their delegation produces 'value for money' for the ultimate beneficiaries.[45]

In practice, several UK pension funds have taken active steps to operationalise this oversight role – through mandate design, regular reporting, and performance-based accountability.[46] In doing so, asset

[42] Section 4.4.1.

[43] See e.g. Aviva Investors, *2021 Responsible Investment Annual Review*, 38 (on file with the author), which refers to acting in the interests of both 'clients and underlying beneficiaries', suggesting awareness of a layered accountability model that extends beyond the immediate asset owner client to end-investors.

[44] UK Code 2020, Principle 8 (Principles for Asset Owners and Asset Managers). The 2012 version of the UK Stewardship Code also made explicit that asset owners 'set the tone for stewardship' and 'cannot delegate their responsibility for stewardship' even though they can 'outsource to external service providers some of the activities associated with stewardship'. See Financial Reporting Council, *The UK Stewardship Code 2012* (2012) [UK Code 2012], 1 and 2.

[45] FCA Handbook COLL 4.5.7, 6.6.20-22, 8.3.5A, 8.5.16-19.

[46] The BT Pension Scheme (BTPS), for example, embeds stewardship expectations directly into its investment management agreements and uses structured questionnaires to evaluate how managers integrate ESG factors and report on stewardship activities. In 2021, BTPS terminated one of its external managers due to inadequate stewardship reporting. See BTPS, *Annual Report and Accounts 2022*, 146 and 148 (on file with the author). Similarly, the Cumbria Pension Fund operates a three-tier monitoring system, including annual meetings with key managers, ESG-specific assessments via questionnaires, and regular reviews of control reports. See Cumbria Local Government Pension Scheme, *Stewardship Report 2021–22*, 49–50 (on file with the author). Another example of manager oversight as part of indirect stewardship is the West Midlands Pension Fund, which employs a 'Red-Amber-Yellow-Green' (RAYG) rating system to score the ESG performance of its external managers and holds quarterly reviews to evaluate the quality of ESG integration and engagement. See West Midlands Pension Fund, *Annual Stewardship Report* (April 2022), 47 and 49–54 (on file with the author).

owners are expected to use their influence to ensure that delegated stewardship is aligned with the long-term interests of their end-investors.[47] Where environmental and social objectives are embedded into these oversight processes, asset owners may also function as sustainability stewards, shaping outcomes not just through their own action but also by governing the stewardship behaviour of others in the investment chain.[48]

In this way, stewardship responsibilities are distributed yet interconnected, requiring both effective delegation and active oversight to ensure that the interests of end-investors – and, increasingly, broader societal interests – are meaningfully represented and protected.

7.4 The Expanding Reach of Stewardship: Assets beyond Public Equity

The scope of investor stewardship has progressively expanded beyond its traditional focus on public equities. In its early form, stewardship was closely tied to institutional investors acting in their capacity as shareholders – hence the term *shareholder stewardship*.[49] This initial model, exemplified by the 1G UK Code and its global counterparts, centred on voting and engagement in listed equities as mechanisms to improve corporate governance, enhance long-term performance, and promote wider economic benefits.[50]

[47] Global soft-law instruments, such as the ICGN's Model Mandate Initiative, have further shaped the expectations around delegated stewardship, offering model terms for integrating ESG, engagement, and accountability mechanisms into manager mandates. These include guidance on mandate design, monitoring frameworks, and stewardship-related Requests for Proposals (RFPs). See International Corporate Governance Network (ICGN), *Model Mandate Appendix A: Requests for Proposals (RFPs) and Due Diligence*, www.icgn.org/model-mandate-appendix-a.

[48] An example of this dual approach – acting directly – engaging with policymakers and coalitions – and overseeing external asset managers and service providers is BT Pension Scheme which reports that: 'BTPSM is responsible for appointing and overseeing external asset managers and stewardship service providers … [and] engages with other asset owners, policy makers, industry bodies, data providers, and regulators on climate change'. See BTPS, *Annual Report and Accounts 2022*, 144 and 145 (on file with the author).

[49] On shareholder stewardship and engagement, see generally contributions to Dionysia Katelouzou and Dan W. Puchniak (eds.), *Global Shareholder Stewardship* (Cambridge University Press 2022) and Harpreet Kaur, Chao Xi, Christoph van der Elst and Anna Lafarre (eds.), *The Cambridge Handbook of Shareholder Engagement and Voting* (Cambridge University Press 2022).

[50] Section 5.3.1.

While this book maintains a particular focus on shareholder stewardship, it is essential to situate this discussion within the broader trajectory of stewardship's evolution. The 2G UK Code marked a pivotal shift by explicitly extending its scope to a wider range of asset classes, including fixed income, private equity, infrastructure, and currency markets.[51] This expansion reflects a growing recognition that institutional investors exert influence across the entire capital structure, and that stewardship responsibilities are not confined to equity ownership alone.

In parallel, the rising urgency of systemic risks – particularly climate change – has further accelerated this shift. In the UK, the implementation of TCFD reporting requirements across all asset classes managed or administered by FCA-regulated asset managers and asset owners underscores the expectation that stewardship addresses climate-related risks holistically and not just within listed equities.[52]

Investor stewardship by creditors, often referred to as 'debtholder stewardship'[53] or 'fixed income stewardship',[54] is gaining traction among institutional investors, regulators, and issuers.[55] While traditionally concentrated in corporate credit, stewardship practices are extending into private and sovereign debt, reflecting a redefinition of the investors' role – not merely as a lender, but as an enlightened steward of systemic resilience.[56] As captured in Topic 3 of the 2020 disclosure sample, stewardship in debt markets now spans the full life cycle of instruments – from pre-issuance framework design to post-issuance monitoring and impact assessment.[57]

[51] UK Code 2020, Principle 12 (Principles for Asset Owners and Asset Managers) and Section 5.3.2. It is notable, however, that this expansion of the stewardship asset is not evident outside the UK. See Dionysia Katelouzou, 'Investor Stewardship: The State of the Art and Future Prospects' in Jeffrey N. Gordon and Wolf-Georg Ringe (eds.), *The Oxford Handbook of Corporate Law and Governance* (2nd ed., Oxford University Press Forthcoming).

[52] FCA Handbook, ESG 2.2.1 on the annual TCFD entity report. For the scope of this rule, see Financial Conduct Authority, *Enhancing Climate-Related Disclosures by Asset Managers, Life Insurers and FCA-Regulated Pension Providers* (Policy Statement PS21/24, December 2021), paras. 1.08–1.12.

[53] Suren Gomtsian, 'Debtholder Stewardship' (2023) 86 *The Modern Law Review* 395.

[54] Financial Reporting Council, *The Influence of the UK Stewardship Code 2020 on Practice and Reporting* (July 2022) 39.

[55] For instance, the Investment Association has published a guide in November 2022 for asset managers undertaking fixed-income stewardship emphasising among others on the need to more effectively integrate stewardship across debt and equity holdings. See The Investment Association, *Improving Fixed Income Stewardship* (November 2022), 6.

[56] See e.g. Dominic Webb, 'Sovereign Engagement: The Next Frontier for Fixed-Income Investors?' *Responsible Investor* (17 August 2022).

[57] Section 6.6.3.5.

Unlike shareholders, bondholders typically lack voting rights, which limits their use of traditional stewardship tools.[58] Nevertheless, corporate bond investors are increasingly asserting influence at the pre-issuance stage, shaping covenant design, sustainability-linked bond structures, and ESG disclosures.[59] Post-issuance, they monitor issuer ESG performance, reporting quality, and progress against objectives, employing contractual escalation tools, such as coupon step-up clauses, to reinforce accountability.[60] These mechanisms help ensure that sustainability commitments are both meaningful and enforceable.[61]

In sovereign debt markets, stewardship is more complex. The absence of formal ownership rights, coupled with multilateral governance and the political sensitivities of public finance, has historically limited direct engagement with sovereign issuers. Nonetheless, institutional investors are identifying context-appropriate avenues for engagement. These include bilateral dialogues with debt management offices, participation in collaborative initiatives addressing systemic concerns such as climate risk, fiscal transparency, and support for green and sustainability-linked sovereign bonds.[62] Additionally, indirect engagement – such as publishing

[58] See e.g. Bluebay, *The UK Stewardship Code 2020, Annual Stewardship Report 2021*, 3 (on file with the author) (acknowledging that 'proxy voting is an immaterial activity for us given we are lenders not owners, although there are instances in which it can occur'). Barings similarly notes that even without voting rights, debt investors can influence ESG outcomes by affecting issuers' cost of capital and participating in amendments or restructurings to shift board and management priorities. See Barings, *UK Stewardship Report, Submission for Calendar Year 2021*, 50 (on file with the author).

[59] See e.g. PIMCO Europe Ltd, *2022 UK Stewardship Code Statement and Report* (October 2022), 60 and 76 (noting over 1,500 corporate bond issuers in 2021, including more than 650 in-depth ESG-focused engagements and regular pre-issuance input on sustainability-linked bonds (SLBs), as well as the associated KPIs, and bond terms).

[60] See e.g. Insight Investment, *Responsible Stewardship, Report to fulfil the requirements of the UK Stewardship Code for the period 1 January–31 December 2021*, 93 (on file with the author) (reporting that '[a]ll our credit analysts regularly meet with issuers to discuss ESG related and non-ESG related issues . . . one of the key inputs into our ESG analysis is the direct information which we receive from companies via engagements that take place').

[61] For instance, PIMCO reported rejecting the credibility of an SLB framework that included a +25 basis point step-up, observing that 'the KPI neglected up to 90% of value chain emissions', thereby undermining the bond's integrity as a genuine sustainability instrument. See PIMCO Europe Ltd, *2022 UK Stewardship Code Statement and Report* (October 2022), 53 (on file with the author).

[62] See e.g. Amundi, *Stewardship Report 2021* (October 2022), 75 (on file with the author); Lazard Asset Management, *2021 UK Stewardship Code Submission, reporting period 1 January–31 December 2021*, 39–40 (on file with the author).

research or engaging with credit rating agencies and standard setters – is emerging as a viable strategy to influence sovereign issuers without direct intervention.[63]

Currency-related risks are also beginning to enter the stewardship frame, especially where they intersect with sovereign ESG performance. Although stewardship in currency markets remains underdeveloped, some investors are incorporating macro-level sustainability considerations – such as governance stability, climate vulnerability, and monetary policy credibility – into currency allocation decisions.[64] In some cases, this includes dialogue with central banks or adjustments to fund structures to reflect clients' hedging needs.[65] While not yet constituting a consolidated stewardship practice, these practices reveal a growing awareness of how ESG risks influence cross-asset investment decisions. They also highlight an important facet of *client stewardship*, namely the alignment of currency exposure with the long-term objectives, risk tolerances, and sustainability preferences of clients.[66]

As stewardship expectations evolve, fixed income investors are increasingly adopting blended stewardship strategies that combine micro-level issuer engagement with portfolio-, system-, and macro-level stewardship. The ASCOR (Assessing Sovereign Climate-related Opportunities and Risks) initiative exemplifies this shift.[67] It provides a structured, transparent framework for evaluating sovereign climate governance – filling a critical gap in a landscape long dominated by equity-focused standards. By equipping investors with a collective tool to guide engagement across jurisdictions, ASCOR supports the

[63] See e.g. Ardea Investment Management, *Ardea Stewardship Policy* (March 2021), 10 (noting the adoption of an indirect engagement approach in sovereign debt markets through peer-reviewed research on climate risk pricing in sovereign yields, as well as thought leadership, academic engagement, and market-facing communications).

[64] See e.g. Mondrian Investment Partners, *UK Stewardship Code Statement 2021* (April 2022), 62 (noting the integration of ESG factors into fixed income and currency research and periodic engagement with sovereign issuers and central banks on green bond issuance and macroeconomic policy risks).

[65] See e.g. Intermediate Capital Group (ICG), *UK Stewardship Code, Statement of Compliance and Disclosure* (October 2022), 22 (on file with the author) (describing the offering of multi-currency fund sleeves to meet clients' needs).

[66] Section 4.4.2.

[67] www.ascorproject.org. For illustrative references to ASCOR within stewardship reporting, see BTPS, *Annual Reports and Accounts 2022*, 154 (on file with the author); Franklin Templeton, *Making Better Connections, UK Stewardship Code Report 2021*, 70 (on file with the author); Western Asset, *Working toward a Shared Future, Stewardship Report* (October 2022), 14, 39, and 72 (on file with the author).

institutionalisation of sovereign stewardship and helps address the persistent absence of standardised reporting frameworks beyond public equities.[68]

'Real estate stewardship' or 'property stewardship' represents another expanding frontier in stewardship practices. As discussed in Chapter 6, while this was the least prevalent in the 2020 disclosure sample (Topic 2), its emergence marks a meaningful evolution: the extension of stewardship principles to illiquid and physical assets, including infrastructure and private markets.[69] Real asset managers increasingly recognise the importance of embedding sustainability across the full life cycle of property ownership – from acquisition and development to ongoing management and divestiture.[70] This life cycle approach seeks not only to preserve long-term financial value but also to advance systemic goals such as urban resilience, energy efficiency, and social inclusion.[71]

Leading institutional investors are increasingly operationalising these ambitions through multifaceted, blended strategies. ESG considerations are systematically integrated into investment decision-making at the acquisition stage, often through structured due diligence and proprietary scoring frameworks.[72] Many such managers retain significant influence over their portfolio companies, frequently holding majority ownership and board representation.[73] During what is often termed the 'active

[68] *The influence of the UK Stewardship Code 2020 on practice and reporting*, 42; *Improving Fixed Income Stewardship*, 16.

[69] Section 6.6.3.6.

[70] PGIM Real Estate, *Annual Stewardship Report, for the year ended 31 December 2021*, 42 (on file with the author) (describing the integration of sustainability considerations across the entire property life cycle: acquisition, active ownership, redevelopment/refurbishment and divestiture).

[71] See e.g. Mayfair Capital, *UK Stewardship Code 2021, Report for Year ended 31 December 2021*, 6 (on file with the author) (describing the use of a proprietary asset scoring model that incorporates long-term ESG trends – such as climate resilience, walkability, and occupier well-being – to align acquisitions with both sustainability and financial objectives).

[72] See e.g. CBRE Investment Management, *UK Stewardship Code Statement 2021* (October 2022), 7 (on file with the author) (noting the integration of ESG considerations early in the investment process through the use of a proprietary ESG Acquisition Tool); Manulife Investment Management, *Stewardship Report 2022*, 66–70 (on file with the author) (outlining the use of a Sustainability and Responsible Investing Toolkit – structured around five pillars: climate stability, ecosystem resiliency, watershed protection, people empowerment, and community prosperity – to guide ESG assessments in land-based real asset investments).

[73] Quinbrook Infrastructure Partners, *Investment Impact and Stewardship Outcomes Report* (2021), 3 (on file with the author).

ownership' phase in stewardship reporting, investors deploy ESG scorecards, net-zero audits, and green leasing provisions to guide asset refurbishment and tenant engagement.[74] These efforts often extend beyond immediate stakeholders such as tenants and contractors to encompass local communities, with a focus on placemaking, sustainable urban design, and socially inclusive development.[75]

To enhance transparency and accountability, investors employ benchmarking systems such as GRESB (Global Real Estate Sustainability Benchmark), invest in ESG training for asset and property teams, and, in some cases, adopt employee co-investment schemes to align internal incentives with long-term sustainability goals.[76] In doing so, real estate stewardship is becoming increasingly institutionalised, reflecting broader trends in the stewardship landscape: integrating fiduciary discipline with public value objectives and extending stewardship across diverse asset classes.

Taken together, the expansion of stewardship beyond public equities – into debt markets, real assets, and even currencies – signals a fundamental redefinition of what it means to be an enlightened investor steward.[77] Yet, as the scope of stewardship widens, a crucial question emerges: what motivates investors to engage in stewardship in the first place? Understanding the motivations behind contemporary forms of stewardship – whether rooted in fiduciary obligations, risk management, reputational positioning, regulatory compliance, or broader societal values – is essential to grasp its evolving nature and legitimacy. It is to these motivations that the next section turns.

7.5 Motivations of Investor Stewardship: Balancing Value, Risk, and Purpose

As with stewardship levels and actors, motivations are a core component of the conceptual typology outlined in Figure 7.1. They provide essential insight into how and why investors adopt specific stewardship

[74] See e.g. PGIM Real Estate, *Annual Stewardship Report, for the year ended 31 December 2021* (on file with the author).

[75] See e.g. Federated Hermes Limited, *Stewardship Report 2021* (April 2022), 43, 78–79 (on file with the author); Principal Asset Management, *2021 UK Stewardship Code Report*, 60–61 (on file with the author).

[76] See e.g. DWS UK Investments Limited, *UK Stewardship Code Report 2021*, 72 (on file with the author); LaSalle, *UK Stewardship Code 2022 Report*, 3 (on file with the author).

[77] See also Section 4.4.3.

behaviours, and into how these behaviours align – or come into tension – with broader institutional objectives. While extrinsic pressures – such as regulatory compliance or reputational incentives – also shape practice, this section focuses on intrinsic motivations: how investors articulate their goals, the values that inform decision-making, and the ways they weight financial outcomes against broader societal and environmental considerations.[78]

Traditionally, stewardship in public equities focused on company-specific concerns – such as business strategy, capital structure, board composition, and executive pay – pursued with the aim of improving long-term financial value.[79] These practices exemplify *value-focused stewardship*, where the central objective is the prudent execution of mandates, financial returns, and liability matching.

As discussed in Chapter 4, however, investor stewardship does not operate through a single, linear relationship. Instead, it unfolds across a network of overlapping stewardship responsibilities – client stewardship, end-investor stewardship, asset stewardship, and sustainability stewardship – each linked to a different group of 'others' whose interests stewards are expected to protect.[80] This layered structure complicates the motivational landscape. It is no longer sufficient to focus exclusively on maximising portfolio value; stewardship increasingly involves balancing multiple, and sometimes competing, expectations across the investment chain and broader society.

Within this expanded context, attention to ESG factors has become a key driver of stewardship.[81] Drawing on patterns observed in stewardship disclosures, *ESG stewardship* is introduced to capture a distinct motivational orientation within the broader stewardship landscape. ESG stewardship refers to the integration of environmental, social, and governance considerations into investment analysis, engagement, and proxy voting – primarily on the basis of their financial materiality.[82]

[78] On how extrinsic motivations shape stewardship, see Sections 4.3.2.3 and 4.4.2.

[79] UK Code 2012, 1 and Principle 3.

[80] Section 4.4.

[81] Evidently, there is not a single stewardship disclosure in the 2020 sample that does not make reference to ESG factors. Data on file with the author.

[82] Investor disclosures illustrate how ESG stewardship is implemented in practice, though not always under that name. See e.g. J. P. Morgan Asset Management, *2021 Investment Stewardship Report, Investor-led, expert-driven* (April 2022) (on file with the author).

While ESG issues often raise broader societal concerns, their treatment within ESG stewardship is primarily instrumental: they are pursued to mitigate long-term investment risks, enhance decision-making, and support risk-adjusted returns. ESG stewardship thus exemplifies a *risk-responsive* form of stewardship – an attempt to align fiduciary responsibility with an evolving risk landscape, using ESG analysis to inform responsible ownership practices, without necessarily redefining the core purpose of investment.[83]

Many institutional investors, particularly under the 1G UK Code, have adopted this approach.[84] Others, however, pursue a more expansive vision. While still framed in terms of long-term value creation, their stewardship strategies extend further – to address systemic risks, shape corporate conduct, and influence regulatory norms. These practices suggest a gradual broadening of stewardship's purpose beyond conventional portfolio metrics.[85]

Within this expanded landscape, *sustainability-oriented stewardship* emerges as a distinct motivational orientation. As used in this chapter, the term refers to an investor's intrinsic commitment to promoting long-term environmental and social outcomes – even when such actions may not generate immediate financial benefit or align with traditional fiduciary expectations.[86]

This motivational concept differs from the sustainability stewardship relationship discussed in Chapter 4, which focused on the direction of stewardship responsibilities – namely towards system-level stakeholders

[83] See e.g. Dodge & Cox, *2021 UK Stewardship Code Report*, 9 (on file with the author) (underscoring that ESG integration is incorporated into their research process, but the *primary investment objective* – long-term financial returns – remains unchanged) (emphasis added).

[84] Section 6.6.2.5.

[85] See e.g. Federated Hermes, *Stewardship Report 2021* (April 2022), 6 (on file with the author) (stating that '[o]ur goals are to help individuals invest and retire better, to help clients achieve better risk-adjusted returns and, consistent with client objectives and applicable requirements, to strive to contribute to positive outcomes in the wider world'); Stepstone, *UK Stewardship Code Report 2021*, 8 (on file with the author) (describing Responsible Investment (RI) as 'a core tenet' of the firm's investment philosophy and fiduciary duty, justified by its potential to enhance 'forward-looking, risk-adjusted returns' and 'maximise overall value for clients'. The report further notes that ESG integration applies to 100 per cent of investments and that private markets are viewed as especially conducive to delivering 'real-world outcomes' aligned with the UK Sustainable Development Goals (SDGs) and systemic goals such as climate action and social equity).

[86] See e.g. Mirova, *2022 Stewardship Report*, 2 (on file with the author) (describing its investment philosophy as seeking to 'reconcile societal and financial performance', positioning ESG integration as a means of delivering positive real-world impact).

and the broader public.[87] In that context, the emphasis was on *for whom* investors are expected to act. Here, the emphasis is on *why* they act: to pursue real-world impact grounded in ethical conviction or in a systems-oriented understanding of long-term financial and societal responsibility.

While the two often align, they are analytically distinct and not always interchangeable. Consider, for example, a boutique ESG investment firm managing a pooled retail fund that explicitly aligns with the UN Sustainable Development Goals (SDGs). Although its legal duty is confined to fund participants, the firm may be deeply motivated by sustainability values and committed to driving real-world impact. In this case, stewardship is sustainability-oriented in motivational terms, but the firm does not necessarily occupy a sustainability stewardship role in the relational sense described in Chapter 4, as its stewardship responsibilities remain directed primarily towards its clients rather than towards system-level stakeholders or the broader public.

By contrast, a large asset owner – such as a pension fund – may be required under regulatory frameworks such as the TCFD or the SFDR (Sustainable Finance Disclosure Regulation) to report on climate-related risks and to consider sustainability in its stewardship activities. In doing so, it may engage on systemic issues and perform the function of sustainability stewardship. However, its underlying motivation may be driven primarily by regulatory compliance, reputational risk management, or long-term financial stability, rather than by intrinsic ethical conviction.[88]

These examples highlight that sustainability orientation and sustainability stewardship are not synonymous: the former describes an internal motivation, while the latter describes an externalised responsibility directed beyond the client relationship. In practice, they can and often do co-exist – but their alignment should not be assumed.[89]

Importantly, the three core stewardship motivations – value-focused, ESG (risk-responsive), and sustainability-oriented – are not mutually exclusive.[90] As illustrated in Figure 7.2, they frequently intersect. Many institutional investors combine these motivations, tailoring their

87 Section 4.4.3.

88 Regulatory compliance does not preclude values-based motivation – but it does not guarantee it either. An institution may act from both instrumental and ethical considerations simultaneously.

89 Motivations within a single institution may be mixed. It is entirely possible for some stewardship activities to be driven by intrinsic sustainability commitments, while others are pursued for regulatory, strategic, or reputational reasons.

90 For instance, there is evidence of mixed motivations behind institutional investors' decisions to incorporate climate risk into their investment decisions. See Philipp

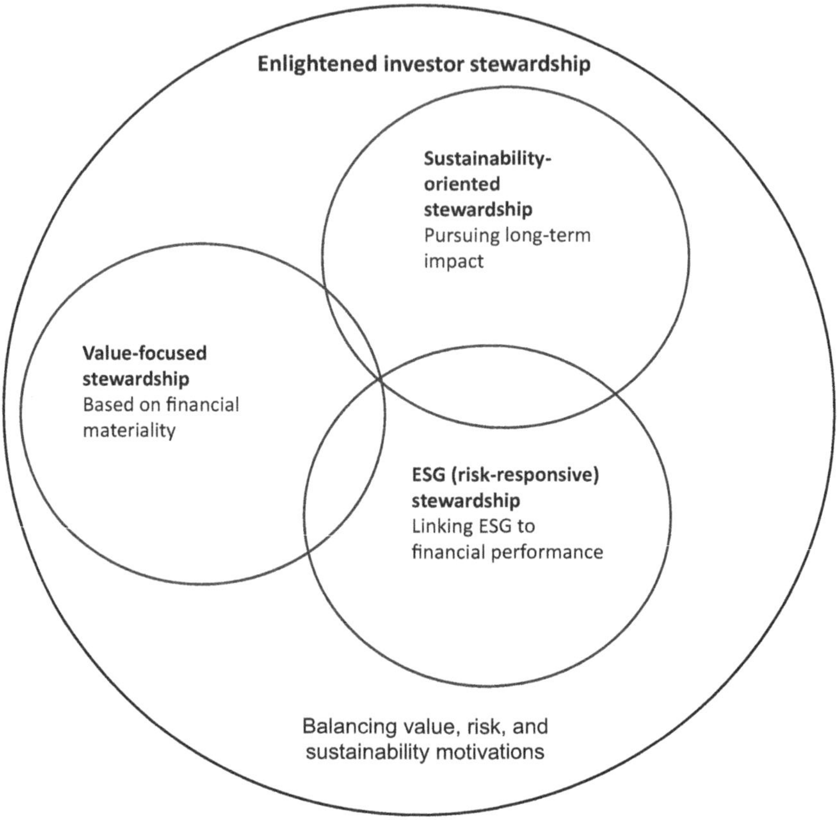

Figure 7.2 Mapping investor stewardship motivations within an enlightened stewardship framework.

stewardship according to asset class, investment horizon, or client mandate. For instance, stewardship disclosures suggest that compared to listed equities, both fixed income and real estate stewardship tend to be more explicitly ESG-oriented – typically framed in risk-responsive terms.[91]

The distinction between these motivations lies less in the issues addressed – since many ESG concerns span all three – than in the underlying purpose, theory of change, and willingness to engage with long-term trade-offs. Value-focused stewards act when issues are clearly financially material. ESG stewards aim to align responsible practices with risk-adjusted performance by

Krueger, Zacharias Sautner and Laura T. Starks, 'The Importance of Climate Risks for Institutional Investors' (2020) 33 *The Review of Financial Studies* 1067.

91 Sections 6.6.3.5, 6.6.3.6, and 7.4.

integrating ESG considerations into investment decisions, often in anticipation of emerging or latent risks. Sustainability-oriented stewards, by contrast, seek to catalyse system-wide change – even where this challenges conventional financial logic or does not promise immediate returns.

Encompassing and connecting these motivational categories is *enlightened investor stewardship* – not a separate category, but an overarching orientation. As introduced in Chapter 4, enlightened investor stewardship refers to an investor's ability to integrate and balance multiple stewardship relationships.[92] Here, the concept is extended to describe how investors reconcile diverse motivations – from delivering financial returns to advancing public value – across the full spectrum of stewardship practice.

Shaped by *values* rather than value alone,[93] enlightened investor stewardship reflects a deliberate effort to align client mandates and performance expectations with long-term environmental and societal goals.[94] It entails a willingness to prioritise meaningful outcomes over procedural compliance and, where necessary, to accept short-term trade-offs in pursuit of lasting impact. This orientation resonates with the broader argument that corporate and investment decisions should aim to maximise 'shareholder welfare' – not merely financial value – by accounting for the preferences shareholders have over social, environmental, and ethical outcomes.[95] In this view, stewardship becomes a mechanism through which investors can express these plural preferences, recognising that long-term welfare depends not only on returns but also on the systemic conditions within which those returns are generated.

While remaining attentive to fiduciary responsibilities and performance benchmarks, enlightened stewards embrace a broader conception of accountability – one that extends beyond proximate clients and beneficiaries to end-investors, including future beneficiaries, as well as investee

92 Section 4.4.3.

93 On the need to distinguish between ESG investing driven by value and values, see Laura T. Starks, 'Presidential Address: Sustainable Finance and ESG Issues – Value versus Values' (2023) 78 *The Journal of Finance* 1837.

94 See e.g. Federated Hermes Limited, *Stewardship Report 2021* (April 2022), 11 (on file with the author) (emphasising financial outperformance through ESG integration, while also framing stewardship as a contributor to societal outcomes: 'There is no conflict between doing good and good investment management – they are one and the same thing'); Robeco, Stewardship Report (01.01.2021–31.12.2021), 9 (on file with the author) (illustrating a balancing approach that aligns fiduciary duty with broader impact, noting that '*[o]ur* stewardship activities are *aimed at long-term value creation in our investments, in addition to creating real-world impact*') (emphasis added); as well as Section 6.6.3.1.

95 See the seminal work: Oliver Hart and Luigi Zingales, 'The New Corporate Governance' (2022) 1 *University of Chicago Business Law Review* 195.

assets, financial markets, and wider societal systems. In this view, investor stewardship becomes a vehicle for delivering both financial discipline and public value. Crucially, enlightened investor stewardship recognises that the motivations underlying stewardship – whether value-driven, ESG-oriented, or sustainability-focused – may be complementary but also come into tension. What defines this approach is not rigid adherence to a singular objective, but the capacity to navigate competing priorities through transparent, accountable, and principled judgement. To understand how this plays out in practice, the next section turns to the means through which investor stewardship is enacted.

7.6 The Means of Investor Stewardship

7.6.1 Upstream Stewardship: Capital Allocation and Investment Design

Stewardship motivations must ultimately be expressed through concrete mechanisms. In practice, institutional investors operationalise stewardship through two core *means*: (i) capital allocation, governance, and investment decision-making; and (ii) engagement, collaboration, and escalation (Figure 7.1). This dual structure reflects a deeper distinction between upstream (ex ante) and downstream (ex post) stewardship means.

Upstream stewardship refers to activities that occur prior to, or at the point of, capital deployment. These include asset selection, ESG integration, investment mandate design, and the establishment of governance parameters that shape the investment process. In contrast, downstream strategies unfold once capital has been committed and typically involve ongoing engagement with investees, voting, collaboration, and escalation. While conceptually distinct, these two phases are closely intertwined in practice. Stewardship influence often flows iteratively across the investment life cycle, with upstream decisions conditioning the scope and effectiveness of downstream engagement.

The 1G UK Code focused predominantly on downstream stewardship – particularly in the context of listed equities.[96] However, the 2G UK Code marked a decisive shift.[97] It explicitly recognises that stewardship begins upstream, with capital allocation, and continues through a range of responsibilities, including asset and service provider monitoring,

[96] Section 5.3.1.
[97] Section 5.3.2.

collaborative initiatives, and the exercise of formal and informal rights across asset classes.[98]

This reframing has expanded how investor stewardship is conceptualised – not as a reactive governance function but as an integrated investment discipline that begins with strategic design.[99] Yet, despite this shift, many 2020 disclosures continue to frame 'stewardship integration' primarily through the lens of ESG risk assessment, positioning ESG factors as performance inputs for managing financial exposure.[100]

A smaller but notable group of investors go further. Their disclosures reflect a more expansive interpretation of stewardship integration – stewardship is not treated solely as a governance overlay, but as an input into buy, sell, and weighting decisions, linking ownership practices more directly to core investment strategy.[101] A few institutions treat stewardship integration as a distinct governance discipline, linked to systemic risk management, public value creation, and long-term planning that transcends traditional ESG metrics.[102]

98 UK Code 2020, 4 and 7.

99 Section 5.4.

100 See e.g. JP Morgan, *2021 Investment Stewardship Report, Investor-led, expert-driven*, (April 2022), 86 (on file with the author) 'describing ESG integration and stewardship as 'complementary practices working in tandem to encourage investing in a way that ultimately benefits clients'); Russell Investments, *UK Stewardship Code* (2021 Report), 45 (on file with the author) (reporting that 'Members of the investment division are trained to integrate ESG considerations and stewardship into our standard investment practice at all stages of our investment process'); Schroders, *Stewardship Code, Reporting on our stewardship activities and outcomes in 2021*, 51 (on file with the author) (mapping how ESG is embedded across the full investment life cycle – from idea generation and portfolio construction to engagement and voting, reflecting a predominantly risk-responsive approach to stewardship integration). See also Section 7.4 (discussing a similarly strong ESG, risk-responsive orientation in fixed income and real estate stewardship disclosures).

101 See e.g. Majedie, *Responsible Capitalism Report 2020 and Stewardship Code 2020 Response, Annual Report to 31 December 2020*, 24 (on file with the author) (noting that '[o]ur fundamental analysis and prioritisation of material issues for each of our holdings links directly to our engagement with those holdings. Furthermore, our analysis and engagement directly impact our conviction levels which affect our buy/ sell/hold and weighting decisions in our funds'); Storebrand Asset Management, *UK Stewardship Code Application, Reporting period 30 September 2020–30 September 2021*, 24 (on file with the author) (stating that '[i]nformation gathered through stewardship has informed acquisition, monitoring and exit decisions').

102 Railpen, *Stewardship Report 2021*, 10 (on file with the author) (articulating stewardship through 'four lenses: improving investment returns, reducing investment risk, impacting Railpen's reputation as a responsible investor, and impacting the future world members retire into' – thereby going beyond ESG metrics to systemic thinking).

Evidence also points to strengthened internal governance. Survey data indicate that smaller asset managers – those managing under £50 billion – are more likely to embed stewardship directly into investment decision-making processes, enhancing team cohesion.[103] Larger managers, by contrast, tend to separate stewardship and investment functions, while establishing formal mechanisms to ensure communication and coordination across teams.[104] Stewardship disclosures reinforce this trend, reflecting a broader institutionalisation of stewardship governance across the investment industry.[105]

7.6.2 Downstream Stewardship: Engagement, Collaboration, and Escalation

While upstream mechanisms have gained traction, downstream engagement continues to anchor investor stewardship practice. Both the 2012 and 2020 iterations of the UK Stewardship Code reinforce expectations for institutional investors – initially framed as shareholders, but now encompassing a wider range of asset holders – to engage with investee companies and other asset classes in ways that promote long-term value creation.[106] As explored throughout this book, stewardship has historically centred on shareholder engagement, taking diverse forms: formal mechanisms such as proxy voting; informal methods including direct meetings, letters, and ongoing dialogue; collaborative initiatives where investors amplify their influence through joint action; and escalation strategies, up to and including divestment.[107]

Disclosures under the 2020 UK Code reveal that investors are expanding and refining their engagement practices. Engagement is no longer conceived as a static or procedural obligation, but as a dynamic,

[103] *The influence of the UK Stewardship Code 2020 on practice and reporting*, 13.

[104] Ibid., 14, 16–17.

[105] See e.g. LGPS Central Limited, *Annual Stewardship Report 2021*, 13 and 30 (on file with the author) (reporting that the Director of Responsible Investment & Engagement (RI&E) is a member of both the Investment Committee and the Private Markets Investment Committee, thereby embedding RI considerations into strategic decision-making, and noting that the RI&E team works closely with the Private Equity team on ESG KPI design, 'reinforcing a shared ownership to RI integration'); UBS Asset Management, *Stewardship Annual Report 2021*, 16 ('[o]ur SI research and stewardship analysts collaborate with our investment teams to provide consistent integration of material ESG factors into investment decisions').

[106] Sections 5.3.1 and 5.3.2.

[107] Sections 3.2, 3.3, 4.3.2, 5.2, 5.3, 6.5, and 6.6.2.1.

context-sensitive process – blending formal and informal tools, tailored strategies, and multi-stakeholder dialogue.

A recurring theme across multiple disclosures is the strategic use of letters – not as stand-alone acts, but as entry points into multi-step engagement processes.[108] Letters frequently serve as initial touchpoints, followed by meetings, calls, or email exchanges. This sequencing is particularly effective when engaging smaller or less familiar issuers, such as small and medium-sized enterprises (SMEs), that may be less accustomed to sustained institutional investor scrutiny.[109] In these contexts, letter writing operates as a flexible entry point that combines informality with intentionality – supporting influence through carefully choreographed, rather than reactive, interactions. Letters are also widely employed in collaborative contexts, where coordinated messaging helps amplify investor voice – particularly on systemic or sector-wide concerns.[110] Notably, their use extends beyond corporate issuers to include national policymakers and public-facing audiences, including media outlets, underscoring their adaptability as a cross-cutting stewardship tool.[111]

Beyond traditional engagement, some investors adopt a quasi-advisory role – especially in asset classes where formal rights are limited, such as fixed income and private markets. Influence in these settings is often exercised through governance participation, board appointments, or

[108] See e.g. WHEB Asset Management, *Stewardship Report* (January–December 2021), 43–44 (on file with the author) (reporting that 42 per cent of its engagements are initiated via letters, particularly around AGM periods).

[109] See e.g. Chelverton Asset Management, *UK Stewardship Code Report* (2021), 20 (on file with the author) (reporting sending over 400 letters sent to companies, many requesting ESG disclosure improvements from SMEs).

[110] See e.g. Storebrand Asset Management, *UK Stewardship Code Application, reporting period 30 September 2020–30* (September 2021), 33–34 (on file with the author) (reporting leadership in a collaborative initiative involving eighty asset managers that issued an open letter urging companies to mitigate human rights risks in Myanmar). However, investors do not necessarily endorse or participate in every collaborative letter issued by coalitions with which they are affiliated. Some, such as Chelverton Asset Management, prefer to raise concerns directly with investee companies. See Chelverton Asset Management, *UK Stewardship Code Report* (2021), 22 and 40 (on file with the author).

[111] See e.g. Robeco, *Stewardship Report*, 01.01.2021-31.12.2021, 63 (on file with the author) (reporting participation in a joint investor letter to the South Korean government through Climate Action 100+, urging the establishment of net-zero pathways); Local Pensions Partnership Investments (LLPI), *Responsible Investment and Stewardship Annual Report 2021/22*, 74 (on file with the author) (describing how LLPI co-signed a letter to corporate boards and also contributed a letter to the Financial Times to raise public awareness of sustainability stewardship).

strategic input into operational decision-making.[112] Others contribute indirectly through structured feedback mechanisms, such as manager assessment questionnaires, client satisfaction surveys, perception studies, or annual advisory councils.[113] While not engagement in the classical sense – that is, directed at investee assets – these tools are increasingly important for shaping stewardship priorities, aligning investment practices with client or beneficiary preferences and values, and influencing market norms. In settings where direct engagement is constrained or system-wide input is sought, such mechanisms can function as subtle yet powerful levers of institutional influence.[114]

Engagement itself is also becoming more adaptive and responsive. Escalation can no longer be understood as a linear or prescriptive process but a context-driven strategy – shaped by issue salience, geography, asset class, and the responsiveness of the investee. In public equity markets, escalation may involve proxy voting, public statements, or shareholder resolutions. In other asset classes, where formal rights may be weaker or

[112] Notably Brown Advisory describes themselves as an 'informal advisor', while Pinebridge refers to its method as 'consultivist', where engagement is not merely for influence but to provide feedback and guidance. See Brown Advisory, *Reflections on Stewardship 2021*, 20 (on file with the author) and Pinebridge Investments, *Financial Reporting Council UK Stewardship Code* (31 October 2022), 39 (on file with the author), respectively. Similarly, Arcus Infrastructure Partners LLP, *UK Stewardship Code Report 2021* (April 2022), 11, 36 and 40 (on file with the author) (reporting the routine appointment of board representatives and the establishment of cross-portfolio advisory committees to influence business strategy, governance structures, and ESG integration).

[113] See e.g. PGIM Real Estate, *Annual Stewardship Report, for the year ended 31 December 2021, aligned with the principles of the UK Stewardship Code 2020*, 38–39 (on file with the author) (describing the use of multiple structured client feedback mechanisms – including fund advisory councils, investor-specific surveys, and quarterly update calls – to inform ESG disclosures and shape investment strategy); and The Universities Superannuation Scheme (USS), *Stewardship Code Report 2022*, 34–35 (on file with the author) (stating that: '[w]e consider our oversight of external managers as stewardship activities as we are "engaging" with them to improve their ESG practices', and describing the use of standardised due diligence questionnaires and scoring frameworks (RAG ratings) for ESG monitoring, as well as participation in advisory committees and face-to-face assessments that inform fund manager selection, continued allocation, or disengagement decisions). Another example is Hayfin Capital Management, a private credit manager, which communicates ESG due diligence scores directly to private equity sponsors via phone or in-person meetings. This feedback loop is designed not only to improve sponsor practices but also to inform the development of Hayfin's own ESG assessment tools. See Hayfin Capital Management LLP, *UK Stewardship Code 2020* (October 2022), 18 and 27.

[114] For example, Robeco's 'Active Ownership Survey' gathers client views to guide external engagement priorities. See Robeco, *Stewardship Report*, 01.01.2021–31.12.2021, 14 (on file with the author).

absent, escalation may take the form of capital reallocation, sponsor dialogue, or eventual divestment.[115] Increasingly, escalation blends private engagement with public pressure and collective action – producing a multi-modal engagement model attuned to both investee behaviour and wider market dynamics.

Engagement beyond listed equities tends to be more tailored and relationship-driven. In real assets, private markets, or credit, influence is often exercised through ESG due diligence, ongoing monitoring, and dialogue with both issuers and intermediaries.[116] At the same time, even shareholder engagement is broadening – extending beyond company executives and fellow investors to include a wider array of stakeholders, such as former employees, customers, suppliers, competitors, non-governmental organisation (NGOs), and regulators.[117] This more inclusive approach enables investors to draw on diverse insights and exert influence through the broader ecosystem, especially when direct access to corporate leadership is limited or ineffective.

At the system- and macro-levels, engagement increasingly takes the form of shaping the rules and norms that govern markets. Several disclosures highlight investor participation in the development of disclosure frameworks and governance standards through collaboration with

[115] For instance, Russell Investments outlines a structured yet non-linear escalation framework that incorporates written concerns, proxy voting, collaborative initiatives, and, where necessary, divestment. See Russell Investments, *UK Stewardship Code* (2021 Report), 74–76 (on file with the author). Similarly, Robeco's 'enhanced engagement' programme – covering thematic areas such as 'Acceleration to Paris' – is explicitly designed to escalate when progress stalls and may ultimately lead to divestment. See Robeco, *Stewardship Report*, 01.01.2021–31.12, 11 (on file with the author). Greater Manchester Pension Fund, through the Local Authority Pension Fund Forum (LAPFF), provides another example of flexible escalation, beginning with letters and moving to public statements or voting alerts where appropriate. See Great Manchester Pension Fund (GMPF), *UK Stewardship Code 2021, Statement of Compliance with the UK Stewardship Code*, 50–51 (on file with the author).

[116] See e.g. Payden & Rygel, *2021 UK Stewardship Code Report*, 45 (on file with the author) (emphasising that in fixed income engagement 'we must rely on relationships with issuers and industry participants to create venues for engagement', and reporting direct engagement not just with issuers, but also with underwriting banks, municipal advisors, servicers, and rating agencies, especially in the context of structured and municipal debt).

[117] See e.g. COMGEST, *UK Stewardship Code 2021, Annual Report* (October 2022), 43 (on file with the author); Newton Investment Management, *Responsible Investment and Stewardship, 2021 annual report* (April 2022), 31–21 (on file with the author). See also Section 3.3.3.

regulators, standard-setters, and civil society.[118] These efforts – ranging from technical committees and industry consultations to co-designing reporting benchmarks – demonstrate how institutional investors are engaging beyond the bilateral firm level to exercise systemic influence.[119]

Taken together, these developments mark a fundamental evolution in engagement practice. Once seen primarily as a post-investment governance tool focused on public equity holdings, stewardship has expanded into a multidimensional strategy – spanning upstream and downstream mechanisms, firm-specific engagement and systemic influence, and both formal rights and informal levers of persuasion. Institutional investors today combine capital allocation with governance input, regulatory engagement with stakeholder dialogue, and targeted action with collaborative escalation.

This shift signals a broader transformation: from shareholder stewardship – centred on equity voting and corporate governance – to investor stewardship, which operates across asset classes, investment horizons, and systemic challenges. Stewardship now encompasses bond issuers, real estate managers, infrastructure providers, and private equity sponsors. It also increasingly engages with public authorities, standard-setters, and multilateral initiatives. As such, stewardship is no longer limited to the rights of shareholders; it is exercised through the influence and responsibilities of capital across the investment chain.

7.7 Conclusion: Stewardship beyond the Shareholder

This chapter has developed a multidimensional typology to illuminate the emerging varieties of investor stewardship. By disaggregating

[118] Chelverton's contribution to the SME Climate Disclosure Framework – developed with CDP and the UK Government – provides a case in point. See Chelverton Asset Management, *UK Stewardship Code Report* (2021), 21 (on file with the author). Another example is Evenlode, which reported active participation in the Corporate Reporting Users Forum (CRUF) and the FRC's Climate Change and Risk Reporting Steering Committees, contributing investor perspectives to the development of guidance on risk and viability reporting. The firm also engaged collaboratively through the FAIRR Initiative, including co-signing an open letter to G20 governments urging the inclusion of agricultural emissions targets in national climate commitments – an effort highlighted at COP26. See Evenlode Investment, *Annual Responsible Investment Report 2021*, 14 (on file with the author).

[119] See e.g. GAM Investments, *Stewardship Report 2022*, 29 (on file with the author) and Insight Investment Management, *Responsible Stewardship at Insight, Report to fulfil the requirements of the UK Stewardship Code for the period 1 January–31 December 2021*, 23, 62–5, 91, and 93–5 (on file with the author) (reporting engaging with sovereign issuers and policymakers through informal dialogue, research trips, and multilateral coalitions). See also Section 7.4 for a discussion of investor engagement with the ASCOR initiative.

stewardship along five analytical axes – the levels at which it operates, the actors who perform it, the assets over which it is exercised, the motivations that drive it, and the means through which it is enacted – the typology reveals a practice that has evolved far beyond its original shareholder-centric form. No longer confined to monitoring and engagement in listed equities, stewardship today constitutes a plural, dynamic field shaped by institutional mandates, asset class characteristics, and competing expectations about the responsibilities of capital.

At its core, the typology captures a fundamental shift in both the scope and ambition of stewardship. The traditional model of shareholder stewardship – grounded in equity ownership and firm-specific engagement – remains foundational. Yet it now operates within a broader investment ecosystem in which institutional investors deploy blended strategies across micro-, portfolio-, system-, and macro-levels. Stewardship increasingly spans asset classes, including debt, infrastructure, private markets, and sovereign bonds, reflecting not only the diffusion of ESG imperatives but also a more expansive understanding of fiduciary purpose.

By making visible the differentiated forms investor stewardship can take – from direct corporate engagement to indirect systemic influence – the typology underscores that shareholder stewardship is only one domain within a wider constellation of investor responsibilities. It clarifies how institutional actors combine direct and delegated influence, navigate value-focused, ESG-responsive, and sustainability-oriented objectives, and activate stewardship at different points along the investment chain.

In doing so, the chapter reinforces the book's central argument: that enlightened investor stewardship cannot be understood in isolation from the broader ecosystem of institutional influence in which it is embedded. *Enlightenment*, in this context, entails the capacity to deliberate and balance competing responsibilities, to exercise principled judgement across time horizons and asset classes, and to align fiduciary, contractual, and regulatory duties with long-term public value.

This typology does not prescribe a singular mode of best practice. Rather, it provides a flexible interpretive framework – one that helps distinguish symbolic compliance from meaningful engagement, and that reveals where stewardship succeeds and where it risks falling short. Such clarity is critical as the boundaries between shareholder value and public purpose continue to blur.

Ultimately, this typology lays the conceptual foundation for the reform agenda developed in the next chapter. Chapter 8 advances the case for a third-generation UK Stewardship Code – one that moves beyond fragmented disclosures and aspirational rhetoric, and towards a coherent institutional framework for stewardship that is truly enlightened in both purpose and practice.

8

The Third-Generation UK Stewardship Code

Realising Enlightened Investor Stewardship

8.1 Introduction

This final chapter turns from what investor stewardship currently is to what stewardship codes are meant to enable. Building on the book's conceptual, empirical, and normative foundations, it makes the case for a third-generation UK Stewardship Code (3G UK Code) – one better equipped to meet the systemic risks, multi-actor dynamics, and expanding responsibilities of contemporary institutional investment. While the second-generation UK Stewardship Code (2G UK Code), introduced in 2020,[1] marked an ambitious shift – away from shareholder-centric, micro-level engagement towards environmental, social, and governance (ESG) integration, systemic risk awareness, and long-term value – the disclosure patterns analysed in Chapter 6 reveal that, despite significant progress, these aspirations have yet to translate into consistent and widespread behavioural change.

The persistence of this ambition–implementation gap reflects more than shortcomings in stewardship reporting. It exposes two interrelated challenges: first, the enduring ambiguity surrounding materiality and fiduciary responsibility, which continues to blur the boundaries of legitimate investor conduct; and second, structural fragmentation across the investment ecosystem, where stewardship practice is shaped less by shared regulatory ambition than by institutional discretion, capacity, and strategic orientation. Despite its expanded scope, the 2G UK Code has often generated a proliferation of narrative disclosures without corresponding gains in coherence or accountability.

This chapter reframes stewardship codes as more than procedural instruments. It argues that they serve a vital normative function – as *norm entrepreneurs* capable of 'crowding in' more ambitious and other-regarding

[1] Financial Reporting Council, *The UK Stewardship Code 2020* (2019) [UK Code 2020].

forms of investor responsibility. This crowding-in function is central to the chapter's analysis: stewardship codes can broaden what counts as legitimate investor conduct, shape internal decision-making, and reorient institutional preferences towards system-wide outcomes, even in the absence of binding mandates. Realising this potential, however, requires clearer normative direction, structural support, and regulatory coherence.

The Financial Reporting Council's (FRC) 2024 public consultation on the future of the UK Stewardship Code offers a critical opportunity to recalibrate the regime. In this context, the chapter advocates embedding *enlightened investor stewardship* as the conceptual and operational core of a 3G UK Code. Enlightened investor stewardship recognises that institutional investors operate not only as fiduciaries but also as actors embedded in broader social, environmental, and financial systems. It offers a principled yet pragmatic framework for reconciling client- and beneficiary-centred duties with the long-term interests of markets, ecosystems, and society.

The chapter unfolds in three parts. First, it diagnoses the limitations of the 2G UK stewardship regime, analysing how definitional vagueness, narrow interpretations of investor duty, and structural asymmetries constrain the Code's transformative potential. Second, it sets out a reform agenda for a 3G UK Code, anchored in a redefinition of stewardship that reflects the multi-relational, multi-level nature of the investment chain. Drawing lessons from Section 172 of the Companies Act 2006, it explores how this redefinition can be operationalised – particularly through narrative reporting – as a means of institutional learning, transparency, and legitimacy. Third, it cautions against the risks of stewardship washing and regulatory minimalism, arguing for differentiated expectations, capacity-sensitive standards, and renewed emphasis on the expressive function of stewardship codes.

Ultimately, this chapter returns to the book's central proposition: that the path to *enlightened investor stewardship* lies in reimagining stewardship not as a technical adjunct to corporate governance, but as a core institutional mechanism for governing the public responsibilities of capital.

8.2 Diagnosing the Gaps: From Governance Tool to Normative Framework

8.2.1 The Crowding-in Function: Stewardship Codes as Norm Entrepreneurs

The typology introduced in Chapter 7 revealed investor stewardship as a pluralistic and evolving practice, expressed across varying levels, actors, asset classes, motivations, and mechanisms.[2] This diversity is grounded in the multi-layered nature of stewardship relationships explored in Chapter 4, which showed that investor stewardship is not a singular or linear responsibility, but one spanning clients, beneficiaries, end-investors, investee companies, financial markets, and society.[3] Taken together, these chapters expose both the interpretive variation and the relational complexity of contemporary stewardship. Yet this pluralism also introduces challenges – most notably, the risks of accountability fragmentation and institutional overstretch.

Confronting these risks requires more than technical adjustments to stewardship practice. It demands a rethinking of investor stewardship's purpose and normative architecture. In particular, it invites reconsideration of the role that stewardship codes can play as vehicles for articulating and embedding shared expectations about the responsibilities of institutional investors.

Traditionally, stewardship codes have been conceived as soft-law complements to the corporate governance toolkit – tools designed to enhance shareholder oversight through engagement and voting.[4] As such, they have often been criticised for failing to transform institutional investors into consistently engaged shareholder stewards.[5] Yet, such critiques risk overlooking a more fundamental point. The primary function of stewardship codes lies not in mandating compliance or enforcing specific behaviours – legal and regulatory duties already exist to bind institutional investors to their proximate clients-and beneficiaries, and increasingly to climate- and ESG-related risks.[6]

Rather, stewardship codes operate as *normative instruments* that help define and institutionalise evolving expectations about the role of institutional investors in shaping economic, environmental, and societal outcomes. By articulating shared principles and legitimising broader interpretations of fiduciary duty, these frameworks act as connective

[2] Section 7.1.

[3] Section 4.4.

[4] See e.g. Dionysia Katelouzou and Dan W. Puchniak, 'Global Shareholder Stewardship: Complexities, Challenges and Possibilities' in Dan W. Puchniak and Dionysia Katelouzou (eds.), *Global Shareholder Stewardship* (Cambridge University Press 2022), 3, 5–9.

[5] For example, Brian R. Cheffins, 'The Stewardship Code's Achilles' Heel' (2010) 73 *The Modern Law Review* 1004; Simon C. Y. Wong, 'Why Stewardship Is Proving Elusive for Institutional Investors' (2010) 7 *Butterworths Journal of International Banking and Financial Law* 406; Arad Reisberg, 'The UK Stewardship Code: On the Road to Nowhere?' (2015) 15 *Journal of Corporate Law Studies* 217.

[6] Section 5.4.

tissue within a complex financial ecosystem. They align organisational behaviour, foster institutional capacity, and support the internalisation of long-term responsibilities that extend beyond conventional shareholder interests.

This is the crowding-in function of stewardship codes: their ability to broaden the domain of legitimate investor conduct, guide internal decision-making towards system-wide outcomes, and influence organisational norms and priorities.[7] They are not weak substitutes for regulation, but adaptive tools that can consolidate emerging governance practices and promote behavioural change across the investment chain – though their voluntary nature necessarily raises concerns about uptake, consistency, and legal effect.[8]

The expressive function of stewardship codes is particularly important. Scholars have shown that law influences behaviour not only through incentives and sanctions but also through *expression and 'preference-shaping'* – by 'making statements' that affirm collective values and shape social expectations.[9] In the stewardship context, these statements help normalise an expanded understanding of fiduciary responsibility – one that extends beyond the narrow pursuit of shareholder primacy and client-first value extraction to include what this book has referred to as *the unseen others*: end-investors (present and future), investable assets, broader stakeholders, ecosystems, and systemic interests often excluded from traditional financial calculus.[10]

This expressive logic stands in sharp contrast to the well-documented 'crowding-out' effect in behavioural economics, which warns that externally imposed rules – particularly financial incentives – can undermine intrinsic motivation.[11] In the realm of investor stewardship, where engagement is

[7] On soft law as norm-setting devices, see further Kenneth W. Abbott and Duncan Snidal, 'Hard and Soft Law in International Governance' (2000) 54 *International Organization* 421.

[8] Ibid. See also Sections 5.4, 8.2.3, and 8.3.1.

[9] See e.g. Cass R. Sunstein, 'On the Expressive Function of Law' (1995) 144 *University of Pennsylvania Law Review* 2021; Robert Cooter, 'Expressive Law and Economics' (1998) 27 *Journal of Legal Studies* 585; Alex Geisinger, 'A Belief Change Theory of Expressive Law' (2002) 88 *Iowa Law Review* 35.

[10] Section 4.3.2.3.

[11] Bruno S. Frey and Felix Oberholzer-Gee, 'The Cost of Price Incentives: An Empirical Analysis of Motivation Crowding- Out' (1997) 87 *The American Economic Review* 746. See also Deborah A. DeMott, 'The Domains of Loyalty: Relationships between Fiduciary Obligation and Intrinsic Motivation the Future of Fiduciary Law Symposium' (2020) 62 *William & Mary Law Review* 1137, 1143–7 (focusing on the crowding-in effect of fiduciary law).

often values-driven and reliant on reputational capital, this concern is particularly acute. Stewardship codes must therefore be careful not to undermine the very motivations they aim to cultivate. Rather than prescribing rigid behavioural norms or relying on extrinsic inducements, these codes are designed to reinforce intrinsic motivation by offering normative guidance, affirming shared values, and fostering spaces for interpretation, deliberation, and institutional learning. As Blair and Stout have argued in their behavioural account of corporate law, trust and trustworthiness are key enablers of cooperative behaviour, and excessive reliance on external controls can weaken these internal motivations.[12]

This insight is reinforced by Eisenberg's theory of law and social norms. He emphasises that legal and quasi-legal instruments exert influence not only through formal enforcement also but through their ability to express, stabilise, and institutionalise shared values. Such instruments act as focal points for behavioural alignment and serve as scaffolds for the internalisation of social norms. For Eisenberg, long-term behavioural change – especially in institutional contexts – depends not on instrumental compliance, but on the internalisation of obligational norms.[13] Stewardship codes operate precisely within this normative register, reinforcing other-regarding commitments and shared accountability across the investment chain.[14]

Similar dynamics are observable across the broader corporate governance landscape. Soft-law mechanisms – such as corporate governance codes – have played a key role in embedding normative commitments to transparency, accountability, and long-term responsibility, particularly in contexts where legal enforcement is weak or politically constrained.[15] These instruments function as scaffolds for the gradual internalisation of norms, enabling institutions to evolve in ways that legal mandates alone may not be able to compel.

Against this backdrop, stewardship codes should be understood as *norm entrepreneurs*: instruments that both reflect and help produce

[12] Margaret M. Blair and Lynn A. Stout, 'Trust, Trustworthiness, and the Behavioral Foundations of Corporate Law' (2001) 149 *University of Pennsylvania Law Review* 1735, 1744.

[13] Melvin A. Eisenberg, 'Corporate Law and Social Norms' (1999) 99 *Columbia Law Review* 1253.

[14] See also Konstantinos Sergakis, 'Shareholder Stewardship: Autonomy and Sociality' (2023) 23 *Journal of Corporate Law Studies* 497.

[15] See e.g. John W. Cioffi, *Public Law and Private Power: Corporate Governance Reform in the Age of Finance Capitalism* (Cornell University Press 2010).

evolving standards of responsible investment. They provide focal points for interpretation, encourage deliberative practices, and support the diffusion of new norms across a heterogeneous and transnational community of institutional actors.

Viewed in this light, stewardship codes are increasingly situated within what has been described as a *regulatory laboratory* of transnational governance.[16] In this setting, hybrid norms emerge through the interaction of public and private actors, as traditional boundaries between hard and soft law, and between national and international regimes, become increasingly blurred. Stewardship codes help crowd in responsible investor behaviour not by mandating it, but by expressing and legitimising evolving priorities. They do so through reputational incentives, interpretive signalling, and the cultivation of shared expectations about the role of institutional investors in the sustainable governance of capital.

The 2G UK Code, as analysed in Chapter 5, partially realises this crowding-in potential.[17] It overlays a public-interest rationale onto a legal architecture still anchored in private fiduciary or contractual relationships. Unlike its 2012 predecessor, which focused narrowly on shareholder stewardship, the 2020 iteration adopts a more outcome-oriented, system-aware perspective. It broadens its remit to include systemic risks, ESG integration, and wider environmental and social considerations.[18] Most notably, it recognises *sustainability stewardship* – alongside client, end-investor, and asset stewardship – as a core dimension of responsible investment.[19] This shift has been reinforced by a growing policy consensus that views investor stewardship as a key mechanism for advancing ESG goals and embedding systemic accountability in financial practice.[20]

Yet this expressive and normative potential tells only part of the story. While stewardship codes articulate evolving expectations about investor responsibility, their practical influence depends on the legal and institutional conditions in which they are embedded. The next section examines how these constraints manifest, focusing on the legal boundaries of other-regarding stewardship in the UK context.

[16] Dionysia Katelouzou and Peer Zumbansen, 'The New Geographies of Corporate Governance' (2020) 42 *University of Pennsylvania Journal of International Law* 1.

[17] Section 5.4.

[18] Sections 5.3.2 and 5.4.

[19] Section 4.4.2.

[20] See e.g. Financial Conduct Authority, *Sustainability Disclosure Requirements (SDR) and Investment Labels* (Policy Statement PS23/16).

8.2.2 *Materiality, Investor Duties, and Constraints on Other-Regarding Investor Stewardship*

Although stewardship codes aim to crowd in broader conceptions of investor responsibility, their normative reach is shaped – and often constrained – by the legal and institutional frameworks in which they operate. This section examines how prevailing interpretations of materiality and fiduciary duty – particularly in the context of trust-based pension schemes – limit the scope for other-regarding forms of investor stewardship.

The 2G UK Code illustrates these tensions. While it expands the stewardship agenda beyond the traditional board–shareholder relationship to include systemic risks, societal challenges, and long-term sustainability objectives, its implementation remains tethered to legal frameworks that bind investor duties primarily to proximate clients and beneficiaries. Despite its more ambitious framing, the 2G UK Code thus continues to operate within a legal architecture inherited from earlier, shareholder-centric models.

This disconnect exposes a deeper regulatory blind spot: the lack of clarity over how expanded stewardship expectations intersect with investor duties under current legal and regulatory regimes.[21] As the 2G UK Code calls on institutional investors to integrate ESG factors and pursue long-term outcomes, a fundamental question arises: what forms of *other-regarding action* are permissible within prevailing duty frameworks? This goes to the heart of how materiality is interpreted. Can institutional investors act in the interests of *others* – such as future beneficiaries, affected stakeholders, or the environment – when those interests are not clearly financially material? And to what extent can investor stewardship target real-world outcomes that do not demonstrably enhance financial returns?

While not all institutional investors operate under fiduciary duties – some are bound instead by contractual or statutory obligations of varying scope[22] – fiduciary norms continue to exert a powerful influence on how stewardship responsibilities are understood and operationalised, particularly among asset owners.[23]

[21] Dionysia Katelouzou, 'The Unseen "Others": A Framework for Investor Stewardship' (2024) 77 *Current Legal Problems* 295, 322–5.

[22] See also Section 4.3.2.3.

[23] In the 2020 disclosure sample analysed in Chapter 6, 61.54 per cent of signatories referred at least once to fiduciary duties. This included 73.47 per cent of asset owners, compared to 58.38 per cent of asset managers – suggesting a stronger reliance on fiduciary framing among trust-based institutions, such as pension funds. Data on file with the author.

Nowhere are these tensions more acute than in the context of ESG investing.[24] UK law broadly accepts the relevance of financially material ESG factors in portfolio management.[25] However, in trust-based pension schemes, considerable uncertainty remains as to whether trustees may also consider environmental or social concerns that lack an immediate or demonstrable financial impact.[26]

Historically, English courts have taken a cautious approach to ESG investing based solely on ethical or moral grounds.[27] The Law Commission has since clarified that trustees may consider non-financial factors if two conditions are met: first, there must be good reason to believe that beneficiaries share the concern in question; and second, the decision must not pose a significant risk of financial detriment to the fund.[28] In practice, however, identifying and aggregating beneficiary preferences – and translating them into investment mandates – remains highly contested and operationally complex.[29]

[24] See e.g. Joakim Sandberg, '(Re-)Interpreting Fiduciary Duty to Justify Socially Responsible Investment for Pension Funds?' (2013) 21 *Corporate Governance: An International Review* 436, 437. For reviews of the mixed empirical evidence on the financial materiality of ESG investing, see Pedro Matos, 'ESG and Responsible Institutional Investing around the World: A Critical Review' CFA Institute Research Foundation; Stuart L. Gillan, Andrew Koch and Laura T. Starks, 'Firms and Social Responsibility: A Review of ESG and CSR research in Corporate Finance' (2021) 66 *Journal of Corporate Finance* 101889.

[25] The Law Commission, *Fiduciary Duties of Investment Intermediaries* (Law Com No 350, 2014) para 6.27. However, in other jurisdictions – most notably in the US – the permissibility of ESG investing, even when framed in terms of risk-return optimisation, remains unsettled. Compare, e.g., Max M. Schanzenbach and Robert H. Sitkoff, 'Reconciling Fiduciary Duty and Social Conscience: The Law and Economics of ESG Investing by a Trustee' (2020) 72 *Stanford Law Review* 381 (arguing that ESG investing is permissible when it aligns with risk-return objectives) with Matt Cole, *Fiduciary Duties of Public Pension Systems and Registered Investment Advisors* (Harvard Law School Forum on Corporate Governance 1 March 2023) https://corpgov.law.harvard.edu/2023/03/01/fiduciary-duties-of-public-pension-systems-and-registered-investment-advisors/ (raising concerns about fiduciary overreach and politicisation).

[26] Juxtapose *Fiduciary Duties of Investment Intermediaries*, paras 5.61–5.62 and Law Commission, *Pension Funds and Social Investment* (2017), para 5.15, on the one hand, with UNEP-PRI, *Fiduciary Duty in the 21st Century: Final Report*, on the other.

[27] *Cowan v Scargill* [1985] Ch. 270; *Harries and Others v. Church Commissioners for England* [1992] 1 W.L.R. 1241.

[28] *Pension Funds and Social Investment*, para 5.15. See also PRI and others Fiduciary Duty in the twenty-first century (2019), www.unepfi.org/wordpress/wp-content/uploads/2019/10/Fiduciary-duty-21st-century-final-report.pdf (asserting the compatibility of ESG incorporation with investors' fiduciary duties).

[29] Benjamin J. Richardson, 'From Fiduciary Duties to Fiduciary Relationships for Socially Responsible Investing: Responding to the Will of Beneficiaries' (2011) 1 *Journal of Sustainable Finance & Investment* 5, 9–11.

Against this backdrop, Principle 7 of the 2G UK Code calls for the integration of material ESG issues – explicitly including climate change – into investment and stewardship.[30] Yet the principle offers no explicit definition of materiality, leaving substantial room for interpretative flexibility. On one reading, the Code suggests a shift towards *double materiality*, under which environmental and social impacts may be relevant even in the absence of direct financial consequences.[31] On a narrower interpretation, however, its repeated references to serving the interests of clients and beneficiaries reinforce a *single materiality* standard – conferring legitimacy only on financially relevant concerns.[32]

The latter interpretation narrows stewardship's remit to actions that either generate firm-level returns (alpha) or contribute to long-term market stability (beta).[33] Public interest goals – such as advancing human rights or mitigating biodiversity loss – risk being dismissed as discretionary or extraneous unless they can be linked to demonstrable financial value. This reflects the UK's regulatory orientation towards a 'single' or 'financial' materiality standard.[34] While financial and sustainability goals may

[30] UK Code 2020, Principle 7 (Principles for Asset Owners and Asset Managers).

[31] Hans-Christoph Hirt, 'The Future of Stewardship: Time to Take a Step Back' in Iris H.-Y. Chiu and Hans-Christoph Hirt (eds.), *Investment Management, Stewardship and Sustainability: Transformation and Challenges in Law and Regulation* (Hart 2023), 319. On how double materiality is embraced by EU policymakers, see Iris H. Y. Chiu, 'The EU Sustainable Finance Agenda: Developing Governance for Double Materiality in Sustainability Metrics' (2022) 23 *European Business Organization Law Review* 87; Félix E. Mezzanotte, 'Corporate Sustainability Reporting: Double Materiality, Impacts, and Legal Risk' (2023) 23 *Journal of Corporate Law Studies* 633.

[32] There are thirty-one references to clients and beneficiaries in the UK Code 2020.

[33] See Section 7.5 on value-focused and ESG (risk-responsive) stewardship.

[34] The Task Force on Climate-Related Financial Disclosures (TCFD) reporting requirements – applicable to both listed companies as well as FCA-regulated asset managers, life insurers, and pension providers – focus on how climate risks and opportunities impact an organisation's financial position and performance. See e.g. Financial Conduct Authority, *Enhancing Climate-Related Disclosures by Asset Managers, Life Insurers and FCA-Regulated Pension Providers* (Policy Statement PS21/24, December 2021). In line with this approach, the UK Sustainability Reporting Standards are based on the disclosure standards developed by the International Sustainability Standards Board (ISSB Standards), which adopt a single, financial materiality perspective rather than the double materiality model embedded in the EU's sustainability reporting standards (ESRS). See Department for Business & Trade, *Framework and Terms of Reference for the Development of UK Sustainability Reporting Standards* (2024). By contrast, the EU's Sustainability Disclosure Regulation adheres to a single materiality approach. See Regulation (EU) 2019/2088 of the European Parliament and of the Council of 27 November 2019 on sustainability-related disclosures in the financial services sector, Article 2(22) defining 'sustainability risk' as 'an environmental, social, or governance

sometimes converge, activities grounded purely in *intrinsic or impact materiality* remain difficult to justify under the prevailing regulatory framework.[35]

Yet, as Chapter 6 demonstrated, not all signatories adhere to this financially bounded logic. Although topic modelling did not isolate a distinct double materiality theme, Topic 6 of the 2020 disclosure sample surfaced a cluster of other-regarding disclosures.[36] Within this group, some institutional investors articulated commitments rooted in normative values and systemic responsibility – even where financial materiality was absent. A small subset explicitly invoked *double materiality*; others implicitly implied its logic, acknowledging both financial risk and real-world impact.[37]

This divergence underscores a deeper problem: the challenge of *regulatory complementarity*. While the 2G UK Code aspires to a multi-layered and multidimensional model of investor stewardship – spanning levels, actors, asset classes, motivations, and means – its implementation remains circumscribed by inherited legal structures that prioritise financial materiality. So long as investor duties are defined primarily by reference to the financial interests of proximate clients or members,

event or condition that if, it occurs, could cause an actual or a potential material negative impact on the value of the investment'. For a comparative analysis of the UK and EU sustainability regimes and their differing treatment of materiality, see Andrew Johnston, 'ESG and Corporate Sustainability: A View from the UK Symposium: Corporate Law, Corporate Governance, and Sustainability' (2024) 52 *Georgia Journal of International and Comparative Law* 576.

35 For a distinction between 'financial materiality', 'impact materiality', 'systemic materiality', and 'intrinsic materiality', see The Investor Forum, *What Does Shareholder Capitalism Mean for Investors?* (January 2022), 40.

36 Section 6.6.3.1.

37 For instance, Amundi explicitly integrates double materiality into its ESG strategy, noting that negative real-world impacts should not be disregarded merely because they do not pose immediate financial risks – thereby affirming a commitment to both financial and societal dimensions of materiality. See Amundi Asset Management, *Stewardship Report 2021* (October 2022), 50 (on file with the author). Similarly, Aon incorporates double materiality into its expectations of asset managers, encouraging disclosures that reflect both financial risks and broader sustainability impacts. See AON, *The UK Stewardship Code* (April 2022), 94 (on file with the author). Cardano also adopts a double materiality lens, explicitly framing its investment approach around both risk-adjusted returns and real-world sustainability outcomes. See Cardano Risk Management Limited, *Stewardship Report 2021* (April 2022), 6 (on file with the author). By contrast, 7IM's emphasis on Scope 3 emissions and supply chain sustainability goes beyond conventional financial risk considerations, though without explicitly invoking the language of double materiality. See 7IM, *Stewardship Report 2021*, 35 (on file with the author).

regulatory inertia will constrain the full realisation of stewardship's broader normative ambitions.

Yet legal constraint is only part of the story. As the next section explores, institutional variation – in form, capacity, size, strategy, and jurisdiction – also plays a significant role in shaping how stewardship is interpreted, prioritised, and operationalised across the investment ecosystem.

8.2.3 The Practice Gap: Fragmentation, Capacity, and Soft-Law Limitations

Beyond legal constraints, the uneven implementation of the 2G UK Code – at least as reflected in public disclosures – reveals a second major barrier to the crowding-in of other-regarding investment norms: deep structural asymmetries in institutional capacity, orientation, and engagement. As Chapter 6 demonstrated, stewardship disclosures vary widely – not only in tone and format but also in substantive focus and strategic ambition.[38] These divergences reflect more than interpretive ambiguity or definitional vagueness. They point instead to underlying structural heterogeneity: differences in institutional form, size, organisational capacity, strategic orientation, and jurisdiction that shape how stewardship is interpreted and enacted in practice.[39]

Investor type is a key differentiator. Asset owners – particularly UK public pension schemes – tend to emphasise trustee-led, system-oriented stewardship, whereas asset managers more commonly foreground bottom-up, firm-level engagement or procedural governance infrastructure. Signatory location also matters: UK-based signatories, likely owing to their proximity to the FRC and the Code's regulatory ecosystem, are more inclined to articulate climate-aligned or other-regarding stewardship narratives than their international counterparts. Organisational scale plays a subtler but still meaningful role: larger institutions have the infrastructure to meet complex reporting demands but often favour scalable, process-driven disclosures over detailed engagement narratives.

Signatory experience further shapes narrative ambition. Investors who signed the first-generation Code in 2012 are more likely to produce climate-conscious and value-driven disclosures in 2020 – suggesting

[38] Sections 6.3, 6.4, 6.5, and 6.6.

[39] Section 6.6.4.

a learning effect over time. Newer signatories, particularly those focused on infrastructure or private markets, often frame stewardship in ways that depart from shareholder-centric norms.

Perhaps most striking is the rhetorical shift among activist signatories. Traditionally associated with firm-level disruption, some now invoke stewardship as a systemic, long-term project. Their disclosures stress market-wide reform and sustainability imperatives, signalling an evolution from adversarial tactics towards norm-shaping engagement.

Yet even these evolutions unfold unevenly. Chapter 6 helps explain variation in disclosure content, but not all dimensions of stewardship capacity are visible through narrative analysis. Scale, for example, does not guarantee capability. Effective investor stewardship depends not only on capital or organisational scale, but also on internal expertise, team coordination, and cultural commitment. Academic research underscores persistent disincentives to engagement – especially for passive funds and index-trackers, where fee structures and business models discourage intensive firm-level stewardship unless the risk is systemic or market-wide.[40]

The structural design of the UK Stewardship Code compounds these challenges. The shift to an apply-and-explain model was intended to elicit more meaningful disclosures and avoid the boilerplate language often associated with comply-or-explain.[41] In practice, however, this has introduced greater interpretive flexibility which – combined with the absence of strong enforcement – has increased the volume of disclosure without always enhancing comparability or rigour. As Chapter 6 showed, some statements align with trustee-led, climate-conscious, or multi-asset stewardship approaches – reflecting greater organisational capacity to extend stewardship beyond listed equities (Topics 2, 3, 5, and 6), while others default to procedural, reactive, or minimal engagement (Topic 4), with limited attention to beneficiary accountability or long-term sustainability outcomes.[42]

The Code's non-statutory nature reinforces this fragmentation. Although the FRC has strengthened its review processes, the Code remains voluntary and lacks binding enforcement.[43] Its soft-law character limits both its

[40] See generally Roger M. Baker and Iris H.-Y. Chiu, *Corporate Governance and Investment Management: The Promises and Limitations of the New Financial Economy* (Edward Elgar 2017).

[41] Section 5.3.2.

[42] Section 6.6.3.

[43] For a detailed analysis of stewardship enforcement, see Dionysia Katelouzou and Konstantinos Sergakis, 'Shareholder Stewardship Enforcement' in Dan W. Puchniak and

regulatory leverage and its ability to drive consistent behavioural change.[44] The future transition to the Audit, Reporting and Governance Authority (ARGA) may signal a firmer approach, but its direction and priorities remain uncertain.[45]

In short, while the 2G UK Code represents a major normative advance, its implementation remains fragmented – shaped by capacity constraints, institutional divergence, and the inherent limits of a largely voluntary regime.[46] This variability is not inherently problematic. As earlier chapters have shown, investor stewardship is a multi-relational and multidimensional practice, shaped by differences in levels of intervention, stewardship actors, asset classes, motivational orientations, and operational means.

But if the aim is to enable more consistent and effective other-regarding investor stewardship, such diversity must be met with clearer guidance, differentiated expectations, and targeted institutional support. Without this calibration, the Code's transformative potential risks being diluted by rhetorical compliance – formal alignment in language without meaningful behavioural change.[47]

This gap between expressive ambition and operational clarity underscores the need for a more coordinated and conceptually grounded framework. The following section turns to one of the key obstacles to such reform: the definitional ambiguity at the heart of the 2G UK Code.

Dionysia Katelouzou (eds.), *Global Shareholder Stewardship* (Cambridge University Press 2022), 572–98.

44 For a broader critique of the UK's soft-law governance framework – and a call to abolish the UK Corporate Governance Code, on which the Stewardship Code model was originally modelled – see Brian R. Cheffins and Bobby V. Reddy, 'Thirty Years and Done – Time to Abolish the UK Corporate Governance Code' (2022) 22 *Journal of Corporate Law Studies* 709.

45 Energy & Industrial Strategy Department for Business, *Restoring Trust in Audit and Corporate Governance: Government Response to the Consultation on Strengthening the UK's Audit, Corporate Reporting and Corporate Governance Systems* (May 2022).

46 On the Code's coerciveness, see Section 5.3.3.

47 On the disjunction between stewardship commitments and behavioural change – illustrated by Blackrock's shifting emphasis on ESG factors – see Jan Fichtner and Eelke M. Heemskerk, 'The New Permanent Universal Owners: Index Funds, Patient Capital, and the Distinction between Feeble and Forceful Stewardship' (2020) 49 *Economy and Society* 493; Giovanni Strampelli, 'Can BlackRock Save the Planet? The Institutional Investors' Role in Stakeholder Capitalism' (2021) 11 *Harvard Business Law Review* 1; Anna Tilba, 'Appearance or Substance of Stewardship and ESG Reporting? The Challenges of Translating "Commitment" into Tangible Outcomes' (2022) 13 *Sustainability Accounting, Management and Policy Journal* 1015.

8.3 Enlightened Stewardship: A Blueprint for the Third-Generation UK Stewardship Code

8.3.1 Definitional Drift: From Vision to Vagueness

As the previous analysis has shown, the uneven implementation of the 2G UK Code cannot be attributed solely to structural asymmetries or reporting burdens. At its core lies a deeper conceptual challenge: the absence of a shared normative anchor capable of guiding investor stewardship practice across a diverse investment landscape. This section examines how the Code's definition of investor stewardship – intended as a unifying vision – has also become a source of interpretive drift.

The 2G UK Code describes stewardship as the 'responsible allocation, management and oversight of capital to create long-term value for clients and beneficiaries, leading to sustainable benefits for the economy, the environment and society'.[48] This marked a significant shift in the UK's stewardship framework, extending its reach beyond firm-specific corporate governance to encompass capital allocation and portfolio management decisions, as well as broader systemic, environmental, and societal outcomes.[49]

Yet this expansive formulation left key questions unanswered. Are environmental and social benefits intrinsic to stewardship's purpose, or merely incidental outcomes? As Chapter 6 showed, this ambiguity gave rise to divergent interpretations. Some signatories embraced a broader, sustainability-oriented conception of investor stewardship, aligned with other-regarding stewardship.[50] Others continued to frame investor stewardship narrowly around firm-specific governance and financial performance.[51]

This definitional ambiguity sits at the heart of the Code's ambition–implementation gap. By widening stewardship's scope – across levels, actors, assets, motivations, and means – without offering a coherent framework for integration or prioritisation, the 2G UK Code invited pluralism but lacked the normative scaffolding needed to coordinate it. Institutional investors were thus left navigating expanding responsibilities

[48] UK Code 2020, 4.

[49] Section 5.3.2.

[50] Sections 6.6.3.1 and 6.6.3.4.

[51] Sections 6.6.3.2 and 6.6.3.3. This also reflects the more governance-oriented conception of stewardship – centred on board-level engagement, proxy voting, and fiduciary alignment with proximate clients and beneficiaries – that was dominant among the 2012 Code signatories. See Section 6.6.2.1.

with limited guidance on how to reconcile competing demands or interpret investor stewardship in a legally and operationally coherent manner.

The FRC's 2024 public consultation on the future of the UK Stewardship Code seeks to address this tension.[52] As a principles-based regulator, the FRC operates through high-level norms rather than prescriptive rules.[53] While this 'new governance' approach – characteristic of the UK's 'regulatory capitalism' – promises flexibility and adaptability, it also carries well-documented risks: interpretive drift, compliance formalism, and uneven implementation.[54] These risks became clearly visible in the disclosures analysed in Chapter 6. Despite the 2G UK Code's broader ambitions, many signatories in the 2020 sample adopted language oriented around risk management and procedural compliance, revealing a gap between rhetorical alignment and substantive practice.

In this context, the challenge facing the FRC is not simply to revise the Code's text, but to address the regulatory conditions that enable superficial compliance. The FRC positions the proposed revisions as a means of responding to these conditions and aligning stewardship with the UK's capital markets growth agenda, though the coherence and adequacy of this vision merit scrutiny.[55] The revisions pursue three interrelated objectives: clarifying stewardship's purpose; streamlining reporting expectations; and better reflecting the roles of different actors across the investment chain. Central to this effort is a revised definition of investor stewardship, framed as 'the responsible allocation, management and oversight of capital to create long-term sustainable value for clients and beneficiaries'.[56]

Notably, the revised definition removes the 2020 Code's explicit reference to societal and environmental benefits. These outcomes are now described only as potential side effects – stewardship 'may lead' to them – but they are no longer positioned as core objectives.[57] The emphasis

[52] Financial Reporting Council, *UK Stewardship Code Consultation* (2024). See further www.frc.org.uk/consultations/stewardship-code-consultation/.

[53] On the concept of 'principles-based regulation', see further Julia Black, 'Forms and Paradoxes of Principles-Based Regulation' (2008) 3 *Capital Markets Law Journal* 425; Julia Black, 'The Rise, Fall and Fate of Principles-based Regulation' in Kern Alexander and Niamh Moloney (eds.), *Law Reform and Financial Markets* (Edward Elgar 2011), 3–34.

[54] On the growth of regulatory capitalism, see generally Iris H.-Y. Chiu, 'An Institutional Theory of Corporate Regulation' (2018) 71 *Current Legal Problems* 279.

[55] *UK Stewardship Code Consultation*, paras. 6–21.

[56] Ibid., para 19.

[57] Ibid., para 19.

shifts firmly towards delivering long-term value for clients and beneficiaries – interpreted as delivering financial returns 'today, without compromising the ability to do so in the future'.[58] This reorientation reinforces a financial materiality logic, under which public outcomes are recognised but remain secondary and discretionary rather than constitutive of intergenerational and systemic investor responsibility.

The result is a narrowing of the normative space in which other-regarding responsibilities can be pursued. Although the definition grants signatories discretion to determine what they consider material to long-term value creation, it places the interpretive burden squarely on individual institutions.[59] Other-regarding aims are rendered permissible but not expected – legitimate but not central.

This approach reflects continued deference to legal, fiduciary, and contractual duties. The FRC affirms that the UK Stewardship Code does not prescribe how such duties should be interpreted or fulfilled.[60] While this regulatory restraint preserves flexibility and facilitates broad uptake, it also highlights the limits of soft law's normative reach. The Code may offer a vision of responsible investment, but it stops short of providing the conceptual scaffolding needed to translate that vision into consistent practice.

As a result, institutional investors face mounting societal expectations – on climate risk, social inequality, and systemic resilience – without a clear interpretive framework. Absent stronger normative guidance, the Code risks repeating the same ambition–implementation gap that limited the 2G regime: expansive rhetoric without meaningful behavioural change.

By contrast, a rearticulated Code – one that embeds public-facing responsibilities within a principled and practicable account of investor stewardship – could offer institutional investors both the legitimacy and guidance they need to engage meaningfully with broader societal objectives. As Chapter 6 illustrated, fragmented implementation should not be read as a rejection of stewardship's regulatory potential. Rather it signals the need for a more coherent framework – one capable of aligning investor duties, institutional diversity, and public purpose in a rapidly evolving investment landscape.

The next section considers how this can be achieved. It explores how the concept of *enlightened investor stewardship*, developed earlier in this

58 Ibid., para 20.
59 Ibid., para 22.
60 Ibid., para 22.

book, can inform the foundations of a 3G UK Code – one capable of reflecting stewardship's multi-relational, multi-actor, and multi-level character, and one of providing firmer normative anchoring at the intersection of finance and the public good.

8.3.2 Embedding Enlightened Investor Stewardship: Lessons from Section 172

To advance other-regarding investor stewardship in a coherent and credible way, the next iteration of the UK Stewardship Code should explicitly embed the concept of *enlightened investor stewardship*.[61] Providing a clear framework for balancing fiduciary duties with broader societal and systemic responsibilities is essential if the Code is to move beyond aspirational rhetoric and deliver meaningful guidance.

Global regulatory and policy developments signal a significant shift towards embedding stewardship practices and ESG considerations within investment frameworks, supported by an expanding corpus of legal and soft-law instruments.[62] Globally, 84 per cent of stewardship codes now reference ESG factors,[63] and recent revisions of non-UK codes reflect a more robust ESG orientation.[64] Yet prevailing models remain largely *risk-responsive*: ESG factors are primarily integrated to mitigate downside exposure, protect long-term portfolio value, and satisfy thresholds of financial materiality.[65] Investor stewardship, in this light, continues to be framed through a prudential, value-preserving lens – rather than one that reconceptualises the purposes of capital allocation itself.

[61] Section 4.4.3. Whether hard law duties can be revised to account for other-regarding stewardship is out of the scope of this article, but a preliminary account is included in Iris H.-Y. Chiu and Dionysia Katelouzou, 'Making a Case for Regulating Institutional Shareholders' Corporate Governance Roles' (2018) *Journal of Business Law* 67.

[62] The PRI's policy regulation database counts 868 policy tools and guidance on ESG. See www.unpri.org/policy/regulation-database.

[63] Dionysia Katelouzou and Alice Klettner, 'Sustainable Finance and Stewardship: Unlocking Stewardship's Sustainability Potential' in Dionysia Katelouzou and Dan W. Puchniak (eds.), *Global Shareholder Stewardship* (Cambridge University Press 2022), 549, 561–5.

[64] For instance, the 2020 version of the Japanese Code includes an ESG-related principle but as explained by Professor Goto investor stewardship in Japan promotes, or at least incentivises, a more short-termist, shareholder-oriented culture among Japanese investors. See Gen Goto, 'The Japanese Stewardship Code: Its Resemblance and Non-resemblance to the UK Code' in Dionysia Katelouzou and Dan W. Puchniak (eds.), *Global Shareholder Stewardship* (Cambridge University Press 2022), 222, 236–8.

[65] This includes a combination of three approaches: integration, screening, and thematic. See PRI, *An Introduction to Responsible Investment Stewardship* (19 February 2021).

Enlightened investor stewardship, by contrast, marks a deeper normative evolution. As developed in Chapter 4, it builds on four stewardship relationships – client, end-investor, asset, and sustainability stewardship – each corresponding to a distinct group of 'others' whose interests investors are expected to consider. Rather than replacing these roles it provides a principled structure for navigating their tensions and intersections. It accommodates diverse motivations – from value-focused and ESG-integrated to sustainability-driven – and aligns responsibility both along the investment chain and outward towards the systemic conditions that underpin long-term value.

Importantly, enlightened investor stewardship is both pragmatic and principled. It enables institutional investors to align financial objectives with social and environmental imperatives, even where these are not immediately financially material.[66] At the same time, it empowers clients, beneficiaries, and end-investors alike to shape capital allocation in ways that recognise systemic risks – without collapsing private mandates into public purpose or undermining contractual responsibilities.

To institutionalise this model, the 3G UK Code could draw inspiration from Section 172 of the Companies Act 2006. Widely recognised as the statutory embodiment of *enlightened shareholder value* (ESV), Section 172 requires directors to promote the success of the company for the benefit of its members as a whole, while 'having regard' to a range of stakeholder interests – including employees, suppliers, the environment, and the long-term consequences of decisions.[67] ESV was envisioned as a 'third way' between strict shareholder primacy and stakeholder pluralism – preserving profit as the guiding purpose, but embedding broader relational accountability.[68]

[66] On materiality, see Section 8.2.2.

[67] The literature on section 172 of the Companies Act 2006 is voluminous. See generally Virginia Ho '"Enlightened Shareholder Value": Corporate Governance beyond the Shareholder-Stakeholder Divide' (2010) 36 *Journal of Corporation Law* 59; Andrew Keay, *The Enlightened Shareholder Value Principle and Corporate Governance* (Routledge 2012).

[68] Cynthia Williams and John M. Conley, 'An Emerging Third Way? The Erosion of the Anglo-American Shareholder Value Construct' (2005) 38 *Cornell International Law Journal* 494. On the regulatory background concerning the scope of interests directors are expected to consider, see Company Law Review Steering Group (1999) *Modern Company Law for a Competitive Economy: The Strategic Framework*, para 5.1.32; Company Law Review Steering Group, *Modern Company Law for a Competitive Economy: Developing the Framework*, DTI (March 2000); Company Law Review Steering Group, *Modern Company Law for a Competitive Economy: Final report*, DTI (June 2001), Chapter 3. On more recent trends that blend section 172-related disclosure

The analogy with investor stewardship is instructive. Like directors, institutional investors exercise delegated authority and are increasingly expected to consider the long-term implications of their decisions. Just as Section 172 frames directors' duties as relational and forward-looking, a revised stewardship framework could encourage investors to act not only in the interests of proximate clients and beneficiaries, but also with awareness of their effects on accountability to investee assets, end-investors, the broader market, and society at large.

Yet the analogy has limits. As the Kay Review aptly noted, 'the company director is not a meta-fund manager, handling a portfolio of investments on behalf of a saver'.[69] Directors owe duties directly to the company as a legal entity; institutional investors operate through private mandates and fiduciary or contractual relationships with clients. These differences underscore the need for a stewardship model that aligns broader responsibilities with existing legal frameworks.

Moreover, the practical experience of Section 172 offers both inspiration and caution. Despite its ambitions, its real-world impact has been modest. Courts have interpreted the duty subjectively,[70] stakeholders lack standing to enforce it,[71] legal practitioners often adopt narrow, risk-averse interpretations,[72] and directors retain wide discretion.[73] As many commentators have noted, ESV has shaped board *rhetoric* more than *behaviour* – largely due to a disconnect between normative ambition

obligations with soft-law mechanisms, see Department for Business, Energy & Industrial Strategy, *Corporate Governance Reform: Green Paper* (November 2016); Department for Business, Energy & Industrial Strategy, *Corporate Governance Reform: The Government response to the green paper consultation* (August 2017).

69 John Kay, *The Kay Review of UK Equity Markets and Long-Term Decision Making* (July 2012) 57.

70 On the common law subjective test, see *Re Smith & Fawcett Ltd* [1942] Ch. 304 at 306, C.A and Regentcrest plc v Cohen [2001] 2 B.C.L.C. 80 at [120]. For a recent analysis of the judicial limits to ESG integration within directors' duties under Section 172, see Luh Luh Lan and Walter Wan, 'ESG and Director's Duties: Defining and Advancing the Interests of the Company' (2023) 23 *Journal of Corporate Law Studies* 537.

71 See e.g. Nicholas Grier, 'Enlightened Shareholder Value: Did Directors Deliver?' (2014) *Juridical Review* 95.

72 Joan Loughrey, Andrew Keay and Luca Cerioni, 'Legal Practitioners, Enlightened Shareholder Value and the Shaping of Corporate Governance' (2008) 8 *Journal of Corporate Law Studies* 79.

73 See e.g. Andrew Keay, 'Tackling the Issue of the Corporate Objective: An Analysis of the United Kingdom's 'Enlightened Shareholder Value Approach' 29 *Sydney Law Review* 577.

and the institutional structures, incentives, and legal constraints that frame corporate governance in practice.[74]

Section 172 illustrates that public-oriented governance can coexist within shareholder-focused frameworks – but it also reveals the limitations of relying on disclosure-based duties without robust mechanisms for accountability. When unsupported by institutional scaffolding, such duties risk becoming symbolic, contributing more to performative compliance than to meaningful change. While the ESV model creates space for directors to integrate societal and environmental considerations into corporate decision-making, it cannot carry this normative burden alone.[75] In the absence of a broader enabling regulatory environment – including more substantive sustainability obligations and stronger enforcement mechanisms – such duties risk becoming overstretched, weakening both their legitimacy and practical impact.

The lesson for the 3G UK Code is clear. If it is to advance other-regarding forms of investor stewardship, it must do more than adopt aspirational language. It must articulate a clear yet flexible vision of stewardship – one that resonates with fiduciary realism while avoiding the vagueness and under-enforcement that have limited the impact of ESV. Responsibilities to *unseen others* – those affected by investment decisions but without direct contractual or legal ties – must be grounded in a conceptual framework that is both normatively compelling and operationally credible.

Within this framework, the enlightened steward emerges not as a fiduciary to all, but as a relational and systemic actor – one who understands that serving clients' and beneficiaries' long-term interests entails broader accountability to the ecological, social, and economic systems upon which those interests ultimately depend, across the

[74] See e.g. John Lowry, 'The Duty of Loyalty of Company Directors: Bridging the Accountability Gap through Efficient Disclosure' (2009), 68 *Cambridge Law Journal* 607; Andrew Keay, 'The Duty to Promote the Success of the Company: Is It Fit for Purpose?' (2011), 32 *The Company Lawyer* 1; Georgina Tsagas, 'Section 172 of the Companies Act 2006: Desperate Times Call for Soft Law Measures' in Nina Boeger and Charlotte Viliers (eds.), *Shaping the Corporate Landscape: Towards Corporate Reform and Enterprise Diversity* (Bloomsbury 2018), 131–50.

[75] Eilis Ferran and Pedro Schillig de Carvalho, 'Reconciling Shareholder Primacy and the Interests of People and Planet' (2025), 141 *The Law Quarterly Review* 463. See also Hans Tjio, 'Sustainable Directors' Duties and Reasonable Shareholders' (2024), 25 *European Business Organization Law Review* 333 (for a nuanced discussion of how directors' duties might evolve to accommodate sustainability goals and the interests of a 'reasonable shareholder').

micro-, portfolio-, system-, and macro-levels of stewardship. A credible investor stewardship regime must acknowledge these interdependencies, balance fiduciary and other legal or contractual obligations with wider public responsibilities, and embed this approach in a definitional anchor that clarifies normative purpose, supports consistent interpretation, and legitimises the integration of sustainability and systemic concerns into core stewardship practice.

8.3.3 Investor Stewardship Redefined: Anchoring the 3G UK Code in an Enlightened Framework

As Section 8.3.1 has shown, the FRC's proposed definitional revision – while intended to improve legal clarity and reporting consistency – risks narrowing the conceptual space within which public value can be meaningfully pursued. By removing explicit reference to broader societal goals, the proposed definition reinforces a financial materiality frame and relegates other-regarding aims to secondary status. If investor stewardship is to become a legitimate and effective mechanism for expanding and coordinating investor responsibilities, it must be capable of responding to systemic risks and rising public expectations where they bear on long-term value creation.

As a soft-law instrument, the UK Stewardship Code plays a crucial role in crowding-in broader interpretations of investor responsibility within the boundaries set by hard law. The definition of investor stewardship is therefore not a mere preamble; it operates as a normative anchor, shaping how institutional investors understand their roles, duties, and the scope of their influence. Any revised definition must reflect the pluralistic realities of contemporary investing – remaining faithful to fiduciary and contractual obligations, while also recognising the broader consequences of investor action and inaction.

A definition grounded in enlightened investor stewardship offers a principled yet pragmatic foundation. It preserves fidelity to existing legal duties while acknowledging that institutional investors are not neutral allocators of capital, but powerful actors whose decisions carry systemic and societal implications. A well-calibrated definition should therefore accommodate diverse stewardship models and asset classes, while affirming that public-facing responsibilities are not incidental but integral to the stewardship function.

To that end, I propose the following revised definition for the 3G UK Code:

> Stewardship is the responsible allocation, management, and oversight of capital to create long-term sustainable value for clients and beneficiaries, and, *in doing so, to have regard to* the interests of broader stakeholders, including end-investors, investee assets, the economy, the environment, and society.

This formulation preserves the centrality of client and beneficiary interests while affirming the interconnectedness of financial value and systemic sustainability, including responsibilities to end-investors over time. It signals that societal and environmental considerations are not externalities but core concerns of effective stewardship. It legitimises a spectrum of motivations – from financial risk management to public interest – without prescribing a one-size-fits-all approach.

Unlike the ESV model, which has been criticised for subordinating stakeholder concerns to shareholder primacy,[76] this definition does not impose a stakeholder mandate by legal fiat. Rather, it expands the space of legitimate investor responsibility without abandoning legal coherence, offering both permission and guidance for institutional investors to act in other-regarding ways. By contrast, definitions that confine investor stewardship to long-term financial value – even when framed broadly – risk overlooking the deeper interdependence between financial systems and societal resilience. A forward-looking definition must therefore affirm that public and systemic responsibilities are not peripheral, but intrinsic to credible and durable stewardship. The formulation proposed here seeks to provide a realistic and operational foundation for stewardship as it evolves to meet both regulatory expectations and public demand.

To embed this expanded vision, the 3G UK Code should also provide practical guidance for navigating overlapping obligations. This includes clarifying how different materiality logics – financial, double, and intrinsic – inform stewardship choices.[77] Drawing on the logic of Section 172 of the Companies Act 2006, the Code could encourage signatories to disclose how they weigh stakeholder interests within their fiduciary and regulatory duties.[78]

Section 172 was never intended to stand alone. It was embedded in a broader framework of narrative accountability, including the Strategic

[76] See e.g. Daniel Attenborough, 'Misreading the Directors' Fiduciary Duty of Good Faith' (2020) 20 *Journal of Corporate Law Studies* 73.

[77] Section 8.2.2.

[78] On the balancing and weighting of stakeholder interests under Section 172, see Andrew Keay, 'Having Regard for Stakeholders in Practising Enlightened Shareholder Value' (2019) 19 *Oxford University Commonwealth Law Journal* 118.

Report requirements,[79] and, from 2019, the Section 172 (1) Statement, which requires large companies to explain how stakeholder interests were factored into board decisions.[80] These disclosure requirements, alongside revisions to the UK Corporate Governance Code – particularly Provision 5 – were designed to make visible how directors considered stakeholder interests in their decision making. While imperfect, they reflect a wider regulatory trend: embedding stakeholder accountability through soft law and narrative disclosure.[81]

The 3G UK Code must take inspiration from this logic. Just as Section 172 was accompanied by narrative mechanisms intended to foster transparency and deliberation, the stewardship definition should be linked to a reporting framework that reflects its expanded normative scope. The goal is not to impose hard rules, but to equip institutional investors with a consistent and credible basis for interpreting – and justifying – their responsibilities across the investment chain.

8.3.4 Making Enlightened Investor Stewardship Credible: Strengthening Reporting

As discussed in the preceding analysis, redefining investor stewardship through the lens of enlightened responsibility is necessary to realign the UK Stewardship Code with the systemic demands of contemporary investment. But conceptual clarity alone, however, is not sufficient. Translating normative ambition into institutional practice requires a reformed Code that is operationalised through credible, reflective, and meaningful disclosure. In a principles-based system with limited enforcement, reporting becomes the principal mechanism through which stewardship norms are articulated, contested, and made visible.

The experience with Section 172 of the Companies Act 2006 offers a cautionary precedent. Though intended to embed stakeholder considerations into directors' decision-making, Section 172's transformative potential has been diluted by weak reporting practices. Supplementary instruments such as the Strategic Report and the Section 172 (1) Statement were designed to illuminate how directors 'had regard' to stakeholders. In practice, however, these disclosures have too often become

[79] Companies Act 2006, sections 414A–414D.

[80] Companies Act 2006, section 414CZA.

[81] UK Corporate Governance Code 2024, Provision 5. See also Barnali Choudhury and Martin Petrin, 'Corporate Governance that "Works for Everyone": Promoting Public Policies through Corporate Governance Mechanisms' (2018) 18 *Journal of Corporate Law Studies* 381.

standardised, backward-looking, and devoid of insight into the deliberative processes that shape boardroom decisions.[82] Rather than fostering meaningful accountability, they risk devolving into boilerplate exercises.[83]

To avoid a similar outcome, stewardship reporting under a third-generation UK Stewardship Code must move beyond procedural compliance. It should encourage differentiated, forward-looking, and self-reflective narratives that align with a revised understanding of stewardship as a system-aware, other-regarding institutional practice. Any credible stewardship regime will therefore require more tailored and structured disclosures, underpinned by clear expectations about *how* reporting should vary across diverse investment models.

The FRC's 2024 consultation marks a meaningful step in this direction. It proposes a more proportionate and modular framework comprising two components: a 'Policy and Context Disclosure', to be updated as needed and reviewed every three years, and an annual 'Activities and Outcomes Report', focused on stewardship practices and results.[84] Crucially, the consultation introduces 'how to report' prompts, differentiated by signatory type and asset class, to foster more targeted, meaningful, and comparable disclosures across a heterogeneous stewardship landscape.[85] These reforms signal a welcome shift away from one-size-fits-all reporting and towards a more interpretive, context-sensitive regime.

Yet, to fully embed enlightened investor stewardship, the 'Activities and Outcomes' component must evolve beyond descriptive inventories. Disclosures should not merely catalogue what actions were taken, but explain *why* they were undertaken, *whose interests* were considered, and *how* those choices align with both long-term financial objectives and broader societal goals. In this way, stewardship reporting becomes a form of public reasoning – one that legitimises investor decisions through visible deliberation.

Here, a richer understanding of fiduciary responsibility proves helpful. Rather than treating impartiality as a static exercise in balancing formal

[82] See e.g. Charlotte Villiers, 'Narrative Reporting and Enlightened Shareholder Value under the Companies Act 2006' in Joan Loughrey (ed.), *Directors' Duties and Shareholder Litigation in the Wake of the Financial Crisis* (Edward Elgar 2012), 97–132.

[83] Katarzyna Chalaczkiewicz-Ladna, Irene-Marié Esser and Iain Macneil, Engaging Stakeholders in Corporate Decision-Making through Strategic Reporting: An Empirical Study of FTSE 100 Companies' (2018) *European Business Law Review* 729.

[84] *UK Stewardship Code Consultation*, para 26.

[85] Ibid., para 36.

entitlements, it can be reinterpreted as a deliberative duty – one that calls on institutional investors to engage seriously with competing interests, even where only some hold formal legal standing.[86] In the context of stewardship, this entails justifying how decisions reflect fairness over time and across different constituencies. Stewardship reporting thus becomes more than a vehicle for information: it becomes a form of public reasoning, through which investors demonstrate how they navigate plural and sometimes conflicting responsibilities in a transparent and accountable way.

To reinforce this deliberative ethos, the 'how to report' prompts should explicitly integrate questions of materiality – not merely in terms of immediate financial impact, but with regard to long-term, systemic consequences. Signatories should be expected to disclose how they determine what is material across different time horizons, asset classes, and stakeholder groups, including ecological, social, and intergenerational concerns. Disclosures should illuminate *when* and *why* certain non-financial issues – such as biodiversity loss or labour standards – are treated as material, even where they are not yet priced by the market, and *how* such assessments shape engagement priorities, voting behaviour, and escalation strategies. This would help recast stewardship reporting as a values-aware, forward-looking practice.

Reporting expectations should also reflect stewardship's multi-level character – encompassing micro (firm-level), portfolio, system, and macro dimensions – and invite signatories to reflect explicitly on normative tensions, competing priorities, and trade-offs across these domains. The aim is to shift the tone of reporting from compliance to reflection, and from procedural box-ticking to institutional learning.[87] Without this evolution, the 3G UK Code risks inheriting the weaknesses of its predecessors: rhetorically ambitious but limited in transformative power.

This imperative is particularly acute in the face of what might be termed *cosmetic stewardship.* Just as greenwashing entails inflated

[86] Amir N. Licht, 'Stakeholder Impartiality: A New Classic Approach for the Objectives of the Corporation' in Arthur B. Laby and Jacob Hale Russell (eds.), *Fiduciary Obligations in Business* (Cambridge University Press 2021), 301–17. See also Section 4.4.3.

[87] For a critique of box-ticking under the UK Corporate Governance Code and a proposal to move towards a principles-based regime aligned with firm-specific accountability and deliberation, see Bobby V. Reddy, 'Thinking Outside the Box – Eliminating the Perniciousness of Box-Ticking in the New Corporate Governance Code' (2019) 82 *The Modern Law Review* 692.

environmental claims without substantive action,[88] *stewardship washing* involves strategically curated disclosures that perform responsibility while avoiding its burdens. Under the guise of stewardship, institutions may project long-termism, ESG integration, or systemic concern, while continuing to prioritise short-term financial returns and procedural compliance.[89] If reporting under a 3G UK Code devolves into symbolic affirmation rather than substantive practice, it risks undermining the legitimacy of the entire regime – especially at a time when institutional investors are increasingly called upon to address systemic risks such as climate change, inequality, and ecological degradation.

This risk is not novel. Scholarship on disclosure-based governance has long cautioned that transparency, in the absence of meaningful accountability, can legitimise inaction rather than correct it.[90] Disclosures become effective only when embedded within broader structures of reputational, professional, or regulatory consequence – structures that enable stakeholders to scrutinise, contest, and influence institutional behaviour.[91] Without such scaffolding, narrative reporting risks reinforcing form over function, visibility over veracity, and intent over impact.

8.4 Conclusion: Reclaiming the Quintessence of Investor Stewardship

This final chapter has argued for a principled and practicable recalibration of the UK's stewardship regime. Anchored in the concept of enlightened investor stewardship, the proposed 3G UK Code is more than a technical update: it offers a normative reorientation that clarifies the purpose, scope, and institutional promise of stewardship. This vision

88 The literature is voluminous: see e.g. Magali A. Delmas and Vanessa Cuerel Burbano, 'The Drivers of Greenwashing' (2011) 54 *California Management Review* 64; Miriam A. Cherry, 'The Law and Economics of Corporate Social Responsibility and Greenwashing' (2014) 14 *UC Davis Business Law Journal* 281; Manuel C. Kathan, Sebastian Utz, Gregor Dorfleitner, Jens Eckberg and Lea Chmei, 'What You See Is Not What You Get: ESG Scores and Greenwashing Risk' (2025) 74 *Finance Research Letters* 106710.

89 See also Giovanni Strampelli, 'ESG, Sustainability Disclosure, and Institutional Investor Stewardship' (2024) 81 *Washington and Lee Review Online* 405 (cautioning that corporate sustainability disclosure requirements are often used instrumentally by institutional investors, reinforcing performative rather than substantive stewardship practices).

90 J. E. Parkinson, *Corporate Power and Responsibility: Issues in the Theory of Company Law* (Oxford University Press 1995), 272.

91 Edward S. Herman, *Corporate Control, Corporate Power: A Twentieth Century Fund Study* (Cambridge University Press 1981), 278.

does not stand alone; it builds on the conceptual frameworks, empirical insights, and normative critiques developed throughout this book.

Across its chapters, the book has traced the evolution of investor stewardship – from its initial grounding in shareholder engagement and corporate governance to its reconfiguration as a multi-level, multi-actor, system-aware practice. This expanded understanding entails broader responsibilities: not only for oversight and engagement, but also for guiding capital allocation across asset classes, extending well beyond public equity. Together, the growing centrality of institutional investors across asset classes, the expansion of stewardship frameworks and disclosure regimes, and the rising salience of systemic risks have reshaped expectations of investor conduct.

At the heart of this transformation lies a central question: what does it mean for an institutional investor to act as a steward of capital in a deeply interdependent world? Drawing on legal doctrine, regulatory frameworks, empirical evidence, and normative theory, the book has shown that narrow, micro-level models of shareholder governance no longer suffice. Nor can investor stewardship be reduced to ESG integration or rhetorical commitments to long-termism. A credible and forward-looking vision must reflect the full complexity of the investment ecosystem – linking clients, beneficiaries, end-investors, assets, markets, and affected communities – and acknowledge the layered responsibilities that flow from those entanglements.

The concept of enlightened investor stewardship offers a framework for this reimagining. It recognises the legal, fiduciary, and contractual constraints that structure investor action, while affirming the legitimacy – and urgency – of broader public-oriented responsibilities. Rather than setting financial and societal aims in opposition, it seeks to align them across multiple levels of stewardship practice: micro, portfolio, system, and macro.

Yet ambition alone is not enough. As this book has shown, the UK's current stewardship regime remains constrained by definitional ambiguity, limited enforcement, and institutional fragmentation. Disclosures vary widely in depth and orientation, shaped as much by organisational capacity as by shared norms. Responsibility is invoked expansively but institutionalised weakly; rhetoric too often outpaces regulatory substance.

Stewardship codes nonetheless possess a distinctive form of power. As soft-law instruments, they shape expectations and coordinate behaviour without relying on formal enforcement. They function as normative infrastructure – quietly guiding how legitimacy, accountability, and ambition are defined within the investment field.

The UK's regime already contains many of the elements needed to fulfil this role. It has moved beyond asset manager primacy, acknowledged sustainability, and begun to differentiate across asset classes and investor types. Its unrealised potential lies in clarifying definitions, strengthening institutional incentives, and reframing stewardship reporting as a site of reflection and accountability rather than procedural compliance.

A 3G UK Code, properly conceived, can meet this challenge. It can provide the interpretive scaffolding investors need to navigate competing expectations. It can embed a richer conception of value – one attuned to systemic resilience and public legitimacy. And it can draw on the empirical insights developed in this book, including the textual and computational analysis of stewardship disclosures, to support reporting practices that are credible, insightful, and meaningfully differentiated.

Ultimately, however, stewardship reform is not only about new codes or improved disclosures. It raises a deeper institutional question: how should capital be governed in a way that aligns investor responsibilities with broader public and systemic outcomes? Investor stewardship should not remain a peripheral mechanism or an annual reporting exercise. It should become a central institutional practice – through which capital is made visible, accountable, and aligned with its broader consequences.

This requires recognising that capital allocation is never neutral; that markets are embedded in society; and that investors – however indirect – shape real economic and social outcomes. Reframed in this light, investor stewardship becomes a bridge between private responsibility and public purpose: anchored in principled definition, enabled by credible practice, and responsive to systemic risk.

At its core, investor stewardship is about building trust – not only between shareholders and corporate managers but also across the entire investment chain, including asset managers, asset owners, and the beneficiaries they represent, not least present and future (intergenerational) beneficiaries.[92] In a period of eroding public confidence, such trust must be earned through coherent, transparent, and accountable stewardship regimes. While some disclosures already gesture in this direction, full institutionalisation remains a work in progress.

The path to enlightened investor stewardship is neither linear nor uncontested. Yet the shift from narrow corporate oversight to a richer,

[92] See also Section 4.3.3.

public-oriented vision of capital governance is both necessary and possible. Meaningful stewardship requires more than firm-level engagement or rhetorical ESG compliance; it demands alignment between capital allocation and systemic resilience, grounded in the recognition that those who steward capital are entangled with those affected by its deployment – including clients, beneficiaries, and the unseen others.

Soft-law instruments like stewardship codes have their limitations, but they also hold untapped potential as tools of behavioural coordination and normative change, particularly within a fragmented or reactive regulatory ecosystem. When grounded in conceptual clarity, supported by institutional capacity, and attuned to the realities of an interdependent world, such codes can help crowd-in other-regarding, enlightened stewardship.

This book therefore offers not merely a reform proposal but also a reorientation – an invitation to reconsider how capital is, and ought to be, governed in the face of systemic risk and societal challenges. The future of investor stewardship remains unwritten. But to meet the demands of our time, it must move beyond aspiration and become commitment. To endure, investor stewardship must look beyond the stewards themselves – to the *unseen others* whose futures are shaped by capital, yet whose voices are too often left unheard.

INDEX

Printed in the United Kingdom by TJ Clays Ltd.